Visionary Journeys

Travel Writings from Early Medieval and Nineteenth-Century China

Harvard-Yenching Institute Monograph Series 78

Visionary Journeys

Travel Writings from Early Medieval and Nineteenth-Century China

Xiaofei Tian

Published by the Harvard University Asia Center
Distributed by Harvard University Press
Cambridge (Massachusetts) and London 2011

Printed in the United States of America

The Harvard-Yenching Institute, founded in 1928 and headquartered at Harvard University, is a foundation dedicated to the advancement of higher education in the humanities and social sciences in East and Southeast Asia. The Institute supports advanced research at Harvard by faculty members of certain Asian universities and doctoral studies at Harvard and other universities by junior faculty at the same universities. It also supports East Asian studies at Harvard through contributions to the Harvard-Yenching Library and publication of the *Harvard Journal of Asiatic Studies* and books on premodern East Asian history and literature.

Library of Congress Cataloging-in-Publication Data

Tian, Xiaofei.
Visionary journeys : travel writings from early medieval and nineteenth-century China / Xiaofei Tian.
p. cm.
ISBN 978-0-674-06252-8
1. Travelers' writings, Chinese--History and criticism. 2. Travel in literature. 3. Foreign countries in literature. 4. Displacement (Psychology) in literature. 5. Visualization in literature. 6. Chinese--Foreign countries--Historiography. 7. China--Civilization--Foreign influences. 8. Literature and history--China--History--Northern and Southern dynasties, 386-589. 9. Literature and history--China--History--19th century. I. Title.
PL2278.5.T72T53 2011
895.1'093251--dc22

2011012642

Index by Eileen Doherty-Sil

Printed on acid-free paper

Last figure below indicates year of this printing
19 18 17 16 15 14 13 12 11

紀念我的祖父
田繼光，字蓋忱
生于清光緒二十七年
卒于民國二十七年

Acknowledgments

Writing this book has been a long and passionate journey in itself, and I have accumulated many debts along the way. It gives me profound pleasure to have this opportunity to express my gratitude for the many colleagues and friends who have helped me, in one way or another, during the process.

Portions of Chapters 1, 2, 3, and 5 in their different incarnations were variously presented at Arizona State University, Beijing University, Columbia University, the École Française d'Extrême-Orient, Fudan University, Harvard University, Princeton University, Suzhou University, and UCLA. I have greatly benefited from the comments and questions from the commentators and the audience. I am particularly grateful for the feedback from David Knechtges, Paul W. Kroll, Robert Gimello, Stephen Bokenkamp, Liu Yuan-ju, Jack Chen, David Schaberg, Fu Gang, Robert Ashmore, Paula Varsano, Chris Nugent, Alan Berkowitz, Chen Yinchi, Cheng Yu-yu, Martin Kern, Sarah Allen, Cheng Zhangcan, Meow Hui Goh, Robert Campany, Yang Lu, Madeline Spring, Stephen West, Joe Cutter, Eugene Wang, Wei Shang, Wang Ping, and Ellen Widmer. I thank my gracious hosts at Suzhou University—Wang Yao, Ji Jin, and Qian Xisheng—for their hospitality. A special note of thanks is due Wendy Swartz for organizing the annual Medieval Workshop, which over the years has provided an interdisciplinary forum for lively discussions among scholars in the field. As an earlier version of Chapter 1 was published in *Asia Major*, I am grateful for the comments of an anonymous reader and for John Kieschnick's suggestions for revision. I also want to thank Kang-i Sun Chang and Pauline Lin for their friendship and inspiration. I feel privileged to be part of this wonderful community of scholars.

The community at my home institution has likewise tremendously enriched both my professional life and my personal life. I thank my colleagues in Chinese literary and religious studies, David Wang, Wilt Idema, Wai-yee Li, and James Robson, for their congeniality and intellectual stimulation. I appreciate Satomi Matsumura for her friendship, and for her insight into the world of plants. Peter Bol and Mark Elliott have both made useful comments on parts of the manuscript. My special thanks go to Philip Kuhn and Michael Puett, former chairs of my department, to William Kirby, former dean of Faculty of Arts and Sciences, and to Diana Sorensen, FAS dean of arts and humanities, for their staunch support and generous encouragement in the crucial stages of this book project. I am beholden to the superb librarians at the Yenching Library, especially James Cheng and Xiaohe Ma, who helped me obtain rare editions of nineteenth-century materials. I am appreciative of the administrative staff at my department—Denise Oberdan, Susan Kashiwa and Gustavo Espada—for their indispensable assistance, warmth, and good cheer. Finally, I would like to acknowledge, with affection and respect, the late Jeremy Knowles, former dean of Faculty of Arts and Sciences: his inspirational speech welcoming the new graduate students touched me deeply when I first entered graduate school at Harvard twenty years ago; his integrity, kindness, grace, humor, and visionary leadership continued to inspire me after I joined the faculty. I cherish his hand-written notes with pictures drawn on them. I will always look up to him as someone to admire and emulate.

I gratefully acknowledge the Scholar Grant conferred by the Chiang Ching-kuo Foundation for International Scholarly Exchange, which, combined with the financial award from Harvard University, enabled me to take a yearlong leave and undertake research for this book in the early stage.

I thank the two anonymous readers of the manuscript for their useful comments and suggestions. With fondness and gratitude I think on John Ziemer, the retired editor of Harvard Asia Center Publications Program, who had shown interest in the manuscript in its gestation and encouraged me to submit it to Asia Center press. I also miss his fine cooking. I am greatly obliged to the current editor, Kristen Wanner, for her hard work on the manuscript and for putting up with my occasional obstinacy. The manuscript reads much better due to her meticulous editing, and I am solely responsible for any remaining error and awkwardness.

The last thanks go to my family, the foundation and joy of my life. To my parents, my brother and sister-in-law, and my mother-in-law, for their love and affection; to my baby son, George, whose impeccable sense of timing allowed me to complete, the day before his birth, the translation of Xie Lingyun's long *fu*, the last piece of this book. But there is no word that could describe my indebtedness to my beloved husband, Stephen Owen, for everything. I feel incredibly fortunate, and immensely grateful, for having him as my fellow traveler. For me, there is no journey worth undertaking without his companionship.

Writing a book about travel often made me think of my grandfather, Tian Jiguang (1901-1938), courtesy name Jinchen, whose life in many ways reflected the vicissitudes suffered by the last generation of the Chinese scholar elite in a turbulent age. At one point, he turned down an opportunity to travel to America for studies because of his aging mother. Later on, he was imprisoned and tortured, and died, for refusing to collaborate with the local authorities under Japanese occupation during the Sino-Japanese War. For the rest of her life, my great-grandmother regretted that he did not leave home for another continent. In commemoration of a journey that never happened except perhaps in imagination, I dedicate this book to my grandfather's memory.

X. F. T.

Contents

Part II

Encountering the World

Appendixes

Reference Matter

Notes on Sources

For early medieval Chinese poetry and prose citations, I use primarily Lu Qinli's 逯欽立 *Pre-Qin, Han, Wei, Jin, and Southern and Northern Dynasties Poetry* (*Xian Qin Han Wei Jin nanbeichao shi* 先秦漢魏晉南北朝詩) and Yan Kejun's 嚴可均 *Complete Prose of Antiquity, the Three Dynasties, Qin, Han, the Three Kingdoms, and the Six Dynasties* (*Quan shanggu sandai Qin Han sanguo liuchao wen* 全上古三代秦漢三國六朝文). These anthologies are divided into different volumes by dynasties, such as *Complete Liang Poetry* (*Quan Liang shi* 全梁詩) and *Complete Liang Prose* (*Quan Liang wen* 全梁文). In identifying the source of a text from Lu Qinli or Yan Kejun's anthologies, I shall not refer to the complete title but cite only the relevant volume title, followed by *juan* and page numbers (e.g., *Quan Liang shi* 1.12). In the notes, the abbreviation *T* is used for *Taishō shinshū Daizōkyō* 大正新修大藏經.

Visionary Journeys

Travel Writings from Early Medieval and Nineteenth-Century China

Introduction

This book examines writings on moving through and seeing the world at two important moments of dislocation in Chinese history. By dislocation I mean not only physical displacement but also intellectual and emotional dislocation that one experiences when encountering and actively engaging with the foreign, the unfamiliar, the strange and unknown. The two moments refer to early medieval China (commonly known as the Northern and Southern Dynasties [317–589 CE]) and modern China—more precisely, the nineteenth century. While it is not uncommon to trace a theme through its history of development, it might seem unconventional to write a book on two periods separated from each other by more than a thousand years. This general introduction thus aims to broadly outline what this book is about, as well as explain my decision to focus on these two periods. But first I would like to ask the reader to engage in a mental exercise.

Suppose that people of the future were to look back to a past age when China came into paradigm-changing contact with the foreign world. It was an age when foreign vocabulary was introduced into every aspect of Chinese life, when foreigners came to China and lived among the Chinese people, trading, studying, lecturing, and training students; it was an age when the Chinese likewise journeyed to distant lands, with some staying on for good, never to return to their native soil. It was an age when a vast amount of foreign material was translated into Chinese and absorbed at all levels of society. Many concepts were lost in translation, but this did not stop people from reaching out, reading, and being profoundly changed by what they read. It was an age of tremendous anxiety that China was going to be enslaved by outside influences and lose its native cultural heritage. It was also an age when many people eagerly embraced those same influences and argued passionately for tolerance and incorporation of foreign ideas into the native culture. It was an age when boundaries became permeable and were crossed, when people traveled to and from many places, even many worlds. It was an age of bold visions and exciting possibilities, when China was, for better or for worse, forever changed.

With very little modification, the above description of early medieval China may very well be applied to the modern era.[1] Although the substance of the period remains vastly different, the transformative experiences of early medieval China have powerful resonance in modern times, when China came into its first full contact with the Western powers in the nineteenth century. Compared to these two periods, no other period in Chinese history engaged in so much translation, absorbed so much of foreign cultures, and witnessed such a complete cultural transformation. More importantly, the new textual knowledge was complemented by travel and exploration undertaken not just by sailors and traders but by members of the elite, who wrote accounts of their journeys for the eager consumption of a home audience.

Traveling to distant lands and returning home to tell the tale was not all that uncommon in premodern China, and numerous writings about travel, both within China and beyond, were produced during the long millennium between early medieval times and the nineteenth century.[2] Several things, however, distinguish the early medieval era. As examples in

1. For convenience I use the term "early medieval China" for this period, even though some scholars use the term in reference to the first century CE through the seventh century.

2. By "China" I mean an imagined Han Chinese polity. The actual borders and political boundaries were in constant flux throughout history. For an anthology of source materials about foreign travels from early to late imperial China, with a brief scholarly introduction and bibliography attached to each source text, see Chen Jiarong, Qian Jiang, and Zhang Guangda, *Lidai zhongwai xingji*. For a survey of Chinese travel writings from early medieval times through the twentieth century, see Mei Xinlin and Yu Zhanghua, *Zhongguo youji wenxue shi*. For an English anthology of premodern Chinese travel writings with an informative introduction, see Strassberg, *Inscribed Landscapes*.

the Prologue to Part I of this book show, more people moved around during this period than ever before. The rise of Buddhism created a major incentive for people to travel far and wide, and as a result, religious seekers journeyed to Central and Southeast Asia alongside members of imperial expedition teams and traders. These new voyagers came back with different kinds of stories. In connection with the phenomenon of increased spatial mobility, the fourth- and fifth-century elite displayed a pervasive curiosity for all things faraway and exotic. In their various forms, travel accounts from this period grew out of, and in turn fed into and stimulated, such curiosity. Rather than impersonally cataloguing local sites, products, and customs, many of these new travel accounts record personal experiences during these journeys. Crystallized in first-person anecdotes as well as in descriptions of movement through specific places at specific times, the individualized element of these travel writings does not aspire to give an "objective" account of what there is to note, but rather presents the world as seen through the eyes of a historical subject, an individual person.

It is this period that produced the first extant travelogue written by a Chinese author about his travels in and throughout Central Asia, South Asia, and Southeast Asia. The author Faxian 法顯 (ca. 340–421) was a Buddhist monk who set out in the year of 399 on an arduous pilgrimage to India; some fourteen years and thirty kingdoms later, he boarded a merchant ship from Ceylon and returned to China. He told the tale of his journey through hell to paradise and back to an enraptured audience. Nevertheless, during this period one did not need to venture so far to encounter the Other, for even traveling through the "interior" Chinese landscape could mean coming into contact with the foreign. Crossing the borders of a politically divided "China" was, simultaneously, a return to textually familiar territory and a venture into the unknown.

From the year 317, which marked the collapse of the Western Jin dynasty to invasion by northern non-Han peoples, to the year 589, in which China became reunified under one dynasty, the Chinese empire was split into northern and southern rival states. The north was dominated by a succession of non-Han polities, and the south by northern refugees and settlers who established a continuation of the Western Jin dynasty and claimed Han Chinese cultural orthodoxy. This dynasty in the south, known as the Eastern Jin (317–420), was succeeded by four short-lived dynasties, Song (420–79), Qi (479–502), Liang (502–57), and

Chen (557–89). The descendants of the northern refugees, born and raised in the south, as well as native southerners, had only read about the famed former capitals of the Chinese empire, Chang'an and Luoyang, but lacked their forebears' firsthand knowledge of these legendary cities. Goethe, who had come to know Rome well through books, visited Rome for the first time in 1786, and thus described his experience: "Wherever I walk I come upon familiar objects in an unfamiliar world; everything is just as I imagined, yet everything is new."[3] Southern courtiers who had a chance to see Luoyang and Chang'an with their own eyes for the first time during this period must have been struck by a similar sentiment.

In many ways, even the landscape in the south represented a new world. Traditionally the south had been considered peripheral to the center that was the Chinese heartland in the Yellow River region. Seen as a land of heat, humidity, pestilential vapors, and "barbarians" (a reference to the various Southern ethnic peoples), it was, in short, a land for exiles. The Southern Dynasties elite, the highest stratum of which consisted of northern immigrant families arriving in the south during the early fourth century, came to inhabit the land as exiles and refugees, but also as settlers and colonial masters. They made the south theirs by giving it a total textual makeover, writing, painting, and elegantly discoursing on the beautiful and yet strange landscape. In the spring of 353, the great calligrapher Wang Xizhi and a group of forty-odd friends gathered at a place called Lanting and composed poems; those who failed to produce a poem were asked to drink three goblets of wine as a penalty. Wang Xizhi then penned the famous "Preface to the Poetic Collection of Lanting," the single most famous example of Chinese calligraphy. This event alone put Lanting on the cultural map of China; to this day, it is a celebrated site in the suburbs of Shaoxing (in modern Zhejiang province), heavily inscribed with Wang Xizhi's calligraphy, complete with a winding stream by the side of which Wang Xizhi and his friends had supposedly sat, just as he described in the preface. The point is that no one who subsequently visited Lanting or Shaoxing could be innocent of this memory, and Lanting came to serve as an allegory for the entire southern landscape: it was new and exotic to the Southern Dynasties elite, who gazed at it with wonder and celebrated it in their writings. During this time Chinese landscape

3. Goethe, *Italian Journey*, p. 129.

poetry and painting began to flourish, igniting a textual and visual tradition that would continuously grow and change, but always bore the impression made during early medieval times. It was also during this time that Buddhism, known as "the doctrine of images," gained influence among members of the elite, and a discourse of visualization and image-making was being formed as they looked at the world with fresh eyes.

The very first representations of seeing a new world are one of the central elements connecting early medieval sightseers and nineteenth-century travelers—more precisely, the first travelers to Europe and America. The reason for restricting our attention to travel outside China in the nineteenth century is obvious: by this point the Chinese empire had been thoroughly explored, and these travels were well documented. In fact, even the adjacent outside lands—Central Asia, South and Southeastern Asia, as well as China's East Asian neighbors Korea and Japan—had long lost much of their exotic flavor for Chinese travelers. Accounts of these regions abound, and in reading them, one often detects a barely concealed contempt or, at best, a patronizing attitude toward the peoples and cultures encountered. All this changed, however, in the first extensive travel accounts of Europe and America from this period. The Western world was new and strange to the mid-nineteenth-century elite Chinese travelers who were the first to venture out that far; the newness and strangeness were in no small measure due to the fact that the Western world was itself undergoing vast transformations brought about by the Industrial Revolution and struggling with the side effects of this first phase of modernity. The Chinese travelers faced a double culture shock—not just stable difference, but difference itself in a radical process of change. In more than one sense, they experienced a profound sense of dislocation, just like their counterparts from the early medieval era.

"Dislocation," a central issue in this study, is literal as well as figurative, physical as well as mental. Early medieval China was a time of expanding intellectual horizons, and Buddhism, a foreign import, played a crucial role in the overall cultural transformation. One of the many changes brought about by Buddhism was a sense of the shift of the traditional Chinese world order in which "China" occupied a central position, as indicated by the phrase "central plains" (*zhongyuan* 中原) or "middle kingdom" (*zhongguo* 中國). In the travelogue authored by the monk Faxian, however, central India was regarded as the "middle kingdom," while

China itself was referred to as "the land on the margin or borderland" (*biandi* 邊地). As his travelogue testifies in unambiguous terms, he had to go through hell to reach the Buddhist heaven that was central India. In many ways the Buddhist conception of the world was inherited by nineteenth-century travelers to Europe and America, in the sense that they saw the Western world either as heaven or as hell, and rarely, if ever, anything in between. And yet, when they did see the Western world as paradise, they were not anchored by the same equilibrium and matter-of-factness experienced by Faxian, who as a devout Buddhist took for granted the superior status of the birthplace of the Buddha. The nineteenth-century travelers meeting the Western world face to face were in a much more complicated situation culturally, politically, and psychologically. Just as in the early medieval times, modern China was profoundly shaken by foreign influences, although this time the responses were more multifarious and less certain, and people struggled to find a sense of grounding and stability amid the turmoil.

One of the ways writers evoked such a safe haven was to use Buddhist words and images liberally. By this time many of the terms originating from Buddhist scriptures had already become part of Chinese everyday vocabulary and had long lost their exotic flavor, but they still retained an aura of "familiar strangeness." In other words, Buddhism, once a quintessentially foreign religion, had by then been completely accepted and appropriated into the native culture—indeed, it is part of the criteria used to describe what is Chinese today. In the nineteenth century, it provided the best domesticating and familiarizing strategy for travelers to make sense of the new world they encountered. In this the nineteenth century once again harkens back to the early medieval period.

Journeys into new territory; a growing circulation of texts, goods, and people; conscious integration and appropriation of foreign influences—these are characteristics shared by the early medieval period and the nineteenth century. This book brings these two periods together not only in their encounters with Others, but also in their active, unprecedentedly large-scale and deep-reaching interactions with Others and their intense fascination with Otherness. More specifically, this book aims to explore modes of seeing the world; such modes, I argue, were established in early medieval times and resurfaced, in permutations and metamorphoses, in the nineteenth-century writings on encountering the Other.

Seeing the world is a complicated matter. Seeing, as we know, is never passive. It begins with an object—a "what"—and a point of view. It is an active process of sorting out, classifying, and comprehending. There is theoretically a "raw" seeing: the encounter of the naked, undifferentiating, innocent eye meeting the world without trying to make sense of it, but it is something not demonstrated or demonstrable, something we can never know or prove. What we do know is seeing as articulated in language. As such, seeing is governed by a body of explicit and implicit laws and codes, beliefs and values, by which members of a society understand and approach the world; it is also mediated by language, by rhetorical strategies, images, and tropes. One major argument of this book is that a set of schemata of seeing the world was first developed in early medieval China. Just as many basic forms of the Chinese cultural episteme took their shape in this period, the paradigm of seeing had far-reaching influence in Chinese culture. It continued well into the nineteenth century, when the first Chinese elite members embarked on voyages to visit distant foreign lands, venturing further than any of their predecessors had ever gone. By this point the familiar framework, with its implicit and explicit codes of understanding and articulating the world "out there," had sustained much pressure to the point of snapping. It is in the tension between existing categories and new realities that we discern both the continuity of the cultural tradition and its radical changes.

This study is divided into two parts. Part I deals with the early medieval Chinese writings on seeing, visualizing, and image-making; Part II focuses on the fresh seeing of the world in the nineteenth century. I leave more detailed accounts of the chapters in the prologues to Part I and Part II, and keep the general introduction of this book intentionally broad.

In several ways this study itself is about breaking boundaries that fragment and compartmentalize knowledge in academe. Not only are there various institutionalized forms of the division of premodern and modern periods in schools and in the field, but even within premodern studies, barriers exist that segregate the study of one "major period" from another. While specialization contributes to depth and precision, it also tends to encourage intellectual isolation and prevent scholars from envisioning the continuity and transformation of a long, unbroken cultural tradition. When the premodern field is unable to speak to the modern, the significance and relevance of our research and teaching are limited; when the modern field fails to connect with the premodern, it cannot adequately understand and explain modern and contemporary China.

This book also brings together different sorts of materials written within one period that might conventionally be shoehorned into separate disciplinary categories of literature, history, and religion. Mine is a deliberate attempt to counteract the artificial nature of the modern disciplinary divide, based on the conviction that textual production does not take place in a neatly partitioned space. I do not deny that there are indeed boundaries between different branches of knowledge even before the formation of modern disciplines, and that different types of works follow different conventions; but it is equally undeniable that modern concepts often prove inadequate to capturing certain historical phenomena (for example, a modern student's understanding of "literature" certainly would not do justice to the conception of "literature," *wen*, in the mind of a member of the early medieval Chinese elite, nor would modern notions of identity—such as "poet"—have been comprehensible to such a person). Furthermore, the production and circulation of writings that fall into different spheres of literature, religion, and history must be considered in the context of the episteme of the particular epoch. Just as a premodern elite male could be simultaneously poet, diplomat, courtier, bureaucrat, historian, geographer, and paradoxographer, certain larger cultural issues and concerns shared by people living in one era often spill into what modern scholars think of as different spheres and different types of texts.

In this book I treat these spheres and texts together in the hope that some of their hitherto neglected aspects can be illuminated. For instance, Chapter 1 juxtaposes poetry, *fu* 賦 (rhymed prose variously translated as "poetic expositions" or "rhapsodies"), Daoist writings, and Buddhist scriptures and commentaries to demonstrate the shared discourse of visualization and imagination in the Eastern Jin. Chapter 2 discusses military campaign records, *fu* on travel, and Faxian's Buddhist travelogue to illustrate two related modes of seeing sights/sites. Then, in Chapter 3, I examine Xie Lingyun's 謝靈運 (385–433) landscape poetry, not only against the background outlined in Chapters 1 and 2 but also in the context of contemporary accounts of journeys to hell and back, so as to shed light on certain characteristics of his poetry that might otherwise escape notice. In Chapter 4 I use historical writing, ethnographic and geographic accounts, poetry, diary, and travelogue to explore several complex issues involved in encountering the foreign: namely, how people attempted to deal with race and gender, order the world, and map the modern city.

In short, I pay special attention to what I call cultural forms of representation and attempt to sort out rhetorical strategies, or modes of seeing the world, that inform these writings. Ultimately this study explores how people negotiate with dislocation when their inherited cultural assumptions undergo profound shake-ups and transformations, and how self and self-knowledge construct one's view of the Other and are in turn changed by encounters with it. My method is close, historicized reading and analysis of diverse texts, but I will not always situate these texts in their familiar disciplinary "surroundings." Instead, I juxtapose. The effect of juxtaposition should be, not unfittingly, a sense of dislocation and defamiliarization. A specialist might find that my approach does not fall into the usual framework of her or his discipline or field of research (for example, a Buddhist scholar may be disconcerted by my broadly cultural reading of Faxian's travelogue in an attempt to sort out the "cultural grammar" underlying the travelogue); but what I hope to accomplish through this approach is to illuminate the texts in unexpected ways, and appeal to readers interested not just in the period of early medieval China or the nineteenth century but also in issues of representation, travel, visualization, and modernity. Without relinquishing disciplinary claims or specialized forms of knowledge, I feel that it is nevertheless useful to allow different kinds of study to coexist with research under the protocols of the sharper and narrower focus of a specialist.

This study also aims to foreground the problem of genre. Much of the materials treated in this book can be classified as "travel literature," but travel literature is a broad, content-defined category that incorporates many genres. One particular genre that concerns us is poetry. The last chapter of Part I of this book focuses on Xie Lingyun, the great fifth-century poet whose poetry breaks through the paradigm of seeing a faraway, exotic landscape in terms of either heaven or hell; likewise, the last chapter of Part II is devoted to the poetry of Huang Zunxian 黃遵憲 (1848–1905), the last great poet of imperial China, and it argues that poetry not only provided a medium that intervened radically in the self's encounter with the Other, but articulated a quintessentially modern experience, stretching the traditional schemata of seeing the world to its utmost limit.

Both in the early medieval period and in modern times, things moved around a great deal, and so did people. Boundaries were constantly crossed; cultures became mixed. One motif recurring in these chapters is that of journeys: journeys of the mind, or physical journeys to foreign lands, to unfamiliar territories within Chinese borders, to the Buddhist paradise known as the Pure Land, and even to hell and back. The recording of the experience of the journey became an occasion to put the chaos of the world into words and to find meaning and pattern in the process. In this sense the title of this book, *Visionary Journeys*, refers to journeys undertaken *in*, and *with*, vision and imagination.

PART I

Visionary Journeys

Prologue

In south China from the fourth to the sixth century, intellectual and geographical horizons were broadening on all sides. The cultural elite were deeply engaged in spiritual pursuits and in metaphysical discourse about the nature of life and death. This was the Golden Age of the spread of Buddhism, and the native tradition of early Chinese thought, spurred on by Buddhism, was at the same time evolving into something more complicated and textured. The eminent cultural figure Zhang Rong 張融 (444–97) asked on his deathbed to be buried with "the *Classic of Filial Piety* and *Laozi* in my left hand and the *Lotus Sutra* in my right hand."[1] It is, however, anachronistic to adhere to a stringent division of "Buddhism, Daoism, and Confucianism" in this period: it is much more fruitful to think of the contemporary intellectual landscape in terms of a series of important and popular texts—the *Analects*, *Laozi*, *Zhuangzi*, and Buddhist scriptures, most notably the *Vimalakīrti-nirdeśa Sūtra*, the *Lotus Sutra*, the Pure Land scriptures, among many others—and in terms of a new hybrid discourse that made generous mixed use of those texts. This discourse was manifested in writings as well as orally in the everyday life of the elite.

In the early fourth century, when the Jin royal house first crossed the Yangzi River to the south to flee the invading northern non-Han peoples, they became, in the words of the founding emperor of the Eastern Jin,

1. Xiao Zixian 蕭子顯 (483–537), *Nan Qi shu* 41.729.

"lodgers in a land belonging to others" (*ji ren guotu* 寄人國土).[2] Settling in a region that had previously been considered barbarian borderland, they faced a frequently hostile native population, including members of the old elite from the former Kingdom of Wu (222–80). When the Kingdom of Wu was conquered by the Western Jin in 280, there had been a clash of cultures that was exemplified, among other things, in the poetry of Lu Ji 陸機 (261–303), a scion of one of the most distinguished Wu families who went to the capital Luoyang and served in the Jin court.[3] The cultural clash had by no means diminished in the early fourth century when the northern settlers established "a colonial regime of a very peculiar sort" in the south.[4] Repelled by the cultural penchant for "pure conversation" (*qingtan* 清談) or "arcane discourse" (*xuanyan* 玄言) brought over from Luoyang, many native southerners condemned the practitioners of "pure conversation" for their open scorn of conventional social norms and their pursuit of empty metaphysics, as opposed to what was perceived as the more useful branches of learning, such as ritual matters and Confucian classics. Yu Yu 虞預 (ca. 270s–330s), Gan Bao 干寶 (d. 336), and Ge Hong 葛洪 (283–343) were among the most outspoken critics of "pure conversation."[5] Nevertheless, their protest against contemporary emulation of the northern cultural fashion, now relocated to the south, demonstrated the extent to which the south fell under the influence of the northern émigrés. Tension between cultures became a cross-fertilization of cultures: the northern elite absorbed much local

2. Liu Yiqing 劉義慶 (403–44), *Shishuo xinyu jianshu* 2.91.

3. For a detailed discussion of the clash between the Wu culture and the northern tradition, and the regional awareness in Lu Ji's poetry, see Knechtges, "Sweet-Peel Orange or Southern Gold?"; Lin Wenyue, "Pan Yue Lu Ji shi zhong de nanfang yishi."

4. Stephen Owen, "Gone South."

5. See Fang Xuanling et al, *Jin shu* 82.2147; Ge Hong, *Baopuzi waipian jiaojian* 25.625–38 and 26.11–19; Gan Bao, "Jin ji zonglun" 晉紀總論, in Yan Kejun 嚴可均 (1762–1843), *Quan Jin wen* 127.2192. Ge Hong was particularly vocal in his disapproval of the imitation of the "the custom of Luoyang," and opposed the abandonment of the ways of one's homeland in favor of those of "the central states" (*zhongzhou* 中州 or *zhongguo*). *Baopuzi waipian*, 26.12–17. For a classic article discussing the differences, and mutual influences, between south and north, see Tang Zhangru, "Du *Baopuzi* tuilun nanbei xuefeng de yitong." For a discussion of Gan Bao and Ge Hong's negative attitude toward "arcane learning" (*xuanxue* 玄學) and their regional affiliations, see Campany, "Two Religious Thinkers of the Early Eastern Jin," pp. 183–86, 220–21.

popular culture and material culture of the south, just as the northerners' love of discoursing on philosophical topics, along with their continued writing of commentaries on texts now labeled as Buddhist, Daoist, and Confucian, persisted throughout the Southern Dynasties.

Besides the expansion of intellectual horizons, this period saw more people engaged in more physical movement than ever before. The political division of China and the constantly shifting and highly permeable border between the north and south led to significant mobility. People were sometimes relocated *en masse* because their native region had fallen into the hands of the enemy state.[6] More often than not, however, the fluid territorial boundary was traversed by three categories of people. The first category consisted of members of Buddhist clergy who traveled for the purpose of spiritual merit: namely, to spread Buddhism by preaching and converting, to seek enlightenment by looking for a famous teacher or holy scriptures, or to see holy sites.[7] The Liang monk Huijiao's 慧皎 (497–554) *Biographies of Eminent Monks* (*Gaoseng zhuan* 高僧傳) records the lives and accomplishments of about five hundred monks in the course of four and a half centuries; few had not traveled extensively both within and beyond Chinese lands. In many cases the monks explicitly advocated the virtue of widely propagating Buddhist doctrine by means of travel. Sengbi 僧弼 (365–442), a native of Wu, went to Chang'an to study with Kumārajīva 鳩摩羅什 (344–413). Afterwards he "traveled through famous places and observed customs everywhere." When asked to stay and take charge of a monastery, he declined, saying, "One should follow one's karma to benefit the world; how could one only improve a single monastery?"[8] A northern monk, Baoliang 寶亮 (444–509), entered the

6. Mentions of large-scale relocation, voluntary or forced, are scattered through dynastic histories of this period. There is also much secondary literature on this topic. An early monograph is *Wei Jin nanbeichao minhu da liuxi* by Li Jiannong; Cao Wenzhu's *Zhongguo liumin shi* and Volume 2 of Ge Jianxiong, Wu Songdi and Cao Shuji's *Zhongguo yimin shi* provide a good overview.

7. For a recent study of the role of the Six Dynasties Buddhist monks in cultural exchanges between the north and south, see Liu Yuejin, "Liuchao senglü." Another interesting article in this regard is Shang Yongqi's "3–6 shiji sengren de liudong yu dili shiyu de tuozhan." Shang's article, though generally informative, contains some serious factual errors.

8. Huijiao, *Gaoseng zhuan*, p. 270.

clerical order at the age of eleven and was deeply attached to his monastery. When he was a grown man, his master urged him to leave, saying, "How can you be so trapped by the net of affection and not contribute to the dissemination of our Way?"[9]

The second category of people who crossed the south/north border consisted of diplomats.[10] After the mid-fifth century, as the north and south established more regularized diplomatic relations, emissaries paid mutual visits to northern and southern courts. These emissaries were not just political but also cultural ambassadors: on both sides they were chosen for their learning, cultural sophistication, literary talent, and oratorical eloquence. In regards to the last qualification, the famous poet Xie Tiao 謝朓 (464–99) had once tried to excuse himself from receiving the northern ambassador on the grounds of being inarticulate.[11] The diplomats' missions included, among other things, exchanging poetry with their hosts and besting their hosts in tournaments of words. A northern official who was also a noted poet and historian was once thrown into prison for having failed to come up with adequate repartee in his verbal jousting with a southern emissary.[12] The third category of travelers consisted of merchants in search of profit, although the imperial emissaries and members of their entourage were often engaged in commercial pursuits as well.[13]

---

9. Ibid., p. 337.

10. A recent study that provides a comprehensive survey of the secondary scholarship on this subject in its Introduction is Cai Zongxian's *Zhonggu qianqi de jiaopin yu nanbei hudong*.

11. Xiao Zixian, *Nan Qi shu* 47.826.

12. The northern official in question was Wei Shou 魏收 (506–72), the compiler of *Wei shu* 魏書. Li Yanshou, *Nan shi* 62.1523.

13. For a discussion of the commercial activities in the border region between north and south, see Chen Jinfeng, *Wei Jin nanbeichao zhongjian didai yanjiu*, pp. 219–32. For a study of the commercial pursuits of emissaries and their entourage, see Horiuchi Junichi, "Nanbeichao jian de waijiao shijie he jingji jiaoliu." Horiuchi's belief that trading was completely banned or rigidly controlled along the Huai River during the Northern and Southern Dynasties and was limited to the border region is, however, an arguable point, as the ban was not always strictly observed, and traders seem to have traveled beyond the border region, for instance between Chang'an and Xiangyang (in modern Hubei), with relative ease. See Fang Xuanling, *Jin shu* 62.1696; Shen Yue et al., *Song shu* 95.2354; Sengyou 僧佑 (445–518), *Chu sanzang ji ji* 9.333. Also see Chen Jinfeng, *Wei Jin nanbeichao zhongjian didai yanjiu* p. 225.

Women, too, traveled in this period, and they did so much more frequently than before. Buddhist nuns especially enjoyed a certain degree of mobility. *The Biographies of Buddhist Nuns* (*Biqiuni zhuan* 比丘尼傳), compiled in 517 by the monk Baochang 寶唱, records a number of nuns who had traveled extensively. For instance, in the year of 348, Minggan 明感 crossed the Yangzi River with a group of ten nuns and arrived in the Eastern Jin capital city Jiankang 建康 (modern Nanjing). Daoyi 道儀 traveled to Jiankang in the 390s because she had heard that many Buddhist lectures were being held in the capital and the collection of Buddhist scriptures there "had gradually become complete." Huiyu 慧玉 (fl. 437), a native of Chang'an, "roamed everywhere to teach and convert, and traveled to all sorts of prefectures and commanderies." She finally ventured south and resided in Jiangling 江陵 (in modern Hubei).[14] There were many others.

Traders and members of Buddhist clergy did not confine their travels to China; they went far beyond, by land or by sea, to South and Southeast Asia, Central Asia, Western Asia, and Europe. Exuberant contact existed between China, the Sassanid Empire, and the Byzantine Empire, attested by Sassanian silver coins and Byzantine gold coins excavated in China throughout the twentieth century.[15] At the same time, foreign traders and foreign monks and nuns poured into China. Many eminent monks whose biographies grace the pages of *Gaoseng zhuan* were of non-Han descent. Some of them mastered the Chinese language and contributed to the translation of Sanskrit scriptures into Chinese; some of them, like the famous Śrīmitra (fl. 320s), relied on interpreters to communicate with the Eastern Jin elite.[16] In the year of 429, a group of nuns from Sri Lanka arrived at Jiankang. Five years later, another group of eleven nuns, headed by Tiesaluo 鐵薩羅, boarded the same merchant ship, came to Jiankang, and joined the earlier group, who by this time had already learned to speak Chinese. These nuns, with their dark complexions and exotic looks,

---

14. Baochang, *Biqiuni zhuan jiaozhu* 1.15, 1.40, 2.52–53. There are two English translations of *Biqiuni zhuan*: *Lives of the Nuns: Biographies of Chinese Buddhist Nuns from the Fourth to Sixth Centuries*, translated by Kathryn Ann Tsai; and *Biographies of Buddhist Nuns*, translated by Li Rongxi, in *Lives of Great Monks and Nuns*, pp. 69–154.

15. See Shi Yuntao's excellent study, *San zhi liu shiji sichou zhi lu de bianqian*, pp. 202–45.

16. Huijiao, *Gaoseng zhuan* 1.30.

must have been quite a spectacle. They carried out exchanges with the local community of Chinese nuns. With their aid, over three hundred Chinese nuns renewed their reception of Buddhist precepts.[17] One of these Chinese nuns, Sengjing 僧敬 (403–86), was so motivated by the presence of these foreign nuns in the southern capital that she decided to seek holy relics overseas. Although she was prevented from going any further than Guangdong, her travels would have not been possible or even imaginable in an earlier era.[18] The limitation of movement inflicted on nuns was not, however, imposed on monks. Faxian, a Buddhist "pilgrim" to India, was the author of the first extant travelogue written by a Chinese about his experiences in the foreign lands.

Scholars in various fields have observed that the fourth and fifth centuries witnessed an unprecedented flourishing of geographical works and travel writings, including the so-called "poetry of mountains and waters" (*shanshui shi* 山水詩) or landscape poetry.[19] It seems natural to ask, why did this happen? The answer partially lies in the social, political, and religious condition of the age: the mobility of people and ideas; the establishment of boundaries and the subsequent yearning to break them down; the formation of regional identities triggered or intensified by conflicts of cultures; the desire for exploration fanned by travelers' tales; and, last but not least, a sense of infinite possibilities for knowing and seeing not just the phenomenal world of the living but also the otherworld, since the Buddhist clergy and lay believers had reported many a visionary journey to paradise or hell during this period. Indeed, such reports began to proliferate at the turn of the fifth century, at about the same time that Faxian was making his pilgrimage to India, and Xie Lingyun, the poet commonly regarded as "the father of Chinese landscape poetry," was writing luminous poems about exotic locales in nature.

The above description sketches a background to the subject treated in the first part of this book, namely, journeys to other worlds in early medieval China and their significance both for contemporaries—how

---

17. Baochang, *Biqiuni zhuan* 2.88.

18. Ibid., 3.124–25.

19. See, for instance, Mei Xinlin and Yu Zhanghua, *Zhongguo youji wenxueshi*, pp. 30–66; Zhou Hanguang and Dai Hongcai, *Liuchao keji*, pp. 236–73; Li Jianguo, *Tang qian zhiguai xiaoshuo shi*, p. 255.

they were changed by undertaking these journeys or by reading and hearing about these journeys—and for those living in later times. Underlying the accounts of these journeys was an intense longing to see new horizons with one's own eyes and to send an eyewitness report to the people back home.

The following chapters in Part I comment on the different ways in which seeing the world was transcribed, theorized, and negotiated in the writings of this period. The first chapter uses the Southern Dynasties elite's engagement with landscape as an entry point to demonstrate the great value attached to the ability of seeing with the mind's eye. The concept of "visualization" or "imagination" (*xiang* 想)—here used in the sense of "mental image-making"—acquired a rich significance in Chinese cultural discourse, and laid the intellectual groundwork for understanding the cultural thought and aesthetics of early medieval China and of later times. In this chapter I also explore how Buddhism, with its emphasis on teaching through images and meditative visualization, exerted a tremendous influence on Chinese epistemology. Its impact on Chinese literature was certainly not limited to providing a treasure trove of colorful images and motifs.

The second chapter seeks to trace out a set of rhetorical schemata of seeing the world, which I roughly divide into the historical mode of seeing and the heaven and/or hell paradigm. A dialectical tension is inherent in both schemes: in the former, space is seen in terms of a dichotomy of the past and present as one moves through layered sites of history; in the latter, a faraway place is seen as either paradise or hell, but rarely something in between. "Faraway" of course implies "far away *from*." In Chinese a common word for "faraway" is *bianyuan* 邊遠, which indicates a peripheral place remote from the center, be it a frontier region or not. It is, however, important to bear in mind that center and periphery are relative, mutually dependent concepts, and during this period center and periphery were constantly shifting.

Although the "heaven and/or hell" paradigm of seeing was a joint product of Buddhism and native cultural tradition, in a number of accounts of the dreams and visions of Buddhist clergy and lay people during this period, journeys to a Buddhist heaven or hell are literalized and thus remain squarely within a religious framework. The proliferation of such accounts, which form an essential part of the larger contemporary picture of the exploration of other worlds, is also discussed in the second chapter.

The third chapter offers a contextualized discussion of Xie Lingyun's poetry, seen for the first time against the manifold journeys to the otherworld or other worlds. Xie Lingyun, the great aristocrat of the fifth century, made it his vocation to write a poetic account of his visionary journeys—visionary in the same vein as those who visited hell in their visions and came back with firsthand eyewitness reports. Xie Lingyun writes a poetry that teeters on the verge of hell but never quite slips into it. His verse hovers at the boundary between the last lingering light of the day and the vast dark shadows of the night; it is a poetry of twilight, a poetry between the otherworldly purity and beauty of paradise and the ghastly horrors of hell. "Purgatory," the notion of which did not come into clear and mature form in Europe until after the seventh century (and some scholars argue not even until after the twelfth century), is known in the Chinese Buddhist cosmic system as an intermediate existence between death and rebirth in another form.[20] Xie Lingyun's poetry may be verily described as a poetry of purgatory. His is a troubled spirit always seeking peace and tranquility, sometimes believing to have found it in the meaning and pattern discerned in nature. The Buddhist term for Xie's journey is *zhongyou zhi lü* 中有之旅: the journey of an unsettled traveler in a transitional state of being searching for a new habitat or reincarnation.

20. For discussions of the origin of purgatory in Europe, see Atwell, "From Augustine to Gregory the Great," and Le Goff, *The Birth of Purgatory*. Buddhism refers to the stage between death and the next realm as "intermediate being" (*zhongyou* 中有) or "intermediate darkness" (*zhongyin* 中陰). Unlike the Christian purgatory, a place that prepares the soul for heaven, the spirit of the deceased in Buddhist "purgatory" will, generally speaking, be reincarnated in another form or sent to suffer in one of the hells, even though the intervention of the family and friends of the deceased in the form of good deeds may deliver the soul from torments and even enable the soul to attain nirvana. For the Chinese Buddhist concept of purgatory, see Teiser, *The Scripture on the Ten Kings*.

CHAPTER ONE

Seeing with the Mind's Eye

This chapter explores a series of acts of the mind in its interaction with the physical world, or more specifically, with landscape (*shanshui*, "mountains and waters") during the intellectually coherent hundred-year period fortuitously coinciding with the dynasty known as the Eastern Jin. The earliest known record of landscape painting dates to the Eastern Jin; landscape was also an essential element in the so-called "poetry of arcane discourse" (*xuanyan shi* 玄言詩) of the fourth century, a poetry drawing heavily upon the vocabulary and concerns of *Laozi* and *Zhuangzi* as well as upon the Buddhist scriptures. How was landscape perceived by the Eastern Jin elite, and how was this mode of perception informed by a complex nexus of contemporary cultural forces? These are the questions to be dealt with in this chapter.

Exploring the Eastern Jin texts about landscape or about the representation of landscape, we discover that one word is repeatedly associated with the appreciation of "mountains and waters," and that word is *xiang*: to visualize the object of contemplation in one's mind, to bring up the image of the object to the mind's eye. A late second-century definition clearly shows the differentiation of *si* 思 and *xiang*, which later were combined into a compound *sixiang* 思想 meaning "thought" or "to think," and highlights the visual nature of the latter:

Where one lodges one's thoughts is called *si*; it is as if one sees the form [of the object of contemplation] right in front of oneself—this is called *xiang*.[1]

意所存曰思,彷佛如睹其容之處前曰想.

The concept of *xiang* is closely related to form or image (*xiang* 相 or *xiang* 象/像) and is key to the cultural and aesthetic thought of the period. For the Southern Dynasties elite, landscape was essentially a grand image (*xiang* 象), and the perception, interpretation, and indeed the very construction of this Image were contingent upon the workings of the mind. Imagination was therefore an active process of image-making, and so in many ways, the rise of landscape representation in the fourth century was as much a movement inward as outward. That is, the heightened interest in the natural world was but an extension of the primary engagement with the inner world of an individual. It is for this reason that imaginary landscapes are such a prominent motif in the Eastern Jin literature. By examining the diverse manifestations of *xiang* as an act of mental seeing and image-making in a series of secular and religious texts, I seek to demonstrate how this concept became dominant in the cultural discourse of the time, and why it is pivotal to our understanding of early medieval China.

Inner Light/Outer Reality

Buddhist scriptures introduced into China from the late second century emphasize the lack of self-nature of all things. That is, things do not have a definitive nature, but are all contingent on causes and conditions. The *Sutra of Perfect Wisdom* (*Daohang bore jing* 道行般若經, also known as *Xiaopin bore jing* 小品般若經), an important scripture first translated into the Chinese by Lokakṣema (Zhi Loujiachen 支婁迦讖) in 179, then again by Zhi Qian 支謙 (fl. 222–54), and finally by Kumārajīva in 408, contains a long passage explicating "causes and conditions" by way of many metaphors, one of which makes use of the phenomenon of echo:

1. See Chen Hui's 陳慧 commentary on the *Sutra of [Five] Skandhas, [Eighteen] Realms, and [Twelve] Loci* (Skt.: *Skandadhātvāyatana sūtra*, Ch.: *Yin chi ru jing* 陰持入經) 1.11, in *T* 33. The sutra was translated by the Parthian monk An Shigao 安世高 (fl. 148).

> It is like the echo in the mountains: it is not realized with one factor, or with two factors. There has to be a mountain, there has to be a person, there has to be a shout, there has to be an ear listening to it: when all these factors are brought together, an echo is realized.[2]

The echo metaphor brings together material as well as subjective conditions of the physical phenomenon: without mountain, person, and shout, there is no echo; and further, in the absence of an ear to hear it, it may not be said to exist either. The existence of the world of matter thus depends on the cognitive subject.

The significance of the cognitive subject is further elaborated in one of the most popular Buddhist scriptures of the Eastern Jin, the *Vimalakīrtinirdeśa Sūtra* 維摩詰所説經.[3] In the first chapter of the sutra, entitled "Buddha's Kingdom" ("Fo guo" 佛國), the Śākyamuni Buddha asserts that Buddha's kingdom is not a place far beyond mortal reach, but is located in the here and now, in this secular world, "the land of people and creatures walking or crawling with their feet and breathing with their mouths." When a bodhisattva is engaged in creating the Pure Land of Buddha's kingdom in the mortal world, he must purify his mind, for "the Buddha's kingdom is only pure as a result of the purity of the bodhisattva's mind." Śāriputra 舍利弗, who is among the vast audience listening to the preaching of Śākyamuni, wonders to himself: "If the Buddha's kingdom is only pure as a result of the purity of the bodhisattva's mind, then when Śākyamuni Buddha was being a bodhisattva, wasn't his mind impure? Otherwise, how could this Buddha's kingdom be so impure?" Śākyamuni immediately knows Śāriputra's thought, and says to him: "What do you think, Śāriputra? Is it the fault of the sun and moon that those who are blind cannot see that the sun and moon are pure?" Śāriputra replies: "No, World Honored One. It is the fault of those who are blind, not that of the sun and moon." The Śākyamuni Buddha says:

---

2. *Sutra of Perfect Wisdom* 10.476, in *T* 8.

3. This scripture was translated four times from the third century to the early fifth century, by Zhi Qian, Dharmarakṣa 竺法護 (239–316), Zhu Shulan 竺叔蘭 (fl. third–fourth centuries), and Kumārajīva. Zhi Mindu 支敏度 (fl. third–fourth centuries) then combined Zhi Qian and Zhu Shulan's translations into a version of his own. See Zhi Mindu's preface preserved in Sengyou's *Chu sanzang ji ji* 8.310.

"Śāriputra, [in the same way,] the fault lies with those people who are sinful and hence cannot see the splendor and purity of the Buddha land of Tathāgata; it is not the fault of Tathāgata. Śāriputra, my land is pure, but you cannot see it." At this point Brahma Śikhin jumps in, saying to Śariputra: "Why, I see the Buddha's kingdom is splendid and pure, just like the highest abode of the dhyāna heavens!" Śāriputra retorts: "When I look at this land, all I see are its hills, knolls, hollows, chasms, thorns, sands, pebbles, soil, rocks—it is littered with rubbish!" Brahma Śikhin answers: "It is because you, my benevolent one, have highs and lows in your mind and do not adhere to the Buddha's wisdom that you see this land as impure." Thereupon the Śākyamuni Buddha touches the earth with his big toe, and suddenly the universe is magnificently bedecked with thousands and thousands of jewels and gems, and everyone in the audience sees oneself as sitting on a throne of jeweled lotus. As Śāriputra marvels at the revelation of the radiance of Buddha's land, the Śākyamuni Buddha reiterates his lesson: "Śāriputra, this Buddha's kingdom is always thus pure. It is only for the sake of helping those inferior beings to achieve enlightenment that it is shown as an impure land with many imperfections. It is like the heavenly gods all eat from the same jeweled vessels but the rice changes color according to the merits of each and every one of them."[4] Sengzhao 僧肇 (384–414), one of Kumārajīva's most talented disciples, wrote succinctly in his commentary on the *Vimalakīrti-nirdeśa Sūtra*: "The Pure Land is but the shadow and echo of one's mind" 淨土蓋是心之影響耳.[5]

This *Vimalakīrti* story, which teaches that what you are determines what you see, illustrates the power of the mind in an unequivocal way. Śāriputra's observation of the mortal world is noteworthy in its matter-of-fact frankness:

> When I look at this land, all I see are its hills, knolls, hollows, chasms, thorns, sands, pebbles, soil, rocks—it is littered with rubbish!

---

4. This translation is based on Kumārajīva's version, in *Vimalakīrti-nirdeśa Sūtra* 1.537–39, in *T* 14. The reference that the rice changes color according to the merits of the heavenly gods can be found in *Dīrghāgama Sūtra*: "For those with the greatest merits, the color of the rice is white; for those with average merits, the color is blue; for those with the least merits, the color is red" 若福多者飯色爲白，其福中者飯色爲青，其福下者飯色爲赤. *Dīrghāgama Sūtra* 長阿含經 20.134, in *T* 1.

5. Sengzhao, *Zhu Weimojie jing* 1.337, in *T* 38.

我見此土，丘陵坑坎，荊棘沙礫，土石諸山，穢惡充滿。

Interestingly, Śāriputra's description presents the very picture of a landscape. It is up to the viewer of this landscape to see how marvelous it truly is.

For the early medieval Chinese, however, nature was not simply "littered with rubbish," but populated with gods, goddesses, spirits, and goblins, and dotted with magical plants. Recluses sought peace and quiet in the mountains; Daoist adepts sought immortality and transcendence. More often than not, however, the two roles were indistinguishable, for many recluses in the third and fourth centuries went into the mountains with the explicit purpose of finding ingredients for making immortality potions and achieving transcendence.[6] Wang Xizhi 王羲之 (321–79), the well-known calligrapher, roamed in the famed mountains along with the Daoist Xu Mai 許邁 in quest of life-enhancing medicinal plants and presumably minerals as well.[7] Ji Kang 嵇康 (223–62), the Western Jin writer, "wandered in the mountains and marshes picking medicinal herbs; when acquiring the right mood, he would forget to return home. From time to time woodcutters ran into him, and all thought of him as a god."[8] The Chinese phrase for "acquiring the right mood" is *de yi* 得意, literally "acquiring the meaning or the concept." It is a loaded term in the "arcane discourse" and denotes the attainment of some sort of ultimate truth. *De*, "to acquire," is of central importance, for acquiring magical plants and hence immortality (*de xian* 得仙) and acquiring an abstract spiritual principle (*de yi*) belong to a coherent category of meaning. In either case, the focus is on obtaining the quintessence of a landscape, in implicit contrast with the woodcutters' procurement of firewood, which is no more than the superficial "skin and hair" or, to borrow a term from *Zhuangzi*, the "dross" (*zaopo* 糟魄) of the mountains.

The Ji Kang story is particularly edifying: as the aristocratic recluse "acquired the meaning" of the landscape, even though he had not yet achieved transcendence, he was already a "god" (*shen* 神) in the eyes of the rustic woodcutters. They would then propagate and perpetuate the myth of encountering deities in the mountains, which would presumably at-

6. For a discussion of the ingredients of the Daoist adept's "alternative cuisine" see Campany, *To Live as Long as Heaven and Earth*, pp. 25–30.

7. Fang Xuanling et al., *Jin shu* 80.2101.

8. Ibid., 49.1370.

tract more aristocratic recluses into the mountains in quest of themselves. The deification of the aristocrat reflects the social and historical reality of early medieval China with its stringent class hierarchy: commoners and gentry were divided by a gap no less wide than that separating mortals and deities. The rigid social grouping and classification even within the gentry class (as demonstrated by the Nine Ranks system established in the second century for evaluating people's characters and assessing their potential for political careers) was behind the conviction that only a select group could ever see the truth of things. This notion gained wide currency in the fourth century and was translated into the renowned poet-monk Zhi Dun's 支遁 (314–66) interpretation of Zhuangzi's chapter on "Free Roaming" ("Xiaoyao you" 逍遙遊). "Free Roaming" is about the possibility of spiritual freedom. Guo Xiang 郭象 (d. 312) and Xiang Xiu 向秀 (ca. 221–300), the two earlier commentators, stipulated that regardless of whether a creature was big or small, as long as it fulfilled its lot and satisfied its desires, it could achieve spiritual freedom;[9] Zhi Dun disagreed, arguing that only the Perfect Man (*zhiren* 至人) was capable of obtaining true spiritual freedom (*xiaoyao*).[10]

To a naïve woodcutter, a wandering gentleman might pass for a divine being, but the wandering gentleman also ran the risk of misperception: to be able to find the magical plant required more than just a trained eye; it was a subtle practice demanding rigorous preparation, without which the seeker would fail to see the magical plant even if it was right in front of him. The Daoist thinker Ge Hong made this point quite clear in his *Inner Chapters of the Master Who Embraces Simplicity* (*Baopuzi neipian* 抱朴子內篇). In the chapter entitled "Drugs of Immortality" ("Xianyao" 仙藥), he described a variety of mushrooms (*junzhi* 菌芝 or *zhi* 芝) that would grant immortality or at least a thousand years of life to those who ingested them. These mushrooms grew "in the deep mountains, or beneath some grand tree, or beside a fountain. Their shapes may resemble palaces and chambers, carriages and horses, dragons and tigers, human figures, and flying birds."[11] Ge Hong warns his readers:

---

9. *Zhuangzi jishi* 1.1.
10. Yan Kejun, *Quan Jin wen* 157.2366.
11. Ge Hong, *Baopuzi neipian jiaoshi* 11.183.

Famous mountains often have these various mushrooms, but mediocre Daoist adepts whose minds are not focused, whose actions are defiled and virtues few, and who do not know the techniques of entering the mountain properly will not be able to recognize their forms even if they have their pictures, and as a result will not be able to acquire the mushrooms. No matter whether a mountain is big or small, there are always spirits and deities residing there; *if the spirits and deities do not want to give the mushrooms to a person, then even when he steps on it, he will not see it*" [italics mine].[12]

此諸芝名山多有之，但凡庸道士，心不專精，行穢德薄，又不曉入山之術，雖得其圖，不知其狀，亦終不能得也。山無大小，皆有鬼神，其鬼神不以芝與人，人則雖蹊之，不可見也。

For instance, a "Stony Elephant Mushroom" was said to be so radiant that one could see its glow "three hundred paces away from it in a dark night," and yet, "unless one has purified oneself and is utterly focused, and unless one carries Laozi's *Five Talismans of Numinous Treasure for Entering the Mountains,* one will not be able to see it."[13] Ge Hong's discussion illuminates the point made in the *Vimalakīrti-nirdeśa Sūtra* from yet another angle: the efflorescence of the landscape is not available to everyone; it is only revealed to those who are worthy of it. This worthiness, as Ge Hong shows, is manifested first of all in one's attitude—a focused mind.

The focused mind acquired a special resonance in Buddhist teachings on meditation, with which two basic concepts are associated: śamatha 止 (calm abiding) and vipaśyanā 觀 (clear observation). The former refers to the stopping and stilling of actions and passions in order to achieve a serene concentration; the latter to the application of the power of concentration to an enlightened observation of the impermanent nature of reality and seeing things as they really are. *Guan* is often used with specific technical connotations, such as in *guanxiang* 觀想, to visualize the object of contemplation in one's mind. One may contemplate the thirty-two forms of the Buddha, or the Pure Land, or even a corpse (so as to recognize the impermanence of the world). The importance of *guanxiang* lies with the belief that visualization *is* realization. In other words, the Buddha himself is no more than a product of one's mind, a figment of the imagination. The mind is so powerful in its highly focused state that it

12. Ibid., 11.183.
13. Ibid., 11.178.

can literally bring the Buddha and his kingdom to realization; and yet, this realization itself is empty, unreal, just as dharma and "dharma-body" (the true nature of Buddhahood) are fundamentally empty. This ingenious formulation—that visualization is realization, and realization is unreal—testifies to the simultaneous reality *and* unreality of the Buddha, an essential teaching of Mahāyāna ("Great Vehicle" 大乘) Buddhism.

The *Pratyutpannasamādhi Sūtra* (*Foshuo banzhou sanmei jing* 佛說般舟三昧經), translated into Chinese at least three times before the Eastern Jin, contains a vivid discussion of the formulation. In this sutra, the Śākyamuni Buddha teaches that the Pure Land will be revealed to anyone who thinks of it for seven days and nights.

It is just like what one sees in a dream: it does not matter whether it is day or night, whether it is inside or outside; one will be able to see it even if it is shrouded in darkness, and one will be able to see it even if it is blocked from one's view. Bhadrapāla, a bodhisattva should think like this: that within the realm of the various Buddha lands, at the various great mountains, including Mount Sumeru, all places of veiled darkness will open up, and there shall be no covering or closure whatsoever. So the bodhisattva does not need to see with the Divine Eye, nor listen with the Divine Ear, nor go to the Buddha land with the Divine Power of Unimpeded Bodily Function, nor be born there; no, but the bodhisattva will see it right here, on this very seat.[14]

譬如人夢中所見, 不知晝不知夜, 亦不知内不知外, 不用在冥中故不見,不用有所弊礙故不見。颰陀和, 菩薩當作是念。時諸佛國境界中, 諸大山須彌山, 其有幽冥之處, 悉爲開闢, 無所蔽礙。是菩薩不持天眼徹視,不持天耳徹聽, 不持神足到其佛刹, 不於此間終生彼間, 便於此坐見之。

The metaphor of the dream underscores the immediacy of the vision as well as the unreal nature of the visualized image.

The Śākyamuni Buddha goes on to say that seeing the Buddha is like seeing one's own visage in a mirror:

"It is like a young good-looking person wearing handsome clothes and desiring to see himself. If he holds a mirror as bright as sesame oil, clear water, or crystal, and sees his own face in it, then shall we say that there is a reflection coming from outside into the mirror, or the sesame oil, or the water, or the crystal?" Bhadrapāla answered: "No, God of all gods, it is because of the purity of the mirror, the sesame oil, the water, or the crystal that one sees one's own reflection. The reflec-

14. *Pratyutpannasamādhi Sūtra* 2.899, in *T* 13.

tion neither comes from inside nor from outside." The Buddha said: "Good, Bhadrapāla. Since the color is clear and pure, what it shows is clear and pure. If one desires the Buddha, then one immediately sees the Buddha."

"譬如人年少端正著好衣服，欲自見其形。若以持鏡若麻油若淨水水精，於中照自見之，云何寧有影從外入鏡麻油水水精中不也?"颰陀和言："不也，天中天，以鏡麻油水水精淨故自見其影耳。影不從中出，亦不從外入。"佛言："善哉颰陀和，色清淨故所有者清淨。欲見佛即見。"

In the last analysis, the Buddha neither exists beyond the human mind nor can be perceived by a clouded mind. If one's mind is as pure as a bright mirror, the mirror naturally reveals the image of the Buddha—one has only to look into it.

The bright mirror reflecting the true form of everything caught the imagination of the famous Eastern Jin monk Huiyuan 慧遠 (334–416), who was intensely interested in the power of meditation and visualization. In the preface to a group of poems entitled *Meditating on the Buddha and Achieving Samādhi* (*Nian Fo sanmei shi ji xu* 念佛三昧詩集序), he elaborates on the mirror metaphor:

So he who enters into this meditation will become oblivious [to the world around him] and forget [secular] knowledge. He will take the object of his contemplation as a mirror; when the mirror is bright, his inner light shines forth, their rays joining, and myriad images are thus born, so that even without the help of ears and eyes, hearing and seeing are accomplished.[15]

故令入斯定者，昧然忘知．即所緣以成鑒，鑒明則内照交映，而萬像生焉；非耳目之所暨，而聞見行焉．

And yet, since the *Pratyutpannasamādhi Sūtra* often makes use of the metaphor of dream to describe the visualized image in one's meditative contemplation, Huiyuan, ever troubled by the Mahāyāna teaching about the lack of reality of the Buddha and the dharma-body, addressed an inquiry to Kumārajīva about the nature of the image rising from the dark recesses of one's mind during meditative visualization of the Buddha. Huiyuan felt that if the Buddha being visualized in one's mind was indeed a vision of the Buddha, then it would be inappropriate to use the metaphor of dream to describe such an experience, for dream represented "the sphere of a common person" ("meng shi fanfu zhi jing" 夢是凡夫之境).

15. Yan Kejun, *Quan Jin wen* 162.2402.

For Huiyuan, who believed in the ontological existence of the Buddha, a clear distinction existed between the Buddha established by the illusion of a real subjective "I" (*wo xiang zhi suoli* 我想之所立) and "the Sage [the Buddha] beyond dreams" (*mengbiao zhi shengren* 夢表之聖人), who had come to the meditating party from outside. In other words, what Huiyuan had wanted to achieve by meditative contemplation of the Buddha was a "real" vision sent by the Buddha, not an "empty" image generated by one's own mind.

In his response, Kumārajīva explained to Huiyuan that the metaphor of dream was merely an expedient way of teaching people about the power of meditation, and that the Buddha had no "definitive image that truly existed" (*juedingxiang* 決定相); any definitive image of the Buddha that truly existed was a product of thoughts, conjectures, speculations, and discriminations (Skt. sañjñā-vikalpa).[16] Kumārajīva's lengthy reply, like his answers to Huiyuan's other questions, once again manifests the profound gap between the two thinkers, a gap that the modern scholar Ren Jiyu considers as marking a profound difference between Huiyuan's background of native "arcane learning" (*xuanxue* 玄學) and Kumārajīva's more radical teachings about the fundamental emptiness of dharma and about the expedient, yet empty, nature of language, names, and concepts.[17] "Arcane learning," based on the works of Laozi and Zhuangzi, postulates a Non-being or Absence (*wu* 無) as the basic substance (*ti* 體) of the world, and "Being" or Presence (*you* 有) as the function (*yong* 用). Both Non-being and Being are believed to possess an ontological reality, a notion with which a Mahāyāna Buddhist like Kumārajīva would not agree. "Arcane learning" also claims that image (*xiang* 象, such as a hexagram) conveys the meaning (*yi* 意) of the Sage and language elucidates image, and so both image and language may be discarded after one "acquires the meaning."[18] The "meaning" itself is, however, regarded to be

16. Huiyuan and Kumārajīva, *Jiumoluoshi fashi dayi* (also known as *Dacheng dayi zhang* 大乘大義章) 2.134–35, in *T* 45.

17. Ren Jiyu, *Zhongguo Fojiao shi*, Vol. 2, pp. 676–701.

18. See, for instance, Wang Bi's 王弼 (226–49) commentary on the chapter "Elucidation of the Image" (*Mingxiang* 明象) of *The Classic of Changes*. As Stephen Owen (*Readings in Chinese Literary Thought*, p. 587) points out, *xiang* is "neither the particular thing. . . . nor the 'idea' of a thing, but rather a sensuous schematization of the normative thing. In literary usage, beginning in the Southern Dynasties, *hsiang* became strongly asso-

something real and constant, which again conflicts with Buddhist teachings. Many members of the Eastern Jin elite were well versed in Buddhist scriptures, but their understanding of Buddhism was often framed by the concepts and concerns of "arcane learning." In a way, Huiyuan's divergence from Kumārajīva was typical of his age, as Huiyuan was pursuing something solid, real, and permanent, an ultimate truth behind the diverse, transitory, and constantly changing phenomena of the universe. What stood out in Huiyuan's writings was his fascination with meditative visualization and the power of image—mental or otherwise. From the bright mirror that is both the contemplative mind and the object of contemplation, a light radiates, illuminating for Huiyuan the "myriad images" of the phenomenal world, including, first of all, the vicissitudes of the landscape. For Huiyuan, as long as one possessed the ability to see correctly, landscape was definitely not "littered with rubbish," but was a grand image that embodied the ultimate truth he was seeking.

Residing at Mount Lu for over thirty years, Huiyuan had had many opportunities to explore the famed beautiful scenery that surrounded him. It is generally believed that he was the leader of an outing to Stone Gate Mountain that took place in 400, an outing at which he was joined by about thirty monks. A preface written for the "Poems on an Excursion to the Stone Gate" ("You Shimen shi xu" 遊石門詩序) authored by an unknown member of this group best demonstrates such a transcendent perception of the landscape. The preface begins with an account of Stone Gate Mountain: where it is located, how its name came about, and why it is little explored ("The road is full of obstructions and going there is hard, which is why few people have passed through it").[19] Then the author relates the purpose of the group's outing (the "Dharma-master" wanted to "write poems about the mountains and waters"), and the immense hardship of their climb to the summit. Upon ascending the mountain, "we began to realize that of all the beauties of Mount Lu's seven peaks, the most wondrous were contained in this place." After a detailed description of the extraordinary scenery of the Stone Gate as well as an expression of the

---

ciated with 'appearances;' and thus the term is sometimes used imprecisely to refer to the phenomenal world."

19. Lu Qinli, *Quan Jin shi* 20.1086. For a complete English translation of the preface, see Strassberg, *Inscribed Landscapes*, pp. 68–71.

intense pleasure felt by those witnessing the beauty of the landscape, the author reflects on the source of their pleasure:

當其沖豫自得	In such serene contentment
信有味焉	there was truly a unique flavor,
而未易言也	yet it was not easy to put into words.
退而尋之	Withdrawing, we thought back upon it.
夫崖谷之間	Among the slopes and valleys,
會物無主	we grasped phenomena that were without governing subjectivity,
應不以情	and our response to them was not through emotion,
而開興引人	yet it initiated a mood of elation and drew us on,
致深若此	bringing us to such profound depths as this.
豈不以	It must have been that
虛明朗其照	cloudless enlightenment lent clarity to our perception,
閑邃篤其情邪	and a sense of calm distance deepened such sensibilities.
並三復斯談	We talked about this over and over again,
猶昧然未盡	yet it was still something dim and obscure, not fully exhausted.
俄而太陽告夕	Soon afterwards the sun announced the evening,
所存已往	and what we had lodged our hearts in disappeared from view;
乃悟幽人之玄覽	only then did we comprehend the dark vision of the recluse,
達恆物之大情	and realize the constant nature of things.
其爲神趣	The appeal was one of spirit,
豈山水而已哉	and not merely of mountains and waters.

This passage makes it clear that a proper mental state—something in the viewer rather than in the view itself—is the key factor in the appreciation of landscape; even more striking is its emphasis on the absence of emotional involvement in such a mental state. The author insists that one must maintain a dispassionate distance from the object of appreciation in order to perceive the beauty of the phenomenal world. In the last analysis, it is the viewer's "dark vision" (*xuanlan* 玄覽) that has the capacity to shed light on the myriad images. It is significant that comprehension (*wu* 悟) occurs after sunset: what the sightseers find "dim and obscure" (*meiran* 昧然) in broad daylight suddenly becomes illuminated in the dark; only after the earthly vision (*rouyan* 肉眼) fails do the Buddhist masters finally see.

Considering the close relationship of the Stone Gate outing with literary composition (the Buddhist masters went on an outing in order to "write poems about mountains and waters"), I should perhaps point out that the term *xuanlan* appears in Lu Ji's "Poetic Exposition on Literature" ("Wen fu" 文賦): "He stands in the very center, observes in the darkness" 佇中區以玄覽.[20] This opening line of the *fu* describes how the writer takes his position in the center of the cosmos and how his mind goes on a mystical journey in order to obtain "an imaginative experience of the things of the world."[21] As Owen notes, "The shift from purely empirical 'things of the world' implicit in earlier literary thought (e.g., in the 'Record of Music') to these 'things of the world' discovered in a spirit journey within the mind parallels the shift from the involuntarism of earlier literary thought to Lu Ji's voluntarism."[22] In contrast, the Buddhist masters speak of a "real" experience of the "real" things of the world, which seems to form the necessary basis of poetic composition. It is, however, imperative that one's seeing is at the same time also an envisioning—a seeing with imagination. In other words, beauty is not a property of the landscape, but rather originates from the interplay of the landscape and the perception of the viewer with "cloudless enlightenment."

That one is supposed to refrain from responding to phenomena emotionally presents a remarkable departure from the earlier model proposed in "The Record of Music" ("Yueji" 樂記) from *The Record of Rites* (*Liji* 禮記), in which the latent emotions in the human mind are "brought out" by external things.[23] Instead, the Buddhist masters of the Stone Gate call for a sense of "calm distance" to respond to the "mindless" things of the world ("phenomena without governing subjectivity"). This is not to say that the viewers are supposed to be unfeeling, but their mood of elation is an intellectual pleasure produced by a profound realization of the true nature of the landscape. This theme later reemerges in the poetry of Xie Lingyun, who was an avid admirer of the Buddhist master Huiyuan.

---

20. Lu Ji, *Wen fu jishi*, p. 20.
21. Owen, *Readings in Chinese Literary Thought*, pp. 87–88.
22. Ibid., p. 88.
23. Ibid., pp. 50–51.

Mind and Locale

The *Vimalakīrti* story teaches that what you are determines what you see, and the Eastern Jin elite understood the message well. The famous writer Sun Chuo 孫綽 (314–71), in his "Stele Inscription for the Grand Marshall Yu Liang" ("Taiwei Yu Liang bei" 太尉庾亮碑), praises the deceased minister for being able to "face the mountains and waters with *xuan*" ("yi xuan dui shanshui" 以玄對山水).[24] *Xuan* 玄, an important concept in *Laozi* that has been variously translated as dark, profound, abstruse, mysterious, esoteric, or arcane, was widely applied in the general religious, philosophical, and cultural discourse in the fourth century, indicating the attribute of the ultimate truth, or, as in Sun Chuo's inscription, the mental state of residing in the ultimate truth. For the Eastern Jin elite, facing the mountains and waters alone was not enough; one must approach them in the right state of mind. Once during an excursion to White Stone Mountain with Yu Liang, Sun Chuo made a contemptuous comment about someone in Yu Liang's entourage: "This fellow's spirit is not concerned with mountains and waters—how can he produce literary writing!"[25] For Sun Chuo, placing a man in front of mountains and waters did not necessarily entail the existence of a relation between the man and the landscape: only with the right spirit could the man be capable of establishing such a relation.

Indeed, the mind was considered so powerful that it could override one's physical environment. The Western Jin poet Lu Ji wrote in his "*Fu* on Responding to the Praise of Reclusion" ("Yingjia fu" 應嘉賦):

茍形骸之可忘	If one could forget one's body,
豈投簪其必谷	there is no need to cast the official's cap in the valleys.
方介邱于尺阜	A foot-long mound is likened to a high mountain,
託雲林乎一木	and the cloudy forest, lodged in a single tree.[26]

An anecdote from the fifth-century compilation *Shishuo xinyu* relates that when Emperor Jianwen of the Jin (r. 371–72) entered the Flowery Grove Park, he said to those in attendance:

---

24. Yan Kejun, *Quan Jin wen* 62.1814.
25. Liu Yiqing, *Shishuo xinyu jianshu* 8.478.
26. Yan Kejun, *Quan Jin wen* 96.2012.

The spot that suits the mind does not have to be far away. Hiding away by any grove or stream, one may quite naturally have a mental image of the Rivers Hao and Pu [where Zhuangzi roamed], and feel that birds and animals, fowl and fish come of their own accord to be intimate with men."[27]

會心處不必在遠,翳然林水,便自有濠濮閒想也.覺鳥獸禽魚自來親人.

A similar sentiment is conveyed in Wang Xizhi's poem composed at the famous gathering of Lanting on the third day of the third month in 353:

三春啓羣品	The spring months have heralded in various things,
寄暢在所因	my sense of expansiveness is lodged in what I encounter.
仰望碧天際	I gaze at the limits of the blue sky,
俯瞰淥水濱	then look down at the edge of the clear waters.
寥朗無厓觀	All is open and bright in a boundless view;
寓目理自陳	as the world meets my eyes, the truth is naturally revealed.
大矣造化功	How great are the accomplishments of the fashioner of things!
萬殊莫不均	Ten thousand different things, but all on the same level.
羣籟雖參差	Although the sounds of nature are various and uneven,
適我無非親	they are all intimate and endearing upon reaching me.[28]

This poem echoes Zhuangzi's discourse on "All Things Being on the Same Level" ("Qiwu lun" 齊物論), but it also stresses the importance of the subject "I" (*wo* 我), which appears in the last line: they are all intimate upon reaching *me*. It is the poet's gaze that reveals the hidden truth and his listening that perceives the sounds of nature as endearing.

For the masters of "arcane learning," the ideal monarch, who is supposed to be "a king without and a sage within" (*neisheng waiwang* 内聖外王), embodies the principle that spiritual freedom may be achieved regardless of one's status and locale.[29] Indeed, according to a contemporary poet:

---

27. Liu Yiqing, *Shishuo xinyu jianshu* 2.120–21. The translation is based on Richard Mather's translation, with modifications. See Liu Yiqing, *Shih-shuo hsin-yü*, p. 60.

28. Lu Qinli, *Quan Jin shi* 13.895. There is an interesting textual variant for the last character of the poem: *xin* 新 (new or fresh) for *qin* 親 (endearing, intimate).

29. *Zhuangzi jishi* 33.1069.

小隱隱陵藪	A lesser recluse hides in the mountains and marshes,
大隱隱朝市	but a great recluse hides in the court and marketplace.[30]

Such an outlook coincides with the Mahāyāna Buddhist teaching that the destiny of a bodhisattva lies within the secular world, not beyond, and a bodhisattva's duty is the salvation of all people, not just oneself. The *Mahāprajñāparamitā Sūtra* 大品般若經 (also known as the *Wisdom Sutra of the Emission of Light* or *Fangguang bore jing* 放光般若經, translated in 291) states:

If one resides alone, away from people, in the mountains and under the trees, that is not necessarily the way of vivarjana [keeping distance from worldly defilements]. . . . For those who carry out my teaching of peace in the secular world, even if they live beside the city wall, it will not be any different from living in the mountains and marshes.[31]

若在山間樹下獨處寂無人中，未必是爲遠離之法……若在人間隨我寂教者，雖在城傍爲與山澤等無有異。

It is not difficult to associate such a statement with the poet Tao Yuanming's 陶淵明 (365?–427) famous lines, which sum it up so well:

結廬在人境	I built my cottage in the human realm,
而無車馬喧	yet there is no noise of horse and carriage.
問君何能爾	How then did you manage to achieve this?
心遠地自偏	When the heart is faraway, the locale naturally becomes remote.[32]

In the fourth century, one of the major Buddhist "schools" or, to use Zürcher's wording, theories flourishing in south China was the so-called *xinwu zong* 心無宗, loosely translated as the "theory of the free mind."[33] This theory, advocated by Zhi Mindu 支敏度 (fl. third–fourth centuries) in the 320s, elevated the power of the mind to a new height. It believed that so long as the mind was free from attachment to things, things would

30. This is a couplet from a poem by the Jin poet Wang Kangju 王康琚, "Fan zhaoyin shi" 反招隱詩. Lu Qinli, *Quan Jin shi* 15.953.

31. *Mahāprajñāparamitā Sūtra* 14.96–97, in *T* 8.

32. Lu Qinli, *Quan Jin shi*, 17.998.

33. For a discussion of this theory, see Zürcher, *The Buddhist Conquest of China*, pp. 100–102. Zürcher renders the phrase *xinwu* as the "non-existence of mind."

retain their empty nature; in other words, it was the mind that made the phenomenal world empty. This left room for the argument that the phenomenal world was not inherently empty, and consequently the theory came under vehement attack from Zhu Fatai 竺法汰 (320–87), Huiyuan, and Sengzhao. And yet, the idea enjoyed great popularity in its day, especially in the area of Jingzhou 荊州 (in modern Hubei). According to the modern scholar Tang Yongtong, even though the school suffered a severe blow after Huiyuan defeated Zhi Mindu's follower Daoheng 道恆 (ca. fourth–fifth centuries) in a public debate in the 360s, it did not entirely lose its hold as Huijiao claimed in his *Biographies of Eminent Monks*.[34] Wang Mi 王謐 (360–407), the grandson of the great statesman Wang Dao 王導 (276–339), challenged Huan Xuan 桓玄 (369–404) on his belief in the "theory of the free mind," to which Huan Xuan wrote a reply; Liu Chengzhi 劉程之 (ca. 354–410), a devout Buddhist layman better known as Liu Yimin 劉遺民, composed "An Explication of the Theory of the Free Mind" ("Shi xinwu yi" 釋心無義). Although these writings are no longer extant, the titles are kept in Sengyou's 僧佑 (445–518) *A Collection of Records of Translated Tripitaka* (*Chu sanzang ji ji* 出三藏記集).[35] Liu Yimin was one of Tao Yuanming's close friends, and Tao Yuanming had addressed two poems to him. It would seem reasonable that the two of them had shared certain intellectual and spiritual concerns, including the conviction that the mind influenced and defined one's locale.

There was, of course, always an emphasis on physical detachment as a precondition for spiritual transcendence. Ge Hong lamented that when he lived in the city, even though he did not call on others, people would call on him, distracting him from his concentration on spiritual matters. "Mountains and forests do not possess the Way," he said, "and yet those ancients who searched for the Way had to enter the mountains and forests, because they desired to keep their distance from noise and clamor and protect their peace of mind."[36]

---

34. Tang Yongtong, *Han Wei liang Jin nanbeichao Fojiao shi*, p. 186; Huijiao, *Gaoseng zhuan* 5.192.

35. Sengyou, *Chu sanzang ji ji* 12.429.

36. Ge Hong, *Baopuzi waipian jiaojian* 50.694.

A fascinating group of poems exchanged between Zhang Yi 張翼 (style name Junzu 君祖, fl. ca. 344–61) and the monk Kang Sengyuan 康僧淵 (ca. fl. 300–350) seems to exemplify the two different strands of thought about mind and locale. Zhang Yi was one of the earliest known "forgers" of Wang Xizhi's calligraphy; his forgery was so good that it almost fooled the great calligrapher himself.[37] He initially addressed a set of three poems to a monk called Zhu Fajun 竺法頵. In the preface to the poems, Zhang Yi explains that Zhu Fajun was going to withdraw to the western mountains for spiritual cultivation, and so he wrote the poems both to say farewell and to "tease" him. The first poem begins by praising the beautiful scenery of the mountains but ends by questioning Zhu Fajun's choice:

外物豈大悲	Is it Great Compassion to leave the world of things?
獨往非玄同	Going alone is not the way of Profound Sharing.
不見舍利弗	Don't you see that Śāriputra
受屈維摩公	has submitted to Vimalakīrti?[38]

Zhang Yi's point is that one should, like Vimalakīrti, stay within the secular world and work for universal salvation, rather than going off to beautiful, remote locales to make spiritual progress that benefits oneself alone. In a manner typical of his age, he uses both Buddhist and Daoist terms to argue for staying within the secular world and working for universal salvation. While the phrase *xuantong* (Profound Sharing) is taken from *Laozi*, the phrase *dabei* (Great Compassion, Skt. mahā-karuṇā) is an attribute of the Buddha, and differs from ordinary compassion in that it not only embodies mercy for others but also accomplishes the very act of deliverance from suffering.[39] Vimalakīrti was a Buddhist layman; his understanding of the Buddha's teachings, however, proved much deeper than that of the monk Śāriputra. The *Vimalakīrti-nirdeśa Sūtra* advocates dwelling in the midst of the secular world both to achieve enlightenment oneself and to help others achieve enlightenment, and opposes the view that one must stay far away from the human realm for one's own spiritual progress. Zhang Yi's reference to these two well-known figures, Vi-

37. See Yu He's 虞龢 "A Memorial on Calligraphy" ("Lun shu biao" 論書表) presented to Emperor Ming of the Song 宋明帝 in 470, in Yan Kejun, *Quan Song wen* 55.2731.

38. Lu Qinli, *Quan Jin shi* 12.893.

39. *Laozi jiaoshi*, p. 228.

malakīrti and Śāriputra, playfully implies a parallel situation between himself, a layman, and Zhu Fajun, a monk.

Zhang Yi makes his point more explicitly at the end of the third poem by appealing to the rhetoric of the self-styled Mahāyāna ("Great Vehicle") Buddhism that advocates universal salvation, as opposed to the so-called "Small Vehicle" school that advocates self-cultivation. Although the differentiation between the "Great Vehicle" and "Small Vehicle" is debated in modern times, it was a rhetorical move made in the *Vimalakīrti-nirdeśa Sūtra* itself, and Zhang Yi uses it in his argument against going off to the mountains.

苟能夷沖心	If one can calm one's mind,
所憩靡不淨	wherever one stays is the Pure Land.
萬物可逍遙	One may roam free in myriad things;
何必棲形影	what's the need to rest one's form and shadow?
勉尋大乘軌	I urge you to seek the tracks of the Great Vehicle,
練神超勇猛	cultivate your spirit, and excel in being courageous.[40]

To be "courageous" is the trait of a bodhisattva, a sentient being of great enlightenment in vigorous pursuit of Buddhahood through the salvation of self and others. In the *Vimalakīrti-nirdeśa Sūtra*, Maṇjūsri Bodhisattva employs a powerful metaphor to convey the importance of residing within the secular world to achieve enlightenment: "The plateau or the highland cannot produce the blue lotus; only in the lowland, in mud, can the lotus grow."[41] Similarly, in Zhang Yi's vision, spiritual perfection is not something to be sought in reclusion; one's state of mind is paramount and has the power to transform a locale.

Zhu Fajun, who was probably not skilled in poetic composition, did not respond to Zhang Yi's exhortations. It was Kang Sengyuan, a monk of non-Chinese descent who was born in Chang'an and spoke perfect Chinese, who replied to Zhang Yi's playful challenge in verse. Defending Zhu Fajun's choice of reclusion and hinting at the superiority of entering into religious orders, Kang Sengyuan retorts:

幽閑自有所	There is naturally a place for seclusion;
豈與菩薩并	how could one claim to be the same as a bodhisattva?

40. Lu Qinli, *Quan Jin shi*, 12.893.

41. *Vimalakīrti-nirdeśa Sūtra* 2.549, in *T* 14.

摩詰風微指 Vimalakīrti revealed the Buddha's subtle intent;
權道多所成 his expedient means accomplished a great deal.
悠悠滿天下 And yet, of all the people in the whole world,
孰識秋露情 who understood the feelings of Śāriputra?[42]

Zhang Yi's poem in response to Kang Sengyuan once again affirms his preference for the enlightened layman Vimalakīrti. The last couplet of the poem explicitly states his conviction that the power of imagination (*xiang* 想) is of primary significance in the pursuit of enlightenment:

三法雖成林 Although the three dharmas constitute a grove,[43]
居士亦有黨 a layman also has his community.
不見虬與龍 Don't you see the krakens and dragons
灑鱗凌霄上 that extend their scales and ascend into heaven?
沖心超遠寄 A calm mind is better than lodging oneself faraway;
浪懷邈獨往 letting one's mind roam takes one further than going off alone.
眾妙常所晞 All wonders are what I constantly desire,
維摩余所賞 but Vimalakīrti is whom I admire.
苟未體善權 If you have not comprehended the principle of expediency,
與子同彿髣 then you and I shall share the same mere approximation.
悠悠誠滿域 There are indeed people all over the world,
所遺在廢想 but where they err is in their neglect of imagination.[44]

Kang Sengyuan did not give up. It seems that he finally had the last word in this spirited game of witty exchange, not by any subtle reasoning, but by sheer persistence and rhetorical flourish. For this reason the poem deserves to be cited in its entirety:

遙望華陽嶺 I gaze afar at the Huayang Ridge;
紫霄籠三辰 the purple heaven embraces the sun, moon, and stars.
瓊巖朗璧室 Alabaster cliffs open up a jade chamber;
玉潤灑靈津 waters of jade splash over the numinous ford.
丹谷挺樛樹 In the valley of cinnabar grow trees with overhanging boughs,

42. Lu Qinli, *Quan Jin shi* 20.1075.

43. The three dharmas refer to sutra 經, vinaya 律, and abhidharma 論; or the three aspects of dharma: teaching 教, practice 行, and realization 證.

44. Lu Qinli, *Quan Jin shi* 12.894.

季穎奮暉薪 even the tiniest tip of a plant strives in the daily-refreshed light.[45]
融飆衝天籟 Harmonious winds dash against the flutes of heaven;
逸響互相因 their trailing echoes follow one after another.
鸞鳳翔迴儀 Simurghs and phoenixes soar and linger;
虬龍灑飛鱗 krakens and dragons extend their scales in the air.
中有冲漠士 In the midst there is a gentleman of serenity,
耽道玩妙均 indulging in the Way, playing with the wondrous equality of things.
高尚凝玄寂 High-minded, noble, and focused on profound stillness,
萬物忽自賓 myriad things suddenly submit to him of their own accord.[46]
棲峙遊方外 Resting in the mountains, roaming outside the secular realm,
超世絶風塵 he transcends this world, beyond the wind and dust.
翹想晞眇蹤 My imagination soars, desiring his distant tracks;
矯步尋若人 raising my steps, I will seek out that person.
詠嘯舍之去 Chanting, whistling, I shall leave this world behind—
榮麗何足珍 glory and luxury are nothing to be treasured.
濯志八解淵 Cleansing my mind in the canyon of the Eight Liberations,
遼朗豁冥神 I become enlightened, opened up, receptive to the mysterious spirit.
研幾通微妙 Studying the subtle truth and grasping the refined essence,
遺覺忽忘身 discarding the senses, I suddenly forget my body.
居士成有黨 A layman indeed has his community,
顧眄非疇親 but as I look around, former associates are no longer intimate.

---

45. Here *xin* 薪 is exchangeable with *xin* 新, and *huixin* 暉薪 is an abbreviated form of the phrase *huiguang rixin* 暉光日新, "daily renewed and refreshed light." The Western Jin writer Zhang Hua's 張華 (232–300) "Encouraging Aspirations" ("Lizhi shi" 勵志詩) contains these lines: "Improve one's virtue and cultivate one's accomplishments, / and one's light is renewed every day" (進德修業, 暉光日新). Lu Qinli, *Quan Jin shi* 3.615.

46. This line is an allusion to *Laozi*: "If princes and lords may hold fast to it [the Way], then myriad things will submit of their own accord" 王侯若能守, 萬物將自賓. *Laozi jiaoshi*, p. 130.

借問守常徒	Let me ask those people who keep to the ordinary:
何以知反眞	what do they know about returning to the genuine?[47]

Structurally, Kang Sengyuan's poem may be divided into four parts. The first ten lines present an attractive picture of the landscape, and the next six lines situate the reclusive monk right in the midst of it. The poet then claims that he will aspire to emulate the reclusive monk by leaving the secular world behind and seeking enlightenment. While Zhang Yi's poem stresses the triumph of imagination over physical locale, Kang Sengyuan underscores the importance of using one's imagination to follow the footsteps of the reclusive monk, "discarding the senses" and "forgetting the body."[48] The last four lines contrast Zhang Yi's exaltation of the lay community with the Buddhist clerical way of life. Kang Sengyuan gives a clever twist on the word *chang* 常, used in Zhang Yi's poem in the sense of "constant" ("All wonders are what I constantly desire"), asking how people holding on to the "ordinary" (also *chang* 常) could ever hope to "return to the genuine." In a way, Kang Sengyuan and Zhang Yi's poetic exchange may be viewed as versified "arcane discourse," as it demonstrates the two opposing attitudes about the mind and locale.[49]

---

47. Lu Qinli, *Quan Jin shi* 20.1076.

48. Such a progressive structure is hardly novel in the poetry of early medieval China: many "poems of wandering immortals" (*youxian shi* 遊仙詩) and poems on reclusion share the same feature, and the grammatical structure of "zhong you XX shi" ("in the midst there is a XX gentleman," XX being an attribute such as "high-minded," "serene," or "in pursuit of the Way") is a standard portrait of a transcendent figure, be it a recluse or an immortal or often both, who is located in the mountains and waters. Vowing to seek and follow such a transcendent man is also a common trope.

49. Zhang Yi and Kang Sengyuan's poems are preserved in *A Continuation of the Collection of Expanding the Light* (*Guang hongming ji* 廣弘明集), a collection of Buddhist writings compiled by the monk Daoxuan 道宣 (596–667) in 664. This collection also includes the three-poem set *Singing of My Feelings* (*Yonghuai shi* 詠懷詩) by Zhang Yi, the first of which contains the following lines: "What is the need for dwelling in seclusion, / wearing the black robe as a sign of leaving the secular world?" The black robe is the monk's attire. It stresses that even if one finds oneself among unworthy people, one should "forget the mixture of pebbles and jade" and strive to "soothe the inner workings of the mind" 要在夷心曲. *Guang hongming ji* 30.359, in *T* 52; Lu Qinli, *Quan Jin shi* 12.891.

Imaginary Mountains

Xie Daoyun 謝道韞 (fl. ca. late fourth century), a female member of the illustrious Xie clan, left a poem entitled "A Song of Mount Tai" ("Taishan yin" 泰山吟):

峨峨東嶽高	How lofty is the Great Peak of the East,
秀極沖青天	so very striking, rising up to the blue sky.
巖中間虛宇	Among the crags is an empty chamber,
寂漠幽以玄	quiet, serene, profound, and mysterious.
非工復非匠	Created neither by workers nor craftsmen,
雲構發自然	its cloudy structures issue forth from What Is Naturally So.
器象爾何物	What sort of things are you—you vessels and images,[50]
遂令我屢遷	that you should frequently transport me so?
逝將宅斯宇	I promise to take residence in that chamber,
可以盡天年	so that I may live out my natural life's span.[51]

Even if the title might not be reliable, the first line of the poem, which makes a reference to the "Great Peak of the East," leaves no doubt that this is a poem about Mount Tai. The only question is: did Xie Daoyun ever set eyes on Mount Tai?

A couplet like "What sort of things are you—you vessels and images, / that you should frequently transport me so?" seems to suggest that she did. And yet, through most of the fourth century, Mount Tai was in the much contested northern territory. Xie Daoyun's poem might very well have been inspired by a real historical event, as the Eastern Jin army, led by none other than her brother Xie Xuan 謝玄 (343–88), had briefly claimed

50. "Vessels and images" (*qixiang* 器象) was a contemporary term for the things of the phenomenal world. See note 66 below.

51. Lu Qinli, *Quan Jin shi* 13.912. "Taishan yin" is a *yuefu* title. Two poems written under this title are recorded in the thirteenth-century compilation *Yuefu shiji* 樂府詩集, but Xie Daoyun's poem is not one of them. Xie Daoyun's poem initially appears in the early Tang encyclopedia *Yiwen leiju* 藝文類聚 (comp. 624) with no title (7.123). A Ming anthology edited by Feng Weine 馮惟訥 (1512–72) compiles it under the title "Ascending the Mountain" ("Deng shan" 登山). *Gushi ji* 古詩紀 47.389. The poem also appears in *A History of Mt. Tai* (*Dai shi* 岱史) (15.83), compiled by Zha Zhilong 查志隆 (*jinshi* 1559) and edited by Zhang Jinyan 張縉彥 (*jinshi* 1631). In *Daojiao yaoji xuankan* 道教要籍選刊, Vol. 7.

the Mount Tai region in 384. Later, it was again recovered by Liu Yu 劉裕 (363–422) during his northern campaign in 410. Ten years before that, however, Xie Daoyun's husband Wang Ningzhi 王凝之 (d. 399) was killed in the Sun En rebellion, and Xie Daoyun "had lived in Kuaiji [in modern Zhejiang] as a widow ever since."[52] It is highly unlikely that Xie Daoyun would have traveled to Mount Tai in person.

Nevertheless, Xie Daoyun did not have to go to Mount Tai to write those lines. A number of literary precedents before her had represented spirit journeys. The most notable example would have been Sun Chuo's "*Fu* on Roaming Mount Tiantai" ("You Tiantai shan fu" 遊天台山賦), which was already a famous piece of writing in its own time. Sun Chuo, however, had not been to Mount Tiantai when he wrote the *fu*. In its unrhymed preface, he gives an account of the occasion of the composition of the *fu*. After explaining that the inaccessibility of Mount Tiantai was the main reason why it was rarely scaled and not listed among the Five Great Peaks, Sun Chuo reflects on his spirit journey to Mount Tiantai:

Not many men alive in an age can scale them; and no prince has a way to perform sacrifices there. Thus notice of them is absent in common texts, and their name is remarked only in accounts of things rare. Even so, should we think it for nothing that there is such an abundance of pictures and illustrations of them? Unless a man gives up the world and practices the right Way, quitting common grains and feeding on asphodel, he cannot lift off in lightness and lodge there. Unless a man gives himself over to things remote and delves into dark mysteries, unless he is someone utterly sincere and in contact with the gods, he can never envision that remote place and hold it fast. It was for this reason that I sent my spirit rushing and worked my thoughts, sang by day and stayed waking by night. And in the interval of a nod, it was as if I had gone up the mountain more than once. Now I will untie these bands of an officer's cap to lodge forever on these crests. I cannot resist the full force of such visions and spontaneous chanting, so let me here make a show of fine phrases to disperse these concerns.

舉世罕能登陟，王者莫由禋祀，故事絶於常篇，名標於奇紀。然圖像之興，豈虛也哉？非夫遺世玩道、絶粒茹芝者，烏能輕舉而宅之？非夫遠寄冥搜、篤信通神者，何肯遙想而存之？余所以馳神運思，晝詠

52. Fan Xuanling et al., *Jin shu* 96.2516.

宵興，俛仰之間，若已再升者也。方解纓絡，永託茲嶺。不任吟想之至，聊奮藻以散懷。[53]

In this preface, Sun Chuo makes it clear that his *fu* is based not on actual experience, but on visualization (*xiang*): he was able to see the place in his mind by intensely contemplating the mountain day and night. Furthermore, the reference to "pictures and illustrations" suggests that Sun Chuo was using visual representations as an aid in his visualization of the mountain. Although the *fu* itself describes in great detail the author's "ascent," the framework is established at the very beginning: it is a spiritual, not physical, pilgrimage.

The *fu* begins by recounting the primordial landscape:

太虛遼廓而無閡	Utter Void, hollow magnitudes, lacking all limit,
運自然之妙有	there worked elusive presence: What Is Naturally So.
融而爲川瀆	It liquefied and formed the streams and channels;
結而爲山阜	it hardened and formed the mountains and knolls.

It then moves on to a specific spot, namely Mount Tiantai. Besides extolling its loftiness and superiority over other famous mountains, the author takes care to tell the reader about its actual geographical location. It is situated in the region of Yue, which falls under the province of the Herder star:

蔭牛宿以曜峰	It shadows the Herder star with glowing peaks,
託靈越以政基	lodged in Yue the Holy for well-set foundation.

It is so far away and so secluded that people lacking imagination do not go there, and those seeking to undertake the physical journey cannot find access to it. The author expresses his scorn for such people, and voices his longing "to mount upward."

邈彼絕域	Remote are these tracts, far flung,
幽邃窈窕	secret recesses well sequestered.
近智者以守見不之	Stuck within senses, short-sighted wisdom goes not thither;

53. Yan Kejun, *Quan Jin wen* 61.1806. Owen's translation. *An Anthology of Chinese Literature*, pp. 185–88. There are several other English translations of this *fu*: see Mather, "A Mystical Ascent of the T'ien-t'ai Mountains"; Knechtges, *Wen xuan,* Vol. 2, pp. 243–53.

之者以路絶而莫曉 since paths run out, those who would go never can know it.
哂夏蟲之疑冰 I scorn such summer bugs, who doubt there is ice,
整輕翮而思矯 I hold light wings straight, I long to mount upward.

The *fu* suggests that an intense desire is all one needs to take off in a fantastic flight. Such a spiritual ascent proves to be a more gratifying experience than entering the immortal realm:

苟台嶺之可攀 If only I might climb to Tiantai's crest,
亦何羨於層城 what craving then would be left for Tiered Walls Mountain?[54]

Then, on top of Mount Tiantai, the author experiences mystical transportation and enlightenment when, at last,

渾萬象以冥觀 I blur the thousands of images by dark observation,
兀同體於自然 my body, insensate, identical with What Is Naturally So.

Zhi Dun, an acquaintance of Sun Chuo, wrote a poem on the same subject: an imaginary ascent of Mount Tiantai. A comparison of the *fu* and the poem highlights the different generic conventions of *fu* and poetry, while showing that both pieces belong to the same cultural discourse of the Eastern Jin, a discourse that was deeply concerned with the issues of visualization and imagination. Structurally, the poem proceeds in the typical configuration discussed earlier in regard to Kang Sengyuan's poem: first a description of the landscape; then the appearance of a transcendent figure in the landscape, punctuated by the familiar line: "In the midst there is a gentleman who seeks the Transformation" ("Zhongyou xunhua shi" 中有尋化士); finally, the expression of the poet's wish to follow the footsteps of such an immortal/recluse. The description of the landscape is, however, preceded by an opening in a modest, ordinary setting, and this setting turns out to be crucial for establishing the tone for the poem. The reader is given to understand that the landscape to be portrayed in great detail in the poem is but a figment of the poet's imagination. The grand, sublime, and mystical mountain exists in an imaginary space, yet the poet

54. Tiered Walls was the highest peak of the mythical Mount Kunlun in the west. In early medieval poetry, it was often used to indicate the enchanted world of the Undying.

has never left his vegetable garden, where he is touched by the eternal return of spring, the passage of time, and the non-cyclical progress of human life:

晞陽熙春圃	The gentle sun shines on the spring vegetable garden,
悠緬歎時往	at leisure, with far-off thoughts, I sigh about the passage of time.
感物思所託	Touched by things, I long for that in which I lodge myself,
蕭條逸韻上	and the air of lofty detachment rises upward.
尚想天台峻	In my mind I see the loftiness of Mount Tiantai;
髣髴巖階仰	dimly, I seem to be gazing at its precipitous stairs.
泠風灑蘭林	A cool breeze spreads in the magnolia grove,
管瀨奏清響	a stream is piping out a clear sound.
霄崖育靈藹	Cliffs touching the sky nurture a numinous mist;
神蔬含潤長	divine vegetables, moist within, are growing.
丹沙映翠瀨	Cinnabar sand glows in the azure brook,
芳芝曜五爽	and fragrant mushrooms shine in five-colored brilliance.
苕苕重岫深	Towering and soaring, layers of peaks recede afar,
寥寥石室朗	revealing a tranquil and spacious stone chamber.
中有尋化士	In the midst there is a gentleman who seeks the Transformation,
外身解世網	placing himself beyond the mortal realm, disentangled from the net of the world.
抱朴鎮有心	Embracing simplicity, he suppresses the thoughts of Being;
揮玄拂無想	wielding the Mystery, dipping in conceptions of Nothingness.
隗隗形崖頹	Steep and towering, the cliffs of the body crumble away;
冏冏神宇敞	with a radiant light, the house of the spirit opens up.
宛轉無造化	Changing with things and transcending Transformation,
縹瞥鄰大象	he suddenly drifts off and becomes a neighbor to the Great Image.
願投若人蹤	I wish to follow that man's tracks,
高步振策杖	walking with big strides, raising my staff.[55]

Translated as "poetic exposition," *fu* first flourished as a form of rhapsodic performance in the Western Han, and had already been firmly es-

55. Lu Qinli, *Quan Jin shi* 20.1081.

tablished as a tradition by the fourth century. As Martin Kern explains, "In Han times, the word *fu* is interchangeable with a series of homophones or near-homophones that all mean 'to display' or 'to spread out,' linking the genre to the poetic mode of 'exposition.'"[56] It is typically rhymed, and aspires to be both all-encompassing and general when describing a place or an object. A *fu* on a mountain or a river, for instance, tends to give lengthy, detailed depiction of every facet of the mountain or the river. In contrast, early medieval Chinese poetry was increasingly focused on specific circumstances and individual situations. The dramatic effect of Zhi Dun's poem depends almost entirely on its opening couplet, which situates the poet at a specific time and in a specific place. The physical locale of the poet—his springtime vegetable garden—forms a striking contrast with the majestic Mount Tiantai with its exotic, numinous vegetation such as the magnolia grove and the fragrant mushroom, bringing out the disparity between the spiritual and the mundane, the transcendental and the ordinary. His body confined to a humble, familiar setting, the poet goes on a spirit journey to a mystical mountain. It is *xiang*, a mental seeing and envisioning, that connects the two vastly different worlds.

The mountain is compared to a human body, with its cliffs as the corporeal form and the stone chamber with the meditating figure as the spirit. That transcendent figure is thus literally the *shen* 神 (soul, spirit, god) of the mountain; to seek and find him symbolizes the achievement of transcendence—both *de Dao* (attaining the Way) and *de xian* (attaining immortality). And yet, as the "cliffs of the body" collapse and the "house of the spirit" opens up, one realizes that what is to be found is not and should not be a physical human being in the stone chamber. For all his vivid imagination, what the poet sets his heart on is the approximation of the Great Image (*da xiang* 大象), which, according to Laozi, "has no shape" (*wuxing* 無形).[57] Therefore, the last couplet does not necessarily indicate a physical journey: following the footsteps of the transcendent figure is a spiritual exercise, and entails no more than "suppressing the thoughts of Being" and "dipping in conceptions of Nothingness." In the last analysis, the stone chamber seems none other than an image of the

---

56. Kern, "Early Chinese Literature, Beginnings through Western Han," Vol. 1, Ch. 1 of Owen, ed., *The Cambridge History of Chinese Literature*, p. 88.

57. *Laozi jiaoshi*, p. 171.

poet's own mind, and the physical self—the cliffs of the body—must collapse for the spirit to be free.

Another poem by Zhi Dun, also entitled "Singing of My Feelings" ("Yonghuai shi" 詠懷詩), reinforces the importance of spiritual progress over physical pilgrimage.[58]

端坐鄰孤影	I sit upright, a neighbor to my lonely shadow;
眇罔玄思劬	intent thoughts on mystery reach far and deep.
偃蹇收神轡	I gather in the reins of the spirit as it bounds off,
領略綜名書	and set out to grasp the principles of famous books.
涉老咍雙玄	Immersing myself in *Laozi*, I delight in the Double Mysteries;
披莊玩太初	opening up *Zhuangzi*, I savor the Grand Beginning.
詠發清風集	As I read the passages aloud, a clear breeze alights;
觸思皆恬愉	all that touches my thought is peaceful and pleasant.
俯欣質文蔚	Bending to read, I am pleased with the splendor of both content and style;
仰悲二匠徂	looking up, I feel saddened by the falling away of the two craftsmen.
蕭蕭柱下吏	Forever gone is the Clerk Standing by the Pillar;[59]
寂寂蒙邑虛	how silent and empty is Mengyi![60]
廓矣千載事	Already distant, these events of a thousand years ago,
消液歸空無	vanish and return to emptiness and nothing.
無矣復何傷	They are gone—but what need is there to lament?
萬殊歸一塗	Myriad differences will all return to one road.
道會貴冥想	As the paths converge, one treasures visualization of the unseen—
罔象掇玄珠	it is Imagelessness who found the Black Pearl.[61]
悵快濁水際	Feeling melancholy on the banks of turbid waters,
幾忘映清渠	I almost forgot to look at my reflection in the clear river.[62]

---

58. Lu Qinli, *Quan Jin shi* 20.1080–81.

59. Laozi had served as a clerk who stood "by the pillar" of the court.

60. Mengyi was said to be the hometown of Zhuangzi.

61. The Yellow Emperor wandered north of the Red River, and he lost his Black Pearl, a symbol of the Way. He first sent Knowledge to look for it, but Knowledge could not find it. He then sent Lizhu (who was keen-sighted) to look for it, then Wrangling Debate, but neither of them could find it. He finally sent Imagelessness, and Imagelessness found it. *Zhuangzi jishi* 12.414.

反鑒歸澄漠	Returning to self-observation and finally to concealment,
容與含道符	letting go of restraints, I harbor the omen of the Way.
心與理理密	The mind is intimate with holding truth as truth;
形與物物疏	the body removed from treating things as things.[63]
蕭索人事去	Human affairs are quietly left behind;
獨與神明居	I live alone with the transcendent spirit.

The poem opens with the solitary figure of the poet engaged in reading and reflection. What he reads are *Laozi* and *Zhuangzi*, slightly unexpected for a Buddhist monk, but not surprising in the diverse intellectual milieu of the fourth century. That the authors of these works are long gone evokes the famous story from *Zhuangzi* about the Wheelwright Bian, who considers the books read by Duke Huan of Qi—books by authors long dead—as the mere "dregs of the ancients."[64] But the poet decides not to be troubled by that, for it is not in the words left by the ancients that one finds enlightenment, but in the "visualization of the unseen" (*ming xiang* 冥想). Just as Sun Chuo declares that myriad images eventually become blurred in the "dark observation," so Zhi Dun believes that the Way ultimately resides in Imagelessness.

The poem exemplifies a process: from the initial "thoughts on mystery" (*xuan si* 玄思) the poet proceeds to reading; from reading he proceeds to the "visualization of the unseen" (*ming xiang*). The contrast between *si* and *xiang* recalls their second-century definition: "Where one lodges one's thoughts is called *si*; it is as if one sees the form [of the object of contemplation] right in front of oneself—this is called *xiang*." The end of the poem returns to the motif of solitude illustrated in the opening couplet. By this time, however, the poet is no longer just "a neighbor" to his lonely shadow, but rather lives "alone with the transcendent spirit."

In many ways, Zhi Dun's poems on reading, contemplative visualization, and flights of imagination anticipate Tao Yuanming's series of thirteen poems on *Reading the* Classic of Mountains and Seas (*Du* Shanhai jing 讀山海經). This series begins with the poet reading in an early summer garden, yet another familiar everyday setting, and goes on to a

62. "Zhuangzi said: 'I keep to my body and forget about my self—this is like looking at myself in the turbid water and becoming confused in the clear river.'" Ibid., 20.698.

63. Ibid., 20.668.

64. Ibid., 13.490.

spirit journey inspired by the exotic, mythical geography of the poet's reading material, as well as the ancient Zhou king's legendary tour to fantastic lands.[65] These poems, along with Sun Chuo's *fu* discussed earlier, descend from the old tradition of the heavenly wanderings of the *Verses of Chu* (*Chu ci* 楚辭), and yet, in these Eastern Jin texts, the roaming is always carried out in the mind. Tao Yuanming's genius is manifested in his unique articulation of the experience of reading. It is as a reader, and by means of words, that he is transported to a different place—a place no more and no less real than Sun Chuo, Zhi Dun, and Xie Daoyun's imaginary mountains.

Painted Mountains

In her poem, Xie Daoyun uses the phrase "vessels and images" (*qixiang* 器象) to describe the landscape. This phrase, when turning up in Eastern Jin texts, always appears as the concrete manifestation or the physical embodiment of the Way or the Mystery (*xuan*).[66] If real mountains and waters are nothing but "vessels and images," then it is more so for a painted landscape. The Eastern Jin was not only an age in which Buddhism, the "doctrine of images" or "teaching using images" (*xiang jiao* 像教), flourished, but also a time when the visual arts were thriving.[67] There may have been more than a tenuous relation between the two phenomena.

---

65. I give a detailed discussion of the cosmic journey in this poetic series in Tian, *Tao Yuanming and Manuscript Culture*, pp. 148–66. For a fascinating discussion of reading in medieval China, see Jack Chen, "On the Act and Representation of Reading in Medieval China."

66. For instance, see Yu Chan's 庾闡 (fl. ca. 339) "Encomium on the Portraits of Yu and Shun" ("Yu Shun xiang zan" 虞舜像贊): "The ultimate Way is mysterious and wonderful, not something that can be conveyed by vessels and images" 至道玄妙, 非器象所載. Yan Kejun, *Quan Jin wen* 38.1680. Also see the monk Daoheng's "A Defense of Buddhism" ("Shi bo lun" 釋駁論): "The wind of the Way is mysterious and distant, not something that can be illustrated by vessels and images" 道風玄遠, 非器象所擬. Yan Kejun, *Quan Jin wen* 163.2406.

67. As far as scholars can determine, the term *xiang jiao* appeared in Chinese writings for the first time in the fourth century. For an excellent study of the visual arts—painting, calligraphy, and sculpture—in the Eastern Jin, see Zhang Keli, *Dong Jin wenyi zonghe yanjiu*.

At first glance, a painted landscape seems to be more "real" than an imaginary landscape, for painting is executed on paper and with ink, visible to the eye and tangible to the touch. And yet, when the *Sutra of Perfect Wisdom* teaches "causes and conditions," it uses painting as an example:

Again, listen to me, the Worthy One. It is like a painter: there is a wall, there are colors, there is the craftsman, and there is a brush. Only when they all come together is a painted figure accomplished.

賢者復聽。譬如畫師，有壁，有彩，有工師，有筆，合會是事，乃成畫人。[68]

In the sense that painting depends on various conditions and causes to exist, it has no "self-nature," and so is unreal. In the sense that it represents the likeness of a person, a horse, or a mountain, but is not the person, the horse, or the mountain itself, a painting is again unreal. A Buddhist story of a painter and sculptor fooling each other with their artwork demonstrates the illusory nature of paintings. In this story, a famous sculptor played a practical joke on a well-known painter by inviting him over to his house and presenting him with a wonderfully made wooden statue of a girl. Taking the statue to be a real maiden, the painter fell in love with her. After he learned the truth, he was humiliated and decided to get back at his sculptor-host by drawing a painting in which he hanged himself and placing it on the wall of his bedroom. The next morning, when the host saw the painting through the window, he thought his houseguest had committed suicide and was terribly frightened. Only later did he realize his mistake. This incident enlightened the two artists to the illusoriness and vanity of the secular life, and served as a catalyst for them to become monks.[69]

The contemplation of painted images therefore leads to the attainment of enlightenment in several ways: for one thing, the illusory nature of the painted image inspires thoughts of emptiness in the viewer; for another, the content of the painting is a meaningful object of reflection. Contemplating a painted image of the Buddha, for instance, helps a per-

---

68. *Mahāprajñāparamitā Sūtra* 10.476, in *T* 8.

69. This story is anthologized in the sixth-century Buddhist encyclopedia *Differentiated Manifestations of Sutras and Laws* (*Jinglü yixiang* 經律異相), compiled in 516 under the auspice of Emperor Wu of the Liang (r. 502–549). See *Jinglü yixiang* 44.229, in *T* 53.

son achieve enlightenment because it is an invaluable aid for meditative visualization (*guanxiang* 觀想), not to mention producing such an image is considered to be of great religious merit.

The large number of extant writings about Buddhist images in the Eastern Jin testifies to the abundance of such images during this period. Zhi Dun composed two eulogies or encomia (*zan* 贊), one on the image of Amitābha Buddha, the other on the image of the Śākyamuni Buddha.[70] Huiyuan's "Inscription on Buddha's Shadow" ("Foying ming" 佛影銘) remains the best-known example.[71] When Huiyuan led 122 disciples and like-minded laymen to take a vow to be reborn in the Pure Land on September 11, 402, the event took place right in front of the image of the Amithābha Buddha in the Wisdom Terrace Chapel (Boretai jingshe 般若臺精舍) on the northern side of Mount Lu.[72]

The Wisdom Terrace Chapel might have been decorated with a series of mural paintings illustrating the Sadāprarudita chapter ("Satuobolun pusa pin" 薩陀波倫菩薩品 or "Changti pin" 常啼品) from the *Sutra of Perfect Wisdom*. The paintings inspired several encomia written by a Wang Qizhi 王齊之, who was associated with the Huiyuan group.[73] Sadāprarudita was a bodhisattva who was so bent on finding the dharma that he was always weeping tears of longing, hence his name Sadāprarudita (Changti 常啼), which means "always weeping." He forsook his family and went into the mountains to seek the Way; then he heard the Buddha's voice in the sky instructing him to go east and find Bodhisattva Dharmodgata (Tanwujie pusa 曇無竭菩薩). When Sadāprarudita finally got to the city where Dharmodgata lived, he put himself up for sale in order to get some money to buy incense and properly worship Dharmodgata. Śakra-devendra (the King of the Heaven of the Thirty-Three Gods, a protector of the dharma) wanted to test Sadāprarudita's sincerity, so he

---

70. Yan Kejun, *Quan Jin wen* 157.2369–370. Although these encomia are included in Yan Kejun's *Quan Jin wen* (*Complete Jin Prose*) instead of Lu Qinli's *Quan Jin shi* (*Complete Jin Poetry*), in form they are completely identical to verses in five-syllable line.

71. Yan Kejun, *Quan Jin wen* 162.2402. Xie Lingyun also wrote an inscription. *Quan Song wen* 33.2618.

72. Yan Kejun, *Quan Jin wen* 142.2279.

73. Wang Qizhi was a member of the Langye Wang clan. He also composed four poems on "meditating on the Buddha and achieving Samādhi" (*nianfo sanmei* 念佛三昧), which are still extant.

transformed himself into a brāhman and asked Sadāprarudita to exchange his blood, flesh, and heart for money. Sadāprarudita willingly complied, but just before he cut out his heart, a noblewoman who had been watching him took pity on him and gave gold, silver, and other treasures as offerings to Dharmodgata on behalf of Sadāprarudita and herself. Upon this Śakra-devendra revealed his true identity and healed Sadāprarudita's wounds. Sadāprarudita went on to see Dharmodgata, listened to Dharmodgata's preaching, and henceforth obtained samādhi (a high level of meditative contemplation).

Wang Qizhi composed one encomium on Sadāprarudita, one on Bodhisattva Dharmodgata, one on Sadāprarudita entering the mountain to seek the dharma, and yet another on Sadāprarudita getting ready to make offerings to Dharmodgata. As the last encomium indicates, the painting presumably presents the visually dramatic scene of Sadāprarudita mutilating his body:

神功難圖	The divine accomplishments are difficult to achieve,
待損而益	and it needs diminution to obtain benefit.
信道忘形	Have faith in the Way and forget one's body,
歡不期適	for happiness does not lie in [physical] comfort.[74]

Tu 圖, to achieve, also means to draw a picture, so the first line could be a double entendre: "The divine accomplishments are difficult to represent in a painting."

Wang Qizhi also wrote an encomium on a painting of the Buddhas ("Zhu Fo zan" 諸佛贊), which seems to have been the last image of the mural series. An explanatory note is attached to the encomium: "Because Sadāprarudita was constantly weeping and visualizing the Buddhas in his mind, the Buddhas revealed their numinous images for his sake."[75] This encomium summarizes nicely the author's attitude toward Buddhist iconography: "It [the painting] transforms but does not distort; / it presents the Image but is not a slavish imitation" 化而非變，象而非摹. *Xiang* 象, used as a verb here, also means "to resemble." It implies an approximation to the Buddha that transcends superficial physical resemblance, and it evokes the term *xiang jiao* 像教, teaching by images, which is sometimes

74. Yan Kejun, *Quan Jin wen* 143.2286.

75. Ibid., 143.2286.

interchangeable with *xiang fa* 像法—the dharma that "resembles" the "correct dharma" (*zhengfa* 正法) and prevails in the world centuries after the Buddha's nirvana.

One of Zhi Dun's poems on the eighth day of the fourth month, the birthday of the Śākyamuni Buddha, provides an apt commentary on the viewer's relation with the painted image of the Buddha:

緬哉玄古思	As one thinks on the remote past,
想託因事生	visualization arises on the occasion.
相與圖靈器	Together we paint the numinous vessel,
像也像彼形	making an image to resemble His form.
黃裳羅帕質	Yellow jacket is of the substance of gauze;
元服拖緋青	black robe, draped with red and blue silks.
神爲恭者惠	The spirit extends grace only to the reverential;
跡爲動者行	traces are activated by those who follow them.
虛堂陳藥餌	In the empty hall are displayed music and food;[76]
蔚然起奇榮	an extraordinary glory appears in full splendor.
疑似垂嚱微	It seems to be revealing great subtlety,
我諒作者情	and I verily understand the feelings of the painter.
於焉遺所尚	At this place, we discard our ordinary pleasures;
肅心擬太清	purifying our minds, we aspire to the Grand Purity.[77]

This poem makes reference to the custom of displaying the Buddha's image on a bejeweled four-wheel cart during a public parade on the eighth day of the fourth month. The custom was called "walking the image" (*xing xiang* 行像), and the famous artist Dai Kui 戴逵 (d. 395) was known for his skill at painting the Buddha's images for such a purpose.[78] The painted image is a "numinous vessel" that contains the spirit of the Buddha, but whether the vessel can become animated and bestow grace on the viewer depends entirely on the viewer's attitude. After all, the image is no more than a "trace" (*ji* 跡) of the Buddha, and here *ji* retains its original meaning of "footprint," which indicates the simultaneous presence and absence of a person. Only those who follow the Buddha's

76. Here *yao* 藥 is a variant character for *yue* 樂 (music). "Music and food" is a reference to the remark in *Laozi*: "Music and food can stop the passers-by" 樂與餌, 過客止. *Laozi jiaoshi*, p. 141. Here they refer to the offerings made to the Buddha.

77. The poem is entitled "Yong bari shi" 詠八日詩. Lu Qinli, *Quan Jin shi* 20.1078.

78. Liu Yiqing, *Shishuo xinyu jianshu* 21.719.

footsteps in the ceremony of "walking the image" can reanimate His traces by literally walking in them.

The contemplation of painted landscape is equally powerful in enabling the viewer to attain transcendence. Zong Bing 宗炳 (374–443), a lay Buddhist and landscape painter, claimed in his "Account of Painted Landscapes" ("Hua shanshui xu" 畫山水序) that "the substance of mountains and waters belongs to the world of physicality and yet they incline toward numinousness" ("shanshui zhi you er qu ling" 山水質有而趣靈).[79] He painted the mountains and rivers he visited and hung the paintings in his room, saying: "Old age and sickness come to me hand in hand, and I am afraid that I cannot get to see all the famous mountains. I shall purify my mind and observe the Way, taking recumbent journeys."[80] Here seeing the famous mountains and observing the Way are treated as one and the same. Recumbent journeys are, however, conducted with one's spirit, not with one's body. Although bodily eyes and "earthly vision" are important, they are secondary. The landscape paintings in this case serve the same purpose as the images of the Buddha: they are an aid to meditative visualization. By looking at them intensely, all of a sudden one is transported to the real places, just as the person who thinks intently of the Amitābha Buddha will find himself or herself in the Pure Land.

On the one hand, in light of the acknowledged illusiveness of paintings, painted landscape is not only no more real than visualized landscape, but furnishes the best illustration of such imaginary landscape: the former is *xiang* 相, images and appearances, while the latter is *xiang* 想, images of the mind and products of the imagination. On the other hand, imaginary landscape and painted landscape are just as real as physical landscape, because physical landscape is transient and illusory. Zong Bing goes so far as to state in his "Account of Painted Landscapes" that painted mountains and waters are on an equal footing with, and perhaps even superior to, real mountains and waters, for what one seeks in mountains and waters is the "spirit" of the landscape or a higher principle, and so if one can grasp the principle and is transported to a higher plane of reality by gazing at a

79. Yan Kejun, *Quan Song wen* 20.2545. For a complete translation of this account, see Bush and Shih, *Early Chinese Texts on Painting*, pp. 36–38.

80. Shen Yue, *Song shu* 93.2279.

landscape painting, then "even if one vainly seeks among the secluded cliffs, what more could one acquire there?"[81]

The famous painter Gu Kaizhi's 顧愷之 (ca. 345–406) essay, "An Account of Painting the Cloud Terrace Mountain" ("Hua Yuntai shan ji" 畫雲臺山記), presents a doubly illusive landscape, for it is at once a painted landscape and an imaginary one. Here the Cloud Terrace Mountain is the one in modern-day Sichuan. Legend has it that Zhang Daoling 張道陵 (or Zhang Ling, d. 156), the founder of the Daoist "Way of the Celestial Masters," had once tested the faith of his disciple Zhao Sheng 趙昇 on this mountain, and this story is the theme of Gu Kaizhi's painting. For all we know, Gu Kaizhi may never have set foot on the Cloud Terrace Mountain in Sichuan. Furthermore, from the way in which his narrative unfolds, it seems that the author is prescribing how to paint the Cloud Terrace Mountain instead of describing an accomplished picture. In other words, he is visualizing a painting in his mind rather than seeing a painting in front of him.

Gu Kaizhi's essay brings to mind the *Imagines*, whose author, Philostratus, was a Greek living in Rome in the third century. This work describes paintings from the gallery of a wealthy art lover in the city of Neapolis, but whether the paintings discussed in great detail in this work were real or imaginary is still an unanswered question. As Norman Bryson puts it, "If the paintings were non-existent, what the *Imagines* in fact describe are codes of viewing in a remarkably pure form: protocols, expectations, and generic rules governing the viewing of pictures, almost in abstraction from its empirical objects. If, on the other hand, the paintings described actually existed in the collection of a Neapolitan amateur, those rules of viewing become anchored in the context of actual Roman art production."[82] This statement is surprisingly pertinent to Gu Kaizhi's text, separated from the *Imagines* by a mere century.

Preserved in Zhang Yanyuan's 張彥遠 (ca. 847) *Record of Famous Paintings of All the Dynasties* (*Lidai minghua ji* 歷代名畫記), the text of Gu's essay was already quite corrupt by the ninth century. Modern edi-

81. *Quan Song wen* 20.2546.

82. Bryson, *Looking at the Overlooked*, p. 18.

tions punctuate the text differently, yielding different readings.[83] Even in its imperfect form, the "Account" is a remarkable text in many ways. The imaginary painting it describes does not so much represent nature in a "naturalistic" or "realistic" manner as depict an artificially constructed fantasy realm of Daoist immortals and adepts. This is a landscape that can only be seen with the mind's eye.

The account begins thus:

The mountain has a face, and so its back has shadows. I shall make auspicious clouds arise from the clear eastern sky and stretch westward.

山有面，則背向有影。可令慶雲西而吐於東方清天中。

The physical substance of the mountain is brought out in the very first sentence, with its emphasis on light and shadow. Shadow, the obstruction of light, eloquently demonstrates the opaqueness and solidity of the mountain, as well as indicates a particular point of time during the day. Thus the Cloud Terrace Mountain immediately assumes a spatial-temporal dimension that grants it a sense of "reality." The second sentence is a startling statement: we know, of course, that the author is talking about making a picture, but the way in which the statement is uttered makes it sound as if he were going to order the clouds about. The painter in his capacity to cause things to appear and disappear is truly acting as the Creator. "Auspicious clouds" are clouds of five colors, associated with the appearance of deity. These clouds hint at the presence of transcendent beings (e.g., the Celestial Master), and so are a sign for those who can recognize it as such. There is nothing accidental or fortuitous in this envisioned landscape. Everything is planned out carefully as a part of the whole, contributing to the symbolic significance of the entire scenery.[84]

---

83. See Sakanishi Shiho, *The Spirit of the Brush*, pp. 30–33; Michael Sullivan, *The Birth of Landscape Painting in China*, pp. 94–101; Bush and Shih, *Early Chinese Texts on Painting*, pp. 34–36; Chen Chuanxi, *Liuchao hualun yanjiu*, pp. 81–93; Okamura Shigeru, *Lidai minghua ji yizhu*, pp. 290–97. The text referred to in this chapter is based on the one given in Yu Jianhua, *Zhongguo hualun leibian*, pp. 581–82. I have, however, modified the punctuation of the text.

84. As Cai Zhenfeng argues, figures, landscape, and objects exist in a web of inseparable relations in this painting, and such a world of correspondences and relations comprises an important part of its meaning. Cai, "Gu Kaizhi lun hua de meixue yiyi shitan," p. 143. The vision of nature as "architectural, purposefully structured, luminously intelligible, and

The sky and waters should all be painted with blue, which should cover the silk above and below, reflecting the sunlight. As for the mountain range stretching westward, one should take care to bring out a sense of its distance. One should begin painting the mountain from its eastern base. Before reaching the midpoint of the mountain, I will paint five or six purple rocks which resemble hardened clouds buttressing the ridge, and the ridge should go up amidst the rocks. I will make the ridge twist and coil like a dragon. It will rise abruptly, straight and high, enfolding the summit. Below I will make layers of hills in such a way that one shall see it as swelling up, burgeoning, and yet solidifying and escalating.

凡天及水色儘用空青，竟素上下以映日。西去山，別詳其遠近。發跡東基，轉上未半，作紫石如堅雲者五六枚夾岡，乘其間而上，使勢蜿蟺如龍，因抱峰直頓而上。下作積岡，使望之蓬蓬然凝而上。

Interestingly, the painter gives the viewer detailed instruction on how to view the painting and even attempts to regulate the viewer's response: "I will make layers of hills in such a way that one shall see it as swelling up, burgeoning, and yet solidifying and escalating." The combination of movement and stillness in the phrase "solidifying and escalating" (*ning er shang* 凝而上) is striking, as the painter tries to convey the dynamism as well as the sheer physical volume of the hills. This same impulse is also manifested in the description of the purple rocks, which echo the color and texture of the "auspicious clouds." In the surprisingly poetic comparison of rocks to "hardened clouds," the clouds are frozen into a stony solidity, which nevertheless retains the momentum of motion. Throughout the passage, the verb "escalate" or "rise" (*shang* 上) recurs with regularity. The impression on the reader is one of ascension: it is as if the landscape were moving of its own accord. The painter's active engagement of the brushwork is hardly distinguishable from the lively energy of the landscape.

Gu Kaizhi then relates the story on which the projected painting is based:

Then there will be another rocky peak. To the east it confronts a steep crest; to the west it is linked with a west-facing cinnabar-red cliff. Below is a deep ravine. I will paint the cinnabar cliff as overlooking the ravine. I will make it magnificently towering and lofty, and bring out the effect of its extreme steepness. The Celes-

---

with each part contributing to the whole" was a distinctly medieval experience. See Owen, *The End of the Chinese "Middle Ages,"* p. 37.

tial Master sits on the top [of the cliff]; the rock on which he sits should extend to the shades. The peach tree in the ravine should grow sideways from amidst the rocks. I will paint the Celestial Master as emaciated in form and yet noble in spirit. He presides over the cliff and points to the peach tree, turning around and addressing his disciples. Two of his disciples bend over and look into the ravine, so terrified that they are sweating and turning pale. I will paint Wang Liang as serenely sitting there and answering the Master's question, while Chao [Zhao] Sheng is dignified and alert, leaning over to gaze at the peach tree.

次復一峰，是石，東鄰向者峙峭，峰西連西向之丹崖，下據絕澗。畫丹崖臨澗上，當使赫巇隆崇，畫險絕之勢。天師坐其上，合所坐石及蔭。宜磵中桃旁生石間。畫天師形瘦而神氣遠，據磵指桃，迴面謂弟子。弟子中有二人臨下到身，大怖流汗失色。作王良穆然坐，答問，而超[趙]昇神爽精詣，俯眄桃樹。

The scene depicted here is the seventh trial Zhao Sheng endured. The Celestial Master (Zhang Daoling) told his disciples that he would reveal the essence of the Way to those who could pick peaches from a peach tree growing sideways from the cliff; none except for Zhao Sheng had the courage to attempt it. The tension-filled moment right before Zhao Sheng jumped off the cliff was clearly chosen for its dramatic potential, as demonstrated by the contrast between the reaction of Zhao Sheng and Wang Liang and that of the other disciples.

After Zhao Sheng returned to the cliff unharmed, the Master said that he would like to go and pick a peach himself. Everyone protested, but Zhao Sheng and Wang Liang remained silent. The Master threw himself into the ravine but ostensibly missed the peach tree. Zhao Sheng and Wang Liang, instead of lamenting with the other disciples, leapt into the ravine after the Master, and found themselves landing safely right in front of him. Zhao Sheng and Wang Liang's leap is portrayed in the next passage of Gu Kaizhi's essay. It is, however, not immediately clear whether Gu Kaizhi was suggesting this as an alternative scene to the one described above, or whether he intended to place the two scenes within the same painting, or whether he was talking about making a separate picture altogether. If it had been his intention to juxtapose the two consecutive scenes within one painting, it would seem that, as Michael Sullivan has said, he was influenced by the "typically Indian method of continuous narration."[85] Such a method, often employed in mural painting, introduces different temporal frames into one painting space; the relation between time and space consequently becomes complicated, and the painted landscape is further removed from naturalism or realism.

Then again I will draw Wang and Zhao hastening [after their master]. One is partially hidden by the slanting rock face of the western cliff, with only the hems of his robe visible; the other is entirely within view in the air,[86] and I will make him seem wondrously weightless and light. When painting seated figures, one should make them seven-tenths [of their full heights], and the colors of their clothes should be sparing and delicate. This is because the mountain is high and the figures are distant.

又别作王趙趨，一人隱西壁傾巖，餘見衣裾，一人全見室中，使輕妙泠然。凡畫人，坐時可七分，衣服彩色殊鮮微，此正蓋山高而人遠耳。

The phrase *lingran* 泠然 was used in *Zhuangzi* to describe the lightness of Liezi's flight in the wind. Its usage here suggests that by taking the courageous leap, Zhao Sheng (or Wang Liang) was well on his way to achieving transcendence.

In the middle section [of the painting], to the east side there is a cinnabar-colored precipitous peak casting its shadow. I shall make it soaring, beautiful, with a solitary pine tree planted on its top. It faces the cliff where the Celestial Master [sits] to form a gorge. The gorge should be very narrow, so that between the two cliffs an affective, sublime and pure ambience is created, which helps establish the dwelling place of the divine and luminous.

中段東面，丹砂絶崿及蔭，當使嵃㠔高驪，孤松植其上。對天師所 [ ] 壁以成磵，磵可甚相近。相近者，欲使雙壁之内悽愴澄清，神明之居，必有與立焉。

Cinnabar is the most important ingredient in making elixir, and the pine tree symbolizes integrity as well as longevity. Both elements contribute to the symbolic nature of the landscape. The "divine and luminous" (*shenming* 神明) may be a reference to gods, immortals, or the Daoist adepts:

85. *The Birth of Landscape Painting in China*, p. 97.

86. I follow Kobayashi Taichirō's emendation of the character *shi* 室 (chamber) to *kong* 空 (air, void). *Chūgoku kaigashi ronkō*, p. 54.

like the transcendental figure in Zhi Dun's poem cited above, they are the spirit (also *shenming*) of the mountains and waters.

The next passage is textually problematic in that it vacillates between the author/painter's vision of his creation and something that reads like a pragmatic description of a real landscape:

I will then set up a purple rock on the summit of the next mountain ridge. The rock stands erect to represent a left watchtower flanking the cinnabar-colored precipitous peak. To the west it is linked with the Cloud Terrace Mountain, and a path is thus indicated. The left watchtower has a crag as its base, beneath which there is sheer void. The rocks pile up to support the crag, and so together they face the eastern gorge. To the west [of the watchtower] a stream appears amidst rocks, and I follow the contour of the steep edges to make it flow through the hills; the hidden stream descends out of sight, but after a while reemerges in the east. It pours downward into the gorge as a rocky creek and thus disappears into the abyss. The reason for making the water flow downward in the west and then east is to make the painted image seem natural.

可於次峰頭作一紫石，亭立以象左闕之夾高驪絶崿。西通雲臺以表路。路左闕峰似巖爲根，根下空絶。並諸石重勢，巖相承，以合臨東磵。 其西石泉又見，乃因絶際作通岡，伏流潛降，小復東出。下磵爲石瀨，淪沒於淵。所以一西一東而下者，欲使自然爲圖。

The painter's eye penetrates the surface of things and sees the hidden course of the stony brook. Such an arrangement shows what Xie He 謝赫 (fl. 500–535) meant by "planning and positioning" (*jingying weizhi* 經營位置), even though the purpose of such artifice is "to make the painted image seem natural."[87]

The last two sections of the painting contain two mythical creatures, the phoenix and the white tiger. A concluding passage sums up some general points about this projected painting:

The west and north sides of the Cloud Terrace Mountain should be surrounded by hills. Above I shall make a pair of boulders to represent left and right watchtowers. On one boulder I will draw a solitary roaming phoenix. It looks as if it were dancing, with beautiful, carefully painted plumage. It raises and spreads its tail feathers and gazes into the deep gorge. The last section has red rocks, which should have fissures and crevices like cracking lightning bolts. Facing the cliff overlooked by the phoenix to the west of the Cloud Terrace, there will be a

---

87. Yan Kejun, *Quan Qi wen* 25.2931.

ravine. Limpid water flows therein. On the side of the cliff, there is a white tiger crouching on the rock and drinking from the stream. Thereafter I shall create a descending effect and bring the painting to a close.

Altogether there are three sections of the mountain, which, though extended in length, should be painted in a compact manner; otherwise it would not be suitable. From time to time one may make use of birds and beasts, which should all have an appropriate pose. In the ravine below, the reflections of things should appear as inverted. A pure vapor should be made to girdle the mountain at about one third of its height or more, so that the mountain is clearly divided into two layers.

雲臺西北二面可一圖岡繞之。上爲雙碣石，象左右闕，石上作孤遊生鳳，當婆娑體儀，羽秀而詳，軒尾翼以眺絶磵。後一段赤岓，當使釋弁如裂電，對雲臺西鳳所臨壁以成磵。磵下有清流。其側壁外面作一白虎，匍石飲水。後爲降勢而絶。

凡三段山，畫之雖長，當使畫甚促，不爾不称。鳥獸中時有用之者，可定其儀而用之。下爲磵，物景皆倒。作清氣帶山下三分倨一以上，使耿然成二重。

Thus ends Gu Kaizhi's envisioned painting of a completely imaginary landscape, whose fantastic, mystical nature is underlined by its realistic details such as an inverted reflection in the water or the winding course of the stony brook. This essay exemplifies a sort of "in-sight"—achieved not so much by the eye as by the mind. That the fissures of the rocks should resemble lightning bolts is both a vividly visual metaphor and a psychological effect the author/painter intends to impress upon the viewer. It is for this reason that the vision of this painting must always surpass its execution, for it is an internally self-sufficient verbal realization of what the painting is and how it should be perceived by an ideal viewer.[88] It seems almost inevitable that the textual execution of a painting remains superior to its visual counterpart, for it incorporates within itself the desired effect of the painting as no actual painting does.

It is interesting to note that the sixth-century art critic Xie He criticized Gu Kaizhi's paintings, saying that "his brushwork did not match up to his intent, and his fame exceeded the reality" (*ji bu dai yi, sheng guo qi*

88. The best-known execution based on Gu Kaizhi's "Account" was carried out by the famous painter Fu Baoshi 傅抱石 (1904–65) in 1941. Fu Baoshi also wrote a paper entitled "Jin Gu Kaizhi 'Hua Yuntai shan ji' zhi yanjiu" 晉顧愷之畫雲臺山記之研究, which was published in 1940. In *Fu Baoshi meishu wenji*, pp. 413–28.

shi 跡不迨意，聲過其實).[89] Modern scholars chimed in, lamenting that "the sharp contrast between the grand description by Ku K'ai-chih of *How to Paint the Cloud Terrace Mountain* and the relatively feeble pictorial accomplishment seen in the mountain section of his painting in the British Museum."[90] Zhang Yanyuan, who saw some of the Six Dynasties landscape paintings, disparaged them in this perhaps unintentionally comic description:

As for those of the famous paintings since Wei and Jin that are still extant, I have seen them all. In their depiction of mountains and waters, the appearance of the peaks is like that of filigree ornaments or combs of rhinoceros horns. Sometimes the river seems barely enough to sail on; sometimes human figures are larger than mountains. The mountains and waters all have trees and rocks that set them off, and the rows of plants are like stretched arms and spread fingers.[91]

魏晉以降，名迹在人間者，皆見之矣。其畫山水，則羣峰之勢若鈿飾犀櫛，或水不容泛，或人大於山，率皆附以樹石，暎帶其地，列植之狀，則若伸臂布指。

The contrast between such a depiction and Gu Kaizhi's grand vision is dramatic, even painfully so, and seems to demonstrate that nothing in reality could quite match the painter's imagination. If, however, we look at it in terms of the Eastern Jin discourse on mind and locale, it is perhaps not the paintings themselves that are inferior or clumsy. Using only his "earthly vision," Zhang Yanyuan may have simply failed to perceive the splendor of early Chinese paintings, just as Śāriputra was unable to perceive the magnificence of the Buddha's kingdom, seeing only "rocks and dirt" instead.

Images of Visualization

In this chapter, I have explored a variety of issues around the central concept of *xiang* 想: to visualize, to see images in one's mind, and to achieve "in-sight" with the mind's eye. Why was *xiang* of such vital importance to the Eastern Jin elite? Perhaps it is as Yu Chan said in the "Encomium on the Portraits of Yu and Shun": "If we abandon traces and reflections, and

89. Yan Kejun, *Quan Qi wen* 25.2931.
90. Lee, *Chinese Landscape Painting*, p. 17.
91. Yu Jianhua, *Zhongguo hualun leibian*, p. 603.

directly penetrate the mysterious truth, then even if one's power of observation is alone resplendent and illuminates the darkness, where would the people of the world focus their ears and eyes?" 若乃廢其軌景，洞其玄眞，雖冥照之鑒獨朗，天下惡乎注其耳目哉?[92]

Truth must be manifested in concrete, material means. Even visualization (*xiang*) itself must be represented as images and expressed in words. The best example is Zhi Dun's poem "On a Buddhist Monk in Meditation" ("Yong chansi daoren" 詠禪思道人), which is based on a painting by Sun Chuo. This poem is not only a meta-contemplation of sorts but may also be considered as a prototype of "poetry on paintings" (*yonghua shi* 詠畫詩), a popular poetic subgenre in later times. "Poetry on paintings" is different from "encomia on paintings" (*huazan* 畫贊) because the latter is usually reserved for figure paintings and focuses on the character of the person being portrayed, instead of on any clearly defined visual quality of the painting. Zhi Dun's poem is to a large extent still devoted to appraising the person portrayed in the painting, but since the person is situated in nature, the poem gives considerable space to describing the landscape, which enables us to catch a glimpse of what the painting was like.

In the preface to the poem, Zhi Dun explains the occasion for the composition:

The Marquis of Changle [Sun Chuo] made a painting of a meditating monk, and composed an encomium on it. He may be said to have lodged his sincerity by means of bending over and facing [the painted image], and he seeks to always see [the principle] on the yoke. Sketching the precipitous effect of cliffs and forests, he visualizes the presence of the meditating person. I marvel at the exquisiteness of his painting and admire his fine composition. Unable to remain silent, I wrote the following poem.[93]

孫長樂作道士坐禪之像，并而讚之。可謂因俯對以寄誠心，求參焉於衡軛；圖巖林之絶勢，想伊人之在茲。余精其制作，美其嘉文，不能默已，聊著詩一首，以繼于左。

"Seeking to always see [the principles] on the yoke" is an allusion to an *Analects* passage:

92. Yan Kejun, *Quan Jin wen* 38.1681.
93. Lu Qinli, *Quan Jin shi* 20.1083.

Zizhang asked the Master about conducting oneself. The Master said, "Let his words be sincere and trustworthy, and his actions be honest and respectful. If this is so, even in the southern or northern barbarian states, his conduct will be appreciated. If his words are insincere and untrustworthy and his actions dishonest and disrespectful, how could he be appreciated even in his own hometown? When he is standing, he should see these two principles in front of him; when he is sitting in a carriage, he should see them attached to the yoke. And then he will be admired." Zizhang wrote this advice on his sash.[94]

In this *Analects* passage, "seeing" (*jian* 見) is the key word. As Zhu Xi's 朱熹 (1130–1200) annotation elucidates, "This means that one should be thinking of sincerity, trustworthiness, honesty, and respectfulness all the time; wherever he goes, he always seems to be seeing them, and cannot keep away from them even for one instant" 言其於忠信篤敬念念不忘, 隨其所在, 常若有見, 雖欲頃刻離之而不可得.[95] Zhi Dun's allusion to this *Analects* passage is therefore directly pertinent to what Sun Chuo's painting intends to convey: the painting is about meditative visualization, about seeing the Buddha and his kingdom with the mind's eye; to make an image of a monk engaged in meditative visualization is itself a visualization of such meditation, which in turn helps the viewer in his own meditation of the Buddhist way.

According to the preface, the monk is sitting in a natural setting, perhaps on a towering cliff with trees around him. Zhi Dun uses the word *xiang* 想 to describe Sun Chuo's visualization of the monk in such an environment. In the poem itself, we are given to understand that *xiang* is the only way of seeing the monk, for he is located in an inaccessible spot where even birds are scarce. The first part of the poem reads:

雲岑竦太荒	Cloudy peaks rise sharply in the great wilderness,
落落英岊布	many and continuous are the tortuous bends of the hills.
迴壑佇蘭泉	A winding ravine takes in sweet springs,
秀嶺攢嘉樹	on the steep summit a grove of lovely trees clusters.
蔚薈微遊禽	The vegetation is luxuriant, admitting few roaming birds;
崢嶸絶蹊路	the mountain so precipitous, trails and paths are cut off.

94. *Lunyu zhushu* 15.138.
95. *Sishu zhangju jizhu*, p. 162.

中有沖希子	In the midst there is a person of serenity and subtlety,
端坐摹太素	sitting upright, emulating the grand plainness.[96]

"Grand plainness" (*tai su* 太素) refers to the original state or the source of the world of Being, but "plainness" (*su* 素) is also as much a painting term as is *mo* 摹: *su* is white silk, the plain background on which a painting is to be drawn, while *mo* refers to sketching out an object's outline.[97] By employing these two painting terms, Zhi Dun is making a comment on Sun Chuo's visualization of the meditative state, a state that recalls the unadorned and undifferentiated state of the universe.

The poem goes on to a lengthy description of the monk's meditation: his breathing technique, his intense concentration and absorption. The second part of the poem, except for the metaphor that compares the monk to the "cold pine," is abstract and devoid of images. Such a movement from the tangibility of physical landscape to the immateriality of meditation and spiritual progress illustrates the idea expressed in the ending couplet:

逝虛乘有來	Going onto Emptiness, with Being as his vehicle,
永爲有待馭	he is the master of contingencies for all eternity.

In the final couplet, Zhi Dun stresses that "Being" or "Existence" (*you* 有) is the very means by which one arrives at spiritual freedom, just as Sun Chuo has to rely on images and words to portray the spirit journey to transcendence. The monk represented as meditating in the midst of painted mountains and waters is ultimately the perfect allegory of the preoccupation with *xiang*—visualization and imagination—during this period.

---

96. Lu Qinli, *Quan Jin shi* 20.1083.

97. The *Analects* records a conversation about *su* and *hui* 繪 (drawing) between Confucius and his disciple Zixia 子夏. See *Lunyu zhushu* 3.26–27. For the definition of *mo* as a painting term, see the commentary in Ban Gu, *Han shu* 1.81. Wei Zhao 韋昭 (204–73), for instance, describes *mo* as "a painter's sketching an outline before applying colors" 摹者如畫工未施采事摹之矣.

CHAPTER TWO

Journeys to Other Worlds

Truth must be manifested in concrete, material means—this much we know about the belief of the Southern Dynasties elite. In the previous chapter I discussed the importance they attached to visualization, perception, and mental image-making. That, however, by no means precludes a burning desire to go out, to see the phenomenal world for oneself, and to experience it firsthand. Sometimes people traversed through a landscape for pragmatic purposes such as finding ingredients for immortality potions; sometimes it was for aesthetic purposes. It was fashionable for the Southern Dynasties elite to talk about their love of "mountains and waters," so much so that one could indeed speak of a cult status of nature during this period. Never before had the phrase "fond of roaming in mountains and waters" appeared quite so often as part of a positive characterization of a person. It also became a stylish excuse used by members of the elite when asking to serve as magistrate of a certain county known for its beautiful landscape.[1]

At the same time, there was a yearning to explore ever more faraway and exotic places. In the year 347, a successful military campaign led by

1. For instance, Sun Tong 孫統 (fl. 326) "loved mountains and waters, so he asked to be Magistrate of Jin [in Zhejiang]; later he was transferred to Wuning. He did not care for administrative duties but indulged in visits to all the famous mountains and beautiful rivers in the area." Fang Xuanling et al., *Jin shu* 56.1543. Wang Hongzhi 王弘之 (365–427) "loved mountains and waters by nature and asked to be Magistrate of Wucheng [in Zhejiang]." Shen Yue, *Song shu* 93.2281.

the general Huan Wen 桓溫 (312–73) crushed the Cheng-Han 成漢 kingdom in the Shu region (modern Sichuan). A young Wang Xizhi excitedly wrote to a friend who had followed Huan Wen on the campaign:

I have read your other letter detailing the various wonders of the mountains and rivers of the region. Yang Xiong's "*Fu* on the Shu Capital" and Zuo Taichong's "*Fu* on the Three Capitals" are quite incomplete in comparison with what you told me.[2] Now I know there truly are many wonders in that part of the empire, and one may let one's eyes roam and content one's mind much more than from reading. If it is possible, I would love to ask you to get me there, but I am afraid you might not have enough men and horses to fetch me. Please do let me know when you will come back. I very much look forward to your return, and a day feels like a whole year. But I imagine you are stationed in that region and there is no way for you to move back just yet. I hope you could take advantage of your stay and ascend the peaks of Min and Mount Emei.[3] *That* would truly be "a splendor that does not decay!" Even as I speak of this, my heart is already there.[4]

省足下別疏，具彼土山川諸奇，揚雄蜀都、左太沖三都，殊爲不備。悉彼故爲多奇，益令其游目意足也。可得果，當告卿求迎，少人足耳。至時示意。遲此期，眞以日爲歲。想足下鎮彼土，未有動理耳。要欲及卿在彼，登汶嶺峨眉而旋，實不朽之盛事。但言此，心馳於彼矣。

Measuring his friend's eyewitness account against book knowledge, Wang Xizhi found previous records wanting, even though those records were penned by great literary masters such as Zuo Si and Yang Xiong, the latter being a native of Shu. A *fu*, as mentioned above, is an extravagant piece of writing that aspires to encompass all aspects of its subject; a "capital *fu*," like Yang Xiong and Zuo Si's works, seeks to represent a metropolis in a most exhaustive and lavish manner. Zuo Si had reputedly spent ten

2. Yang Xiong 揚雄 (53 BCE–18 CE) was a Western Han writer and scholar who hailed from Chengdu. His "*Fu* on the Shu Capital" is one of the earliest examples of the "capital *fu*," a subgenre of *fu* that praises the glory of a metropolis. See Yan Kejun, *Quan Han wen* 51.402. Zuo Taichong was the style name of Zuo Si 左思 (ca. 250–305), who composed poetic expositions on the capitals of the Three Kingdoms: Shu, Wu, and Wei. For his "*Fu* on the Shu Capital," see Yan Kejun, *Quan Jin wen* 74.1882–884. For an English translation, see Knechtges, "Shu Capital Rhapsody," in *Wen xuan*, Vol. 1, pp. 341–72.

3. The Min mountains are to the northeast of Chengdu. Mt. Emei is to the south of Chengdu.

4. This and the other letters cited below can all be found in Yan Kejun, *Quan Jin wen* 22.1583, 25.1604.

years working on his "*Fu* on the Three Capitals." He criticized previous *fu* writers for their lack of precision in descriptions of places, and claimed to have researched his subject thoroughly: "For the mountains and rivers, cities and towns, I checked maps; for flora and fauna, I substantiated in local gazetteers."[5] And yet, Wang Xizhi complained of the "incompleteness" of these previous writings. For him, the goal was to be able to go there and see it for himself.

Wang yearned to travel afar, but even as he spoke of "letting his eyes roam" amidst the mountains and waters of the Shu region, his mind had already taken off on a flight of imagination as he carried out his own mental inspection tour of the landscape. Such was the power of visualization discussed in the previous chapter. Realizing that it might be unrealistic for him to go in person, he beseeched his friend to visit the famous Shu mountains almost as if in his stead or on his behalf. His letter notably describes the ascension of those mountains as "a splendor that does not decay." This is the very phrase used by Cao Pi 曹丕 (187–226), Emperor Wen of the Wei, to describe literature: "Literary works are the supreme achievements in the business of state, a splendor that does not decay."[6] Ascending a mountain is supposed to be an occasion for literary composition, as reflected in the Han saying: "He who is able to compose *fu* upon climbing to a high place can become a grand master" (*deng gao neng fu keyi wei dafu* 登高能賦可以為大夫).[7] In this letter, however, Wang Xizhi transfers the grand quality of literary writings to the occasion of composition, so that the occasion becomes an end in itself, not just a means to an end.

In this letter Wang Xizhi also uses the word *qi* 奇 (strange, wondrous, or extraordinary) twice; his sense of curiosity indeed matches the Chinese phrase for it—*hao qi* 好奇, literally "love of the strange." Wang Xizhi belonged to the first generation born and raised in the south after the Jin royal house crossed the Yangzi River. For someone like him, the Shu was the stuff of legend: he had read about it but had never been there, and unlike the generation before him, he never experienced the sense of a

---

5. Yan Kejun, *Quan Jin wen* 74.1882.

6. Cao Pi, "Lun wen" 論文, in Yan Kejun, *Quan Wei wen* 8.1098.

7. Ban Gu, *Han shu* 30.1755.

"unified empire" with Shu belonging to it, however briefly.[8] When the news of the conquest of Shu first reached the Eastern Jin capital, it must have caused quite a sensation. Several other missives penned by Wang Xizhi to his friend or friends in Shu at this time attest to his intense desire to know the newly accessible region. This desire often takes the visual form:

I know a lecture hall from the Han dynasty is still there, established during the reign of Emperor He [r. 89–105]. I hear that in the hall there are some exquisite paintings of all sorts of things that have existed since the High Antiquity and that they are quite worth looking at. Are there good painters there to produce a copy? Can I get hold of a copy of the paintings? Pray do let me know in detail.

知有漢時講堂在，是漢和帝時立此。知畫三皇五帝以來備有，畫又精妙，甚可觀也。彼有能畫者不？欲摹取，當可得不？須具告。

Another letter inquires after the scions of the former local worthies:

They say Qiao Zhou has a grandson, a noble-minded recluse who will not come out and serve. Does this gentleman get to realize his wish? It fills me with longing to meet him. Pray do tell me in detail. Do Yan Junping, Sima Xiangru, and Yang Ziyun all have descendents?[9]

云譙周有孫，高尚不出，今爲所在其人有以副此志不？令人依依。足下具示。嚴君平、司馬相如、揚子雲皆有後否？

It is almost as if the descendents of the Shu luminaries might form a living link between Wang Xizhi and the past. The other link is the ancient sites in the city of Chengdu:

I once met Zhuge Yong in the capital, and asked him in great detail about the Shu region. He told me that the city walls and gates and the various towers and terraces of Chengdu were all built by Sima Cuo in the Qin times. I visualized

8. The Shu-Han regime founded by Liu Bei 劉備 (r. 221–23) was conquered by the Western Jin in 263. About forty years later, the Li family of Shu declared independence from the Jin and established the Cheng-Han kingdom there.

9. Qiao Zhou (199–270) was a Shu-Han statesman. For an excellent study of his influence, see Farmer, *The Talent of Shu*. Sima Xiangru (ca. 179–117 BCE), like Yang Ziyun (the style name of Yang Xiong), was a great *fu* writer and a native of Shu. Yan Junping (fl. ca. 34 BCE) was Zhuang Zun 莊遵 (Zhuang was changed to Yan to avoid duplicating the personal name of Liu Zhuang 劉莊, Emperor Ming of the Han). Zhuang Zun, another native of Shu, made a living by telling fortunes in the Chengdu marketplace and lectured on *Laozi* after closing shop for the day. Ban Gu, *Han shu* 72.3056–57.

them from afar and was quite moved. If this is not true, pray do tell me about it in detail. I would love to expand my knowledge of novel things.

往在都見諸葛顒，曾具問蜀中事，云成都城池門屋樓觀皆是秦時司馬錯所修，令人遠想慨然。爲爾不信，一一示，爲欲廣異聞。

Sima Cuo was a general working for the state of Qin in the Warring States period. He argued for attacking Shu, and the King of Qin took his advice. After conquering Shu in 316 BCE, Qin became a much more powerful kingdom. In 301 BCE, Sima Cuo was sent to Shu to suppress a rebellion; he pacified the region and killed the rebel leader.[10] Part of an eventually unified China, Shu was one of the first states to be subsumed into the Qin empire. For someone like Wang Xizhi, the fact that Chengdu might still retain architectural structures from the Qin times, constructed by a well-known historical figure, was an important piece of information, for it enabled him to visualize from afar (*yuan xiang* 遠想) the cityscape of Chengdu as familiar and recognizable on the cultural map of a unified empire from the Qin and Han times. The word *yuan* 遠, "from afar," indicates both spatial and temporal distance from a Chengdu that was built in the fourth century BCE; and yet, the existence of physical evidence of a remote past that Wang had only read about in dynastic histories was more than enough to affirm the sense of a cultural continuity.

The statement at the end of the letter, "I would love to expand my knowledge of novel things," is repeated verbatim in another of Wang's letters, which asks about the famous "salt wells" and "fire wells" of Shu. A salt well is a well with salty water from which salt can be extracted; a fire well is a brine pit from which natural gas can be obtained. Both terms appear in Yang Xiong's and Zuo Si's poetic expositions on the Shu capital:[11]

---

10. See Sima Qian, *Shi ji* 5.207, 210.

11. Yang Xiong mentions "fire well" 火井 and "salt springs" 鹽泉 in "*Fu* on the Shu Capital." Yan Kejun, *Quan Han wen* 51.402. *Han shu* mentions a Shu merchant who "monopolized the profit of salt wells" 擅鹽井之利 and made a fortune. Ban Gu, *Han shu* 91.3690. Zuo Si writes "Fire wells store flames deep in hidden springs" 火井沈熒于幽泉 and "Every family has a brine-spring well" 家有鹽泉之井 in his version of "*Fu* on the Shu Capital." Yan Kejun, *Quan Jin wen* 74.1882–883. Knechtges' translation. *Wen xuan*, Vol. 1, pp. 344–45, 353.

Are there both salt wells and fire wells there? Have you seen them with your own eyes? I would love to expand my knowledge of novel things. Pray do tell in detail.

彼鹽井火井皆有不？足下目見不？爲欲廣異聞，具示。

Wang Xizhi's curiosity about salt wells and fire wells is indicative of his intense desire to learn about "novel things" (*yiwen* 異聞), which can also be rendered as "unusual or extraordinary things," as evidenced by his prodding his friend for information in the form of visual evidence and narrative details. Equally notable is the fact that Wang was in the habit of pressing his correspondent for an eyewitness account. Wang Xizhi may be said to represent the very essence of "people back home," people with an insatiable desire to broaden their horizons through those who have seen the outside world with their own eyes.

Wang Xizhi's friend or friends must have written back and given him the detailed accounts he required. Although we no longer have those replies (Wang Xizhi's own hand-written epistles would not have been preserved had it not been for his fame as a calligrapher), we may safely assume that many such correspondences took place during this period, as more and more people were traveling to hitherto little-explored or completely new territories. What ensued in the subsequent decades was a repetition of the pattern established above through Wang Xizhi's letters: the audience back home played the role of eager consumers of geographical information, and the travelers supplied it with accounts guaranteed to be authentic—"witnessed with my very own eyes." The accounts are dazzling in their diversity: those of travels to north China; to the deep south; to Central Asia, India, and Southeast Asia; to hell; to "grotto heaven"; or to the Buddhist paradise. In these accounts we come to discern some of the foundational paradigms of "seeing the world" to be drawn on in later times.

Sites of History: Accounts of Military Campaign

Wang Xizhi's letters provide a window into an important aspect of social life in south China, which was frequent military action undertaken by Eastern Jin generals against neighboring regions. One of the most prevailing stereotypical views of the Southern Dynasties is that they suffered from an effeminate weakness in comparison with the northern states. The reason for such a stereotype is quite simple: the south was eventually conquered by a northern dynasty, the Sui, in 589, which was succeeded by another northern dynasty, the Tang. In the official histories written by the conquest dynasties, the defeated were portrayed as decadent, sensuous, and ineffectual. This portrait of the south is, however, far from the truth. If we can go beyond "the effeminate southerner" as the umbrella term invented as an ideological counterpart to the "macho northerner," which is no less of an ideological construct, we see regional differences perceived and mapped out by contemporaries that show a much finer understanding of local situations. Soldiers from Xuzhou (in modern Jiangsu), for instance, had a reputation for being tough and courageous.[12] The people of Jiangling, the provincial capital of the Jingzhou prefecture (in modern Hubei), were said to be mortally afraid of the powerful army of Xiangyang (also in modern Hubei).[13] The Liang prince Xiao Gang 蕭綱 (503–51), who as Governor of Yongzhou lived in Xiangyang for several years, described the local people years later as "valuing their swords and thinking nothing of death" in a letter to a cousin who was assigned to a post at Yongzhou.[14]

The conquest of the Cheng-Han kingdom in 347 was just one of the many military exploits undertaken by the southern troops. Though not always successful, the Eastern Jin army made repeated attempts to recover lost territories,[15] and throughout the Song, Qi, and Liang dynasties, the desire to conquer the north was never absent from the machinations of the southern court. It is also worth noting that on a number of occasions the southern army penetrated deeply into the northern heartland and captured the former capitals Chang'an and Luoyang. By way of comparison, no northern army had ever been able to come close to Jiankang, the southern capital for more than two hundred years. Even Hou Jing 侯景 (d. 552), the northern general whose rebel army took Jiankang in 549, was only able to do so because he had first capitulated to the Liang court and

12. "Men from Xuzhou were generally tough and plucky. Huan Wen often said: 'The ale of Jingkou is drinkable; the soldiers of Jingkou are usable'" 徐州人多勁悍, 溫恒云: 京口酒可飲, 兵可用. Fang Xuanling et al., *Jin shu* 67.1803.

13. Yao Cha and Yao Silian, *Liang shu* 1.4, 10.187.

14. Yao Cha and Yao Silian, *Liang shu* 22.349. Yan Kejun, *Quan Liang wen* 9.3000.

15. In 352, Yin Hao 殷浩 went on a military campaign against the north. He was defeated several times, and consequently was demoted to a commoner in 354. Fang Xuanling et al., *Jin shu* 8.198–200.

was subsequently granted a place in the south. In other words, his army rose against the Liang from within the southern territory rather than coming directly from the north.

The military campaigns undertaken in the fourth and fifth centuries were important to the southern elite in a number of ways, as they opened up new vistas and were as much sensational cultural events as landmark military and political affairs. It is important to bear in mind that a new generation was raised in the south after the wave of immigration and settlement in the early fourth century, and this new generation related to north China in a way that was quite different from their parents, who grew up in the north and cherished vivid memories of life there. To someone like Wang Xizhi, the north was a textual memory rather than a personal memory. And yet, with the military campaigns against the northern regimes, visiting the north in person became a distinct possibility for many southerners. The cities, towns, and landscapes that had existed for them only as images in reading and imagination suddenly came alive in front of their eyes. To parody the famous words of Julius Caesar: "They came, they saw, they recorded." And the need to record was partially a response to the demand of the audience back home, as we have seen in Wang Xizhi's case.

A poem entitled "To Chief of Staff Yang" ("Zeng Yang zhangshi" 贈羊長史) written by Tao Yuanming in the year of 417 conveys the mood of "people back home" from a slightly different perspective than Wang Xizhi's letters.[16] Earlier that year, Liu Yu, the general who would later force the abdication of the Eastern Jin emperor and establish the Song dynasty, defeated the Later Qin, a northern state founded by the Qiang people, and captured its capital, Chang'an. Chief of Staff Yang was dispatched as an emissary by the Eastern Jin court to visit Liu Yu's troops, and Tao Yuanming wrote the poem upon his departure:

愚生三季後	My ignorant self was born long after the Three Dynasties:
慨然念黃虞	I think with longing of the ancient kings.
得知千載外	To learn of an age a thousand years ago
正賴古人書	All we have are the books the ancients wrote.
賢聖留餘跡	The traces that are left of the worthies and sages

16. Lu Qinli, *Quan Jin shi* 16.979. I use James R. Hightower's translation with slight modifications. *The Poetry of T'ao Ch'ien*, pp. 86–87.

事事在中都	Are one and all be found in the capital region.
豈忘游心目	I never lost my wish to wander there,
關河不可踰	But the road was blocked by rivers and passes.
九域甫已一	Now that all Nine Regions are united,
逝將理舟輿	I would surely prepare my boat and carriage.
聞君當先邁	I hear that you will have to go ahead
負痾不獲俱	While I am sick and cannot go along.
路若經商山	If your journey takes you past Mt. Shang,
爲我少躊躇	Do me a favor: stop there long enough
多謝綺與甪	To pay my deep respects to Qi and Lu—
精爽今何如	Is their spirit still vigorous these days?
紫芝誰復採	Does anyone pick the purple mushrooms now?
深谷久應蕪	Their hidden valley is long since overgrown.
駟馬無貰患	No coach-and-four will buy you free from care;
貧賤有交娛	It's poverty and low estate bring joy.
清謠結心曲	Their pure song is kept fast in my heart's recesses,
人乖運見疏	But the men are distant, and our times are not alike.
擁懷累代下	Harboring these feelings so many ages after,
言盡意不舒	I've exhausted my words, but cannot express what is on my mind.

The poem is about the impossibility of communication and the desire to break down barriers posed by a divided empire, time, and the inadequacy of human language. It begins by relating how the poet has long been reading about the renowned city of Chang'an and yearning to see it. Feeling regret that he is unable to go in person, the poet asks his friend to linger a while at Mt. Shang in the capital region and pay homage to the famous recluses ("Qi and Lu") who once lived there. He mentions a song attributed to the recluses that speaks of picking mushrooms in the valley, a song passed down in those "books the ancients wrote." As he contemplates the difference between then and now, the song only serves to remind him of the vast distance, both temporal and spatial, that separates him from the ancient recluses. Finally, his attempt to respond to the song with one of his own—this very poem he gives to his friend—only brings him more disappointment, for even if he has said everything he can, he fails to express what is deeply on his mind.

Tao's poem represents an understanding of geography in historical terms. The spatial remoteness of Mt. Shang is configured as a temporal gap that is impossible to bridge. The physical landscape is supposed to bear visual evidence of textual knowledge, but even if the poet is not hindered from going there by his failing health, the valley is now overgrown and more hidden from sight than ever, not to mention its "spirit"—the recluses—is long gone. Texts are all one has to learn of a past era, and yet, as the poet indicates at the end of the poem, they are an unreliable passage to the minds of their authors. Communication is fraught with problems, and obstacles are created not just by a divided empire. For someone like Tao, perhaps the best kind of travel is done through imagination, not by means of boat or carriage. Nevertheless, the very existence of the poem belies its pessimistic message: Tao seems to understand that poems like this are "traces" or "footprints" (*ji* 跡) left behind in the overgrown valley of time, just like the songs of the vanished recluses.

The Traveler's Memories

While Tao Yuanming largely remained at home during these exciting years, the other great turn-of-the-century poet, Xie Lingyun, eagerly seized the opportunity to travel when he, like Chief of Staff Yang, was sent by the Jin court to visit General Liu Yu at Pengcheng (in modern Jiangsu) just before Liu set out on the campaign against the Later Qin. Xie Lingyun left the capital Jiankang in the winter of 416 and returned in the early spring of 417. He gave a lengthy account of his trip in "*Fu* on My Journey" ("Zhuanzheng fu" 撰征賦), which is included in his biography in the *Song History* (*Song shu* 宋書) compiled by Shen Yue 沈約 (441–512) in the 480s.[17]

Prior to Xie Lingyun's time, there had been a long tradition of writing poetic expositions on one's travels. One of the earliest specimen is "*Fu* on a Northern Journey" ("Beizheng fu" 北征賦) by Ban Biao 班彪 (3–54), a distinguished member of the scholar-official class. This poetic exposition exemplifies a pattern that can be observed through subsequent poetic expositions on travel, that is, it relates all the famous historical sites the author sees during his journey. As David Knechtges points out, it is an "excellent example of the theme of *lan gu* 覽古, or 'contemplation of antiquity.' In its common form, the poet describes his visit to a place that

17. Shen Yue, *Song shu* 67.1743–53. For a complete English translation, see Appendix I, pp. 287–340.

is associated with a famous historical event or person and reflects upon it."[18] In this type of writing, space is perceived through time, and yet time is ordered by space, for the history connected with the places the poet traverses is configured not chronologically but rather spatially, based on the itinerary of the poet.

Xie Lingyun adds a new twist to the long tradition of travel *fu* by combining reflection on dynastic history with family history. Xie came from an illustrious clan. His great-grand-uncle Xie An 謝安 (320–85) was one of the most powerful ministers of the Eastern Jin, who saved the state from an impending crisis by winning a historical battle against the northern invaders in 383. Xie An's nephew, Xie Xuan, personally led the defense army and was made a duke as a reward for his victory. Xie Lingyun, being Xie Xuan's grandson, inherited the ducal title in 399. The history of the Xie clan was thus closely intertwined with the fate of the Jin state. By Xie Lingyun's time, however, the glory of the Xie clan had faded, and the Jin court had fallen completely under the control of Liu Yu, who took the throne for himself not long after his successful northern campaign of 417. Not surprisingly, Xie's poetic exposition is infused with nostalgia for the past on both private and public levels. He states in the preface, "As I looked back upon the sites of old, feelings swelled in my bosom" ("Juanyan guji, qihuai yiduo" 眷言古跡, 其懷已多).

The poetic exposition begins by tracing the ancestry of the Xie clan and giving an account of Xie's own position within the genealogy. It then relates the suffering of the Jin house at the hands of the non-Han regimes, Liu Yu's decision to undertake the northern campaign, and Xie's role as an emissary from the court to Liu's army stationed at Pengcheng. The poet's journey commences in Jiankang:

爾乃	Thereupon
經雉門	I passed through the Pheasant Gate,
啓浮梁	and the Pontoon Bridge opened up for me;
眺鍾巖	I gazed far at Bell Mountain,
越查塘	as I sailed over Zha Pond.

The Pheasant Gate is a generic name for the gate of the imperial palace, here a likely reference to the gate of the Palace City (Taicheng 臺城), the

18. Knechtges, "Poetic Travelogue in the Han *Fu*," p. 140.

walled palace compound inside the city of Jiankang. The Pontoon Bridge refers to the Red Sparrow Bridge over the Qinhuai River to the south of Jiankang. Both Bell Mountain and Zha Pond were located in the capital region. As the poet embarks on his journey from the capital, he relates a brief history of the Eastern Jin—hence the next dozens of lines recount the fall of the Western Jin and Emperor Yuan's reestablishment of the Jin court in Jiankang in 317, the accomplishments of various Eastern Jin emperors hereafter, and the Sun En Rebellion that destabilized the regime from 399 to 411. Next, as he gazes at the Foundry City (Yecheng 冶城) to the southwest of Jiankang, the site of the old third-century foundry, the poet reminisces about Wang Dao, the great Eastern Jin statesman who set up his headquarters there.[19] Then, before he moves on to Wang Dun 王敦 (266–324), a cousin of Wang Dao's and a rebel general in the early years of the Eastern Jin, the poet's thoughts go further back in time to the Kingdom of Wu founded by Sun Quan 孫權 (182–252), because at this point of his journey his boat has moored at the Stone Fortress to the west of Jiankang. In the passage below, he muses over the rise and fall of the Kingdom of Wu:

次石頭之雙岸	Mooring my boat at the banks of the Stone Fortress,
究孫氏之初基	I investigated the foundation of the house of Sun.
幸漢庶之漏網	Rejoicing in his survival as a commoner of the Han,
憑江介以抗維	Sun Jian took the south as his powerbase to uphold law and order.
初鵲起於富春	At first soaring like a magpie at Fuchun,
果鯨躍於川湄	in the end he leapt like a whale from the Yangzi River.
匝三世而國盛	In three generations, the kingdom flourished,
歷五僞而宗夷	but the clan was finally destroyed after five pretenders to the throne.
察成敗之相仍	I examined the cycle of success and failure:
猶脣亡而齒寒	the teeth feel cold when the lips are gone—
載十二而謂紀	a period of twelve years is known as one full cycle;
豈蜀滅而吳安	how could Wu be safe when Shu had fallen?
眾咸昧於謀兆	Yet all remained oblivious to what was destined to be;
羊獨悟於理端	Yang alone recognized the sign from the beginning.

19. Liu Yiqing, *Shishuo xinyu jianshu* 26.827. Emperor Ming of the Jin referred to Wang Dao as the "Lord of the Foundry City" (Yecheng gong 冶城公). Also see Pei Qi 裴啓 (fl. mid-fourth century), *Yu lin*, pp. 87–88.

請廣武以誨情	With his sincerity, he convinced the Baron of Guangwu,
樹襄陽以作藩	and cultivated the city of Xiangyang as a fence.
拾建業其如遺	Taking Jianye was as easy as picking up something from the ground,
沿萬里而誰難	the army sailed ten thousand miles without encountering obstacles.
疾魯荒之詖辭	I loathed the lies of Duke Huang of Lu;
惡京陵之譖言	I detested the slandering of Jingling;
責當朝之憚貶	I disapproved of how those powerful men feared responsibility—
對曩籍而興歎	facing the records of the past, I heaved a sigh.

This passage gives a succinct summary of the entire history of the Kingdom of Wu. It relates the accomplishments of Sun Jian 孫堅 (156–92), a native of Fuchun (in modern Zhejiang) who established the foundation for the rise of the Sun clan. The "three generations" refer to Sun Jian and his two sons Sun Ce 孫策 (175–200) and Sun Quan. Sun Ce was Sun Quan's elder brother, not his father, which makes the phrase "three generations" seem a little out of place; nevertheless, Sun Ce was the leader before his untimely death, and Sun Quan was his appointed successor. The "five pretenders to the throne" in the next line refer to Sun Ce, who was given the posthumous title Emperor Wulie 武烈皇帝; Sun Quan, the founder of Wu; Sun Liang 孫亮 (r. 252–58); Sun Xiu 孫休 (r. 258–64); and Sun Quan's grandson Sun Hao 孫皓 (r. 264–80), the last ruler of Wu. The poet sees the fall of Wu as an inevitable consequence of the fall of Shu, which was conquered by the Jin army in 263. It is not immediately clear what he means by the line, "a period of twelve years is known as one full cycle," but it probably refers to the historian Chen Shou's 陳壽 (233–97) comment that one of the admirable accomplishments of the last Shu ruler was to rule for twelve years without changing his reign title.[20] In the next couplet, the poet praises the crucial role played by the general Yang Hu 羊祜 (221–78) in the conquest of Wu. Although few at court shared his conviction, Yang Hu always believed that Jin would eventually conquer Wu. During his tenure as the governor of Jingzhou in Xiangyang, Yang Hu actively made military preparations for the war.[21] Zhang Hua,

20. Chen Shou, *Sanguo zhi* 33.903.

21. See Yang Hu's biography in Fang Xuanling et al., *Jin shu* 34.1013–25.

the famous Western Jin minister and writer, was the only one who supported Yang Hu's plan. Two years after Yang Hu died, the Jin army captured the Wu capital Jiankang, then named Jianye, and unified China; Zhang Hua was made the Baron of Guangwu for his endeavors.[22]

The poet then turns his attention to the villains. Duke Huang of Lu was Jia Chong 賈充 (217–82), the Jin emperor's favorite. He was made commander-in-chief of the Jin army in the campaign against Wu. Fearing a negative outcome, he repeatedly wrote the emperor stating the impossibility of the mission; at one point he even asked the emperor to execute Zhang Hua, the pro-war minister. After Jia Chong's death, the officials in charge planned to give him the derogatory posthumous title "Huang" 荒 (neglectful of duty and indulgent in sensual pleasures), which was rejected by the emperor, so they changed his posthumous title to "Wu" 武 (meaning "martial"). Here Xie chose to use the posthumous title rejected by the emperor to pass judgment on Jia Chong.[23] "Jingling" refers to the general Wang Hun 王渾 (223–97), the Duke of Jingling. He and another general Wang Jun 王濬 (206–86) were both instrumental in the conquest of Wu; however, Wang Hun was jealous of Wang Jun's achievements and slandered him in his many letters to the emperor.[24] In the last couplet, the poet openly expresses his disapproval of the small-mindedness of these two highly placed men.

The reflection on history in this passage is typical of most travel *fu*. At first it seems that the poet embarks on a journey going back in time in reverse chronological order, but it soon becomes clear that chronology is distorted to fit the spatial configuration of historical events, as the poet first passes through the sites of the Western Han, then those of the Three Dynasties in antiquity, and then again those of his own dynasty. In other words, history is organized by geography. In Xie's poetic exposition, dynastic time and familial time are also closely intertwined, as the sites prompting his musings are often places where the poet's ancestors, in particular Xie An and Xie Xuan, had left indelible marks. Thus we have an example of a travel *fu* that affirms the position of the author, the heir to

22. Fang Xuanling et al., *Jin shu* 36.1070.
23. See Jia Chong's biography in Fang Xuanling et al., *Jin shu* 40.1165–171.
24. See Fang Xuanling et al., *Jin shu* 42.1202.

the ducal title earned through defending the state, at the culmination of a dual history—dynastic and familial.

In the passage cited above, verbs such as "investigating" (*jiu* 究) and "examining" (*cha* 察) are applied to historical events rather than to topography. The last line, "facing the records of the past, I heaved a sigh," effectively collapses physical and textual landscapes into one. Although Xie Lingyun is occasionally given over to depictions of nature in this poetic exposition, his main concern is with the visible or invisible traces of the past. The following lines, joining physical travels with textual knowledge, best illustrate the most prominent characteristic of this type of poetic exposition:

紛征邁之淹留	With much lingering in the course of my journey,
彌懷古於舊章	Even more did I think on the past manifested in the writings of old.

The poet's survey of the landscape proves to be the totalitarian point of view that strings disparate places and times together into a unified whole stamped with a strongly personal imprint. Even though he is seeing the landscape for the first time, it is always already a re-view, as he is constantly conjuring up places he has never seen before.

The Function of Anecdotes

Xie Lingyun's poetic exposition is not the only example of a poetic exposition on the subject of travel from this period. The Eastern Jin military campaigns to the north provided many opportunities for writers to write on such a topic. For instance, Yuan Hong 袁宏 (ca. 328–76) wrote a "*Fu* on the Northern Campaign" ("Beizheng fu" 北征賦) in 369 when he followed the general Huan Wen on one of his many northern campaigns. Only fragments of this work are extant, but even in these fragments, one can nevertheless detect similarities to Xie's "*Fu* on My Journey." At the same time, another type of travel writing, written in plain unrhymed prose and often referred to as a "record" or "account" (*ji* 記), began to make its appearance in the Eastern Jin; documents of this type were produced in rather large quantities at the turn of the fifth century.

These travel accounts were very much associated with the frequent military campaigns that took place in this period. For instance, Fu Tao

伏滔 (ca. 317–96), a famous writer of the time and a member of Huan Wen's staff, wrote *A Record of the Northern Campaign* (*Beizheng ji* 北征記); an otherwise obscure figure named Meng Ao 孟奥 wrote an account of the same event with the same title. The second surge of campaign records appeared between 409 and 418. In 409, Liu Yu undertook a successful campaign against the Southern Yan in the old Qi region (modern Shandong), a fact that does not go unmentioned in Xie Lingyun's "*Fu* on My Journey." In honor of this campaign, Wu Jizhi 伍輯之 wrote *An Account of Going with the Army on Campaign* (*Congzheng ji* 從征記), and Qiu Yuanzhi 丘淵之 wrote *A Record of Qi* (*Qi ji* 齊記), alternatively known as *A Record of the Journey to Qi on a Campaign* (*Zheng Qi dao ji* 征齊道記 or *Zheng Qi daoli ji* 征齊道里記). Within a decade, Liu Yu's campaign against the Later Qin again was documented in a number of accounts, including *A Record of the Western Campaign* (*Xizheng ji* 西征記) by Dai Yanzhi 戴延之 (also known as Dai Zuo 戴祚), *A Record of the Northern Campaign* (*Beizheng ji* 北征記) by the famous historian Pei Songzhi 裴松之 (372–451), a work of the same title by Xu Qimin 徐齊民, and *An Account of the Campaign* (*Su zheng ji* 述征記) by Guo Yuansheng 郭緣生. Some of the records in circulation at the time focus on one particular place visited during the campaign rather than on the entire journey, such as *A Record of Luoyang* (*Luoyang ji* 洛陽記) by Dai Yanzhi, or *A Record of the Divine Soil* (*Shenrang ji* 神壤記) by Huang Min 黄閔, which is dedicated to the city of Xingyang 滎陽 (in modern He'nan).[25] The best known of these accounts, *A Record of Ye* (*Yezhong ji* 鄴中記) by Lu Hui 陸翽, was written during this period. None of these records is extant today, but many fragments are preserved in encyclopedias and commentaries, especially the *Commentary on the Classic of Waterways* (*Shui jing zhu* 水經注) authored by the northern writer Li Daoyuan 酈道元 (d. 527).

Unlike *fu*, by this time a high literary genre with a long-established tradition, a *ji* is written in straightforward unrhymed prose that allows its author much freedom in the selection of materials. A *ji* typically gives exact locations of notable geographical features and famous sites, explains a place name, recounts the past and present of a place, and records pertinent local lore. Its most noteworthy feature is the inclusion of anecdotes. Although it

25. The Eastern Jin Emperor Jianwen's mother, Zheng Achun 鄭阿春 (d. 326), was a native of Xingyang.

is true that the *fu* began to show "the increasing specificity of time, place, and voice" from the end of the Western Han, it never goes into everyday detail, personal or otherwise, in narrating a journey the way a *ji* does.[26] Some examples below illustrate this point.

In *A Record of the Western Campaign*, Dai Yanzhi relates an incident in which two army officers were punished for their misconduct:

Several miles to the north of Mount Jiaoshi, there is a grave mound constructed for the Metropolitan Commandant of the Han Dynasty [Lu Jun 魯峻, d. 172]. However, when his family was opening up the mountain to bury him, they saw a white snake and a white rabbit, so they had him buried to the south of the mountain instead. When they were digging his grave, they found metal, and thereupon named the hill "Metal Land." The hill is quite steep. In front of the grave mound there is a stone shrine as well as a stone temple. . . . There was also [once] a stone settee. It was eight feet long, smooth and shiny. If one knocked on it, its sound could be heard near and far. Fu Zhenzhi, Retainer Gentleman, and Zhou Anmu, Administrative Advisor, both on the staff of the Grand Marshall [Liu Yu], broke the stone settee, and each took half of it. They were sued by the descendants of Mr. Lu, and both were dismissed from office.[27]

焦氏山北數里有漢司隸校尉冢，穿山得白蛇、白兔，不葬，更葬山南，鑿而得金，故曰金鄉山。山形峻峭。冢前有石祠、石廟……又有石床，長八尺，磨瑩鮮明，叩之，聲聞遠近。時太尉從事中郎傅珍之、諮議參軍周安穆，折敗石床，各取去，爲魯氏之後所訟，二人並免官。

This passage explains the origin of the name of a mountain, documents a local site and the related lore, and gives an almost journalistic account of a contemporary incident, all three elements presumably being of great interest to the audience back home.

Another incident was supposedly an auspicious omen that foretold Liu Yu's ascension to the throne; it later found its way into dynastic history as well as Buddhist compilations:

Wang Zhixian, Administrative Advisor to the Duke of Song [Liu Yu], made a stop at the Cypress Valley. He dispatched a messenger back to the Duke bearing a letter from the monk Huiyi. According to the letter, there would be the auspice of gold and jade disks. The Duke sent men to go and fetch them. The army

26. Knechtges, "Poetic Travelogue in the Han *Fu*," p. 142.
27. Li Daoyuan, *Shui jing zhu shu* 8.777–80.

advanced and camped to the east of Mount Xiao. When the gold and jade disks arrived, the Duke had an altar constructed, and received them with respectful bowing.[28]

宋公諮議參軍王智先，停柏谷，遣騎送道人惠義疏云有金璧之瑞。公遣迎取。軍進次于崤東，金璧至，脩壇拜受之。

Although a travel *fu* can certainly tell a grand story such as the rise and fall of a kingdom or the beginning and end of a journey, it aims to sketch a broad outline of events rather than elaborate on specific details. As a rule, incidents of mere anecdotal interest and minor figures do not make any appearance in it. If a writer deems something like the omen of gold and jade disks worthy of inclusion, he is likely to devote one or two succinct, lyrical, and perhaps also cryptic lines to it, but no narrative detail will be given. This is why commentaries written in plain unrhymed prose are often considered necessary for a poetic exposition: apart from glossing difficult words, they supply information of an explanatory nature to the highly condensed lines. Zuo Si's "*Fu* on the Three Capitals" inspired three commentaries soon after its completion.[29] Xie Lingyun, as far as we know, was the first writer to provide a commentary on his own poetic exposition, namely the "*Fu* on Dwelling in the Mountains" ("Shanju fu" 山居賦). As Francis Westbrook points out, "No doubt the main function of the commentary is to make the *fu* more comprehensible and enjoyable to contemporary readers, and this is accomplished by more subtle means than merely glossing difficult words and identifying allusions."[30]

The level of narrative detail in a *ji* turns out to be a striking feature in the recounting of personal experience. During the campaign in 417, the author Dai Yanzhi, along with a colleague Yu Daoyuan 虞道元, sailed upstream on the Luo River at Liu Yu's command to investigate the river course. Dai and Yu went as far as Tanshan Fort 檀山塢, which was located to the southwest of Luoyang. They passed by a town called Sanle.

28. Ouyang Xun et al., *Yiwen leiju* 84.1434. Mount Xiao lies to the west of Luoyang, and the Cypress Valley to the west of Mount Xiao. The incident occurred in the thirteenth year of the Yixi era (417) and was recorded in the *History of the Song Dynasty* (Shen Yue, *Song shu* 27.784). For Huiyi's biography, see Huijiao, *Gaoseng zhuan* 7.368.

29. Fang Xuanling et al., *Jin shu* 62.2376.

30. Westbrook, "Landscape Description," p. 222.

Sanle's men and women, old and young, had never seen a boat before. Hearing that the Jin emissaries were sailing upriver, they all came out and gathered like ants on the riverbanks, looking at us and doubling over with laughter.[31]

三樂男女老幼，未嘗見舡，既聞晉使溯流，皆相引蟻聚川側，俯仰傾笑。

It is hard to believe that these people of Sanle living by the Luo river had never seen a boat, but Dai and Yu were probably sailing in a particular type of boat unknown or uncommon in the north, such as the four-masted lug-sail boat.[32] In any case, this incident, though apparently trivial, is intriguing and amusing, as it conveys a vivid local detail that would never have found its way into a poetic exposition, which is usually given to expression of feelings on a more lofty or philosophical plane. It is, however, details like this that constitute the texture of life in early medieval China.

Likewise, the following remark contains nothing of grand historical or philosophical significance but was of personal importance to Dai Yanzhi, and presumably of interest to his home audience as well:

I saw pigeons for the first time in my life when I reached Yongqiu [in modern He'nan]. They were about the size of a pheasant, with color like that of a parrot, and played in pairs.[33]

祚至雍丘始見鴿，大小如鳩，色似鸚鵡，戲時兩兩相對。

---

31. Li Fang et al., *Taiping yulan* 770.3544. I have emended "old and *weak*" 老劣 to "old and *young*" 老幼 based on the variant version in Xiong Huizhen's 熊會貞 (1863–1936) commentary on *Shui jing zhu*. See Li Daoyuan, *Shui jing zhu shu* 15.1296.

32. The southerners likely learned to use four-masted lug-sail boats from the Cantonese or Annamese in the third century. See Needham, *Science and Civilization in China*, Volume IV, Pt. 3, pp. 600–601. During this campaign Liu Yu's army also used a type of fast warship called *mengchong* 蒙衝 ("covered swoopers"). This type of ship had its back roofed over with a covering, and both sides of the ship had oar-ports (Ibid., p. 686). As *Song shu* records, "The oarsmen were all inside the ship. The Qiang people [of the Later Qin] only saw the ships sail upstream on the Wei River but could not see any oarsman propelling them. The northerners had never had such boats, and everyone was awed and marveled at them, thinking they were superhuman" 行船者悉在艦內，羌見艦泝渭而進，艦外不見有乘行船人，北土素無舟楫，莫不驚惋，咸謂為神. *Song shu* 45.1369.

33. Li Fang et al., *Taiping yulan* 923.4228.

A *fu* sub-genre known as "*fu* on things" (*yongwu fu* 詠物賦) became quite popular in the third and fourth centuries, with one of the standard topics being birds. One may easily write a poetic exposition on the pigeon, describing its shape, color, habits, and habitat as required by generic conventions, but the admission to seeing pigeons for the first time in one's life is a highly personal and individualistic statement, and certainly no part of the traditional topical repertoire of a poetic exposition. A typical travel *fu*, as we have seen in the case of Xie Lingyun's "*Fu* on My Journey," reflects on grand historical events taking place at famous sites and presents an itinerary on a cultural map. In it, the significance of geography is superseded by that of history, which is nevertheless organized along the continuum on the axis of space. In contrast, a travel account written in plain unrhymed prose can and often does incorporate the minutiae of the author's personal history. Rather than delineating the history of a dynasty or even that of a clan, a prosaic travel account interspersed with anecdotes provides glimpses into the life of one person, not just in the sense of "how I feel," but also on the level of "what I am like."

To modern mainstream historians, anecdotes may be, to quote Catherine Gallagher and Stephen Greenblatt, "no-account items: tolerable, as rhetorical embellishments, illustrations, or moments of relief from analytical generalizations, but methodologically nugatory."[34] In dynastic histories of imperial China that adopt biographies as their basic format, anecdotes are important trivia and central marginalia, as they are carefully chosen for inclusion to illustrate a point or shed light on the character of a biographical subject. But anecdotes in early medieval prosaic travel accounts were much more than mere illustrations. Prior to the emergence of these accounts in the Eastern Jin, the poetic exposition had been the major form in which to record one's response to traveling. In order to adhere to the generic conventions, the author of a poetic exposition must follow a prescribed itinerary of dynastic history, express appropriate feelings at the appropriate historical sites, and define the present by the past. In contrast, a *ji* superimposes an individual's experienced time upon political time, and turns the author from the solemn, all-knowing narrator into a colorful historical person with curiosities that are not always satisfied or

---

34. Gallagher and Greenblatt, *Practicing New Historicism*, p. 49.

anxieties that are not always resolved. The author of a *fu* is someone who is always the active agent of looking, examining, investigating, and reflecting, like Xie Lingyun; but the author of a *ji* can easily become the object of looking, examining, amazement, wonder, and even ridicule, like Dai Yanzhi. The acknowledgment of a different perspective in the prose travel account allows room for the existence of the Other, which would be inadmissible in the travel *fu* with its singular perspective. This is of no small significance in the history of Chinese narrative.

When commenting on the "minutely detailed" passage of narrative time from the thirteenth-century work *La Vie de Saint Louis*, Mary Campbell said, "This reverence for the minutiae of time is essential to the concerns of the novel."[35] Anecdotes in an early medieval Chinese prose travel account are none other than the "minutiae of time" in a narrative organized by movement across space. Unlike in a *fu*, whose generic conventions prescribe the author's movement, movement in a *ji* becomes unpredictable very much like in real life, opening up the possibility of adventure. We are of course still a long way off from the modern novel, but as we will see in the next section, the turn of the fifth century witnessed the emergence of a narrative unified by a subject who observes but is also the object of observation, and who moves and changes through space and time.

Paradise Gained and Lost: Faxian's Passage to India

At about the same time that Xie Lingyun and Dai Yanzhi were writing their travel accounts, a Buddhist monk, Faxian, was writing his. It bears remarkable similarities to Xie's and Dai's travelogues, especially to Dai's; it also shows intriguing departures that would produce far-reaching influence and help establish the paradigm of seeing the world for later times. In this section, I demonstrate how Faxian's travelogue embodies what I call a cultural narrative of going through hell to enter paradise that exists in many contemporary written and oral accounts. To this narrative Faxian adds the element known as "longing for home" (*sigui* 思歸). Both the hell/paradise structure and the motif of "longing for home" were familiar to Faxian's contemporaries, but their combination results in a

35. Campbell, *The Witness and the Other World*, p. 135.

travel account that is drastically different from those discussed in the previous section.

By a cultural narrative I refer to a "story" that can appear in different kinds of texts across genres and is well-known to members of the society, who may or may not be aware of its narrative structure on a conscious level and whose recognition of the narrative structure needs never to be articulated as such. The story of going to heaven through hell, with the element of "longing for home" thrown in to create an interesting twist, is centered around the Buddhist notions of hell and paradise, and mixed with long-standing motifs and images from the native tradition.

Faxian's travelogue is, notably, a first-person narrative. Admittedly, it could be difficult to distinguish first- and third-person narrative in classical Chinese writings because an author often invokes his own name in self-reference, but the intimate details recorded in Faxian's account points to an intensely personal account. In the midst of his dispassionate recording of places, temples, Buddhist holy sites, and their related lore, the author intersperses anecdotes and observations colored with his own feelings. Preserved more or less in its entirety, Faxian's travelogue marks a new level of individuality and subjectivity achieved in travel writing.

Egeria and Faxian

Before discussing Faxian, we will first look at another religious traveler, a female contemporary of Faxian from another continent, with the purpose of bringing out the particular nature of Faxian's journey by placing him in a comparative framework.

In the late nineteenth century, a manuscript was found in Italy that turned out to be the middle section of a late fourth-century account of a Christian pilgrimage to the Holy Land. The pilgrim was a woman named Egeria—at least this is the name that most scholars agree upon—and the account of her journey was apparently a letter she wrote to her sisters back home somewhere on the Atlantic coast.[36] Egeria's letter is, in the words of Mary Campbell, "the first narrative of travel produced by the Christian, European, Western world we still live in."[37] It begins with the fragment,

36. *Egeria's Travels to the Holy Land*, pp. 3, 235–36.
37. Campbell, *The Witness and the Other World*, p. 21.

"ostendibantur juxta scripturas," which is translated as "were shown according to the Scriptures."[38]

Such a fortuitous opening sets the tone for Egeria's entire extant account, as physical landscape holds little interest or attraction in her eyes except as holy sites that provide visual evidence for the stories recorded in the Bible. What has been said of the anonymous pilgrim from Bordeaux who visited Palestine in the year of 333 is equally true of Egeria: "The land the pilgrim visits is only meaningful in relation to scripture, and its landmarks acquire their significance by being interpreted in the light of the Biblical text which is the pilgrim's principal resource."[39] If a place is of no scriptural significance, Egeria does not see it and does not record it, the two processes—seeing and recording—being one and the same. The typical sentence in her account reads: "We were also shown the place where Lot's wife had her memorial, as you read in the Bible." To this statement she quickly adds, "But what we saw, reverend ladies, was not the actual pillar, but only the place where it had once been. The pillar itself, they say, has been submerged in the Dead Sea—at any rate we did not see it, and I cannot pretend we did."[40] In other words, even though the place is empty and has no pillar, it is *known* to Egeria—in the sense of being recognized as well as comprehensible—as the place where a biblical event once happened. The landscape of the Near East is an opened Holy Book, and Egeria is traveling as a reader. Even her account is meant to be an aid in reading and meditating, as she writes to her sisters at home:

> I know it has been rather a long business writing down all these places one after the other, and it makes far too much to remember. But it may help you, loving sisters, the better to picture what happened in these places when you read the holy Books of Moses.[41]

Scholars ascertain that the time of Egeria's travel likely fell between 381 and 384. Some fifteen years after Egeria visited the East, Faxian embarked on a long journey in search of the complete Vinaya Piṭaka, a text that outlines rules and regulations for Buddhist monks and nuns. The land jour-

38. Campbell, *The Witness and the Other World*, p. 23. *Egeria's Travels to the Holy Land*, p. 91.

39. "Introduction," in Elsner and Ribiés, *Voyages and Visions*, p. 16.

40. *Egeria's Travels to the Holy Land*, p. 107.

41. Ibid., pp. 97–98.

ney took him through many states of Central Asia and India; thirteen years later, in the year of 412, he finally returned to China via the sea route. In the following year, he arrived at the capital of the southern empire, Jiankang. Faxian became the "first Chinese traveler to describe the main geographical features of the Indo-Gangetic depression. He is also credited with being the first to explore and describe the island he called 'the Country of the Lion' (Sri Lanka)."[42]

Faxian apparently authored an account of his travels shortly after arriving in China, but it seemed too brief to satisfy the curiosity of his readers. A few years later, he was prompted to relate his travels in greater detail:

> At lecturing assemblies, I repeatedly asked Faxian about his travels. A reverent and modest man, he always spoke the truth. Thereupon I urged him to write a thorough account of what he had roughly summarized before, and so Faxian once again related his experience from beginning to end, this time in an exhaustive manner.[43]

> 因講集之際，重問遊歷。其人恭順，言輒依實。由是先所略者，勸令詳載。顯復具敘始末。

This passage appears in the colophon that was penned by an anonymous author in 416 and appended to Faxian's account, now commonly known as the *Record of the Buddhist Kingdoms* (*Foguo ji* 佛國記).[44]

---

42. Boulton, *Early Chinese Buddhist Travel Records*, p. 280.

43. *Faxian zhuan kaozheng*, p. 299. I have consulted a number of editions, particularly Adachi Kiroku's *Faxian zhuan kaozheng* 法顯傳考證 (1937); Zhang Xun's *Faxian zhuan jiaozhu* 法顯傳校注 (1985); and Yang Weizhong's *Xinyi Foguo ji* 新譯佛國記 (2004). For English translations of this work, see Samuel Beal's *Si-yu Ki* (1884); Herbert A. Giles' *The Travels of Fa-hsien* (1959); James Legge's *A Record of Buddhistic Kingdoms* (1965 rpt.); and, most recently, "The Journey of the Eminent Monk Faxian" in *Lives of Great Monks and Nuns*, trans. by Li Rongxi and Albert Dalia (2002). The most up-to-date translation of this work appears in German: Max Deeg's *Das Gaoseng-Faxian-Zhuan als religionsgeschichtliche Quelle* (2005). The page numbers of the quotations in this chapter correspond to Adachi Kiroku's collated edition.

44. Like many early medieval works, Faxian's account has several variant titles; *Foguo ji* 佛國記 and *Faxian zhuan* 法顯傳 are the most commonly used. Sengyou (*Chu sanzang ji ji* 2.55) mentions a work named *Buddha's Travels through India* (*Fo you Tianzhu ji* 佛遊天竺記) and brought back by Faxian, which several scholars believe to be one and the same as Faxian's own travel account. See Cen Zhongmian, *Zhongwai shidi kaozheng*, pp. 151–63; Zhang Xun, pp. 5–8. This, however, is doubtful. In his bibliography, Sengyou lists

In many ways, Faxian forms a perfect parallel with Egeria. Both authors are considered "pilgrims" by modern scholars, although the accuracy of this term is debatable; both have a matter-of-fact narrative style that does not resort to much rhetorical embellishment, if at all; last but not least, both are interested in topography only as it relates to seeing holy sites where an event of scriptural significance once occurred. Faxian does describe the hardship and perils of traveling, but once he enters India, his seeing is focused on various holy sites, or "traces," left behind by the Buddha. In the following passage, he describes one of the Buddhist kingdoms called Kuśanagara; its narrative mode is typical of the entire account.

Going east for twelve yojanas, we came to the City of Kuśinagara. To the north of the city, between the two śāla trees by the Hiraṇyavati River, the World Honored One, with his head toward the north, achieved parinirvana. There were also the place where Subhadra, the last of the Buddha's disciples, obtained enlightenment; the place where a golden coffin was offered to contain the body of the World Honored One for seven days; the place where the Vajrapāṇi laid down his golden vajra-club; and the place where the eight princes divided the Buddha's relics. At each of these places a stupa was built, along with a monastery. They are all still there today. The inhabitants in the city are few and far between; there are only Buddhist monks and the households working for the monasteries.[45]

復東行十二由延到拘夷那竭城。城北雙樹間希連河邊，世尊于此北首而般泥洹。及須跋最後得道處，以金棺供養世尊七日處，金剛力士放金杵處，八王分舍利處，諸處皆起塔，有僧伽藍，今悉現在。其城中人民亦稀曠，正有衆僧民户。

---

twelve titles as brought back by Faxian but then states, "There are eleven titles altogether." Zhang Xun argues that this is because Faxian's own travel account is not included. However, the "eleven titles" may simply refer to "eleven titles *of Buddhist scriptures*"; *Buddha's Travel through India*, being a secular title, is not included in the list of sutras in a bibliography of *tripitaka*—the "three divisions of the Buddhist canon." This is an interesting point because Faxian's own account contains passages that overlap with *Buddha's Travel through India*, whose fragments are preserved in other works. These passages all concern Buddhist sites and their related lore, not Faxian's personal experience. If *Buddha's Travels through India* was indeed a separate work brought back from India by Faxian, as claimed by the monk Fajing's 法經 *Bibliography of Various Sutras* (*Zhongjing mulu* 衆經目錄, comp. 594), then Faxian may have used it as a reference when he composed his own travel account.

45. *Faxian zhuan kaozheng*, p. 168.

The unadorned style of narration and the discovery of the past in the present evoke contemporary campaign records or even the travel *fu*; the difference is that Faxian's account is located squarely within a religious temporal framework.

When she first arrived at a holy site, Egeria made it her regular practice to say a prayer and read a relevant passage from the Bible. For instance, she spent a night at a church near the Burning Bush "out of which God spoke to holy Moses," and though it was too late to offer a sacrifice, she nevertheless said a prayer in the church and also in the Garden by the Bush, and read an appropriate passage from the Book of Moses.[46] Similarly, Faxian spent a night on the Vulture Hill, where the Buddha and his disciple Ânanda once sat in meditation. He brought incense, flowers, oil, and a lamp to make an offering to the Buddha:

> I was deeply moved and saddened. Drying my tears, I said: 'The Buddha was once here teaching the *Śûrângama Sūtra*. I, Faxian, do not live at the same time as the Buddha, and I only get to see the traces left by the Buddha and the place where He once was.' I thereupon recited the *Śûrângama Sūtra* aloud in front of the stone cave, and spent the night there.[47]
>
> 慨然悲傷，收泪而言："佛昔于此住，説首楞嚴。法顯生不值佛，但看遺迹處所而已。"既于石窟前誦首楞嚴，停止一宿。

Faxian and Egeria both sought to establish a close relationship to the past. For them, texts represented the vital link between the past and present, and they must rely on the texts to reenact the past.

Another resemblance of Faxian to Egeria is a negative one. Although both are referred to as pilgrims, neither exhibits the typical characteristics of a pilgrim. In their seminal work *Image and Pilgrimage in Christian Culture*, the anthropologists Victor Turner and Edith Turner regard pilgrimage as an "inward movement of the heart."[48] Using Arnold van Gennep's paradigm of separation, limen, and aggregation that describes all rites of passage, the Turners see pilgrimage as "the great liminal experience of the religious life."[49] The objective of pilgrimage is the spiritual, and of-

46. *Egeria's Travels to the Holy Land*, pp. 96–97.

47. *Faxian zhuan kaozheng*, p. 212.

48. Turner, *Image and Pilgrimage in Christian Culture*, p. 8.

49. Ibid., p. 7.

ten physical as well, transformation of the pilgrim, who is elevated to a higher spiritual plane of existence through going on a pilgrimage, and whose bodily ills can be healed while undertaking the penitential and therapeutic journey:

> In the paradigmatic Christian pilgrimage, the initiatory quality of the process is given priority, though it is initiation to, not through, a threshold. Initiation is conceived of as leading not to status elevation (though in practice it may often have that effect) but to a deeper level of religious participation. A pilgrim is one who divests himself of the mundane concomitants of religion—which became entangled with its practice in the local situation—to confront, in a special "far" milieu, the basic elements and structures of his faith in their unshielded, virgin radiance. It is true that the pilgrim returns to his former mundane existence, but it is commonly believed that he has made a spiritual step forward.[50]

Measured against this description, neither Egeria nor Faxian should be considered a true pilgrim. Egeria was more of a tourist roaming the biblical landscape. Her narrative maintains an unvarying tone throughout, "reflecting no inner process of transformation and no gradual accumulation of insights or depth of feeling."[51] To be fair, her letter frequently expresses her delight at being shown a holy site, and the adjectives she uses to describe the Holy Land indicate her amazement, admiration, and pleasure as she encounters an "endless" and "really huge" valley, a "large and beautiful" church, or a "plentiful" and "beautifully clear" spring "with an excellent taste." A particularly charming description of the fish in the pools inside the palace of King Abgar of Edessa reads: "I have never seen fish like them: they were so big, so brightly colored, and tasted so good."[52] Egeria's sense of delight and wonder, while childlike, is evenly sustained throughout the narrative: there is no culmination point, climax, or defining moment of enlightenment. She may have seen firsthand all the places she had read about in the Bible, but whether that did anything to help her achieve "a deeper level of religious participation" is not immediately apparent from her narrative.

---

50. Ibid., pp. 14–15.
51. Campbell, *The Witness and the Other World*, p. 27.
52. *Egeria's Travels to the Holy Land*, p. 116.

As for Faxian, his journey was more precisely a book quest. His account opens with the following statement:

When I, Faxian, was in Chang'an, I deplored the incomplete and imperfect state of the Vinaya Piṭaka. Therefore, in the *jihai* year of the Hongshi era [399], Huijing, Daozheng, Huiying, Huiwei and I, who were of the same mind, went on a journey to India to look for scriptures on discipline.[53]

法顯昔在長安，慨律藏殘缺，于是遂以弘始二年歲在己亥，與慧景道整慧應慧嵬等同契至天竺尋求戒律。

Faxian's journey had a fixed destination, but it was certainly not a specific pilgrim center, such as a city, a town or a village associated with a particular shrine. Many of the most important Buddhist holy sites, including the Buddha's birthplace, were in central India, but Faxian's six-year sojourn there seems to have been an accident rather than a deliberate decision:

My original aim was to seek copies of the Vinaya Piṭaka. In the kingdoms of northern India, however, the scriptures were transmitted orally from one master to another, and there was no written copy to transcribe. Therefore I went on to central India.[54]

法顯本求戒律，而北天竺諸國皆師師口傳，無本可寫，是以遠步乃至中天竺。

Faxian did not go to central India just to pay homage to the holy sites; instead, he was motivated by a pragmatic objective—obtaining the scriptures.

Paradise Gained

With such a clear objective for his journey, Faxian's travel account is not mere narration, but a narrative. This is one of the most important features of Faxian's account. On the surface, the narrative is structured around an individual's quest for Buddhist scriptures; it has a beginning (the decision to undertake the quest and departure), a middle (the hardship of travel), and an end (the successful completion of the quest and return). But when

53. *Faxian zhuan kaozheng*, p. 29. The "second year" of the Hongshi era in the original text should be emended to the "first year," which was a *jihai* year.

54. Ibid., p. 245.

we look closely, we see a second level: underlying Faxian's account is a journey through a demonic landscape to the ultimate paradise. The contrast between the demonic landscape and paradise overlaps with that of periphery and center. Before I begin a discussion of the hell/paradise paradigm in Faxian's travelogue, it is necessary to briefly go over the representation of center and periphery in the Chinese tradition.

In the early poetic collection known as the *Verses of Chu*, two texts—"Summoning the Soul" ("Zhao hun" 招魂) and "Great Summons" ("Da zhao" 大招)—describe the shamanistic ritual of calling back the wandering soul of the dying or the deceased.[55] In these texts, death is configured spatially: the body is situated in the center, surrounded by regions with inhospitable climates, man-devouring beasts, and nightmarish landscapes in the six directions (that is, north, south, east, west, above, and below). The soul is first warned about the unspeakable horrors of those foreign territories on all sides and then invited to return to the security and sensual pleasures of home. The soul-summoning ritual described in the two texts was, however, interpreted by the commentator Wang Yi 王逸 (d. 158) as a political allegory. According to Wang Yi, these texts represent attempts to call Qu Yuan 屈原, the loyal but slandered minister, out of exile and back to the capital.[56] In such an interpretation, death and exile become connected: both are a departure to the outlying wilderness, to the periphery, and in both cases there is a motivation to return—to the body, the corporeal residence of the soul, and to the capital, the political and cultural center of the state. Being banished to remote provinces meant going into oblivion and experiencing a form of political death, and indeed many exiled officials were unable to physically survive the harsh living conditions, the climate, or the hardships of travel to such remote places. A poem by Jiang Yan 江淹 (444–505), written during his exile to the Jian'an Commandery (in modern Fujian) in 474, makes the connection between death and exile quite explicit. The poem is entitled "Crossing the Spring Peak and Emerging on Top of Various Mountains" ("Du Quanqiao chu zhushan zhi ding" 渡泉嶠出諸山之頂). Its last couplet reads: "In the

55. The current versions of these two texts are from the first century BCE at the latest. See *Chuci buzhu* 9–10.197–226. For an English translation, see Hawkes, *The Songs of the South*, pp. 219–38.

56. *Chuci buzhu* 9.197, 10.216.

south, the sky is ablaze, / O soul, come back" 南方天炎火，魂兮可歸來.[57]

Center and periphery are, however, a pair of relative, mutually dependent concepts that have no stable substance. In his account, Faxian states: "Central India is known as the Central Kingdom" 中天竺所謂中國.[58] It is very likely a direct translation of the Sanskrit term Madhyadésa (in Pāli, Majjhima-desa), which means "the Middle Country." In both Pāli and Sanskrit Buddhist texts, India is divided into five regions, which are not always stated definitely except in the case of Madhyadésa. As Debarchana Sarkar explains, "The reason behind the supreme importance attached by the Buddhists to this division lies in the fact that Gotama attained enlightenment or Bodhi and became the Buddha in an eastern district of this division and 'the drama of his whole life was staged on the plains of the Middle Country.'"[59] Buddhist scriptures sometimes reverse the argument, saying that the Buddha could only be born at the center of the world because otherwise his powerful substance would tip the earth off balance.[60] In any case, the Chinese rendering of Madhyadésa, *Zhongguo* 中國, uses the same compound that in the native tradition had always been reserved for the north Chinese heartland; it is also the term indicating "China" in modern times. According to the Buddhist geography, however, Faxian and his fellow travelers were regarded as men from the "borderland" (*biandi* 邊地).[61] In the kingdom of Pitu (Bhida), the local people marveled at the sight of Faxian and his companions:

> When they saw us Qin monks, they were greatly moved. They said: "How could these men of the borderland become ordained as monks and travel such a great distance to seek the Buddhist Law?"[62]

> 見秦道人往，乃大憐愍，作是言："如何邊地人能知出家爲道遠求佛法?"

---

57. Jiang Yan, *Jiang Wentong ji huizhu*, p. 115.

58. *Faxian zhuan kaozheng*, p. 79.

59. Sarkar, *Geography of Ancient India in Buddhist Literature*, p. 65.

60. See, for instance, *Fo shuo taizi ruiying benqi jing* 佛說太子瑞應本起經, in *T* 3: 1.473.

61. For a detailed discussion of "center/periphery," see Liu Yuan-ju, "Sheyuan yu guifan" pp. 319–54.

62. *Faxian zhuan kaozheng*, p. 112.

At the Jetavānā Monastery, Faxian and his fellow traveler Daozheng are again called "men from the borderland":

The monks came out and asked us: "Where did you come from?" We answered, "We came from the land of the Han people." The monks said with a sigh, "How extraordinary is it that men from a border country should come to this place for the sake of seeking the Law!" They said among themselves: "None of our teachers has ever seen a Han monk coming to our place."[63]

彼衆僧出問顯等言："汝從何國來?" 答曰: "從漢地來。" 彼衆僧嘆曰："奇哉，邊國之人乃能求法至此。" 自相謂言："我等諸師和上相承以來未見漢道人來到此也。"

This term was not only used by Indian monks to refer to foreigners like Faxian, but also by Faxian and his companions to refer to themselves:

When Daozheng and I first arrived at the Jetavānā Monastery, we reflected on how the World Honored One had lived here for twenty-five years. We felt sad that we had been born in the borderland and had had to travel through many kingdoms to come here, and that by this time some of our companions had gone back and some had passed away. Today we finally saw the place where the Buddha had once lived, and we were deeply moved.[64]

法顯、道整初到祇洹精舍，念昔世尊住此二十五年，自傷生在邊城，共諸同志游歷諸國，而或有還者，或有無常者，今日乃見佛空處，愴然心悲。

The acknowledgement of central India as the center of the world and China as borderland was not universal in Faxian's time, and indeed it was a source of contention among Faxian's contemporaries.[65] For Faxian and his fellow travelers, however, this was not an issue up for dispute. The most telling example is Daozheng's decision:

After he came to the Central Kingdom, Daozheng witnessed the rules of conduct observed by the Buddhist clergy, and saw that the dignified demeanors of those monks were worthy of observing under all sorts of circumstances. He recalled

---

63. Ibid., p. 137.

64. Ibid., p. 137.

65. He Chengtian 何承天 (370–447), a prominent anti-Buddhist scholar, debated this point with a monk in Jiankang in the early fifth century. The identity of the monk varies in different records, but one of the candidates was Zhiyan 智嚴, who had joined Faxian in his travels. See Zheng Cheng and Jiang Xiaoyuan, "He Chengtian wen foguo lishu gushi de yuanliu ji yingxiang," pp. 61–71.

with regret that in the borderland of the state of Qin, rules and regulations in Buddhist monasteries were incomplete. He vowed not to be born in the borderland again until he achieved Buddhahood. He thereupon remained in India and never returned.[66]

道整既到中國，見沙門法則，衆僧威儀，觸事可觀，乃追嘆秦土邊地，衆僧戒律殘缺，誓言自今已去得佛，願不生邊地，故遂停不歸。

The journey from borderland to center was by no means easy. As Faxian leaves Chang'an for India, the first part of his quest reenacts the dreadful journey to the outlying wilderness prescribed in the Chinese texts on summoning the soul. The landscape is demonic and fraught with perils, and some kingdoms are inhospitable or downright hostile. The desert to the west of Dunhuang, for instance, is described as follows:

In the River of Sands, there were many evil demons and hot winds. Travelers who encountered them all perished without a single survivor. Up above there was no flying bird, and down below there was no running beast. One looked around as far as one could for a path through, but one knew not which direction to go; skeletons of the dead were all one had for road markers.[67]

沙河中多有惡鬼熱風，遇則皆死，無一全者。上無飛鳥，下無走獸，遍望極目，欲求度處，則莫知所擬，唯以死人枯骨爲標幟耳。

Faxian then recounts that after a seventeen-day journey, they arrived at the Kingdom of Shanshan 鄯善, "a country rugged and hilly, with a thin and barren soil." The next kingdom they passed through was little better, as "the people of Wuyi were not attentive to etiquette and propriety, and treated visitors very poorly." Some of Faxian's companions had to return to Gaochang to seek financial support; Faxian and the others kept going southwest: "There were no inhabitants along the way. The travel through sands was very hard. The miseries we suffered were incomparable in human experience."[68]

The Kingdom of Yutian (Khotan) and several other states after Khotan offered a welcome respite, but the Onion Range and the river Indus were again dangerous and dreadful:

66. Ibid., pp. 245–46.
67. Ibid., p. 34.
68. Ibid., pp. 36–39.

The Pamir Mountains had snow in winter and summer. There was also a poisonous dragon. When offended, it would spew out a poisonous wind and cause rain, snow, and sandstorm. Not one out of ten thousand travelers who encountered such calamities was able to survive.[69]

葱嶺冬夏有雪。又有毒龍，若失其意，則吐毒風雨雪，飛沙礫石。遇此難者，萬無一全。

We traveled southwest along the Pamir range for fifteen days. The road was difficult and rugged, the crags extremely steep and dangerous. The mountain had nothing but rocks; it rose up several thousand meters high. One felt dizzy when looking down over the edge of the cliff. If one wanted to advance, there was no place to put down one's foot. Below was a river called the Hindus. In the past, people chiseled the rocks and opened a path that had seven hundred steps. After climbing the steps, we crossed the river on a suspension bridge made of ropes.[70]

順嶺西南行十五日，其道艱岨，崖岸嶮絶。其山唯石，壁立千仞，臨之目眩，欲進則投足無所。下有水名新頭河。昔人有鑿石通路施傍梯者，凡度七百。度梯已，躡懸絙過河。

The hardships of travel culminated in the tragic end of one of Faxian's two remaining companions:

The Snow Mountain had snow on it in winter and summer. On the shaded north side of the mountain, a fierce wind suddenly began to blow, and we were all freezing and shivering. Huijing could not go any further. A white froth came out from his mouth. He said to me: "I cannot live anymore. You should get going now. Don't stay here and die with me." With these words he breathed his last. I held him and cried sadly. His wish was not fulfilled—this was fate; what could be done about it![71]

雪山冬夏積雪。山北陰中，遇寒風暴起，人皆噤戰。慧景一人不堪復進，口出白沫，語法顯云："我亦不復活，便可時去，勿得俱死。"于是遂終。法顯撫之悲號。本圖不果，命也奈何！

Soon after Huijing's death, Faxian and Daozheng reached central India, which marked a watershed in Faxian's journey. No further description of danger and hardship appears after this point. There might have been a place or two in central India that had few inhabitants and seemed desolate,

69. Ibid., pp. 57–58.
70. Ibid., p. 67.
71. Ibid., p. 112.

but it was nothing as horrible as what the travelers had endured before. From the moment he entered central India, it was as if Faxian had left hell behind and entered the earthly paradise.

The southern region from this point on was called the Central Kingdom. In the Central Kingdom, the climate was temperate, and there was no frost or snow. People were numerous and happy. There were no household registers, no official codes of law; only those who plowed the king's land paid tax on it. If they wanted to leave, they could leave; if they wanted to stay, they could stay. The king ruled without capital punishment or any other form of corporal punishment. Offenders were only fined according to the nature of the offense. Even for those who committed the gravest crimes, the punishment was no heavier than cutting off of the right hand. The royal guards and attendants all enjoyed a regular salary. Throughout the kingdom, the people did not kill any living creature, drink alcohol, or eat scallions and garlic, except for the caṇḍālas. The caṇḍālas were wicked men who lived apart from the others. When they came to a city or a marketplace, they would strike a piece of wood to distinguish themselves, so that the others knew who they were and avoided coming into contact with them. In the Central Kingdom, the people did not raise pigs and chickens, nor did they sell livestock. There was no butcher shop or taverns that sold ale in the marketplace. They used cowries in buying and selling. Only the caṇḍālas were fishermen and hunters who sold meat.

從是以南，名爲中國。中國寒暑調和，無霜雪。人民般樂，無户籍官法，唯耕王地者乃輸地利。欲去便去，欲住便住。王治不用刑斬，有罪者但罰其錢，隨事輕重。雖復謀爲惡逆，不過截右手而已。王之侍衛左右皆有供祿。舉國人民悉不殺生，不飲酒，不食葱蒜，唯除旃荼羅。旃荼羅名爲惡人，與人別居。若入城市，則擊木以自異，人則識而避之，不相搪突。國中不養猪鷄，不賣生口，市無屠估及沽酒者。貨易則用貝齒。唯旃荼羅漁獵師賣肉耳。

The high status accorded to the Buddhist clergy completes the picture of a Buddhist paradise:

Since the Buddha's parinirvana, the kings and nobles built monasteries for the priests, and provided them with land, houses, gardens, orchards, service households, and cattle. The grants were engraved on metal plates to be passed from king to king, and nobody dared to invalidate them; they remained valid till the present time. The priests had no lack of housing, bedding, food, drink, and clothing. It was the same everywhere in the Central Kingdom.[72]

---

72. Ibid., p. 117.

自佛般泥洹後，諸國王長者居士爲衆僧起精舍，供給田宅、園圃、民户、牛犢，鐵券書錄，後王王相傳，無敢廢者，至今不絶。衆僧住止房舍、床褥、飲食、衣服都無闕乏，處處皆爾。

In many ways, Faxian's portrayal of central India, like Marco Polo's account of the wonders of the East, serves as a reversed mirror image of the Chinese regimes at the time. Corporal punishment was an important part of punitive law; even government officials could not avoid it.[73] Throughout the third and fourth centuries, there were repeated discussions of restoring more serious forms of corporal punishment, such as the cutting off of a foot.[74] Household registers were another important issue, because registered households were the taxpayers on whom the state relied for income and corvée labor. Many people tried to evade being registered by secretly moving to another place; more often than not they attached themselves to elite landholders and thus received exemption from taxation. The state fought constantly against such practices, and the freedom of going or staying at will, enjoyed by the people in central India, was quite unimaginable. Just as Marco Polo's exotic East represented Europe's dream ideal, the same kind of wish-fulfillment could certainly be said of Faxian's idealized account of central India.

According to Faxian's biography in the *Biographies of Eminent Monks*, when Faxian decided to spend a night on Vulture Hill, he was first warned of the dangers of the mountain and then abandoned by the two monks who served as his guides, because they were afraid of the wild beasts roaming the mountainside. Later that night, Faxian was surrounded by three black lions. Faxian reportedly kept reciting sutra, and the lions finally left him in peace.[75] This incident, likely apocryphal, does

---

73. In south China, Wang Meng 王濛 (309–47) declined the appointment of Senior Aide to the Minister of Education because the ranking of this post was not high enough to avert public whipping if the holder of the post violated the law. Fang Xuanling et al., *Jin shu* 93.2419. Corporal punishment continued to be meted out according to a person's social standing in the fifth century: "[If anyone breaks the decree,] a member of the gentry will be deprived of his office, and a commoner will be whipped one hundred times." Xiao Zixian, *Nan Qi shu* 56.978. It also existed in the north: "In the early years of the Wei, the law was quite austere, and many courtiers had received whipping for their offense." Wei Shou, *Wei shu* 48.1089.

74. Fang Xuanling et al., *Jin shu* 30.938–42.

75. Huijiao, *Gaoseng zhuan* 3.88.

not appear in Faxian's own travel account. One modern scholar believes that this is because, on the one hand, Faxian was too modest to boast of his bravery, and on the other hand, he had undergone so many trials during his travel that this incident on Vulture Hill was not considered worthy of mention.[76] One cannot help observing that the absence of this incident from Faxian's account is consistent with his by-and-large euphoric description of central India: it was a land of temperate weather and kind-hearted people, absent of personally experienced danger.

Peril appears again only during the return journey from Sri Lanka back to China. Faxian's description of this difficult sea voyage is about eight hundred words long, taking up no small portion of an account of ten thousand words. The narration is also more detailed than in many other places of the account. One passage summarizes the perils of the sea:

> There were many pirates on the sea, and if one encountered them, there was no escaping alive. The great sea was vast and boundless, and one could not tell east from west. All one could do was to look to the sun, moon, and stars for direction. When it was cloudy and rainy, the boat followed wherever the wind blew without any definite course. In the darkness of the night, one could only see the great waves crashing into one another, which emitted a glistening light like the color of flames, with giant turtles, tortoises and water monsters all about. The merchants were fearful and did not know which way to go. The sea was infinitely deep, and there was no place to moor the boat. One only knew east and west when the sky cleared up; only then could one advance in the right direction. If the boat were to bump into any hidden rock, then there was no hope of survival.[77]

> 海中多有抄賊，遇輒無全。大海彌漫無邊，不識東西，唯望日月星宿而進。若陰雨時，爲逐風去，亦無所准。當夜暗時，但見大浪相搏，晃若火色，黿鱉水性怪异之屬。商人荒懅，不知那向。海深無底，又無下石住處。至天晴已，乃知東西，還復望正而進。若値伏石，則無活路。

In addition to this passage, Faxian vividly narrates two particularly dangerous incidents on the sea, both caused by a great storm. In the first incident, the merchants aboard the vessel all threw their bulky goods into the sea to lessen the load; Faxian, too, threw away his kendi (a jar for

76. Faxian, *Xinyi Foguo ji*, annot. and trans. Yang Weizhong, p. 155.
77. Ibid., p. 274.

drinking water), wash basin, and other things as he prepared for the worst. In the second incident, the Brahmans aboard the vessel contemplated leaving Faxian on some island, for they believed that having a monk on board had brought them bad luck. He was saved only by his patron's intervention.

By portraying the horrors and tragedies attending his journeys to and from central India, Faxian sequesters central India off as a heavenly kingdom surrounded by perilous terrains and treacherous seas. It is a land of promise that is barely within reach. Cosmas Indicopleustes, a seafaring Greek merchant who traveled to India and Sri Lanka about a century after Faxian, has left behind a fascinating work called *Christian Topography*. In this work, Cosmas postulates that the earth we inhabit is surrounded by ocean, and that beyond the ocean lies another earth, which is the seat of paradise.[78] The earthly paradise is forbidden territory in Cosmas' vision; it seems less inaccessible in Faxian's Buddhist worldview, but one must still go through hell to reach it. As we shall see in the following section, such a trajectory was both fresh and familiar to Faxian's contemporaries.

The Paradigm of Heaven and Hell

The native Chinese tradition had developed notions of the otherworld long before Buddhism arrived in China,[79] but certainly no known literature in the pre-Buddhist period gives such elaborate descriptions of heaven and hell as the Buddhist scriptures do. The so-called Pure Land Buddhism, which flourished in south China in the fourth and fifth centuries, attracted many followers among the elite.[80] Pure Land Buddhism advocates belief in the Pure Land of Amitābha Buddha, the Buddha of In-

---

78. *The Christian Topography of Cosmas*, p. 33.

79. Much has been written about this. See, for example, Ying-Shih Yu, "'O Soul, Come Back!'" pp. 381–86; Thompson, "On the Prehistory of Hell in China," pp. 27–41; McClenon, "Near-Death Folklore in Medieval China and Japan," pp. 326–27. McClenon describes near-death experiences that involve visits to heaven prior to the import of Buddhism. For recent Chinese scholarship on the native Chinese conception of the otherworld, see Hou Xudong, "Dong Jin nanbeichao Fojiao tiantang diyu guannian de chuanbo yu yingxiang"; and Wang Qing, *Xiyu wenhua*, pp. 195–202.

80. Ren Jiyu, *Zhongguo Fojiao shi*, Vol. 2, pp. 618–23; Wang Qing, *Wei Jin nanbeichao shiqi de Fojiao xinyang yu shenhua*, Chapter 3.

finite Life and Infinite Light, who resides in the Western Paradise or the Pure Land as opposed to the "impure land" of the mortal world. One of its major texts is the *Sutra of Infinite Life* (*Wuliangshou jing* 無量壽經), which, judging from the many different translations produced between the third and fifth century, was immensely popular.[81] In this sutra, the Pure Land of Amitābha Buddha is described in sumptuous terms. It is a land of instant gratification. Delicious food and drink appear and disappear as one wishes. A breeze blows the jeweled trees, making a pleasant music and spreading a delightful aroma for those who wish to indulge the senses; those who do not wish so will hear and smell nothing. Everyone bathes in jeweled pools. After emerging from the pool, each sits on a lotus flower.

The topography of the Pure Land is worth noting. The following passage is from the version translated by Lokakṣema in the late second century:

> Its kingdom has no Mount Sumeru. . . . It has no big sea nor small sea; it has no streams or rivers or the Ganges, nor does it have mountains, forests, brooks, and valleys; there are no dark and hidden places. The land, made of Seven Jewels, is all level and flat. There are no birds and beasts and hungry ghosts from hell, no flying insects or crawling insects. . . . There are no Asuras, dragons, demons, and gods. There is never a time of great rain, nor are there spring, summer, autumn, and winter. There is neither great cold nor great heat. The weather there is always temperate and balanced; it is incomparably pleasant and good.[82]
>
> 其國中無有須彌山……其國土無有大海水，亦無小海水，無江河洹水也，亦無山林溪谷，無有幽冥之處。其國七寶地皆平正。無有泥犁禽獸餓鬼蜎飛蠕動之類也，無阿須倫諸龍鬼神也，終無有大雨時，亦無春夏秋冬也。亦無有大寒，亦不大熱。常和調中適，甚快善無比。

---

81. This scripture was first translated into Chinese by Lokakṣema in the late second century; it was translated again in 252 by Kang Sengkai 康僧鎧. The other extant early translation was completed by Zhi Qian, also from the third century. Subsequently there appeared several more translations.

82. *T* 12: 1.283. This version is known as *Foshuo wuliang qingjing pingdeng jue jing* 佛說無量清淨平等覺經. Some scholars believe that this is one and the same with the version entitled *Wuliangshou jing* translated by Dharmarakṣa, and so the extant version post-dates Zhi Qian's version. This theory is not entirely convincing. See Ren Jiyu, *Zhongguo Fojiao shi*, pp. 441–42.

The absence of steep cliffs, unfathomable watery depths, hidden caverns, and dark corners in the Pure Land evokes Faxian's description of the topography of central India:

The land between the Indus River and south India, and indeed from the Indus River all the way to the South Sea, stretches about forty or fifty thousand miles. It is all flat and level. There is no big mountain or large river; there are only rivulets.[83]

自度新頭河，至南天竺，迄于南海，四五萬里皆平坦，無大山川，正有河水。

Even the eternally temperate climate in the Pure Land of Amitābha Buddha corresponds to Faxian's description of central India as a land with mild weather, described as "cold and heat in harmony" (*hanshu tiaohe* 寒暑調和). The veracity of Faxian's account is not in question here; the point is that he is already conditioned to see and recognize what he has learned to see and recognize. As Gombrich said, "Artists don't go into the field to paint what they see but to see what they already know how to paint."[84]

Knowledge about the Pure Land was widespread during the Eastern Jin. Zhi Dun was moved to write an encomium on a painting of Amitābha Buddha ("Amituofo xiangzan" 阿彌陀佛像讚). In the preface to the tetrasyllabic encomium, he thus describes the Pure Land:

According to the Buddhist scriptures, there is a kingdom in the west named Peaceful Nourishment. The road leading to it is meandering and remote, and the miles are as numerous as the grains of sand in the Ganges. Excepting those who do not depend on anything, no one can roam its territories; excepting those who do not rush, how can one reach it speedily?[85] The Buddha of that kingdom is called Amitābha, which means "Infinite Life" in the Jin language. The Kingdom has no king's law or official ranking, for the Buddha is the King, and the Three Vehicles are their teachings. Men and women there are all born from lotus blossoms, and there is no filth of pregnancy and childbirth. All the halls, mansions, and palaces are decorated with the Seven Jewels; moreover, they are naturally

83. *Faxian zhuan kaozheng*, p. 118.

84. Cited in States, *Dreaming and Storytelling*, p. 180.

85. "Bu ji er su" 不疾而速 is a phrase found in the *Classic of Changes*. See *Zhou yi zhengyi* 7.155.

structured without human artifice. In the parks, gardens, pools, and ponds there grow numerous extraordinary flowers.[86]

佛經記西方有國，國名安養，迴遼迴邈，路踰恆沙。非無待者，不能遊其疆；非不疾者，焉能致其速。其佛號阿彌陀，晉言無量壽。國無王制班爵之序，以佛爲君，三乘爲教。男女各化育於蓮華之中，無有胎孕之穢也。館宇宮殿悉以七寶，皆自然縣搆，制非人匠。苑囿池沼，蔚有奇榮。

Not surprisingly, there are many contemporary near-death experience accounts of devout Buddhists, both priests and lay people, attaining to the Pure Land, particularly in the case of those concentrating on it in their meditative visualization.[87]

At the same time, extensive accounts of journeys to hell were also circulated in the fourth and fifth centuries.[88] In many ways, hell is the other side of heaven, and the otherworldly beauty of the Pure Land must be complemented and reinforced by the horrors of hell.[89] One well-known story about the journey to hell is that of Zhao Tai 趙泰, who "died" on August 20, 370, and came back to life after ten days to give a detailed "eyewitness account" of hell. Zhao Tai's story is recorded in at least two "anomaly accounts" (*zhiguai* 志怪) of the fifth century. The first of the accounts is *Records of Worlds of Darkness and Light* (*Youming lu* 幽明錄), compiled under the auspices of Liu Yiqing 劉義慶 (403–44), Prince of Linchuan; the second is *Signs from the Unseen Realm* (*Mingxiang ji* 冥祥記), put together by Wang Yan 王琰.[90] A passage from the *Mingxiang ji* version gives a typical scene of hell narrative as "reportage literature":

---

86. Yan Kejun, *Quan Jin wen* 157.2369.

87. For instance, see Huijiao, *Gaoseng zhuan* 6.234, 7.273–74, 11.401, 11.416, 11.437, 12.468. Also see McClenon, "Near-Death Folklore."

88. See Campany, "Return-from-Death Narratives in Early Medieval China"; and Campany, "To Hell and Back."

89. Michihata Ryōshū discusses this in *Chūgoku Bukkyō shisōshi no kenkyū*, pp. 93–94.

90. Both versions are cited in the tenth-century *Taiping guangji* 太平廣記 (109.739–41 and 377.2996–998). I follow the Tang monk Falin's 法琳 (572–640) "Bian zheng lun" 辨正論 commentary in identifying Zhao Tai as a man of the Eastern Jin rather than of the Song (*Taiping guangji* 109.740). The Eastern Jin dynasty does not have the reign title Taishi 太始, which I emended to Taihe 太和 (366–71).

At the time, there were about fifty to sixty relatives who were waiting upon Zhao Tai, and they all heard Tai's account. Tai himself committed his experience to writing to show his contemporaries. . . . When his contemporaries heard that Tai had died and then come back to life and had seen much of the punishment and reward in the underworld, they all paid visits to him and asked him about it. Ten of the visitors, including Sun Feng of Wucheng, who was Superior Grand Master of the Palace, and Hao Boping of Changshan, who was the Marquis of Guannei, gathered at Tai's place and inquired about it in great detail. They all became fearful and were converted to Buddhism right then and there.[91]

時親表內外候視泰者五六十人，同聞泰説。泰自書記，以示時人……時人聞泰死而復生，多見罪福，互來訪問。時有太中大夫武城孫豐、關內侯常山郝伯平等十人，同集泰舍，款曲尋問，莫不懼然，皆即奉法。

The interest in Zhao Tai's underworld journey is similar to the general public's curiosity about Faxian's overseas travels. Death is the ultimate foreign country, from which few travelers come back to tell the tale, and when they do, it is a sensational story.

The description of hell presents something that is rarely seen in classical Chinese literature, namely, an ugly and dreadful landscape:

There was a blazing tree with a circumference of about fifty paces and a height of a thousand yards. There were swords all around it. Flames burst from the tree top. Underneath the tree, dozens of people fell upon the flaming swords, which pierced their bodies.[92]

有火樹，縱廣五十餘步，高千丈，四邊皆有劍，樹上然火，其下十十五五，墮火劍上，貫其身體。

There were towering trees of swords, whose height was immeasurable. Their roots, trunks, branches, and leaves were all made of knives and daggers. People swore at one another as they all climbed up the trees as if with pleasure, but then their heads were severed from their bodies, and their bodies were all cut up in small pieces.[93]

劍樹高廣，不知限量，根莖枝葉，皆劍爲之。人眾相訾，自登自攀，若有欣意，而身首割截，尺寸離斷。

---

91. Wang Yan, *Mingxiang ji*, in *Taiping guangji* 377.2998. For a complete English translation of Zhao Tai's story, see Kao, *Classical Chinese Tales*, pp. 166–71.

92. Liu Yiqing, *Youming lu*, in *Han Wei liuchao*, p. 740.

93. Wang Yan, *Mingxiang ji*, in *Taiping guangji* 377.2997.

In one account, a man named Cheng Daohui 程道惠 (361-429), like Zhao Tai, went on a guided tour of hell. His good karma allowed him to walk on a "straight and flat" road, while "on both sides of the road there were dense and thick bramble thorns that one could hardly step into. Sinners were driven into the thorns, which pricked their flesh. The sound of their painful cries deafened the ears."[94] The motif of bramble thorns is prominent in the imagination of hell. Another account relates the journey through hell of a man named Shi Changhe 石長和, who, being a Buddhist believer, also walked on a level road, but "both sides of the road were lined with brambles and thorns as sharp as eagle's claws. Shi saw throngs of people, old and young, running along among the brambles as if being driven. Their bodies were all wounded, and there was congealed blood on the ground."[95]

A description of the infernal landscape appears in the section on hell in the *Pearl Grove of the Garden of Dharma* (*Fayuan zhulin* 法苑珠林), a Buddhist encyclopedia compiled by the monk Daoshi 道世 (ca. 596–683) in 668:

> The forest of daggers rises up to the sun; the peaks of swords touch the sky. Waves surge in cauldrons of boiling water; flames flare up from the blazing furnaces. The iron city wall is shut tight during the day, and copper pillars are burning bright at night.[96]
>
> 刀林聳日，劍嶺参天。沸鑊騰波，炎爐起焰。鐵城晝掩，銅柱夜然。

The topography of hell is usually diametrically opposed to the Western Paradise: the land is hilly and craggy, the vegetation thorny and deadly, and the temperatures extreme, with slabs of ice as large as sheets falling and scattering and hitting people.[97] When we read Faxian's journey to India in terms of the preponderance of hell stories, often accompanied by visual images, which were widely circulated as oral accounts and as part of

94. Wang Yan, *Mingxiang ji*, in *Taiping guangji* 382.2041. For a complete English translation of Cheng Daohui's story, see Kao, *Classical Chinese Tales*, pp. 172–75.

95. Liu Yiqing, *Youming lu*, in *Han Wei liuchao*, p. 746. For a complete English translation, see Appendix II, pp. 341–43.

96. Daoshi, *Fayuan zhulin*, p. 227.

97. The sixth-century Buddhist encyclopedia *Jinglü yixiang* has a couple of sections devoted to various forms of hell collected from diverse scriptural sources (*juan* 49–50, in *T* 53).

the Buddhist preaching of this period, it is not difficult to see how Faxian's travel report could easily find powerful resonance in the contemporary cultural imagination about the otherworld.

James McClenon rightly points out that Chinese and Japanese near-death folklore "reveals a bipolar effect," with some accounts focusing on hell and others on heaven.[98] And yet, heaven and hell are not two polar opposites that never intersect with each other. When Zhao Tai was in hell, he saw three sinners delivered from their sufferings because their living family members were praying in a Buddhist temple for their redemption. The three people were taken to a mansion in the south. Zhao Tai followed them and saw a splendid hall, in which a god sat on a jeweled throne and the governor of hell was paying respects to him. Zhao Tai asked a clerk who that godly figure was, and the clerk replied, "That is the World Honored One, the Teacher who enlightens and redeems people" (*Haoming Shizun, duren zhi shi* 號名世尊, 度人之師). In Zhao Tai's vision, the grand mansion where the Buddha sat was not far away from hell; indeed he walked there with apparent ease, following the trail of the three pardoned sinners. Liu Sahe 劉薩荷, a soldier and a hunter, also met with Bodhisattva Avalokiteśvara during his tour of hell.[99]

Journeys to hell and stories about journeys to hell, it seems, are meant to lead the traveler and the audience to heaven, and more often than not they do. Paradise is not a given; it has to be "gained" through much suffering and conscious effort. Faxian's travel account is structured on the basis of the paradigm of heaven and hell established in early medieval China.

Paradise Lost: The Image of a Fan

What happens when one finally gains paradise? One can certainly stay there, as Daozheng, Faxian's fellow traveler, did; and that would be the end of the story. Faxian, on the other hand, chose to go back to the "bor-

98. McClenon, "Near-Death Folklore," p. 327.

99. Liu Sahe was the late fourth-century monk Huida 慧達. Accounts of his journey to hell, his conversion from a sinner to a devout Buddhist monk and his miraculous experiences can be found in a variety of early medieval sources, most notably in *Mingxiang ji*. See Daoshi, *Fayuan zhulin* 86.2483–486. His biography is also included in Huijiao, *Gaoseng zhuan* 13.477–79.

derland." He had a noble purpose: "My original aim was to seek the Vinaya Piṭaka and have it circulated in the land of the Han people, so I went on the return journey alone."[100] But within the account there is a hidden narrative that places Faxian in a unique position. Because of this hidden narrative, Faxian is no longer just the depersonalized bearer of an itinerary or the faceless recorder of a catalogue of exotic places; his travel account becomes a first-person narrative imbued with an unmistakable subjectivity.

In *Image and Pilgrimage in Christian Culture*, Victor and Edith Turner describe how the pilgrim undergoes the hardship of the journey to arrive at a profoundly spiritual experience. Surrounded by "symbolic structures" such as religious images and buildings, "often described and defined in sacred tales and legend," the pilgrim is initiated into a "new, deeper level of existence than he has known in his accustomed milieu." Victor and Edith Turner argue that the trials of the long journey make the pilgrim particularly vulnerable and receptive:

> Religious images strike him, in these novel circumstances, as perhaps they have never done before, even though he may have seen very similar objects in his parish church almost every day of his life. The innocence of the eye is the whole point here, the "cleansing of the doors of perception." Pilgrims have often written of the "transformative" effect on them of approaching the final altar or the holy grotto at the end of the way.[101]

Near the end of his journey, Faxian was indeed struck by an image while he was visiting a monastery in Sri Lanka, but it was not a religious image, and the transformative impact it produced was more emotional than spiritual:

> In the monastery there was a hall decorated with gold and silver and finished with various precious stones. Inside there was a statue of the Buddha in green jade, which was about thirty feet tall and shone forth with the glow of the Seven Jewels. Its majestic form was solemn and dignified beyond description. In its right palm was a priceless pearl. I had been away from the land of the Han people for many years. All the people I associated with were foreigners; my eyes had not seen familiar mountains, rivers, trees, and plants for a long time. My traveling companions had all left me: some stayed behind and some had died. There was

100. *Faxian zhuan kaozheng*, p. 246.
101. Turner and Turner, *Image and Pilgrimage*, p. 11.

only me looking upon my shadow, and my heart was constantly filled with melancholy. All of a sudden, in front of this jade statue, I saw a white silk fan from the land of Jin, presented by some merchant as an offering to the Buddha. At that moment I could not help my tears.[102]

起一佛殿，金銀刻鏤，悉以衆寶。中有一青玉像，高三丈許，通身七寶炎光，威相嚴顯，非言所載，右掌中有一無價寶珠。法顯去漢地積年，所與交接，悉異域人。山川草木，舉目無舊。又同行分披，或留或亡。顧影唯己，心常懷悲。忽于此玉像邊，見商人以晉地一白絹扇供養，不覺凄然，淚下滿目。

The statue of the Buddha with its indescribable magnificence aroused awe and admiration in Faxian; but what *touched* him turned out to be a secular object—the image of a fan. The contrast between the opulent splendor of the precious jewels and the plain white silk fan is at once striking and poignant. If the first part of the passage evokes an impersonal catalogue of exotica commonly seen in an account of a foreign country or a faraway place, then the second part of the passage embodies an intensely personal and lyrical moment.

The lyricism of the moment is largely due to the fact that the white silk fan is one of the quintessentially poetic images in early Chinese classical poetry. In the Southern Dynasties, a widely known poem attributed to Lady Ban (d. ca. 6 BCE) compares the fate of an aging palace lady to an abandoned fan in autumn. There was also a popular set of romantic southern songs centering on the image of a white round fan in the fourth and fifth centuries.[103] As such, the image of a white silk fan would have especially resonated with Faxian's southern audience. In an account that is otherwise characterized by a dispassionate style and often given to long narration of Buddhist lore, Faxian's reaction to the fan is remarkable in its emotive self-representation.

In his campaign account, Dai Yanzhi similarly shared personal experiences, such as seeing a pigeon for the first time. Such observations serve to give a full account of what one sees during one's journey more than to relate

102. *Faxian zhuan kaozheng*, p. 255.

103. The southern song set, "Round Fan Lover" ("Tuanshan lang" 團扇郎歌), is attributed to the mistress of the Eastern Jin minister Wang Min 王珉 (361–88). See Lu Qinli, *Quan Jin shi* 19.1052. The fan poem attributed to Lady Ban was included in the sixth-century literary anthologies *Wen xuan* 文選 and *Yutai xinyong* 玉臺新詠. Lu Qinli, *Quan Han shi* 2.116–17.

heartfelt responses. Compared with Dai Yanzhi's account, Faxian's writing betrays something deeply emotional, a subjectivity rarely seen in a travel account from this period.

During a journey lasting fourteen years and crossing many foreign kingdoms, one is bound to find so many things worthy of attention that to see something or not to see it (seeing, that is, as represented in a travelogue and memoir) becomes a deliberate choice instead of a random act. Faxian's seeing of the fan is much more than a mere passing mention of an interesting personal anecdote. His response to the image of the fan was certainly not very Buddhist: desire, longing, homesickness—these are all emotions and forms of attachment that a Buddhist priest should learn to purge in the process of self-cultivation, but they played a key role in Faxian's life as a traveler. It was from Sri Lanka that Faxian finally embarked on his homecoming voyage. His seeing of the fan in some ways serves, if not as a catalyst for his decision to go home, then as a narrative preparation for that decision.

Faxian's encounter with the fan is structured as a powerful emotional response to a visual stimulus followed by an ensuing action. Such a narrative structure would not have been strange to his audience in south China, who were familiar with a number of contemporary stories structured along a similar continuum. The best-known example is perhaps the story about Liu Chen 劉晨 and Ruan Zhao 阮肇, which appears in Liu Yiqing's *Records of Worlds of Darkness and Light*. In the story, Liu Chen and Ruan Zhao of Shan county 剡縣 (in modern Zhejiang) went into Mount Tiantai in the year of 62 CE. There they encountered two beautiful women, who addressed them by name and seemed to be expecting them. The women invited them home, where many maids were preparing a sumptuous feast for them. A group of young women showed up at the banquet, each bringing some peaches and congratulating the two women on the arrival of their bridegrooms. That night the two men paired off with their brides. The story records that after ten days the men requested to leave, but the women persuaded them to stay, so they remained there for half a year. Then it was spring:

> All kinds of birds were singing, and the two men were filled with a stronger homesickness than ever. They again asked to go home, this time with urgency

and persistence. The women said, "You are pulled by your sins. What can be done about it?"[104]

百鳥啼鳴，更懷悲思，求歸甚苦。女曰："罪牽君，當可如何？"

What happened afterwards follows a Rip Van Winkle storyline: they discovered that during their six-month absence from home, many years had passed in the mortal world, their friends and relatives had long since died, and their hometown had changed beyond recognition. They finally located their seventh-generation descendants, who told them their ancestors had gone into the mountains and gotten lost, never to return. In the year 383, they vanished again without a trace.

A similar story is recorded in *A Sequel to* In Search of the Supernatural (*Xu* Soushen ji 續搜神記 or Soushen *hou ji* 搜神後記), a collection of anomaly accounts attributed to Tao Yuanming.[105] The names of the two men in this story are Yuan Xiang 袁相 and Gen Shuo 根碩, but the location of their encounter with the divine women remains the same. Just like in the Liu/Ruan story, the goddesses were difficult to reach: Liu and Ruan had to swim upstream for two or three miles, and Yuan Xiang and Gen Shuo had to pass through a "very narrow and precipitous" stone bridge. Once they crossed over to the other side and went through a grotto, they found themselves in a "level and vast space inside, with all the trees and plants emitting a fragrance." Like in the Liu/Ruan story, the goddesses were expecting the two mortals, and they lived together as husband and wife. One day the two women went out to congratulate a friend whose bridegroom had just arrived (one wonders if this is a tongue-in-cheek intertextual reference to the feast prepared for Liu and Ruan upon their first arrival). After the women left, Yuan Xiang and Gen Shuo tried to escape. The two women already knew of their plan and caught up with them; they were not angry but gave them a parting gift instead. Besides the parting gift, the most significant divergence from the Liu/Ruan story is that the Rip Van Winkle effect is missing, as Yuan and Gen returned home and resumed their lives as before. One day, when Gen Shuo was plowing, his family brought him lunch and found him standing still in the

104. Liu Yiqing, *Youming lu*, in *Han Wei liuchao*, p. 697. For a complete English translation of Liu Chen and Ruan Zhao's story, see Kao, *Classical Chinese Tales*, pp. 137–39.

105. The original *Soushen ji* was compiled by Gan Bao.

field; upon closer examination, they saw "an empty shell of the man like the shed skin of a cicada."[106]

Several other stories in Tao Yuanming's and Liu Yiqing's collections follow a similar narrative structure. In one of the stories in Tao's *Sequel*, a person accidentally fell into a huge grotto in Mount Songgao. After groping his way around the darkness for several days, he emerged into an open space and saw two chess players. They gave him some "white-colored juice" to drink and asked him to stay. He declined their invitation and was given instructions about how to get back. Later he learned that the chess players were immortals.[107] Similarly, a story in Liu's *Records* relates the romantic encounter of a man named Huang Yuan 黃原 with a goddess named Miaoyin 妙音. After several days together, Huang Yuan asked Miaoyin for permission to return home temporarily, whereupon he was told that he and his lover would be separated forever.[108]

The common element in these stories is the moment of "longing for home" (*sigui* 思歸) experienced by the protagonist. If being in paradise is a prolonged state of bliss, the very act of remembering the mortal world is a sound of discord that breaks off the enchantment. In meditative visualization, one must focus on the thought of the paradise or of the Amitābha Buddha or Bodhisattva Avalokiteśvara continuously and ceaselessly without disruption, a state of concentration that is described as one "without break for even a single thought-instant" (*niannian xiangxu* 念念相續).[109] Any pause in this constant state of absorption, any distraction at all, terminates the magic forever. Paradise lost can sometimes be regained, but the answer is always ambiguous—nobody knows for sure if or when it will happen.

In his article entitled "Empyreal Powers and Chthonian Edens: Two Notes on T'ang Taoist Literature," Edward Schafer distinguishes the mystical and romantic encounter of Liu Chen and Ruan Zhao from "An Account of Peach Blossom Spring" ("Taohuayuan ji" 桃花源記) written by

106. Tao Yuanming, Soushen *hou ji*, pp. 2–3.

107. Ibid., p. 2.

108. Liu Yiqing, *Youming lu*, in *Han Wei liuchao*, p. 699. For a complete English translation of Huang Yuan's story, see Kao, *Classical Chinese Tales*, pp. 139–40.

109. Fu Liang et al., *Guanshiyin yingyan ji sanzhong yizhu*, p. 121. For a detailed exploration of meditative visualization and its influence on the poetics of the early medieval period, see Chapter 5 of my *Beacon Fire and Shooting Star*.

Tao Yuanming.[110] The latter appears in *A Sequel*, though it is much better known as an independent piece of literary writing, indeed one of the best-known stories in the Chinese literary canon. The two stories, however, are more similar than is commonly recognized, as they share the narrative structure of entering a paradisial space and then leaving it of one's own accord. I certainly do not intend to downplay the literary significance of the account of Peach Blossom Spring; and yet, instead of treating it as a singular work of pure literary genius existing within a cultural vacuum, a different approach is to consider it as one of numerous similar stories in circulation at the time. In other words, we should think of the Peach Blossom Spring story as part of the anomaly accounts collection compiled by Tao Yuanming, who was known as a lover of "strange tales," rather than *merely* as part of the literary collection written by Tao Yuanming the great poet. When we do this, it becomes easier to see the story as part of a much larger story cycle that was immensely popular at the turn of the fifth century. It is perhaps a misguided attempt to try to find a single source for a popular story like this in medieval China, when stories and texts were circulated in a much more messy way than in late imperial times; there is no neat textual filiation, only morphing and crossing. A story goes through metamorphosis and is written down by different hands. Names, locations, and costumes may change, but the central characters and basic plot remain the same.

In such a context, it is anachronistic to attempt to demarcate the Buddhist, Daoist, and Confucian "schools of thought." Scholars may contend that Tao Yuanming was a believer in Confucian values or an admirer of Zhuangzi, and so could not possibly have been influenced by Pure Land Buddhism in spite of Tao's close association with several lay members of the monk Huiyuan's Mount Lu community; but any writer is always writing from within a complex social and cultural system, in which values are constantly exchanged across artificial boundaries invented only later as a way of trying to make sense of the system. If we forego the rigid division of the "three schools" imposed by convention and reinforced by modern academic disciplines, it becomes clear that the story of Peach Blossom Spring, in which the fisherman voluntarily departs from the paradisial land, never again to find his way back, is a variation of the "paradise lost"

110. Schafer, "Empyreal Powers and Chthonian Edens," pp. 667–77.

theme that is repeated in many contemporary tales as well as in Faxian's travel account.

The key element of such tales is the element of free will. The renunciation of paradise is always voluntary, and it is almost always the consequence of longing to return to the mortal world. Longing for home, *sigui*, felt either by a soldier on military campaign or by an official traveling on the king's business, is a familiar pathos in classical poetry. In the poem "Li Sao" 離騷 from the *Verses of Chu*, the poet goes on a cosmic quest for a worthy lord. Toward the end of the poem, just as his chariot is galloping through heaven, he pauses in mid-flight to look back on the mortal world:

陟陞皇之赫戲兮 I was mounting aloft to such dazzling splendor—
忽臨睨夫舊鄉 all at once I glanced down to my homeland of old.
僕夫悲余馬懷兮 My driver grew sad, my horses felt care,
蜷局顧而不行 they flexed looking backward and would not go on.[111]

The "Li Sao" was not an unfamiliar text to members of the Southern Dynasties elite, and yet, to find oneself already in paradise (as opposed to being on the road like the "Li Sao" speaker) and longing for the mortal world became a recurring narrative motif only in the fourth and fifth centuries. Faxian's work is unique in that it presents this paradigmatic structure in a first-person travel account. It is not like the travel *fu* that records, in an emotionally even tempo, the author's progress from one site of history to another; nor is it a catalogue of exotic customs and products that serve the political, economic, and military interests of the empire. Faxian's singular feat is the fact that he manages to turn his travel account into a personal epic. He does this first of all by adding vivid details about himself to the more impersonal descriptions of Buddhist sites and lengthy relation of Buddhist stories. Granted, those details are only brief glimpses into the life of Faxian, but they are enough to provide a sketch of Faxian as a real man traveling in a real world of dangerous, unfamiliar territory. Even more importantly, Faxian achieves the effect of a personal epic by incorporating a narrative structure of paradise gained and lost, which would have been familiar to early medieval Chinese readers from various stories in circulation at the time, and yet was couched in a new framework, namely that of the travel account. Suddenly, instead of an infinitely ex-

111. *Chuci buzhu* 1.47; Owen's translation. *An Anthology of Chinese Literature*, p. 175.

pandable list of places visited, what we have is a story with a beginning and an end and a dramatic turning point in between.

In the later tradition, stories appear in which gods and goddesses, rather than the mortals stumbling upon the immortal realm, "long for the human world" (*si fan* 思凡).[112] In a moment of weakness, a god or goddess succumbs to the temptation of the sensual pleasures of the human world, is henceforth cast out from heaven and born as a mortal being, and invariably must undergo considerable vicissitudes to regain paradise. The remote beginning of this popular theme in late imperial Chinese fiction and drama lies in early medieval times.

112. Examples are numerous, from vernacular stories to novels such as *Journey to the West* and *The Dream of the Red Chamber*. That the male and female protagonists of a work of fiction often turn out to be divine beings who choose to descend to the mortal world or are banished to the mortal world due to the stirring of "mortal sentiments" (*fanxin* 凡心) is a recognized narrative strategy in late imperial Chinese fiction. See, for instance, Shen Jie, "*Sanyan* zhong daojiao shenxian gushi de xushi zhuti moshi."

CHAPTER THREE

Xie Lingyun, Poet of Purgatory

After Faxian arrived at Jiankang, among those who were fascinated by his journey and sought out his companionship was a haughty aristocrat. This was the young Xie Lingyun, who had yet to embark on his own famous journeys. Xie Lingyun was well versed in the Buddhist doctrine, and yet he was never quite able to extricate himself from what Buddhists regard as two of the greatest human weaknesses, namely, wrath and obsession. Two years after he composed his "*Fu* on My Journey," he learned of an affair between his favorite concubine and one of his retainers; in a fit of rage, he killed the retainer and dumped his body into the Yangzi River. When the matter became known to the public, Xie Lingyun was dismissed from his office—a light punishment by today's standards, but this was the fifth century, and Xie Lingyun was descended from one of the most prestigious clans of the Southern Dynasties. The following year, Liu Yu ended the rule of the house of Jin and became the founding emperor of the Song dynasty, and Xie Lingyun was pardoned and reinstated in his former post.

He did not stay there long. Liu Yu died in 422, and his young heir succeeded to the throne. Xie Lingyun, unable to get along with the regents in power and under suspicion for conspiring with another imperial prince, was sent away from the capital to a provincial post at Yongjia 永嘉 (in modern Zhejiang). This was the first of several demotions Xie would experience through the remainder of his tumultuous public career. Within a year of his arrival at Yongjia, Xie Lingyun resigned and returned to his home estate in Shining 始寧 (in modern Zhejiang). He was summoned to the court and served again, resigned again, was subsequently accused by an enemy and went to the capital to absolve himself, and was appointed once more to a provincial post. A series of troubled moves led to further conflicts with the authorities and ended in the poet's final exile to the far south, where he was accused of rebelling against the ruling dynasty and executed in the marketplace of Guangzhou. That was in the year of 433; the poet was forty-eight years old.

Xie Lingyun traveled a great deal during the last decade of his life; the bulk of his extant poems are from this period and describe his sojourns far and near. We tend to forget, in the comfort and ease of modern travel, what a difficult enterprise it was to travel in those times, when mountains had no paved roads or footpaths but were filled with overgrown vegetation that blocked progress. Xie Lingyun not only had an insatiable curiosity for new scenery but, being a nobleman with an extensive estate, possessed the material and human resources that enabled him to travel to out-of-the-way, little-frequented places. Once he deployed several hundred of his retainers to cut down trees and open a path through the mountains that led all the way to the county of Linhai 臨海, a commandery about a hundred miles to the south of Shining. They made such a commotion that the magistrate of Linhai was quite alarmed, believing that a large band of mountain robbers had descended on his jurisdiction. The magistrate calmed down only after he learned that it was just Xie Lingyun and his crew. Xie invited the magistrate to join him in his expedition, but the magistrate refused. This anecdote provides a good illustration of the repeated lament in Xie Lingyun's poetry that "I regret there is no one who shares what I feel, / and together with me climbs the ladder to blue clouds" 惜無同懷客，共登青雲梯.[1] It is rather remarkable how such a poignant sense of loneliness should permeate Xie Lingyun's poetry, considering the large entourage of retainers traveling with him and working for him. The issue of social class no doubt underlies the poet's complaint about his lack of companionship.

Nevertheless, people like the Linhai magistrate, who turned down Xie Lingyun's invitation to go on an expedition with him, might very well have been among the most avid readers of Xie Lingyun's landscape poetry

1. From Xie's poem "Climbing the Very Highest Peak of Stone Gate" ("Deng Shimen zuigao ding" 登石門最高頂). Lu Qinli, *Quan Song shi* 2.1166.

produced from his adventures. According to Xie Lingyun's biography in the dynastic history,

Every time a poem of his reached the capital region, people high and low vied with one another to make a copy of it, and the poem would reach all gentry members and commoners overnight. His writings were admired far and near, and his reputation made quite a stir in the capital.[2]

每有一詩至都邑，貴賤莫不競寫，宿昔之間，士庶皆遍。遠近欽慕，名動京師。

Xie Lingyun's travel poems, in the way in which they were eagerly consumed by a home audience, are the poetic equivalent of contemporary accounts of journeys to distant lands, be they foreign countries, north China, paradise, or hell. They were produced in the same intellectual and cultural milieu and satisfied a keen public appetite for what was far away, exotic, and inaccessible. The mountains Xie Lingyun visited were not necessarily easy to reach, even for people who possessed the physical prowess and the desire to travel. Just like in the modern world, travel, especially travel for pleasure, was an indicator of social status and economic power. The "pleasure" part is an important element in Xie Lingyun's travel writings, as it marks Xie Lingyun's departure from the traditional model of "loyal minister in exile" established by the archetypal figure of Qu Yuan, the putative author of the "Li Sao." If the figure of Qu Yuan is largely legendary and shadowy, then Jiang Yan, the poet much closer to Xie Lingyun's time, is playing the role of Qu Yuan to the tee in his exile poem cited in the previous chapter. Unlike Jiang Yan, Xie Lingyun rejects or at least gives a new twist to the "loyal minister in exile" theme by constantly and consciously seeking out new scenery and enjoying it. His poetry reveals an insatiable desire for new things, coupled with a sense of urgency. The author says as much himself:

懷新道轉迥	Yearning for new prospects, I find the road grow ever longer;
尋異景不延	the daylight is not prolonged for seeking out wonders.[3]

2. Shen Yue, *Song shu* 67.1754.

3. From Xie's poem "Climbing the Lone Hill in the River" ("Deng jiangzhong guyu" 登江中孤嶼). Lu Qinli, *Quan Song shi* 2.1162.

Xie Lingyun's biography presents the image of an aggressive mountain climber who invests in innovative travel gear:

When exploring mountains, he made a point of reaching secluded and precipitous spots. Even if there were a thousand layers of crags and hills, he would exhaust them all. In climbing he always wore wooden clogs, taking off the front cleats of the clogs when going uphill and taking off the back cleats downhill.[4]

尋山陟嶺，必造幽峻。巖嶂千重，莫不備盡。登躡常著木履，上山則去前齒，下山去其後齒。

Frequently taking detours on his way to a provincial post or back to his home estate in Shining, Xie Lingyun sometimes lingered for weeks on a mountainside, as he did at Mount Lu during his term at Linchuan 臨川 (in modern Jiangxi) in 432:

山行非前期	This mountain trip is not planned;
彌遠不能輟	the further I go, the more unable I am to stop.
但欲淹昏旦	I had only wanted to stay for a morning and night;
遂復經盈缺	by now the moon has waxed and waned again.[5]

The claim of spontaneity in traveling—being drawn onward, almost as if against the poet's will, by the beauty of nature—was a novel phenomenon, and so was the repeatedly expressed desire for seeking new sights and fresh scenery. It was no doubt a manifestation of the poet's individual temperament—intensified, however, by a socio-historical context in which there was a prevailing desire for seeing more of the physical world beyond established boundaries. When people could not go into uncharted territories themselves, they would avidly read about them in travelogues written by others.

If Faxian writes about an earthly paradise, and many Buddhist miracle tales speak of touring through hell, then Xie Lingyun always lingers in the middle. Suspended between heaven and hell, it is a space in the midst of the "human realm" (*renjian* 人間). The poet was constantly in transit from one place to another in the last decade of his life, a period that saw the production of most, and certainly the best, of his extant poems. Fur-

---

4. Shen Yue, *Song shu* 67.1775.

5. From the poem "Climbing to the Highest Peak of Mount Lu and Looking at the Various Ridges" ("Deng Lushan jueding wang zhuqiao" 登廬山絕頂望諸嶠). Lu Qinli, *Quan Song shi* 3.1179.

thermore, his poetry reflects an obsession with the *process* of traveling, the vigorous, strenuous movement from point A to point B. Sometimes he is literally in an intermediate state, neither here nor there, like in a poem written at the beginning of his trip to Yongjia entitled "My Neighbors Saw Me Off at Square Hill" ("Linli xiangsong zhi Fangshan" 鄰里相送至方山).[6] Square Hill is a small hill just south of the capital city of Jiankang.

祗役出皇邑	Accepting my service I left the imperial city;
指期憩甌越	soon enough I expect to repose in Ou and Yue.
解纜及流潮	Undoing my moorings, I catch the tidal currents,
懷舊不能發	yet I cannot set out for my attachment to old friends.

"Repose" (*qi* 憩) implies an interruption of normal activities, an interim state and a pause; it is certainly an odd word to describe the life of a magistrate. The poet seems to indicate that the destination of his journey, Ou and Yue, is not a permanent dwelling but a temporary resting stop before he moves on to somewhere else; but even before he reaches it, he is helplessly enthralled in feelings of nostalgia for old friends left behind in the capital. Although he unties the moorings, he cannot (*bu neng* 不能) undo the human attachments, and Square Hill becomes a limbo for a soul that wishes to wander off to faraway lands but is unable to break free. There is a tension between *yi* 役, service, and *qi*, repose, in the opening couplet. Xie Lingyun's magisterial term at Yongjia is both *and* neither—he is precariously poised between the two modes of existence, and his lingering at Square Hill mirrors such an unsettled state of being.

On his way to Yongjia, Xie Lingyun made a detour to visit his family estate in Shining, where he wrote a poem entitled "Stopping by My Villa in Shining" ("Guo Shining shu" 過始寧墅). As Owen says, "Everywhere he goes, he is only 'stopping by.'"[7] The anticipated continuation of his journey after a brief respite at home is symbolic of the poet's life and work at large: the poet always occupies the middle point, the intermediate existence between death and rebirth that characterizes not only his spatial and temporal self-positioning, but also the configuration of psychological topography in his poetry.

---

6. Lu Qinli, *Quan Song shi* 2.1159.

7. Owen, "The Librarian in Exile," p. 219.

Xie Lingyun's most famous poem, "Climbing the Tower by a Pool" ("Deng chi shang lou" 登池上樓), was written when he was in Yongjia. It once again opens with the description of such an intermediate state:[8]

潛虬媚幽姿	Its hidden form lends charm to the sunken kraken,
飛鴻響遠音	the soaring swan sounds off its far cries.
薄霄愧雲浮	One reaches high skies, and I am shamed before the drifting clouds;
棲川怍淵深	the other rests in watery depths, and I am humbled by the deep ravine.
進德智所拙	My wisdom was inept in improving my virtue,
退耕力不任	yet my strength could not bear retiring to plow.
徇祿及窮海	In pursuit of salary, I have come all the way to farthest sea's edge;
臥痾對空林	now, lying ill, I face the barren woods.

While the sunken kraken is a figure of reclusion, the soaring swan represents advancement in one's official career. The poet is instead a creature of the land, as he lies ill and gazes at the winter woods. He admits his inadequacy in the improvement of virtue, which is a euphemistic way of saying that he has failed to achieve an illustrious public career; at the same time, he freely acknowledges that he is not cut out for the life of a recluse, either. Xie Lingyun explicitly rejects the two traditional paths taken by members of the elite and emphasizes an alternative personal choice.

No less than his older contemporary Tao Yuanming, Xie Lingyun frequently seeks to justify his lifestyle in his poetry. A pattern begins to emerge. In another Yongjia poem, entitled "Reading in My Study" ("Zhai zhong dushu" 齋中讀書), Xie Lingyun once again emphasizes the uniqueness of his situation by explicitly setting it against the two conventional choices:[9]

既笑沮溺苦	I laugh at the hardships of Changju and Jieni,
又哂子雲閣	but I also scoff at Ziyun in his tower.
執戟亦以疲	"Holding the halberd" is wearying enough;
耕稼豈云樂	how could they find delight in harvesting and plowing?
萬事難并歡	In everything it is hard to enjoy the best of both worlds;
達生幸可托	I am lucky I can devote myself to understanding the principle of life.

8. Lu Qinli, *Quan Song shi* 2.1161.

9. Ibid., 2.1168.

Changju 長沮 and Jieni 桀溺 were recluse-farmers who had been plowing together when Confucius sent his disciple to them to "inquire after the ford."[10] Ziyun was the style name of Yang Xiong, who continued to serve under Wang Mang 王莽 (45 BCE–23 CE), the usurper of the Han throne, as a collator in the Tianlu Tower. Later on, he was implicated in the case of one of his disciples. When Wang Mang's arresting officers came for him, Yang Xiong threw himself out of the tower in a panic and almost died.[11] "Holder of the Halberd" was a low-ranking imperial guardsman that became associated with Yang Xiong in Cao Zhi's 曹植 (192–232) "Letter to Yang Dezu" ("Yu Yang Dezu shu" 與楊德祖書): "In the past Yang Ziyun was but a holder of the halberd."[12] Expressing disapproval of both lifestyles embodied in the persons of Changju/Jieni and Yang Xiong, Xie Lingyun offers a phrase from *Zhuangzi*, "understanding the principle of life" (*da sheng* 達生), as his own solution. The chapter in *Zhuangzi* bearing this phrase as its title is about nonattachment to things of the world; it also contains a remark attributed to Confucius that furnishes an appropriate comment on Xie's poem: "Do not go inside and hide; do not go outside and manifest yourself; rather stand like a piece of dry firewood in the middle" 无入而藏，无出而阳，柴立其中央.[13] Though written during Xie Lingyun's term as magistrate of Yongjia, this poem certainly presents a unique vision of public service: claiming an absence of lawsuits and a dearth of official business, the poet stresses reading and writing as acts of both leisure and pleasure. This particular style of governing earns him the place in the middle, halfway between hiding and manifesting oneself.

The poetry Xie Lingyun wrote after his resignation from his post at Yongjia continues to avoid any simple version of antithesis. A poem entitled "To the South of My Fields I Set Up a Garden, into Which I Diverted a Stream and for Which I Erected a Wall" ("Tiannan shuyuan jiliu zhiyuan" 田南樹園激流植援) begins with such a statement:

---

10. *Lunyu zhushu* 18.165.
11. See Ban Gu, *Han shu* 87.
12. Yan Kejun, *Quan Wei wen* 16.1140.
13. *Zhuangzi jishi* 19.647.

樵隱俱在山	Though woodcutters and recluses are both in the mountains,
由來事不同	their doings have never been the same.
不同非一事	Not the same, yet not in just one way—
養痾亦園中	one may also convalesce in one's garden.

Li Shan 李善 (630–89) cites the lost *History of the Jin Dynasty* (*Jin shu* 晉書) compiled by Zang Rongxu 臧榮緒 (415–88): "Hu Kongming once said, 'A recluse is in the mountains; a woodcutter is also in the mountains. Although they are both in the mountains, their doings in the mountains are quite different.'"[14] To this Xie Lingyun adds yet another way of being in the mountains—convalescing. His illness could be real, or it could be a pretext. The very ambiguity, as opposed to the woodcutter's profession and the recluse's ideological decision, creates a unique identity for the poet.

The intermediate existence is a particular stage. Located between the point of origin and destination, it defers ending and projects an aura of eternal transition that yearns for fulfillment in its final completion and oblivion. It is, indeed, the perfect description of desire, travel, and narrative. Xie Lingyun's obsession with the intermediate state naturally extends to landscape. A Yongjia poem entitled "Climbing the Lone Hill in the River" ("Deng jiangzhong guyu" 登江中孤嶼) gives an account of a hill literally situated in the middle of a river:[15]

江南倦歷覽	To the south of the river, I have grown weary of sightseeing;
江北曠周旋	it has been a while since I last frequented north of the river.
懷新道轉迴	Yearning for new prospects, I find the road grow ever longer;
尋異景不延	the daylight is not prolonged for seeking out wonders.
亂流趨孤嶼	Cutting across the current I hurry to the Lone Hill,
孤嶼媚中川	the Lone Hill that lends charm to mid-stream.
雲日相輝映	Clouds and sun gleam on one another,

14. Xiao Tong (501–31), *Wen xuan* 30.1397.

15. Lu Qinli, *Quan Song shi* 2.1162. According to Gu Shaobo, the Lone Hill is the name of a hill on an isle in the Ou River to the north of Wenzhou, the modern name of the old county seat of Yongjia. See Xie Lingyun, *Xie Lingyun ji jiaozhu*, p. 84.

空水共澄鮮	sky and water share purity and freshness.
表靈物莫賞	It manifests a numinous spirit, but none appreciate it;
蘊眞誰爲傳	it harbors Genuine Beings, but who tells the tale?
想像昆山姿	With my mind's eye I see the form of Mount Kunlun,
緬邈區中緣	remote from me now, the causality of this limited world.
始信安期術	Now for the first time I believe in Anqi's techniques
得盡養生年	that may help me live out my natural lifespan.

The opening couplet sets out two antithetical geographical locations—the south and north of the river. *Zhouxuan* 周旋, a phrase translated as "to frequent" in this context, also has the meaning of socializing; it is as if the poet were talking about associating with an old friend. We realize that he is quite familiar with both sides of the river by now, and his decision to go north is in fact a decision to go *back* to a former haunt, rather than explore a new territory. This creates a tension with the second couplet, in which the poet expresses in unambiguous terms his desire for new, unusual, and ever-changing scenery. The poet seems to have exhausted all possibilities, and his return to the north of the river is a gesture of desperation.

As he observes the long road and the waning daylight, we hear one of Xie Lingyun's favorite texts, the "Li Sao" in the *Verses of Chu*: "On and on stretched my road, long it was and far, / I would go high and low in this search that I made."[16] There is also a faint echo of the words of another man of Chu, Wu Zixu 伍子胥, who was so intent upon avenging his father's and brother's deaths that he brought the enemy's army to destroy his home state. When an old friend censured him for going too far in his scheme for revenge, he said: "The daylight is receding, and my road is long; I therefore have to go against the current."[17] In both earlier texts, there is a strong sense of urgency: time is passing, and yet much remains to be sought after. Xie Lingyun's poem is neither about a cosmic quest such as in the *Li sao* nor about family vengeance such as in Wu Zixu's case, and yet, the resonance of the earlier texts gives a weight and poignancy to what should have been mere pleasure trips.

---

16. *Chuci buzhu* 1.27.

17. Sima Qian, *Shi ji* 66.2177. In Xie Lingyun's time, temples dedicated to Wu Zixu were scattered throughout south China, especially in the former Wu/Yue region where Yongjia was located.

Something happens along the way, as it always does. The poet's desire to see new prospects is unexpectedly fulfilled on his way back to the north side of the river, as he sees the Lone Hill from a distance and hurries toward it. The Lone Hill has a name that reflects its location: as clouds and sun refract light on each other (*xiang* 相) and sky and water "share" (*gong* 共) purity and freshness, the Lone Hill stands solitary in the middle of the river, belonging neither to one side nor to another. Perhaps it is for this reason that it manifests a "numinous spirit" and harbors "Genuine Beings." As he gazes at the hill, the poet sees with his mind's eye the Lone Hill's true match—the legendary Mount Kunlun where immortals dwell.

The accidental nature of the poet's discovery of a hill that harbors immortal beings recalls the utopian realm stumbled upon by the hapless fisherman in Tao Yuanming's famous account of Peach Blossom Spring. That the poet is inspired by the sight of a small hill to see in his mind a grand mythical mountain also recalls the older poet. In the prose preface to a poem entitled "An Excursion to Xie Brook" ("You Xiechuan" 游斜川), Tao Yuanming explains why he prefers a little hill to the much more majestic Mount Lu:

> About South Mountain [Mount Lu], its name is truly old now, so it is not worthy of our sighs. As for the Tiered Wall, it has nothing around it, and rises alone out of the isle in mid-stream. As I visualize the numinous mountain from afar, I am charmed by the lovely name of this hill.[18]
>
> 彼南阜者，名實舊矣，不復乃爲嗟歎。若夫曾城，傍無依接，獨秀中皋。遙想靈山，有愛嘉名。

Like Xie Lingyun, Tao Yuanming writes about a hill located in the middle of a stream whose name, "Tiered Wall," reminds him of Mount Kunlun, since it is also the name of Mount Kunlun's highest peak. If Tao Yuanming's ascent of the hill is purely optical, then Xie Lingyun's is an actual physical act.[19] In both poems, the physical landscape is transformed into a magical and spiritual landscape seen by the mind's eye, and the poet is transported to a different plane of reality. Tao's poem follows the tradi-

---

18. Lu Qinli, *Quan Jin shi* 16.975. Depending on which textual variant one follows, this poem and its preface were either written in the year of 401 or 421. In the latter case, it would have been only two years before Xie Lingyun wrote his poem on the Lone Hill.

19. See the detailed discussion of this poem in my book, *Tao Yuanming and Manuscript Culture*, pp. 142–46.

tion of feast poetry with its theme of *carpe diem* and ends with the resolve to enjoy the day's pleasures to the fullest. Xie Lingyun, on the other hand, turns to the tradition of poetry on "wandering immortals" that speaks of the quest for transcendence and immortality in the mountains.

In many ways, the Lone Hill in the middle of the stream is the poet's self-projection. Xie Lingyun is fascinated with the intermediate state—a suspension between this world and the other world, between heaven and hell. This happens not only in the spatial configuration but also on the temporal level. Many of Xie's poems are set at twilight, a time delicately balanced between day and night, light and darkness. It is a time of pause in his active traveling, a time of growing still and contemplative. "Fuchun Isle" ("Fuchun zhu" 富春渚), a poem written on his way to Yongjia, exemplifies Xie Lingyun's unique ability to mix physical geography and textual knowledge to describe his inner journey.[20]

朝發漁浦潭	In the morning we set out from Fisherman's Deeps,
暮宿富春郭	at night we rested on the outskirts of Fuchun.[21]
定山緬雲霧	Steady Mountain far and faint in clouds and fog,
赤亭無淹薄	at Crimson Pavilion there was no tarrying.
溯流觸驚急	Countering currents, I bashed through swift dashings;
臨圻阻參錯	close by the bank I was blocked by strewn rocks.
亮乏伯昏分	In truth I lacked Bohun's endowments,
險過呂梁壑	while the peril surpassed that of Lüliang's canyon.
洊至宜便習	"To pooling it cometh"—best to be inured;
兼山貴止托	"mountains joined"—value halting and lodging.
平生協幽期	Lifelong affinity with designs for withdrawal,
淪躓困微弱	floundering, fumbling, trapped by weaknesses.
久露干祿請	Long evincing appeals for preferment,
始果遠游諾	only now fulfilling a pledge for far wandering.

20. Lu Qinli, *Quan Song shi* 2.1160. Owen's translation with modifications. *An Anthology of Chinese Literature*, pp. 319–20.

21. The opening couplet in the *Wen xuan* version reads: "By evening we passed over Fisherman's Deeps, / in the morning we reached Fuchun" 宵濟漁浦潭，旦及富春郭 (*Wen xuan* 26.1240). Almost all modern editions have adopted this version. I follow the *Taiping yulan* version here, as night travel was rare except under extraordinary circumstances, especially when, according to the poem, the upriver journey has been so difficult. Xie Lingyun was a leisurely traveler who had taken his time to arrive at Yongjia—there was no reason why he should press the boatmen to undertake a night voyage. See Li Fang et al., *Taiping yulan* 46.353.

宿心漸申寫	My perennial heart progressively unfolds,
萬事俱零落	myriad matters all fall away.
懷抱既昭曠	Now that my concerns are bright and expansive,
外物徒龍蠖	external things may contract like a dragon or an inch-worm, all in vain.

The poet has sailed up the Fuchun River, passing through Crimson Pavilion, Steady Mountain, and Fisherman's Deeps, until he reaches the outskirts of the city of Fuchun, where he moors his boat for the night. The upriver journey has been difficult and indeed more perilous in the eyes of the poet than Lüliang's canyon, where "even fish, turtles, and crocodiles could not swim," and the poet states that he is no Bohun Wuren who could calmly walk backwards until his feet were half over the edge of a deep abyss.[22] The next couplet contains two references to the *Classic of Changes*: water flows continuously over difficult terrain because it is accustomed to it; the hexagram of "mountains joined" urges one to be still and not reach beyond one's position.[23] J. D. Frodsham relates these *Yijing* references, ostensibly alluding to the poet's perilous river voyage, to Xie's recent ousting from the court. This is certainly true,[24] but the textual echoes are also pertinent to Xie's physical movement on a more literal level: "halting and lodging" alludes to his stopping over at Fuchun for the night instead of persisting in struggling with the current and braving the foggy weather.

Mooring outside the city of Fuchun on a dark, misty night, the poet is inspired to reflect on his life. He declares his "lifelong affinity with designs for withdrawal," with *youqi* 幽期 literally meaning "darkling expectations" or "darkling appointment." "Floundering, fumbling, trapped by weaknesses" again evokes the difficult journey during the day, but somehow, at the day's end, in the rising fog and the descending darkness, the poet discovers the true meaning of "halting and lodging," and achieves an enlightenment that illuminates his inner state of being.

---

22. Both stories are recorded in *Liezi*, a Daoist work of uncertain date. It resurfaced in the fourth century with a commentary by Zhang Zhan 張湛, who was roughly Xie Lingyun's contemporary. *Liezi* was a work familiar to the Eastern Jin elite. *Liezi jishi* 2.62. 2.51–52.

23. *Zhou yi zhengyi* 4.71–72, 5.116.

24. Frodsham, *The Murmuring Stream*, Vol. 2, p. 119.

The last line of the poem is yet another reference to the *Classic of Changes*: "The inchworm contracts its body in order to advance; dragons and snakes hibernate in order to preserve their lives" 尺蠖之屈以求信也，龍蛇之蟄以存身也.[25] Since in the source text both the inchworm and the much larger creatures like dragons and krakens are described as either "contracting" or "hibernating," the metaphorical implication of "dragon and inchworm" in Xie's line can only be "to shrink and hide."[26] The modern commentator Gu Shaobo's paraphrase of the final couplet is quite appropriate: "No matter how hard the others may compete for an official salary, I will never again follow suit."[27] And yet, the power of this couplet does not lie in paraphrasing, but in the interplay of images: the illumination and expansion of his inner being is contrasted with the shrouding darkness and the contraction, shrinking, and falling away of myriad things around him.

Another poem written during his journey to Yongjia, "Seven-League Rapids" ("Qili lai" 七里瀨), again expresses the feeling of confinement and the eventual spiritual liberation achieved by imagination.[28]

羈心積秋晨	The traveler's heart is gathered up on autumn mornings;
晨積展游眺	the morning's gathering is unfolded in his roaming gaze.
孤客傷逝湍	The solitary wanderer feels wounded by the swift currents passing on,
徒旅苦奔峭	the lone wayfarer suffers from rocks crumbling down from the shore.

Ji 積 means "to gather together, to pile up, to contain," an unusual verb for describing the "traveler's heart." Its antonym that appears in the corresponding position in the next line is *zhan* 展, to unfurl. As the traveler lets his gaze roam to release his pent-up feelings, he only sees things that depress him more: swift currents recalling Confucius' exclamation about

25. *Zhou yi zhengyi* 8.169.

26. The eighth-century *Wen xuan* commentator Liu Liang 劉良 interprets the couplet as follows: "Though a dragon may soar and an inchworm may contract, the poet treats them equally" 雖龍騰蠖屈,不爲殊觀也. See Xiao Tong, *Liuchen zhu* Wen xuan 26.498. The modern commentator Li Yunfu also takes "dragon and inchworm" as meaning "to be active and still, to stretch and shrink." See *Xie Lingyun ji*, p. 33. My interpretation differs from these.

27. *Xie Lingyun ji jiaozhu*, p. 47.

28. Lu Qinli, *Quan Song shi* 2.1160.

the ceaseless flow of time, and crumbling rocks that make the water journey dangerous.[29] Time and space are both relentless forces that oppress the traveler. Once again the poet finds himself facing nightfall:

石淺水潺湲	Over stony shallows the waters froth,
日落山照曜	when the sun sets, the mountains glow.
荒林紛沃若	In the wild forests, thick and leafy,
哀禽相叫嘯	mournful birds call to one another.

Right before the darkness falls, the mountain is filled with light and sound and seems to be coming to life. It is a time for the birds to return to their nests, and a time for the human traveler to stop for the night and pause for reflection:

遭物悼遷斥	Encountering things of the natural world, I lament my exile;
存期得要妙	longing for the time of withdrawal, I attain the marvelous.
既秉上皇心	Having acquired the state of mind of the Sage Emperors,
豈屑末代誚	how could I care in the least for the mockery of this late age?

With this resolution he looks toward the rapids where the Eastern Han recluse Yan Guang had fished, but sees a much grander fishing in his imagination:

目睹嚴子瀨	With my own eyes I have witnessed Master Yan's Rapids,
想屬任公釣	my mind's eye, however, sees the fishing of Lord Ren.
誰謂古今殊	Who claims that past and present differ?—
異世可同調	different ages can share the same mode.

Lord Ren is a fictitious character in *Zhuangzi* who fished in the Eastern Sea, using fifty oxen as his bait. After a year of getting nothing, he finally caught a gigantic fish whose meat fed all the people of the region.[30] As is typical of Xie Lingyun, the image in his mind expands to gargantuan proportions and overwhelms everything that appears in front of him. The "unfolding" in the first couplet is finally completed, and the darkness that closes in on the poet becomes irrelevant, unimportant.

---

29. *Lunyu jizhu* 9.80.
30. *Zhuangzi jishi* 26.925.

It is hard not to relate the image of the large fish to the famous *Zhuangzi* passage:

The fish trap exists because of the fish; once you've gotten the fish, you can forget the trap. The rabbit snare exists because of the rabbit; once you've gotten the rabbit, you can forget the snare. Words exist because of the meaning; once you've gotten the meaning, you can forget the words. Where can I find a man who has forgotten the words so I can have a word with him?[31]

荃者所以在魚，得魚而忘荃；蹄者所以在兔，得兔而忘蹄；言者所以在意，得意而忘言。吾安得夫忘言之人而與之言哉？

One may indeed forget about the fish trap if one catches a fish as big as Lord Ren's. And yet, in his more somber moments, the poet sees nothing but emptiness and impending darkness in the surrounding landscape; the hills that have lost their "numinous spirit" and the "Genuine Beings" are compared to an empty fish trap. In the poem entitled "Entering Huazi Hill, the Third Valley of Hemp Stream" ("Ru Huazi gang shi Mayuan disangu" 入華子崗是麻源第三谷), after he finally makes his way to the mountain top, the poet discovers, to his disillusionment, "Of the feathered folk there is not the least trace; / Cinnabar Hill is only an empty fish trap" 羽人絶彷彿，丹邱徒空筌.[32]

In "Entering the Mouth of the Pengli Lake" ("Ru Pengli hu kou" 入彭蠡湖口), the poet's pent-up feelings find no release.[33] Like "Climbing the Lone Hill in the River," the poem begins with the statement of weariness, this time not just with experience itself but also with writing about that experience. Unlike in "Climbing the Lone Hill," however, there is no more yearning for new prospects or the active seeking of wonders, and the second half of the poem finds the poet standing in a landscape deprived of its numinous creatures, precious things, and strange beings:

客游倦水宿	In his journey the traveler wearies of spending nights on water.
風潮難俱論	It is hard to tell all of the winds and tides.
洲島驟回合	Sandbars and isles suddenly turn and merge;

31. *Zhuangzi jishi* 26.944. Watson's translation, in *The Complete Works of Chuang Tzu*, p. 302.

32. Lu Qinli, *Quan Song shi* 3.1178.

33. Ibid., 3.1178.

圻岸屢崩奔 shores and banks frequently crash down.
乘月聽哀狖 In moonlight I listen to the plaintive gibbon;
浥露馥芳蓀 Drenched in dews, I inhale the scent of sweet iris.
春晚綠野秀 As spring grows late, the green fields are flowering;
巖高白雲屯 On the tall cliffs, white clouds mass.
千念集日夜 A thousand cares gather by night and day,
萬感盈朝昏 myriad sentiments fill dawn and dusk.
攀崖照石鏡 I climb a slope to see my reflection in the Stone Mirror,
牽葉入松門 pulling on leaves I enter Pine Gate Mountain.
三江事多往 The events of Three Rivers are mostly bygone,
九派理空存 the principle behind the Nine Tributaries survives by itself.
靈物吝珍怪 Numinous creatures begrudge their precious marvels,
異人秘精魂 strange beings keep their souls in secret.
金膏滅明光 The bright rays of the Golden Oil are extinguished;
水碧輟流溫 Liquid Sapphire ceases its flowing warmth.

Finally, the poet tries to relieve his feelings of melancholy by playing music, but "in vain do I play the song of 'A Thousand Miles,' / when music stops, my cares become even heavier" 徒作千里曲，弦絶念彌敦.

At other times, too much is "gathering up" and "piling up" not only in his mind but also in the physical world, and the landscape becomes claustrophobic. "Climbing the Very Highest Peak of Stone Gate" ("Deng Shimen zuigaoding" 登石門最高頂), written between 428 and 431 during his second extended stay at his home estate in Shining, thus describes his lodge on the mountaintop:[34]

疏峰抗高館 On the cleared peak is raised up a high lodge,
對嶺臨回溪 facing ridges look down on a winding creek.
長林羅戶庭 Tall forests stand in front of doors and in courtyards,
積石擁階基 heaps of boulders crowd around stairs and foundations.
連巖覺路塞 In those joined cliffs I sense the blocking of the road,
密竹使徑迷 the dense bamboos cause a person to stray from his path.
來人忘新術 Those who come forget their recent roads;
去子惑故蹊 those who leave grow confused as to their former trail. . . .

Another poem, supposedly also written during this period, bears the lengthy title, "A Newly Constructed Residence at Stone Gate, Surrounded by High Mountains, Winding Creeks, Stony Rapids, Dense For-

34. Ibid., 2.1165–166.

ests, and Tall Bamboos" ("Shimen xinying suozhu simian gaoshan huixi shilai maolin xiuzhu" 石門新營所住四面高山迴溪石瀨茂林脩竹).[35] A sense of confinement is inherent in the seclusion of the poet's mountain residence. The opening couplets describe the residence in a spot that is difficult to reach:

躋險築幽居	I mount steep crags to build a secluded dwelling,
披雲臥石門	pushing through cloud, I lie at the Stone Gate.
苔滑誰能步	The moss is so slippery, who can walk on it?
葛弱豈可捫	the rattan so weak, how could anyone grab hold of it?

These lines recall Tao Yuanming's verse: "This isolated alley keeps away deep ruts, / and turns back the carriages of old friends" 窮巷隔深轍，頗回故人車.[36] Deep ruts are created by large carriages, the means of transportation for the rich and famous. Although the settings of the two poems are rather different, both imply that the inconvenient locations of the poets' homes discourage their friends from visiting. While Tao Yuanming sings the praises of the rustic pleasures of his everyday life, Xie Lingyun's loneliness is intensified by a landscape darkened by overgrown plantation:

早聞夕飆急	Early I hear the swiftness of the evening wind,
晚見朝日暾	late I see the dawn sun brightening.
崖傾光難留	Where the slope overhangs the light will not linger,
林深響易奔	in the depth of the woods echoes easily flee away.

The descending darkness that surrounds the poet, and the perils of nature with its impenetrable vegetation, evoke contemporary accounts of journeying through hell.

Xie Lingyun's landscape, though verging on the horrific, never turns hellish. One of his Yongjia poems, "Climbing the Green Screen Mountain in Yongjia" ("Deng Yongjia lüzhang shan" 登永嘉綠嶂山), exemplifies the mood that is typical of his poetry.[37]

35. Ibid., 2.1166.
36. Lu Qinli, *Quan Jin shi* 17.1010.
37. Lu Qinli, *Quan Song shi*, 2.1162–63.

裹糧杖輕策	I wrap provisions and take my light staff;
懷遲上幽室	with yearning I mount the secluded chamber.[38]
行源徑轉遠	As I walk to the source of the stream, my path grows further;
距陸情未畢	even when I reach the mountaintop, my mood is not spent.
澮潋結寒姿	Ripples form in cold beauty;
團欒潤霜質	lithe, bamboo's substance is moistened by frost.
澗委水屢迷	As the ravine wounds, the waters are often lost from sight;
林迥岩逾密	the trees stand tall, and the cliffs grow mysterious.
眷西謂初月	I look westward, and think it is the new moon;
顧東疑落日	turning to the east, I take the glow for the setting sun.
踐夕奄昏曙	Toward evening, darkness turns to light,[39]
蔽翳皆周悉	everything veiled and covered becomes illuminated.
蠱上貴不事	"Decay" above—value not serving the prince;
履二美貞吉	"Tread" in the second place: praise constancy that brings good fortune.[40]
幽人常坦步	The recluse always walks on the level road;
高尚邈難匹	his noble aims are lofty and hard to match.
頤阿竟何端	Nourishment on the mountaintop—what is its sign?
寂寂寄抱一	In quiet and stillness, I give myself to embracing the One.
恬知既已交	Now that serenity and knowledge are conjoined to nourish each other,
繕性自此出	from this point on, our mended nature emerges.

---

38. All Chinese commentators have taken *huaichi* 懷遲 in the second line as meaning "winding and zigzagging," perhaps considering it as interchangeable with *weichi* 委遲, a common compound with the same meaning. But the Middle Chinese pronunciation of *huaichi* does not make it homophonous with *weichi*. I choose to read *huaichi* as a verb-object phrase that forms a parallel with the verb-object phrase *guoliang* 裹糧 ("to wrap provisions") in the corresponding position in the first line.

39. *Jian xi* 踐夕 has a textual variant, which is *can xi* 殘夕 (at the end of the evening). Commentators usually take *hun shu* 昏曙 as a unit, meaning "day and night." But it does not work with "toward evening" or "at the end of the evening." I take the third and fourth characters, *yan hun* 奄昏, as one phrase, which means "dark." A precedent is a couplet from a Han *yuefu* song: "He did not live a full lifespan, but approached the dark underworld early" 天年不遂，蚤就奄昏. This song was recorded in "The Monograph on Music" ("Yuezhi" 樂志) in *Song shu* 21.622, and was part of the Jin court music repertoire. See the sixth-century *Gujin yuelu* 古今樂錄 cited in Guo Maoqian, *Yuefu shiji* 39.574.

40. "Decay" (*gu* 蠱) and "Tread" (*lü* 履) are the names of two hexagrams in the *Classic of Changes*.

The landscape in this poem is difficult, confusing, and cold. At first the poet is sustained by his characteristic enthusiasm for exploring new scenery. The phrase *julu* 距陸 in the fourth line, here rendered as "reach the mountaintop," is taken from the "Fisherman" chapter of *Zhuangzi*.[41] The fisherman image echoes Tao Yuanming's account of Peach Blossom Spring, in which the fisherman, like the poet here, follows a mountain stream to its source. What awaits the poet is, however, not a utopian community secluded from the madding crowd, but a thick bamboo grove that obstructs his view. Nor does he seem to have located the true source of the stream, as the ravine twists and turns and disappears from sight. The tall trees make the crags seem increasingly *mi* 密, a word with multiple meanings: mysterious, hidden, quiet, and enclosed. The entry on "mountains" in *Erya* glosses *mi* as describing a hill that looks like a hall or chamber;[42] the poet has indeed entered a "secluded chamber" just as he set out to do.

Surrounded by dense vegetation and a winding ravine at the end of the day, the poet feels a sense of claustrophobia and disorientation. When light suddenly streams down through the forest, for a moment he thinks the moon is rising in the west and the sun is setting in the east. He is in fact experiencing the phenomenon known as "sunlight cast back" (*huiguang fanzhao* 回光反照)—that is, the setting sun casts its light back and illuminates, for a brief moment, the entire sky before the world sinks into darkness. This intense albeit temporary brightness penetrating the forest strips the mountain cracks and crannies of all shadows. All of a sudden, "everything veiled and covered becomes illuminated."

At the very moment when light brightens up the mountains, the poet achieves spiritual enlightenment: he reaches the resolution of withdrawing from public service and keeping to "quiet and stillness." He understands that as long as he remains constant in his resolution to eschew public life, he will always be able to "walk on the level road." This is a poetic realization of the *Yi* hexagram, "Tread": "He treads on the level road; the recluse practicing constancy has good fortune."[43] The poet's declaration recalls contemporary accounts of journeying to the underworld in which

---

41. *Zhuangzi jishi* 31.1023.
42. *Erya zhushu*, p. 116.
43. *Zhou yi zhengyi* 2.41.

the Buddhist disciple alone walks on the great level road while unenlightened sinners struggle with bramble thorns along the roadside.

Modern scholarship has accustomed us to think of these texts as belonging to neatly demarcated spheres labeled as "philosophy," "religion," and perhaps "literature," even though early medieval accounts of journeys to the underworld can hardly be considered "literature" in its modern sense. Such boundaries, however, did not exist in Xie Lingyun's time. A historicized reading of Xie's poem should be what I call a "thick reading" that places the text in its full context and crosses, where necessary, modern disciplinary boundaries. For Xie Lingyun, reader, translator, and expounder of Buddhist scriptures, the passage from the *Pratyutpanna-samādhi Sūtra* cited earlier in this book could certainly be heard in the background. In that passage, when the Buddha's kingdom is revealed to its seeker,

> It is just like what one sees in a dream: it does not matter whether it is day or night, whether it is inside or outside; one will be able to see it even if it is shrouded in darkness, and one will be able to see it even if it is blocked from one's view. Bhadrapāla, a bodhisattva should think like this: that within the realm of the various Buddha lands, at the various great mountains, including Mount Sumeru, all places of veiled darkness will open up, and there shall be no covering or closure whatsoever.

The vision of the Pure Land is accomplished through intensely focused contemplation and visualization. In Xie's poem, the ultimate enlightenment is brought about by his perseverance on a solitary path and by a physical act that triggers further textual echoes. The phrase *yi'e* 頤阿 in line 17 deserves our attention, as it is a difficult phrase that has generated multiple readings. My reading is different from that of previous scholars but supported by internal textual evidence as well as by Xie's copious references to the *Classic of Changes* in his poetry in general and in this poem in particular. Instead of trying to read *yi* or *e* as a loan character, I gloss *yi* as "nourishment," the name of a hexagram in the *Classic of Changes*. The "Judgment" of the hexagram is given as follows:

Yi is such that constancy here means good fortune. Observe his nourishing and how he seeks to fill his own mouth.[44]

頤，貞吉。觀頤，自求口實。

The Commentary on the image of the hexagram says:

Thunder going on under the Mountain: this constitutes the image of Nourishment. In the same way, the noble man is careful with his language and practices restraint in his use of food and drink.

山下有雷，頤；君子以愼言語，節飲食。

The basic meaning of the word *yi* is "jaws," and the image of "thunder going on under the mountain" is interpreted as "activity below but stillness above" (*shangzhi xiadong* 上止下動), thus figuratively evoking the upper jaw that does not move (i.e., mountain) and the lower jaw that does (i.e., thunder). Thunder also indicates the coming of rain that nourishes myriad things. As its name indicates, the hexagram is about "nourishment" (*yiyang* 頤養): a "noble man" should be mindful of the food and drink he takes in through his mouth, as well as of the words that come out of his mouth, for caution in one's speech avoids trouble, and restraint in eating and drinking cultivates good health. As such, the line in Xie Lingyun's poem is a literal realization of the image of the hexagram: standing on the mountaintop, the poet nourishes his body with the provisions he has brought with him; the physical nourishment leads to his resolution that he will withdraw from public service and give himself to spiritual nourishment.

The intricate web of textual references culminates in the last couplet: "Now that serenity and knowledge are conjoined to nourish each other, / from this point on, our mended nature emerges" 恬知既已交，繕性自此出. This couple alludes to the *Zhuangzi* chapter entitled "Mending One's Nature" ("Shan xing" 繕性). The opening passage of the chapter is directly relevant to Xie's poem:

Those who mend their nature through common learning in order to return to the Beginning, and those who multiply their desires through common thinking in order to obtain Enlightenment: they are called the blinded and benighted

44. *Zhou yi zhengyi* 4.69. Translation by Richard John Lynn in *The Classic of the Changes*, p. 27.

people. In antiquity those who practiced the Way nourished their knowledge through serenity. Knowledge was born, but they did not do anything with knowledge: this is called nourishing serenity with knowledge. When serenity and knowledge nourish each other, harmony and order emerge from one's nature.[45]

繕性於俗，學以求復其初，滑欲於俗，思以求致其明：謂之蔽蒙之民。古之治道者，以恬養知；知生而無以知爲也，謂之以知養恬。知與恬交相養，而和理出其性。

The key words in this passage, as in Xie's poem, are "nourishment" (*yang* 養) and "blinded and blighted" (*bi meng* 蔽蒙). The mutual nourishment of serenity and knowledge is echoed by the poet's "nourishment on the mountaintop," and *bi meng* is echoed by the phrase in Xie Lingyun's poem, *bi yi* 蔽翳, "veiled and covered." This poem is ultimately about vision: the poet's journey leads him to the spot where "everything veiled and covered becomes illuminated" and lucidity is restored.

Despite its ominous tone, Xie Lingyun's landscape never becomes entirely hellish. It is redeemed from ugliness and horror by an inherent luminous pattern, embodied by that of the cold ripples on top of the Green Screen Mountain. Xie Lingyun is not the eyewitness reporter on the horrors of hell, but is the poet of purgatory. Ever tormented and anguished, he nevertheless remains eternally hopeful. His world is crepuscular, as he, the active, aggressive traveler, invariably stops and becomes still and pensive in the twilight. Xie Lingyun is not a poet who brings happiness to his readers as Tao Yuanming does, but he shows them—the ones who stay back home—what he sees from unusual vantage points in the wilderness.

Modern literary scholarship on Xie Lingyun often repeats the statement that his landscape poetry is burdened with a "tail of arcane discourse" attached to the body of a poem devoted to landscape description. The "tail of arcane discourse" refers to the last part of a poem containing the *Laozi*, *Zhuangzi*, and *Classic of Changes* terminologies; it is considered stiff and unnatural, an ending that mars an otherwise pretty landscape poem. Such a perception is, however, a fundamental misunderstanding of the poetics of Xie Lingyun's landscape poetry. Wang Bi, whose third-century commentary on the *Classic of Changes* was certainly familiar to

45. *Zhuangzi jishi* 16.547–48.

Xie Lingyun, wrote the following on the chapter "Elucidation of the Image":

> The Image is what brings out concept; language is what clarifies the Image. Nothing can equal Image in giving the fullness of concept; nothing can equal language in giving the fullness of Image. Language was born of the Image, thus we seek in language in order to observe the Image. Image was born of concept, thus we seek in Image in order to observe the concept. Concept is fully given in Image; Image is overt in Language.[46]
>
> 夫象者，出意者也。言者，明象者也。盡意莫若象，盡象莫若言。言生於象，故可尋言以觀意。象生於意，故可尋象以觀意。意以象盡，象以言著。

Wang Bi is speaking of the hexagram "images" here, which consist of broken and solid lines. In Xie Lingyun's poetry, *xiang* (image) is the hexagram image fully embodied in the image of landscape; realized by language, it brings out "concept"—the meaning inherent in the world and seen with the mind's eye.

46. Stephen Owen's translation. *Readings in Chinese Literary Thought*, p. 33.

Coda

Yuan Song 袁崧 (d. 401), an older contemporary of Xie Lingyun, wrote *An Account of Yidu* 宜都記, which contains an enthusiastic description of the beauty of the Three Gorges:

I had often heard that the water in the gorges flows rapidly. Written records and oral accounts all warn people about the perils of river travel, but no one has ever said anything about the beauty of these mountains and waters. When I came to this place, I was absolutely delighted. Only then did I believe the saying that hearing about something could never compare to seeing it in person. The layered crags and striking peaks, with their strange and extraordinary forms, are beyond description. The trees and plants, growing ever so lushly, rise above the cloud vapors. No matter if one looks up or down, the more one gazes upon it, the better the view is. I lingered there for several days and nights, and quite forgot to return. I have never seen anything like it in my travel experience. I was pleased with myself for having acquired this marvelous view. If the mountains and waters had consciousness, they would certainly marvel at me, too, as the first person in a thousand years who understood and appreciated them.[1]

常聞峽中水疾，書記及口傳，悉以臨懼相戒，曾無稱有山水之美也。及余來踐躋此境，既至欣然，始信耳聞之不如親見矣。其疊崿秀峰，奇構異形，固難以辭敘。林木蕭森，離離蔚蔚，乃在霞氣之表。仰矚俯映，彌習彌佳。流連信宿，不覺忘返，目所履歷，未嘗有也。既自欣得此奇觀，山水有靈，亦當驚知己于千古矣。

1. Quoted in Li Daoyuan, *Shuijing zhu shu* 34.2845.

This passage summarizes many of the issues discussed in the foregoing chapters: the emphasis on firsthand experience, the sense of exploration and discovery, and the notion that one should cultivate an appreciation of the beauty of landscape. In the Southern Dynasties, people were not only expanding their horizon of vision to hitherto unfamiliar territories, but also seeing with new eyes. There was an emphasis on subjectivity, both in terms of the capacity for visualization and imagination and in terms of an increased level of individuality and personal engagement in seeing the world. In many ways, this age of adventure and discovery embodied both an inward turn and an outward turn.

Two major rhetorical paradigms of seeing the world prevailed during this period: one was the seeing of the past in the present; the other was heaven versus hell. The former could be found in poetic expositions on travel as well as campaign accounts in plain unrhymed prose. The campaign accounts, however, contain many personal anecdotes, which give them an autobiographical flavor; the proliferation of such accounts changed the nature of travel writing as exemplified in poetic expositions. In these campaign accounts, instead of an itinerary with a preconceived, familiar structure, what we have are unpredictable narratives of accident and adventure.

Many early medieval accounts conceptualized the otherworld, here defined in a broad sense, as either a heavenly realm or a land of terror and peril. The foreign, be it central India or a goddess dwelling in the mountains or hell itself, was represented in romanticized, fantastic, and never entirely human terms. This basic rhetorical strategy of seeing was to have far-reaching influence on the cultural consciousness of successive generations of writers.

Interlude

An interest in seeing the world anew, as manifested in Xie Lingyun's poetry, continued into the sixth century during the Liang dynasty, but by that time a shift had occurred. The grand vista favored by Xie Lingyun was reduced in scope in the Liang court poetry. Focused attention to the minutiae of everyday life and the details of the phenomenal world characterizes the poetry known as Palace Style Poetry (*gongti shi* 宮體詩), written by the then Crown Prince Xiao Gang, his younger brother Xiao Yi 蕭繹 (508–55), and their salon members in the 530s and 540s. Deeply influenced by the Buddhist discourse, the Xiao princes and their courtiers represented in their poetry a seeing of the world as it truly was: a sensuous fleeting illusion.

Xie Lingyun is often hailed as the father of Chinese landscape poetry. His landscape, teetering on the verge of the abyss as it does, nevertheless resists slipping into total darkness, inasmuch as we can discern in it a luminously traced pattern. Classical Chinese poets after Xie were almost always intent on representing the beauty of nature, and few manifested a taste for the aesthetics of ugliness. When someone did, it stood out. The early ninth-century poet Meng Jiao 孟郊 (751–814) is one such distinguished exception. A series of Meng Jiao's poems entitled "The Lament of the Gorges" ("Xia ai" 峽哀) depict nature in demonic terms. The Three Gorges are described as sharp-toothed monstrous entities, drooling and reeking, hungry for all living creatures, even hacking up the sun and moon. With coffins hanging on the cliffs and bones jutting out from them, poisonous krakens in the waves waiting to devour travelers, and gibbons and birds crying mournfully, the Three Gorges are presented as a living hell on earth. Yuan Song would have been shocked if he had read these poems, but even he would have had to acknowledge that Meng Jiao was the "first person in a thousand years" who understood and appreciated the terror and ugliness of the Three Gorges.

Poem No. 5 of "The Lament of the Gorges" ends with a reference to Xie Lingyun and his clansman Xie Tiao, who were both renowned landscape poets:

峽螭老解語	Old krakens understand how to talk,
百丈潭底聞	you can hear them at the bottom of hundred-yard pools.
毒波爲計校	In waves of poison, they makes their plots
飲血養子孫	and nurture their offspring by drinking blood.
既非皋陶吏	Since they are not Gao Yao's wardens,[1]
空食沉獄魂	they merely eat the souls sunken in prison.
潛怪何幽幽	How hidden those sunken demons are!—
魄說徒云云	in vain their dark-soul discussions are thus.
峽聽哀哭泉	Listening in the gorges, weeping and wailing springs,
峽弔鰥寡猿	lamenting in the gorges, widow and widower gibbons.
峽聲非人聲	The sounds of the gorges are no human sounds,
劍水相劈翻	sword-waters cleave and crash.
斯誰士諸謝	Here who can enlist the Xies
奏此沉苦言	to present these sinking bitter words?[2]

It is ironic that the Meng Jiao poem best known to modern Chinese readers—best known because it is widely anthologized and even included in elementary school textbooks in mainland China—is a sweet little poem praising maternal love and filial piety.[3] The characteristic Meng Jiao poem is, however, angry, bitter, and belligerent. He reminds one of Śāriputra in the *Vimalakīrti-nirdeśa Sūtra*, who says to the Śākyamuni Buddha: "When I look at this land, all I see are its hills, knolls, hollows, chasms, thorns, sands, pebbles, soil, rocks—it is littered with rubbish!" Brahma Śikhin instructs Śāriputra that he sees this land as impure only because his mind is full of impurities. What you are determines what you see: this les-

1. Gao Yao was the legendary Emperor Shun's minister in charge of punishments and imprisonment.

2. *Meng Jiao shiji jiaozhu*, p. 489.

3. The poem is entitled "A Ballad of the Wandering Son" ("Youzi yin" 游子吟).

son, so well-learned by writers in early medieval times, is perhaps one of the major reasons why description of ugly landscape occurs so rarely in Chinese literature.

In late imperial China, "ugliness," either in landscape terms or in human terms, sometimes appears as a debunking of the high poetic discourse, usually in less elevated genres such as vernacular fiction or song suites. A typical example is Chen Duo's 陳鐸 (ca. 1454–1507) song suite satirizing the brothel in north China, which begins: "In front of her door, a stream of mule carts passes by; / Dust flies— / now where can you find / Riding home amidst flowers, my horse hooves are fragrant?"[4] The line "Riding home amidst flowers, my horse hooves are fragrant" is from an anonymous poem presumably written in the tenth century.[5] As courtesans are often referred to as "flowers," this poetic line takes on a double meaning. In the fifteenth-century song, dust and mule carts are the "real world" substitute for the stylish horse-riding and sweet aroma permeating one's clothes: there is no romance or panache in this world. What deserves note is the linguistic "framing" of the poetic line within a colloquial question, with *nali you* 哪里有—"where can you find"—being a vernacular expression on a lower linguistic register that highlights and debunks the high romantic image of riding amidst flowers.[6] The world is seen in binary terms: elegant and vulgar, elite and common, spiritual and physical, beautiful and ugly.

The nineteenth-century novel *The Precious Mirror of Ranking the Flowers* (*Pinhua baojian* 品花寶鑒), which focuses on male homosexual love, creates a split between platonic love and physical passions. The former is all purity, romance, and poetry; the latter, all fleshly needs and sexual desires, deliberately depicted in explicitly obscene language. The split is stressed to such an extent that somaticity is squarely situated in the realm of ugliness by an accentuation of bodily functions and bodily dis-

4. Xie Boyang, *Quan Ming sanqu*, p. 694.

5. Chen Shangjun, *Quan Tang shi bubian*, p. 1549.

6. Such debunking of high poetic elements appears prominently in the sixteenth-century vernacular novel, *The Plum in the Golden Vase* (*Jin ping mei* 金瓶梅). Many scenes in the novel are based on conventional motifs and imageries in poetry about beautiful ladies in a luxurious boudoir setting, but the novelist always gives a "real life" twist to these motifs and imageries to highlight the lower-class background of a nouveau-riche household, and the effect is both ironic and comical. For a detailed discussion of this phenomenon, see Tian, *Qiushuitang lun* Jin ping mei.

charges whenever physical desire is being portrayed; needless to say, the division between body and mind coincides neatly with that between social classes. The hierarchy of "upper body" and "lower body" is thus superimposed on the hierarchy of the upper class and lower class. Chapter 13, for instance, mimics such a division in formal terms. The first half of the chapter is devoted to a depiction of the romantic attraction between a young member of the scholar elite and a good-looking actor, who turns out to be a descendant of a scholar-official but whose family fortune has declined; their connection is portrayed in purely spiritual terms, with their conversation centering on such graceful topics as the love of "fair weather, lovely landscape, good books, and poetry written out of 'true feelings.'" The second half of the same chapter, however, goes from heaven to hell: an ugly, vulgar, and sexually depraved middle-aged merchant pays a visit to the handsome actor, but is tricked by the actor into drinking too much and falling asleep next to the friend accompanying him. A comic scene of mistaken identity ensues in the middle of the night, complete with descriptions of urine and vomit, filth and stink. It forms a stark contrast with the upper-class youth and the actor, a pair of lovers who spend that night in the same bed but sleep "fully clothed" and have "no wicked thoughts" in their minds.[7] Such a contrast is maintained throughout the novel.

The binary of high versus low and spiritual versus carnal is often superimposed on the spatial structure of inside versus outside. In the famous eighteenth-century novel *The Dream of the Red Chamber (Honglou meng* 紅樓夢), the Grand View Garden is a paradise in which the male protagonist Jia Baoyu 賈寶玉, an upper-class teenage boy, happily lives with his sisters, female cousins, and maids. One day, however, Baoyu is struck with discontent and grows listless in his carefree existence. Who but his male servant—a member of the lower class—introduces Baoyu to vernacular fiction and drama, many of which are erotic novellas about ancient beauties. Despite the servant's enjoining of him "not to take them into the Garden," Baoyu chooses a few of the "more refined" works to bring inside, leaving those "coarse and indecent" ones in his study outside the garden. He is subsequently caught reading a romantic play, quite appropriately entitled "An Account of Encountering the Goddess," by the heroine Lin Daiyu 林黛玉, Baoyu's younger female cousin and soul mate,

7. Chen Sen, *Pinhua baojian*, pp. 103–12.

who is, at the moment, burying fallen flowers. When Baoyu asks her why she does not simply sweep the flowers into the stream, Daiyu answers that the stream is clean enough inside the garden, but once it flows out of the garden, the water will become soiled, and so will the fallen flowers.[8]

The mass of fallen blossoms has rich cultural associations: one thinks of the fallen peach flowers that lead the fisherman to the utopian community in Tao Yuanming's "Account of Peach Blossom Spring," or the flower petals thickly covering the ground of the Pure Land and celebrated by the poet Gong Zizhen 龔自珍 (1792–1841) in his "Song of Fallen Flowers in the Western Suburbs" ("Xijiao luohua ge" 西郊落花歌).[9] While the fallen flowers in the Pure Land are regularly blown away by a powerful wind that leaves the ground completely clean, the fallen flowers in this artificially constructed "paradise in the midst of the human realm"—the Grand View Garden—must be consciously and vigilantly protected from the filth of the mortal world. And yet, Daiyu's desire to preserve the purity of the fallen flowers inside the garden is already compromised by the invasion of the outside world. The invasion does not begin with the importation of romantic reading materials that awaken love and desire in the inhabitants of this Chinese version of Eden; it begins instead with the very presence of Baoyu himself, a self-proclaimed "impure creature" (*zhuowu* 濁物) whose flesh is "made of mud."

In *The Dream of the Red Chamber*, the segregation of cleanliness from filth and beauty from ugliness is consistently configured spatially. One of the masterful touches of this novel is its insistence that the segregation fails, as the boundary is being constantly transgressed and permeated. A maid servant finds a perfume bag embroidered with an erotic image inside the garden; an intimate article of clothing of Baoyu's maid, the first girl who has had sex with him, leaves the garden and falls into the hands of an actor who later marries her; last but not least, Miaoyu 妙玉 the Buddhist nun, the only girl in the garden who is even more obsessed with cleanliness than Daiyu, is drug-raped by a burglar, and, in one version of the novel, sold into the brothel, which is commonly described as the world of "wind and dust" (*fengchen* 風塵).

---

8. Cao Xueqin, *Chongjiao bajia pingpi* Honglou meng, pp. 489–91.
9. *Gong Zizhen shixuan*, pp. 85–89.

The inside/outside division that recurs throughout *The Dream of the Red Chamber* had a particular resonance in the nineteenth century, as Qing China was reluctantly coming into contact with the "outside world." In the course of over a millennium between the early medieval period and the nineteenth century, many travelers had, like Faxian, ventured into foreign lands, the best known of them being the Tang monk Xuanzang 玄奘 (602?–64) and the eunuch general Zheng He 鄭和 (1371–1433); but it was only during the nineteenth century that members of the elite and high office-holders first went as far as the Western nations and wrote extensive records of their trips. The mode of seeing the world established in early medieval China was still a basic paradigm in the writings of these writers, but the world around them had changed.

From the early twentieth century until today, both in and out of academic circles, people who are interested in China tend to give a great deal of consideration to the process of "Westernization" of China in modern times, but largely ignore the fact that Europe and America likewise underwent tremendous change very close to the time when China came under the influence of the outside, and that European countries did not all develop and "modernize" at the same pace. As Gillian Tindall says,

> The great drama of the nineteenth century, and thus of nineteenth century literature, is that of technological change and the social change it brought in its wake: industrialisation, urbanisation, the colonization of the globe. The potential landscape, or landscapes, of many people's lives expanded greatly; at the same time, in another sense, the world shrank. . . .[10]

The English were no less amazed by the fast-traveling train and the penetration of railways into their countryside than the Qing Chinese visitors. Industrialization, for better or for worse, transformed human life across the world, and its impact was felt everywhere. It was the dawn of a new age for humankind. We must now turn our attention to how the very first elite Chinese travelers in Europe and America fared in this violent storm that shook up the world, including China—a civilization that had, despite numerous changes and transformations, managed to maintain a sense of cultural continuity and confidence for many centuries.

---

10. Tindall, *Countries of the Mind*, p. 58.

PART II

Encountering the World

Prologue

In the late 1860s, the scholar Wang Tao 王韜 (1828–97), who had assisted the noted Scottish sinologist James Legge (1815–97) in translating the Chinese classics into English, wrote a poem on suffering from eye disease when he was staying in England. A couplet from the poem reads,

口耳俱窮惟恃目	Mouth and ears both blocked, I can only rely on my eyes;
喑聾已備慮兼盲	already deaf and mute, I worry about going blind as well.[1]

To this couplet Wang Tao appended an explanatory note saying: "I do not know the local tongue." It is obvious that when Wang Tao talks about the use of his eyes, he is referring to looking at the world around him rather than reading.

Wang Tao's experience was typical of many of the Chinese travelers who went to Europe and America in the nineteenth century. Looking is always the primary mode of getting to know a foreign country, particularly so for those who have little or no knowledge of its language. The renowned scholar and writer Qian Zhongshu 錢鍾書 (1910–98) once commented, with no small amount of irony, that the late Qing travelers' use of their eyes was rather limited, since they demonstrated little interest in the literature and arts of the West, focusing instead on technology,

1. The poem is entitled "Eye Disease" ("Mu ji" 目疾). It is included in Wang Tao's *Henghua guan shi lu* 蘅華館詩錄, in *Xuxiu siku quanshu*, Vol. 1558, p. 476. This is a photo-reprint of the 1880 edition of Wang Tao's *Taoyuan congshu* 弢園叢書.

political systems, museums, zoos, or circus shows.[2] Qian Zhongshu's criticism is certainly justified, but we must bear in mind that looking, not reading, was an explicitly articulated major purpose of these late Qing travelers' journeys. In a memo to the throne regarding the first delegation to be sent abroad, Prince Gong (Aisin-Gioro Isin 愛新覺羅奕訢, 1833–98), famous for his dealings with Westerners, described the intended mission as one of "observing the customs and human relationships of the said country [England]" 一覽該國風土人情.[3] In other words, the first elite travelers to the Western world were dispatched as the "eyes" of the Manchu government. They were asked to see and to record, and they did.

The travel writings of the nineteenth century discussed in the following chapters, like earlier travel writings, operate by a set of schemata of writing about seeing the world. There was, however, a jolt to the system, so to speak. Despite being late-comers in a long tradition, these travelers were pioneers in several senses. Their journeys extended far beyond the normal orbit of previous Chinese travelers; they were not only among the first to leave written accounts of Europe and North America but were also members of the scholar elite. To date, we know of only three Chinese accounts of Europe and America before the Manchu government dispatched formal delegations in the 1860s. The earliest account of Europe, written by a Christian named Fan Shouyi 樊守義 (1682–1753), was never printed or circulated beyond the Qing court and remained almost completely obscure well into the twentieth century; as a result, it never impacted the Chinese populace as the nineteenth-century accounts did.[4]

---

2. Qian Zhongshu, "Hanyi diyishou Yingyu shi 'Rensheng song' ji youguan ersanshi" 漢譯第一首英語詩《人生頌》及有關二三事, in *Qizhui ji*, p. 131–33.

3. In the same memo, dated February 22, 1866, Prince Gong further states that the emissaries should "pay attention to everything during their travels, record the geography, customs, and human relationships of the said country along the way, and bring the record back to China" 沿途留心將該國一切山川形勢風土人情隨時記載帶回中國. Wen Qing, Jia Zhen, and Bao Yun, *Chouban yiwu shimo* 39, in *Xuxiu siku quanshu*, Vol. 419, pp. 689–90.

4. Wang Zhongmin 王重民 discovered Fan Shouyi's account in the Biblioteca Nazionale Centrale of Rome in 1936 and mentioned it in his "Luoma fangshu ji" 羅馬訪書記. This essay was first published in *Tushu jikan* 圖書季刊 in December 1936 and reprinted in *Lenglu wensou*, Vol. 2, p. 799–809. Yan Zonglin 閻宗臨 (1904–1978) copied, punctuated, and annotated the manuscript, which was subsequently published in *Saodang bao* 掃蕩報 in 1941 and reprinted in *Zhongxi jiaotong shi* 中西交通史 (pp. 187–196) in 2007.

The second account, *The Record of the Seas* (*Hai lu* 海錄), was transcribed from the oral account of Xie Qinggao 謝清高 (1765–1821), a Cantonese trader. The third was composed by Lin Qian 林鍼 (pronounced by some scholars as Lin Zhen), a native of Fujian who went to America in 1847 as a translator. It seems that Lin Qian had received the best classical education of all three, although he could by no means be called learned.[5] None of these authors was a member of the scholar elite trained in traditional literary learning like the diplomats and dignitaries sent abroad by the Qing court.

The nineteenth-century Chinese travelers went to Europe and America at a time when the Western countries were experiencing the shocking effects of the Industrial Revolution and the dawning of the modern age. These accounts therefore represent an encountering and engaging with the Other in both spatial and temporal terms: traveling from China to distant lands across the ocean, and from a pre-industrial age to an industrial age. What happens, then, when a brave new world is imposed on the received schemata of writing about seeing the world? What happens when the codes and values by which one perceives the world are also interrupted by a drastically different social formation? The Buddhist "heaven/hell" picture of the universe, established in the Six Dynasties, remained a powerful paradigm of seeing the world in the nineteenth century, but the paradigm became infinitely more complicated, and eventually broke under pressure.

In Chapter 4, I examine a group of nineteenth-century elite travelers' accounts against the received tradition, focusing on the rhetoric of encountering the foreign. My study largely focuses on the first such travelers who went overseas in the 1860s, namely Bin Chun 斌椿 (b. 1804) and Zhang Deyi 張德彝 (1847–1918), because at that time they had few previously published travelogues to turn to, and their seeing of the Western world was not yet preconditioned by a quickly growing textual tradition. Bin Chun, the first emissary officially dispatched to Europe by the Qing government, mentioned that Xu Jiyu 徐繼畬 (1795–1873) gave him a copy of *A Short Account of the Maritime Circuit* (*Yinghuan zhilüe* 瀛環志

---

5. See Zhong Shuhe's discussions in *Zouxiang shijie*, pp. 39–59.

略) before his departure.[6] During his long voyage, Bin Chun primarily consulted Xu's work, supplemented by maps of various countries, to understand the geography and history of the places he passed through, because, as he was quick to point out, territories beyond Sri Lanka "could no longer be found in [other] records."[7] Xu Jiyu's work was, however, largely based on the information he collected from Western missionaries and consular officers, and Xu himself had never traveled to the Western world.

One may very well compare Bin Chun with, for instance, the female elite overseas traveler Shan Shili 單士厘 (1858–1945). As Ellen Widmer observes, though not the first woman traveler outside of China, Shan was "the first of her class to do so, and she was the first to write about her travels in an extensive way."[8] Shan's account of Japan and Russia, *Travelogue in 1903* (*Guimao lüxing ji* 癸卯旅行記), mentions that she had read many travelogues about Siberia, and "the shape of *Guimao lüxing ji* suggests a broad acquaintance with Japanese travel writing" as well.[9] Unlike Bin Chun, who was more than fifty years her senior, Shan Shili belonged to the generation that had access to many more travelogues and geographical treatises about the Western world. Although any given place in Europe she visited might not yet have had much written about it, if at all, in Chinese—and was therefore not yet burdened with layers of what Hu Ying calls "textual accumulation"—the framework of seeing the Western world had been well established by the early twentieth century, which was the time when Shan wrote her travelogues.[10] In contrast, the first elite travelers to the Western world had to engage in a more extensive negotiation between existing categories and new realities. They had to find language for things outside of their system of knowledge and conception of the world.

---

6. For a biographical treatment of Xu Jiyu, including a translation and study of the major portions of his work, see Drake, *China Charts the World.*

7. Zhong Shuhe, *Zouxiang shijie congshu*, Vol. 1, pp. 100–101. Bin Chun's travel writings, as well as Zhang Deyi's records of the first two overseas trips he undertook, are all included in this volume, which was published in 1985. All subsequent citations refer to this 1985 edition unless otherwise noted. I have also consulted several nineteenth-century printed editions, which will be noted in the case of significant textual variants.

8. Widmer, "Foreign Travel through a Woman's Eyes," p. 767.

9. Ibid., pp. 769–70.

10. Hu Ying, "'Would That I Were Marco Polo,'" p. 147.

Chapter 5 addresses the issue of genre, for in more than one case the nineteenth-century travelers not only took notes of their journeys in prose but also composed poetry along the way. During his seven months of travel, Bin Chun kept a day-to-day diary, *Record from the Raft* (*Chengcha biji* 乘槎筆記), as well as wrote over 130 poems in two collections, *Roaming in the Oceanic Kingdoms* (*Haiguo shengyou cao* 海國勝遊草) and *Sail Returning from the Horizon* (*Tianwai guifan cao* 天外歸帆草). What does poetry do in a case like this? Was the writing of poetry simply a fulfillment of the conventional behavior expected from a member of the scholar elite? Was it a reflex that was second nature for an educated Chinese traveler? I argue that poetry played a special role in articulating the experience of the Other for nineteenth-century Chinese writers. The canonical statement that poetry serves to express the poet's aims and feelings, always an ideal or a theoretical formulation rather than a description of reality, proved even more inadequate in a full representation of such a special role. The nineteenth century was a moment of profound shock to the Chinese elite: they witnessed an unprecedented world order that was, in fact, as new to the Western countries as to China. This was the beginning of the modern age, and people from both sides of the globe had to come to terms with it. In some ways, nothing helped the Chinese elite grapple with the complexities, the trauma, and the conflicted feelings induced by such a shocking experience better than writing poetry.

CHAPTER FOUR

The Rhetorical Schemata of Seeing

Historical accounts of China covering the nineteenth and early twentieth centuries have often focused on the imperialist advances made by Western nations into Chinese territory. While not denying the impact of imperialism on China, we would miss a big part of the picture if we were to ignore the other side of this story of cultural confrontation: in detailed accounts of their journeys to Western countries, elite Chinese travelers made the West at once the target of intense scrutiny, analysis, probing, and distortion and the object of desire, admiration, contempt, and loathing. Jacques Derrida discusses writing as "the possibility of the road and of difference" violently inscribed on paper and "the essential confrontation that opens communication between peoples and cultures, even when that communication is not practiced under the banner of colonial or missionary oppression" as an "anthropological war."[1] In this sense, I might describe the mid-nineteenth-century Chinese travel accounts of Europe and America as a metaphorically "colonialist" discourse that commits acts of violence to the encountered world by imposing on it their own conceptual categories and system of classification. Language and representation have their share, indeed a powerful one, in the colonial enterprise.

Historians and literary scholars have already written about Qing China as a colonialist/imperialist presence in relation to non-Chinese

---

1. Derrida, *Of Grammatology*, pp. 107–8.

peoples on both material and discursive levels.[2] Here, however, I am not speaking of the Qing state's dealings with frontier regions such as Taiwan, a place they overpowered and explicitly attempted to "civilize," but of their much more uneasy confrontation with the Western nations that were in no way disadvantageous in material resources and military might vis-à-vis the Qing empire. It is particularly interesting to observe how members of the Chinese elite represented remote lands whose very existence had been doubted by some Qing officials not long before—lands that, compared to China's close neighbors, had been little explored but now were recognized as a complex, powerful Other. The unprecedented pressure exerted by such a tension-filled power relationship on the schemata of seeing the world led to intriguing results. In the following sections, I analyze the various received rhetorical strategies of representing the foreign and how they were deployed, transformed, and complicated in nineteenth-century Chinese travel accounts.

The Utilitarian Mode

> Like the prudent bee, which arises in the summer-time at dawn from its beloved cells and, directing its course in swift flight through the unknown ways of the air, alights upon many and various blossoms of herbs, plants and fruits, and finds and carries home what pleases it most, he [King Alfred] turned afar the gaze of his mind, seeking abroad what he had not at home, that is, in his own kingdom.
>
> —Asser (d. 908), The Life of King Alfred

The first comprehensive history of China, the *Historian's Record* (*Shi ji* 史記), gives a detailed description of the peoples and places in Central Asia in the words of the famous Han explorer Zhang Qian 張騫 (fl. 130–119 BC). It begins with Dayuan 大宛, a kingdom in the Ferghana Valley:

Dayuan is to the southwest of Xiongnu and exactly to the west of the Han. It is about ten thousand leagues from the Han realm. Its people are sedentary; they

2. See, for instance, Perdue, "Comparing Empires"; Hostetler, *Qing Colonial Enterprises*"; and Teng, *Taiwan's Imagined Geography*.

EPIGRAPH: In Douglas, *English Historical Documents*, p. 294.

plow fields, grow wheat and barley, and produce grape wine. They have many fine horses that sweat blood and are the descendants of Heavenly Steeds. They have walled cities and houses. The kingdom has over seventy cities and towns. The population numbers in the several tens of thousands. Their soldiers shoot arrows and use halberds on horseback.[3]

大宛在匈奴西南，在漢正西，去漢可萬里，其俗土著，耕田，田稻麥，有蒲陶酒，多善馬，馬汗血，其先天馬子也。有城郭屋室，其屬邑大小七十餘城，眾可數十萬，其兵弓矛騎射。

Significantly, Zhang Qian's matter-of-fact description of Dayuan and the other Central Asian kingdoms is framed in a conversation between him and the Han emperor as an oral report, indeed an eyewitness account, made to the emperor. The description was designed to inform, to present basic data about a place that was of potential use to the state, and to entice and allure. Geographical location and distance in relation to the Han, local products, administrative systems, population, and the strength of the army: all this is practical knowledge of great economic and military value to the empire. Zhang Qian intended to persuade the emperor to "do something" about the foreign places: to send emissaries, open trade routes, and secure an ally against the Xiongnu people, with whom the Han had fought over the frontier regions for years. Toward that end, he offered signposts and itineraries. His persuasion worked well. The emperor was impressed, "much pleased," and dispatched four groups of emissaries to seek out the kingdoms that had "many strange things."[4]

The form of Zhang Qian's report is typical of what I call a utilitarian mode in seeing and representing a foreign place. "Elsewhere" is to be used and exploited through trade or through conquest and colonization. For this reason, natural resources and local products are a standard feature in such reports. As the English literature scholar Sealy Gilles says of the two ninth-century Old English accounts about the White Sea and the Baltic Sea made to King Alfred: "Foreign territories and alien peoples have relevance and familiar use. They can be evaluated and made to fit, and rather than threatening the text's host cultures and its values, they are used to expand and enrich it."[5]

3. Sima Qian, *Shi ji* 123.3160.

4. Ibid., 123.3166.

5. Gilles, "Territorial Interpolations in the Old English Orosius," p. 92.

This mode of narration, mixing ethnographic observations and practical geographical directions, continues throughout premodern Chinese history. Particularly illustrative of this mode is an account of the realm of Majapahit on the island of Java in a fifteenth-century travelogue authored by Gong Zhen 鞏珍, a native of Nanjing who accompanied Admiral Zheng He during one of his famous maritime expeditions in the early 1430s. This work, entitled *A Record of the Foreign Kingdoms of the Western Ocean* (*Xiyang fanguo zhi* 西洋番國志) with a preface dated 1434, is one of the three extant accounts of Zheng He's voyages. The other two accounts, respectively written by Fei Xin 費信 and the Muslim interpreter Ma Huan 馬歡, are much better known and have been translated into English.[6] Gong Zhen's work, according to his preface, is based on the interpreter's record; the interpreter presumably was none other than Ma Huan, since Gong's work bears many similarities to Ma's *Overall Survey of the Ocean's Shores* (*Yingya shenglan* 瀛涯勝覽).[7] Nevertheless, Gong Zhen's is a consciously edited and polished version, offering more details in some places than the other two accounts; it also includes three imperial edicts (of January 13, 1421, November 10, 1421, and May 25, 1430, respectively) that do not appear in the other two accounts.

Gong Zhen's account of the realm of Majapahit unfolds in a detailed, orderly fashion by first describing the location of Majapahit:

Take a small boat from Sulumayi [Surabaja] and proceed for eighty miles, and you will arrive at a port called Zhanggu [Changkir]. From here you travel on land for half a day toward the southwest and arrive at Manzheboyi [Majapahit], where

---

6. See Ma Huan, *The Overall Survey of the Ocean's Shores* (*Yingya shenglan jiaozhu* 瀛涯勝覽校注); Fei Xin, *Description of the Starry Raft* (*Xingcha shenglan jiaozhu* 星槎勝覽校注). Both editions were edited and annotated by the Chinese scholar Feng Chengjun 馮承鈞. W.W. Rockhill's "Notes on the Relations and Trade of China" includes translations of Fei Xin's *Description of the Starry Raft* (preface 1436) and Ma Huan's *The Overall Survey of the Ocean's Shores* (1451). A new translation of Ma Huan's account, with introduction, notes, and appendices, was made by J.V.G. Mills and published as *Ying-yai sheng-lan: The Overall Survey of the Ocean's Shores* in 1970. Mills's translation of Fei Xin's account was published under the title *Hsing-ch'a-sheng-lan: The Overall Survey of the Star Raft*. Both accounts were partially translated in Paul Wheatley's *The Golden Khersonese*, pp. 88–103.

7. Gong Zhen, *Xiyang fanguo zhi*, p. 13. In his introduction to this edition, the modern scholar Xiang Da speculates that the interpreter was Ma Huan. *Xiyang fanguo zhi*, p. 8.

the king lives. There are two or three hundred aboriginal households, with seven or eight chieftains assisting the king.[8]

從蘇魯馬益小舡行八十裏，到埠頭，名漳沽。登岸向西南行半日，到滿者伯夷，則王居處也。其處有番人二三百家，頭目七八人輔王。

It then recounts the climate and local products:

The weather is hot like summertime throughout the year. There are two harvests of rice annually, and the grains are fine and white. There grow sesame and mung beans, but no barley and wheat. The local products include sapanwood, Rudraksha, white sandalwood, nutmeg, long pepper, cantharides, fine iron, Green Turtle shell, Hawksbill Sea Turtle shell; they also have cockatoo as big as hens, red and green parakeet, five-colored lory, and myna bird, which can all imitate human speech.

天氣長熱如夏，田稻一年二熟，米粒細白。芝麻菉豆皆有，惟無大小麥。土產蘇木，金剛子，白檀香，肉豆蔻，華茇，班猫，鑌鐵，龜筒，玳瑁，鸚鵡大如母鷄，及紅綠鶯哥，五色鶯哥，鷯哥，皆能效人言語。

After giving a lengthy list of flora and fauna, the author goes on to comment on local eating and drinking customs:

Their people have no beds or chairs, no spoons or chopsticks. They use plates for food and pour ghee on it; they eat with their hands. Fish, shrimp, snakes, earthworms, and maggots are all eaten after being roasted over fire. When they get together for a drinking party, they all sit on the ground and drink nipa palm wine and coconut wine contained in earthen jars.

國人坐臥無床凳，飲食無匙箸。飯用盤盛，沃以酥汁，手撮而食。凡魚蝦蛇蚓蛆蟲等物，以火燎過即啖之。或有聚飲者，列坐于地，酒乃茭蕈椰子所釀，盛于瓦罌。

This is followed by an explanation of the three different classes of people at Majapahit: the Muslims, the Chinese immigrants from Canton and Fujian, and the autochthones. A fantastic account of the origin of the autochthones, clearly obtained from the local lore, is given. Next the author describes the Majapahit calendar (the tenth month was considered the

8. For the passages cited here, see Gong Zhen, *Xiyang fanguo zhi*, pp. 7–10.

beginning of spring) and a festive celebration of spring ("Bamboo Spear Assembly"), where men fought with sharpened bamboo poles. Then the author relates marriage customs, funeral customs, the monetary system, writing and language, weight measures, and forms of entertainment. The section closes with a description of the kinds of merchandise that would appeal to the Majapahit people:

These people love, most of all, such goods as blue and white porcelain, musk, embroidery, ramie cloth, and glass beads. They often collect local products and send them to China as tributary gifts.

國人最喜青花磁器並麝香、花繡、紵絲、硝子珠等貨。國人常采方物遣使進貢中國。

Language specifying the kingdom's relation with China as a tributary state is ubiquitous in all three fifteenth-century travelogues. In Gong Zhen's work, seventeen out of the twenty accounts of various kingdoms of the "Western Ocean" contain this statement. The confirmation of the subordinate status of a foreign territory at the end of an account aims to bring an alien culture and people effectively into the system of values established by the "Central Kingdom." For the fifteenth-century explorers, those territories exist only in relation to the country of origin, and are meaningful only in terms of their resources and economic usefulness.

Such a discourse of superiority persisted well into the nineteenth century, but gradually became limited to China's close neighbors. When passing through Saigon in 1890, the poet and diplomat Huang Zunxian reminisced about Emperor Qianlong's (r. 1735–96) imperialistic ventures in Vietnam and China's subsequent concession of rights to France in 1885, after the Sino-French War, with a hardly concealed nostalgia about the "good old days":

神功遠拓東西極	The divine accomplishments reached the eastern and western limits;
聖武張皇六十年	our sagely martial emperor's splendid rule lasted sixty years.
不信王師倒戈退	Who would believe the imperial army should turn back and retreat,

翻將化外棄南天	giving up this land beyond civilization in the far south![9]

Although he regretted its loss, Huang Zunxian nevertheless referred to Vietnam as a "land beyond civilization." In the nineteenth century, a hierarchy was established between these neighboring states and the European powers. This can be seen more clearly in the first of Huang's "Twelve Miscellaneous Poems on Singapore" ("Xinjiapo zashi shiershou" 新嘉坡雜詩十二首):[10]

天到珠崖盡	The sky reaches its end at the Pearl Cliff,
波濤勢欲奔	where the breakers are galloping along.
地猶中國海	The place is still within the China Sea,
人喚九邊門	but people call it the Gate to the Nine Frontiers.
南北天難限	Even heaven cannot divide the south and north,
東西帝並尊	yet the emperors of the East and West are equally revered.
萬山排戟險	Ten thousand mountains range like perilous halberds—
嗟爾故雄藩	alas, you used to be a mighty vassal state.

Typical of Huang Zunxian's heavy use of allusions, the middle section of the poem contains several textual references. "Nine Frontiers" was a term coined in the Ming to refer to the nine frontier regions. In 1885, Singapore and the nearby islands under the control of England were considered the gateway for the British Empire and referred to as the "Gate of the Sea" (Haimen 海門). In the third century, Cao Pi, Emperor Wen of the Wei, was preparing for an attack on the Kingdom of Wu; upon seeing the raging Yangzi River, he remarked that the mighty river was designed by heaven to be a dividing line between the south and north.[11] During the Warring States period, the King of Qin in the West and the King of Qi in the East were revered as "the Western Emperor" and the "Eastern Emperor"—here a reference to the sovereigns of China and England.[12]

The poem presents a complex picture of geography and sovereignty. While the sky (*tian* 天)—or the protection of heaven (*tian*) that is the

9. The poem is one of the quatrains entitled "Thoughts upon Passing through Saigon, Vietnam" ("Guo Annan Xigong yougan" 過安南西貢有感). The sagely martial emperor refers to Emperor Qianlong. Huang Zunxian, *Renjinglu shicao*, p. 162.

10. Ibid., pp. 210–11.

11. Chen Shou, *Sanguo zhi* 47.1131.

12. Sima Qian et al., *Shi ji* 5.212.

imperial court—stops at the Pearl Cliff in the far south, the ocean extends far beyond the present boundary of the Qing empire, which makes the poet think of a time when the territory of the empire was likewise much wider. Now, within the watery expanse of what is still known as the "China Sea," the island of Singapore has nevertheless become the gateway for the British. This signifies a discrepancy between "Name" and "Reality," a divide warned against by Confucius, which to the poet is as painful as it is inappropriate. The third couplet is a continued reflection on the conflict between nature and culture: nature has no effective boundary to mark territorial waters, but the human realm is divided into the East and the West, presided over by two "equally revered" monarchs.

The declaration that displaces China and Britain into the model of "Warring States" would not have been imaginable in an earlier, more sinocentric age; nevertheless, there is no doubt in Huang Zunxian's mind to which nation Singapore should belong, even in such a reconfigured world map. He does not disguise his disappointment that it is no longer a "vassal state" of the Chinese empire. Thirty-four years earlier, in 1867, when passing through Singapore on his way to England and witnessing the large Chinese population flourishing there, Wang Tao had entertained a similar sentiment:

> Suppose our Dynasty could send one single emissary to its land to propagate the imperial grace, relying on our great prestige and power, so that they may willingly submit and happily subject themselves to our use—wouldn't we be establishing a "screen and hedge territory" overseas?[13]
>
> 使我朝能以一介之使式臨其地，宣揚恩惠，憑藉聲靈，俾其心悅誠服，歸而向我，樂爲我用，豈非于海外樹一屏藩哉?

To rule over a people who "happily subject themselves to our use" is every imperialist's dream, and "use" (*yong*) is the key word in this imperialistic fantasy.

13. Wang Tao, *Manyou suilu*, p. 67. Wang Tao in fact believed that all "the various small states in the Southeast Asia" were once upon a time the vassal states of China, and lamented, when visiting Penang, how they were gradually taken by European powers from the mid-Ming on, so that the "screen and hedge territories overseas" were all gone by his time. Ibid., p. 70.

Love of the Strange

In his account of the "Western Regions" in the *History of the Han Dynasty* (*Han shu* 漢書), the historian Ban Gu 班固 (32–92) states:

The kingdoms from Qiemo [Cherchen] onward all plant the five grains. Their topography, soldiery, flora, and fauna are about the same as in the land of the Han. I will therefore only record what is different from us.[14]

自且末以往皆種五穀，土地草木畜產作兵略與漢同，有異乃記云。

To record only the differences from one's native country may be a necessary writing strategy when one gives an account of dozens of kingdoms, but such a strategy often becomes a way of making another culture seem more alien. In other words, when encountering the foreign, people are fascinated by what is *yi* 異, a word that means both "different" and "strange." Ultimately it is difference that constitutes strangeness, and anything that seems familiar goes unmentioned because it is not deemed noteworthy. Excessive "love of strangeness" (*hao qi* 好奇) must by necessity keep the sense of unfamiliarity alive and thereby impedes a sympathetic understanding of the foreign.

In the early eras of the Qing, the famous poet and playwright You Tong 尤侗 (1618–1704) was responsible for putting together the "Account of Foreign Countries" ("Waiguo zhuan" 外國傳) for the *History of the Ming Dynasty* (*Ming shi* 明史). Much of the account is based on the travelogues written by Fei Xin and Ma Huan. Upon completing the account in 1681, You Tong composed 110 "Bamboo Branch Songs on Foreign Countries" ("Waiguo zhuzhici" 外國竹枝詞). A "bamboo branch song" is a quatrain in seven-syllable lines that had supposedly originated among the southern aboriginal people and was appropriated by literati poets in the ninth century; it later became a poetic subgenre that was employed to describe local customs and particularities of a region or even scenic sites such as the West Lake in Hangzhou. You Tong's "Bamboo Branch Songs" are unique in that they describe foreign places that the poet had only visited in his reading, and so he could not claim firsthand local knowledge as previous writers of bamboo branch songs had done before him. A comparison of the travelogues by the fifteenth-century writers,

14. Ban Gu, *Han shu* 96.3879.

You Tong's reworking of these sources in the dynastic history, and his poetic retelling of the same material, demonstrates the distorting power of the "love of the strange."

One telling example is the rendering of Majapahit funeral customs. According to Gong Zhen,

If a parent is about to die, the children ask the parent whether after death he or she would like the body to be devoured by dogs or cremated or cast away in water. The children will then do as the parent wishes. If the parent wishes the body to be devoured by dogs, then the children will carry the body to the seashore or to the wilderness. A dozen dogs will come to devour the body. It is considered best if the entire body is consumed; if not, then the sons and daughters will cry sadly and cast what remains of the body in the water. If a wealthy man or a noble who is about to die has a beloved concubine, she will make a vow, saying: "I will follow you onto death." At the funeral, a pyre is prepared to burn the body. When the flames are blazing, two or three beloved concubines, with flowers on their heads and wearing kerchiefs of five-colored patterns, climb onto the pyre, wail loudly, and then throw themselves into the fire to be burned with the body of their lord. Such is their funeral rite.[15]

父母將死，則問父[死]後欲犬食，欲火化，或欲弃水中，隨父母所願欲而行之。若欲犬食，則舁尸至海濱或野外，有犬十數來食其肉，盡爲好，食不盡，子女皆悲號哭泣，弃其餘水中而歸。又富翁及貴人將死，有所愛婢妾，輒與誓曰：死則同往。及死出殯，積柴薪焚主翁尸，及火焰盛，所愛妾二三人皆戴草花披五色花手巾，登跳號哭，遂投火中，同主尸燒化，以爲送葬之禮。

This elaborate description is simplified into a terse passage in the *History of the Ming Dynasty*:

After a parent dies, the children carry the body to the wilderness and feed it to dogs. If the body is not completely consumed, the children are greatly saddened and burn the remains. Wives and concubines are in most cases burned to death to accompany their deceased husband.[16]

父母死，舁至野，縱犬食之；不盡，則大戚，燔其餘。妻妾多燔以殉。

15. Gong Zhen, *Xiyang fanguo zhi*, p. 9. Ma Huan's description (*Yingya*, pp. 13–14) is more verbose but relates more or less the same information..

16. *Ming shi* 324.8405. Fei Xin's description (*Xingcha*, p. 14) leaves out the part about funeral rites for parents.

The changes are revealing. The fifteenth-century sailors were clearly struck by the peculiarities of the Majapahit funeral arrangements, and they laid out in detail what they considered *yi*—different and strange. The dynastic history makes the custom sound even more alien to a Han Chinese reader by omitting the mention of the dying parent's wish, so that the feeding of a parent's remains to dogs seems to be a heartless decision made by the barbaric children.

The same is true of the depiction of self-immolation. In contrast with Gong Zhen's description in seventy-one characters, the *History of the Ming Dynasty* retelling is in six characters. Narrative economy is considered a virtue in classical prose; it is nevertheless significant to notice what has been left out in the dynastic history. According to the fifteenth-century travelogues, self-immolation was practiced among the noble and wealthy by "beloved concubine(s)" who voluntarily made a vow to the dying. By erasing these specifics, the *History of the Ming Dynasty* version creates an impression that the custom was pervasive and compulsory in the Majapahit society, accentuating the brutality of a "primitive" people. Difference from "us" is not only inscribed as strangeness but also as barbarity, and the Han Chinese culture is implicitly upheld as what is humane and civilized while the Other is dehumanized.

Switching from the role of historian to that of poet, You Tong selects the most bizarre and exotic elements from a plethora of details to feature in his poetry. One of his two poems on Zhan City 占城 (Champa) reads:

金花冠上戴三山	The king has on his head a golden-flower "three-hill" crown,
玳瑁装鞋束寶鐶	and he wears shoes of tortoise-shell and a bejeweled belt.
任爾通身都是膽	You may be full of guts, from head to toe, but what would you do
那堪黑夜遇尸蠻	when you run into the "corpse-head barbarian" on a dark night?[17]

You Tong clearly made use of Fei Xin's travelogue, which is the only account that mentions the "tortoise-shell shoes" of the Champa king; the

17. Wang Shenzhi and Wang Zijin, *Qingdai haiwai*, p. 9.

other sources all describe the king as walking around barefooted.[18] The last couplet of the poem refers to two local legends. The first one tells of how each year, the Champa king would demand a jar of gallbladders that were cut out from living people and marinate them in wine. He then drank the wine and/or bathed himself in it, believing that it could make a person "gutsy."[19] The second legend is about a female ghoul known as the "corpse-head barbarian" (*shitou man* 屍頭蠻). Her only marked difference from ordinary human females was her empty eye sockets. At night her head would fly away from her body and eat human feces. Those whose feces were eaten would die.[20]

In You Tong's poem, the gaudy outfit of the Champa king is offset by dark practices; the color contrast of gold on black brings out the effect intended by the poet. The king might very well dress up, in Zhou Daguan and Fei Xin's words, like a vajrabodhisattva, Buddha's warrior attendant, or, in the less flattering comparison drawn by Ma Huan and Gong Zhen, like an actor in a Chinese opera; but underneath the glitter beats the terrifying "heart of darkness." By connecting two folk tales that are unrelated in their original sources, You Tong creates a picture of Champa that is both exotic and frightening.

As mentioned above, You Tong had never traveled to the places he wrote about. His use of eyesight was limited to his reading the pages of books that were available to him. But the impulse to see what is "different and strange" is as strong in an armchair traveler as in eyewitness accounts of faraway lands. Zhang Zuyi 張祖翼 (1849–1917), a renowned calligra-

---

18. Fei Xin, *Xingcha*, pp. 1–2. For the other sources, see Zhou Daguan's 周達觀 (fl. 1295–1346) *Zhenla fengtu ji* 真臘風土記, p. 76; Ma Huan, *Yingya*, p. 2; Gong Zhen, *Xiyang fanguo zhi*, p. 2.

19. This is recorded in the Yuan dynasty sources from the fourteenth century: Zhou Daguan's *Zhenla fengtu ji*, p. 177; Wang Dayuan's 汪大淵 (1311–50) *Daoyi zhilüe* 島夷志略, p. 55. Also see Fei Xin, *Xingcha*, p. 3; Ma Huan, *Yingya*, p. 5; Gong Zhen, *Xiyang fanguo zhi*, p. 3. The *Ming shi* also records the tale. It is interesting to notice that Zhou Daguan's *Zhenla fengtu ji* states that they would not take the gallbladder of any Chinese person, because one year they did so and all the gallbladders in the jar turned rotten. The *Ming shi* (324.8393), however, claims that "whenever they place the gallbladder in a container, the gallbladder of the Chinese person always comes up on top, so they especially prize the Chinese gallbladder." I have not been able to locate the source for this claim.

20. This tale is recorded in all of the sources cited in the previous note except for Zhou Daguan's *Zhenla fengtu ji*.

pher and a cultural conservative, wrote a set of poems entitled "Bamboo Branch Songs on London" ("Lundun zhuzhici" 倫敦竹枝詞).[21] In these poems, Zhang Zuyi focuses his attention on anything that strikes him as strange. Sometimes a phenomenon may very well be a singular instance and does not represent the norm of the local society; to include the report of such a phenomenon in a collection that is ostensibly designed to convey the overall picture of a foreign country to a home audience endows the phenomenon with a more general quality than is justified. In a few cases, even Zhang Zuyi's own rhetoric betrays the bias and limitation of his seeing. He says, for instance, in the note appended to poem No. 92:

Many European women have moustaches, which look just like a man's. But no more than one or two out of ten thousand women have it.[22]

泰西婦女多有生鬚者，其鬚與男子無異，然萬中不過一二也。

"Many" and "no more than one or two out of ten thousand" cannot be easily reconciled. It leads one to suspect that Zhang had only seen "one or two" women with facial hair, but the impression so overwhelmed him that he felt compelled to record it. After all, what could better mark an *essential* foreignness than what is considered an abnormal physical trait?

Poem No. 39 is about what must have seemed a shocking custom to the nineteenth-century Chinese: paintings of nudes in both family spaces and public places. A note appended to the poem states, "Painted beauties, no matter whether they are in colors or in ink, are all stark naked only with their private parts covered. Such paintings are displayed in halls and stud-

21. These poems are reprinted in Wang Shenzhi and Wang Zijin, *Qingdai haiwai*, pp. 207–29. They were first printed under the pseudonym Juzhong menwai han 局中门外汉 in the *Guanzide zhai congshu bieji* 觀自得齋叢書别集 series compiled by Xu Shikai 徐士恺 (1844–1903). In a note appended to one of the poems (No. 4), the poet says, "This year is the fiftieth anniversary of Queen Victoria's reign." Queen Victoria's Golden Jubilee was celebrated on June 20–21, 1887. However, the author's colophon is dated to the *jiashen* year of the Guangxu era (the year 1884). This suggests that the poet had begun to write the poems as early as 1884 but did not finish the set until 1887, and that the poems were likely not composed all at one time. See Zhang Zuyi, "Lundun zhuzhici," 1b and 24a, in Xu Shikai, *Guanzide zhai congshu bieji* Vol. 24. Wang Shenzhi and Wang Zijin, *Qingdai haiwai*, pp. 207, 228.

22. Zhang Zuyi, "Lundun zhuzhici," 22a, in Xu Shikai, *Guanzide zhai* 24. Wang Shenzhi and Wang Zijin, *Qingdai haiwai*, p. 227.

ies and no one seems to be bothered by them."[23] Zhang's statement gives the impression that all portraits of women are nudes, which is of course far from the truth. Zhang might be exaggerating to create a sensational effect, or he might simply be so overwhelmed by what he saw that he could not and did not see anything else. He also seems to have failed to notice male nudes, an equally prominent subject of European paintings and statues. The poem reads:

家家都愛挂春宮	Every family loves to hang "Spring Palace" paintings on the wall;
道是春宮卻不同	you might say they are "Spring Palace," but then they are not quite the same:
只有横陳嬌小樣	there is only the charming posture of lying stretched across a bed,
絶無淫褻醜形容	but there is no repulsive demeanor of lust or lewdness.

China does not have a tradition of painting nudes; visual representation of nakedness is more often than not associated with erotic pictures called *chungong* 春宮 (literally "Spring Palace"). Seeing paintings of nude figures on public display was such a profoundly alien experience that Zhang Zuyi lacked the language for it. He had to resort to the existing native cultural vocabulary to describe it for his home audience, but what he saw far exceeded the term he brought to it, and he could only say that they were "not the same" (*butong* 不同).

It was relatively easy to accurately describe a train and a camera, no matter how novel these technological inventions seemed to be at the time of their first appearance; an oil painting of a nude figure was something else. It had an entirely different cultural and aesthetic tradition behind it. Zhang's struggle to find adequate language to describe such paintings provides a perfect example of the inadequacy of existing categories and concepts in one's native culture to articulating the fundamental "difference" (*butong*) of an alien culture. Zhang made no attempt, however, to further understand the phenomenon except to marvel at its difference. The love of strangeness must by necessity preserve the strangeness in or-

23. Zhang Zuyi, "Lundun zhuzhici," 10a, in Xu Shikai, *Guanzide zhai* 24. Wang Shenzhi and Wang Zijin, *Qingdai haiwai*, p. 216.

der to keep its mystique alive. As the following section demonstrates, a closely related aspect of the love of strangeness in encountering the foreign is to see everything in contrasting colors of heaven and hell.

Heaven and Hell

With the exception of fictional narratives such as *Journey to the West*, religious travel writings like Faxian's *Record of the Buddhist Kingdoms* are conspicuously absent in late imperial Chinese travelogues. Nevertheless, the heaven-or-hell paradigm of seeing and inscribing the world, frequently couched in Buddhist vocabulary, persisted well into the nineteenth century. In discussing the poet Huang Zunxian's "exotic allusions" drawn from Buddhist texts or from monographs on foreign lands in dynastic histories, J. D. Schmidt speculates that "exotic allusions must have caused Huang Zunxian special difficulties," because "although in some cases he may have intended the allusions to make his foreign descriptions seem more accessible to his audience, they may have had the opposite effect."[24] The sources of many of those "exotic allusions," however, may not have seemed so exotic or unusual to a Chinese reader as Schmidt suggests, for Buddhist terms used by Huang Zunxian had by this time long lost their foreign flavor and become part and parcel of the Chinese cultural lore. They were, and still are, easily accessible in Chinese popular culture. The effect of using Buddhist terms in depicting the foreign is to make it acceptably alien. In other words, the vocabulary evoking the Pure Land or Avîci Hell provides familiar and comforting images of unfamiliarity and strangeness, so that the alien nature of a foreign culture may be effectively conveyed and comprehended without causing shocks to the foundation of one's native conception of the universe.

As in earlier literatures, heaven and hell are typically strictly segregated so that a foreign place is either paradisial or hellish. What this means is that a foreign place is kept just slightly out of human reach. Bakhtin says of the epic that "the represented world of the heroes stands on an utterly different and inaccessible time-and-value plane, separated by epic distance." He adds that to "portray an event on the same time-and-value plane as oneself and one's contemporaries . . . is to undertake a radical

24. Schmidt, *Within the Human Realm*, pp. 97–98.

revolution, and to step out of the world of epic into the world of the novel."[25] The heaven-or-hell paradigm of seeing a foreign land is in many ways not unlike stepping into an epic world, but this paradigm took on some new characteristics in the nineteenth-century writings about encountering the foreign. Segregation occurred in close relation to considerations of race, class, and gender on several levels: the establishment of a hierarchy among cultures based on their technological development and material well-being, the problematized representation of gender and sexuality, and the mapping of the modern city.

Ordering the World

In the nineteenth century, the first leg of the sea route from China to Europe stopped at Saigon, Singapore, Ceylon, Aden, and Suez. This was the route followed by the first Qing delegation sent to Europe consisting of the senior Manchu official Bin Chun and, among others, Zhang Deyi, who was a nineteen-year-old student of Tongwen guan 同文館 (School of Language) established by the Manchu government in 1862. Later Zhang made seven more extended trips to Europe, North America, and Japan, as interpreter, attaché, and finally ambassador, respectively. He has left seven extensive volumes of diaries, which provide detailed descriptions of things seen, events experienced, and people encountered during these trips.[26]

The diary for his first trip is entitled *An Account of the Strange across the Ocean* (*Hanghai shuqi* 航海述奇); the subsequent diaries are named *The Second Account* (*Zai shuqi* 再述奇), *The Third Account* (*San shuqi* 三述奇), and so forth.[27] Zhang Deyi was no poet, nor was he deeply educated in traditional literary learning, but he possessed common sense, keen powers of observation, and an ability to spin out lucid prose. He was a member of the team led by Bin Chun to "see and record" eleven Euro-

25. Bakhtin, *The Dialogic Imagination*, p. 14.

26. Zhang Deyi kept eight diaries, one for each trip; however, the seventh diary about his trip to Japan in 1901 is no longer extant.

27. Only the first, fourth, and eighth diaries were printed during Zhang Deyi's lifetime. Zhang's definitive manuscript versions of the diaries, revised and copied out in his own hand in the last years of his life, were photo-printed as *Gaoben Hanghai shuqi huibian* 稿本航海述奇匯編 in ten volumes by Beijing Tushuguan chubanshe in 1997.

pean countries in 1866; a year later, he was chosen to join the first formal diplomatic mission, headed by Pu Anchen 蒲安臣 (Anson Burlingame, 1820–70) and known as "the Burlingame Mission," to the United States, and then again to participate in the first diplomatic mission to the principal European nations in 1868. The European diplomatic mission was headed by a Manchu official, Zhi Gang 志剛, who also kept a diary; it was published later as *An Account of My First Mission to Europe* (*Chu shi Taixi ji* 初使泰西記).[28]

Upon closer examination, we can see an interesting tendency emerging in these writings. The travelers established a strict hierarchy among the foreign nations. While the European nations were marveled at and glorified, South Asian and African people were disparaged and demonized. This tendency is reminiscent of a passage in Gong Zhen's travelogue about the Majapahit kingdom:

> There are three kinds of people in the kingdom. The first kind is Muslims from the Western land, who live here as merchants; their daily food and drink are quite clean. The second kind is Chinese people from Canton or from Zhangzhou and Quanzhou of Fujian who are seeking refuge here; their food is also clean, and they have all been converted to Islam. The third kind is that of the autochthones. They are dark-skinned and ugly, have faces resembling monkeys, walk around with bare feet, and worship demons. Theirs is what the Buddhist scriptures refer to as the "demon kingdom." Their food and drink are filthy, as they eat snakes, ants, insects and earthworms without hesitation. The dogs kept in their households eat food from the same container as their masters, and sleep with their masters in the same bed, and nobody is bothered by it.[29]

> 其國人有三等。一等西番回回人，因作商賈流落于此，日用飲酒清潔；一等唐人，皆中國廣東及福建漳、泉州下海者，逃居于此，日用食物亦潔淨，皆投禮回回教門。一等土人，形貌醜黑，猱頭赤脚，崇信鬼教，佛書所謂鬼國即此地也。其人飲食穢惡，蛇蟻蟲蚓，食啖無忌。家畜之犬與人共食，夜則同寢，恬不爲怪。

Frederick Lugard (1858–1945), a British explorer and colonial administrator who served as Governor of Hong Kong (1907–12) and Governor-

28. Zhi Gang's diary is included in Vol. 1 of *Zouxiang shijie congshu*, edited by Zhong Shuhe and published in 1985. Zhang Deyi's *Zai shuqi*, also included therein, is entitled *Ou Mei huanyou ji* 歐美環遊記 in this edition.

29. Gong Zhen, *Xiyang fanguo zhi*, p. 8. Ma Huan, *Yingya*, pp. 11–12.

General of Nigeria (1914–19), once divided the natives of British Tropical Africa into three classes: primitive tribes, advanced communities, and Europeanized Africans. Lugard advocated indirect colonial rule in Africa by employing Africans, and the division of the natives into three classes was meant to be of practical use to colonial administration in a number of ways.[30] The classification was, however, first of all meant as a way of knowing the natives and understanding the situation of the country he lived in; in this aspect, the Ming travelers' impulse to classify the Javanese people was not much different from Lord Lugard's.

Citing the Buddhist scriptures as an authority, the Ming travelers managed to evoke a sense of familiar foreignness and find a place for the aborigines in an established system of classification. The nineteenth-century travelers Bin Chun and Zhang Deyi looked at the natives of Vietnam and Singapore and saw the same "demon kingdom." Zhang Deyi thus describes the people he saw at Saigon: "The people are born short and small, with haggard complexion and dim eyes. They love to chew betel nut. Men and women, old and young, open their mouths, which are red and big, frequently; their voices are coarse like a frog's."[31] One of Bin Chun's "Miscellaneous Poems on Vietnam" describes Malay coach drivers in this way:

御者猙獰形可怖	The driver is hideous and ferocious, his form terrifying:
文身斷髮鬢蓬鬆	his body is tattooed, his hair cut short and scruffy.[32]

"Tattooed body and cut hair" is an old phrase used as early as in the *Zuozhuan* and *Shi ji* to describe the "barbarian" people in the south. It is more evocative than mimetic.

In Singapore, Bin Chun makes the following observation about the local fauna as well as the natives:

The smaller monkeys are no more than a foot tall. The island is particularly rich in precious birds of all colors. People from our boat bought as many as hundreds of them; they are extremely pleasing to the eye. *It is just that the uncivilized,*

30. See his book *The Dual Mandate in British Tropical Africa*, published in London in 1922.

31. Zhang Deyi, *Hanghai shuqi*, p. 461.

32. Bin Chun, *Haiguo shengyou cao*, p. 159.

primitive natives of the island, with their dark skin and red teeth, are quite a frightful sight. If Liu Zihou had come here, he would certainly have said: "Ah, how strange it is that the numinous energy of the maker of things should be invested in birds rather than humans!"[33]

猿猴小者不盈尺。珍禽尤夥，五色具備，舟人購畜者以數百計，大可悅目。惟土人則黑肉紅牙，獉獉狉狉，殊堪駭人。使柳子厚至此，必曰：異哉，造物靈秀之氣，不鍾於人而鍾於鳥！

Liu Zihou was the style name of Liu Zongyuan 柳宗元 (773–819), the Tang writer who penned a series of eight famous landscape essays when he was in exile in Yongzhou 永州 (in modern Hu'nan). One of the essays, entitled "An Account of the Little Stone Wall Hill" ("Xiaoshichengshan ji" 小石城山記), contains the following remarks:

I have doubted the existence of the maker of things for a long time. Now when I come here and see this hill, I even more firmly believe there is indeed one. Yet I wonder why he does not fashion this hill in the Middle Region but locate it in the barbarian land instead, so that for hundreds of years it could not showcase its talent. This truly is useless labor that is unworthy of a god. If so, then might there not be a maker of things? Someone said, "This hill is to comfort worthy men who are humiliated and trapped in this place." Someone else said, "The numinous energy of the natural transformation does not fashion great men but is invested in making things like this. For this reason the southern Chu region has very few talented men but very many extraordinary rocks." These two opinions—I am not yet ready to believe either of them.[34]

吾疑造物者之有無久矣，及是愈以爲誠有。又怪其不爲之中州而列是夷狄，更千百年不得一售其伎，是故勞而無用，神者倘不宜如是，則其果無乎。或曰：以慰夫賢而辱於此者。或曰：其氣之靈，不爲偉人而獨爲是物，故楚之南少人而多石。是二者，予未信之。

Bin Chun attributed the second opinion cited in Liu's essay to Liu himself, but this hardly matters; what matters is that Singapore now replaced Yongzhou as the "barbarian" (*yidi* 夷狄) space. Just like in the earlier travel accounts of Java, the only worthy humans in these godforsaken

33. Bin Chun, *Chengcha biji*, p. 99. The italicized part appears in the version included in the series *Xiao Fanghu zhai yudi congchao* 小方壺齋輿地叢鈔 compiled by Wang Xiqi 王錫祺 (1855–1913) and printed in 1891, Series I, Vol. 11, 42b. It is, however, deleted from the 1981 and 1985 editions.

34. *Liu Zongyuan ji*, p. 773.

places were immigrants and settlers from outside; the natives were a "frightful" sight, lower on the hierarchy than "precious birds." In the 1981 and 1985 editions of Bin Chun's diary, the editor Zhong Shuhe deleted this passage, no doubt finding it offensive or embarrassing.[35] Ironically, the modern press that published these editions in the 1980s was located in none other than the "southern Chu region" that was regarded "barbarian" by the Tang writer Liu Zongyuan.

As the travelers journeyed on, comparison and gradation continued. In a diary entry for April 10, 1866 (by Bin Chun's record, the twenty-fifth day of the second month on the fifth year of the Tongzhi era), Bin Chun wrote:

> Boat passengers have increased to more than 170 people. There is no extra room left. They are from twenty-seven nations and speak seventeen different languages. Their appearances and clothes are all bizarre and outlandish, each in one's own way. There are tall ones, huge and massive ones who weigh 200 catties, ones with sideburns and beards and disheveled hair. They are all dressed in colorful cloth like in a Chinese martial opera or in the Lamaist ritual of "Beating the Devil." Only those from various major European nations are mostly nice-looking and elegant; their women are also quite pretty. They wear dresses of light gossamer and fine silk, which are particularly beautiful.[36]

> 船客增至一百七十有奇，無餘地矣。計二十七國人，言語不同者十七國，而形狀服飾之詭異，亦人人殊。有頎而長者，有碩大無朋，稱重二百斤者；有鬚鬢交而髮蓬蓬者。衣裙多用各色花布，似菊部之扮演武劇，又如黄教之打鬼。惟泰西諸大國，則端正文秀者多，婦女亦姿容美麗，所服輕綃細縠，尤極工麗。

The sharpest contrast occurs in the description of the sumptuous court assembly taking place at Buckingham Palace. According to Bin Chun, there were about 1,200 lords and ladies present at the party; later on, he participated in a dinner hosted by the British crown prince and princess. Bin Chun was overwhelmed by the visual splendors of the court banquet:

---

35. Zhong Shuhe mentioned the deletion in the preface to the 1981 edition of *Chengcha biji*. See *Chengcha biji (waiyizhong)*, p. 3. He did not mention the deletion in the 1985 edition. In an article about his correspondence with Qian Zhongshu regarding the *Zouxiang shijie* series, Zhong reminisced that Qian had expressed disapproval of Zhong's editorial censorship. See Zhong Shuhe, "Ji Qian Zhongshu zuoxu," p. 76.

36. Bin Chun, *Chengcha biji*, pp. 100–101.

I almost thought that this body of mine was at the Jasper Pool in paradise, and that those who conversed with me were heavenly gods in golden armor and goddesses from the Pistil Pearl Palace, and that I was no longer in the mortal world.[37]

幾疑此身在天上瑤池，所與接談者皆金甲天神，蕊珠仙子，非復人間世矣。

This happens to be the other passage excised from Bin Chun's diary by Zhong Shuhe. It is interesting that of the two passages Zhong Shuhe decided to remove, one speaks of "hell" and the other regards "heaven." Both extremes are a source of discomfort to the modern editor, who probably perceived them as "politically incorrect" because one is too denigrating to the natives and the other too complimentary to the British royals.

A passage from Wang Tao's travel account, *Jottings from Wanderings* (*Manyou suilu* 漫遊隨錄), presents an even clearer picture of hierarchy:

I began my trip in Hong Kong and passed through Singapore, Penang, Ceylon, Aden, and then Suez, where finally I felt a renewal of scenery: the residents' skin color had become increasingly yellow, and the climate had also become cooler; the eyes and hair of the people at Suez were black, looking no different from the Chinese. The men and women there were also largely good-looking. Egypt has been regarded a civilized country since the ancient times; there are indeed good reasons for such a claim. We then passed through Cairo and Alexander, sailed across the Mediterranean, and moored at Messina. Unfortunately we were not able to go on the shore. This place had many volcanoes and was rich in sulfur. Then we arrived at the French harbor city of Marseilles, and the vista immediately expanded into a grand view. It was almost like entering another universe. Cities such as Leon and Paris had numerous famous scenic spots, and it is nearly impossible to record them all. By the time we reached London, once again it felt like coming into yet another grotto heaven. As for the gathering place of all luxuries and splendors, the ultimate altar of sightseeing, nothing could rival the Great House of Glass [i.e., the Crystal Palace].[38]

余自香港啓行，由新嘉坡而檳榔嶼而錫蘭而亞丁而蘇彝士，至此始覺景象一新：居民面色漸黃，天氣亦稍寒，睛髮俱黑，無异華人，士女亦多清秀。古稱埃及爲文明之國，洵不誣也。復歷基改羅，經亞勒山大，渡地中海而泊墨西拿，惜未及登岸。其地多火山，產硫磺。既抵

37. Bin Chun, *Chengcha biji*, in *Xiao Fanghu zhai yudi congchao*, 49a. This is in the entry for the twenty-third day of the fourth month of the fifth year of the Tongzhi era (June 5, 1866).

38. Wang Tao, *Manyou suilu*, p. 101.

法埠馬賽里，眼界頓開，幾若別一宇宙。若里昂，若巴黎，名勝之區，幾不勝記。逮至倫敦，又似別一洞天。其爲繁華之淵藪，游觀之壇場，則未有若玻璃巨室者也。

Wang Tao's description, beginning from the least desirable and steadily moving up until finally culminating in London's Crystal Palace, may be summarized by the Chinese phrase, "gradually entering the realm of delight" (*jianru jiajing* 漸入佳境). When Wang Tao first arrived in Hong Kong, he found the city revolting: "The hills are bald and reddish, the water runs fast; the people are stupid and their language incomprehensible. Upon first arrival it was almost unbearable" 山童赭而水汩減，人民椎魯，語言侏離，乍至幾不可耐.[39] Egypt won his begrudged approval, because the Egyptians with their black eyes and hair looked Chinese. Egypt's reputation as "a civilized country" no doubt also helped. France was like "another universe," and London was "yet another grotto heaven," a Daoist term referring to earthly paradise. Departing from the brutal heat and hideous landscapes of hell, going through the "cooler" and "largely good-looking" purgatory, Wang Tao finally made his way into heaven.

On the other end of the spectrum, Zhang Deyi reported a decline toward what he perceived as a lower rung in the ladder in human civilization. Sailing from San Francisco to New York during his second trip abroad, his boat stopped first at Acapulco and then Colón, Panama, also called Aspinwall by the U.S. emigré community (transcribed as A-si-bang-e 阿斯浜額 by Zhang Deyi). Zhang Deyi described what he saw in Panama:

> The houses use bamboos for supporting structure and tree leaves for roof tiles; they are low, cramped, and shabby, even worse than the houses in Saigon. As for the natives, they have large and obese faces, flat noses, and big bones; some are dark and some are yellow-skinned. Men and women, old and young, all look like ghouls, truly a shocking and frightful sight.[40]

房皆竹作間架，葉代陶瓦，矮小鄙陋，遜于西貢多矣。人則面目肥大，扁鼻大骨，黑黄不一。男女老幼望之如鬼，駭然可畏。

The image that persists in these descriptions is that of *gui* 鬼, variously translated as demons, ghouls, or devils—or that of some other creature,

39. Ibid., p. 59.

40. Zhang Deyi, *Ou Mei huanyouji*, p. 650.

such as frogs or birds. In either case, the foreign peoples are portrayed as subhuman or non-human. Entertaining himself during the long ocean voyage by composing mediocre verses, Bin Chun wrote a poem about the black laborers working in the boiler room on the boat. It is entitled "A Ballad of the Blacks" ("Heiren yao" 黑人謠):

山蒼蒼	The mountains are of a dark green,
海茫茫	the seas stretch endlessly,
阿非利加洲境長	the territory of the African continent is enormous.
黑人肌肉黝如墨	The muscles of the black people are as dark as ink,
啾啾跳躍嘻炎荒	they twitter and hop around, having fun in the fiery wilderness.
冰蠶不知寒	The ice-silkworm does not know cold;
火鼠不畏熱	the fire-rat is not afraid of heat.[41]
黑人受直傭舟中	The black men who are hired to work in the ocean-liner
敢嚮洪爐當火烈	dare to face the great furnace and scorching fire.
洪爐烈火金鐵鎔	The great furnace and scorching fire can melt metal;
赤身豈怯光焰紅	with their naked bodies, these men do not fear the blazing flames.
臨陣沖鋒稱敢死	When fighting in battles, they claim to risk death;
食人之祿能輸忠	when taking a salary from their lord, they pay back with loyalty.
吁嗟乎	Alas,
蹈湯赴火亦不怨	they don't mind walking into boiling water or burning fire,
其形雖惡心可讚	their form may be ugly, their heart is admirable,
願以此爲臣子勸	I hope to use this ballad to urge all subjects.[42]

The opening lines deliberately echo the famous "Song of Chi Le" ("Chi Le ge" 敕勒歌). It is purportedly a Sarbi song from the sixth century, which ends with a remarkable image of the steppe:

41. "Ice-silkworm" and "fire-rat" are legendary creatures. For more about ice-silkworm see Wang Jia's 王嘉 (fl. fourth century) *Shiyi ji* 拾遺記, 10. 228. Fire-rat is believed to come from the far south, and its hair can be woven into asbestos. See Zhang Bo's 張勃 (fl. third century) *Wu lu* 吳錄 in Li Fang, *Taiping yulan*, 820.3782. This couplet is almost taken verbatim from Su Shi's 蘇軾 (1037–1101) poem entitled "Xu Dazheng Xianxuan" 徐大正閑軒: "The ice-silkworm does not know cold; / the fire-rat does not know heat" 冰蠶不知寒，火鼠不知暑. *Su Shi shiji* 24.1283.

42. Bin Chun, *Chengcha biji*, pp. 192–93.

天蒼蒼	The heavens are of a dark blue,
野茫茫	the wilds stretch endlessly,
風吹草低見牛羊	the wind blows, the grasses bend, revealing sheep and cattle.[43]

In Bin Chun's poem, instead of "sheep and cattle," we see the black workers. The implicit comparison becomes explicit when Bin Chun proceeds to compare the workers to "ice-silkworm" and "fire-rat." Those legendary creatures are so used to their native elements that they have no awareness of cold or heat, just like, in Bin Chun's opinion, the black people who are "having fun in the fiery wilderness" of the African continent. In Bin Chun's eyes, this characteristic makes them ideal for working in the boiler room in the tropical weather: a job, as he sees it, sanctioned and justified by the laws of Nature. One year later, Zhi Gang, another Manchu official, passed through Panama and heard that twenty thousand Cantonese laborers working on the railway construction had died of poor living conditions in the hot tropical weather. He remarked: "How cruel! It would have been so much more appropriate to employ people from the hot land of Africa [for this kind of job]."[44] Like Bin Chun, Zhi Gang appealed to laws of Nature to justify human exploitation and social hierarchy.

The description of the African people presents an idealized picture of "children of nature," as innocent and carefree as they are ignorant and uncivilized like birds that "twitter" or animals that "hop around." What Bin Chun finds admirable about the black people, despite their "ugly" appearances, is their "loyalty" as "subjects." This "loyalty" no doubt also stems from their utter innocence. This is the closest the Chinese ever come to the concept of "noble savage." It is a rhetorical strategy that is still employed today in writings both within and outside Chinese academia to idealize non-Han Chinese peoples in history as well as in modern times, a condescending, damning praise that places them just underneath the forces and benefits of civilization. The Edenic vision is always a double-edged sword; it projects one's desire for "purity and simplicity" onto a foreign people, so that one may both envy them for their "untainted" state

43. Lu Qinli, *Quan bei Qi shi* 全北齊詩 3.2289.
44. Zhi Gang, *Chu shi Taixi ji*, p. 267.

and reassure themselves of their own cultural superiority by claiming sophistication and refinement.

By hailing the black laborer as a role model for "all subjects," Bin Chun placed himself, a subject of the Qing, into the system that meshes social and racial hierarchies. Needless to say, he considered the Chinese as several rungs above the African people. Such a view was, and in fact still is, not uncommon in China.[45] In 1880, Huang Zunxian wrote an indignant poem in response to the passing of the Chinese Exclusion Act in the United States, which prohibited or limited the immigration of Chinese workers. The poem contains the following lines:

皇華與大漢	The celestial emissaries and the great Han people
第供異族謔	are reduced to a mere laughing-stock to the foreign races.
不如黑奴蠢	Surely it is better to be as stupid as the black slaves
隨處安渾噩	who, unenlightened, are content with their lot anywhere.[46]

Hun'e 渾噩, here translated as "unenlightened," is an ambiguous word sometimes used in a positive sense to refer to a simplicity associated with a legendary high antiquity. Although the loss of such primitive simplicity is lamented in *Laozi* and *Zhuangzi*, Confucianism put great stock in "teaching and civilizing" (*jiaohua* 教化). Zhang Deyi, after taking a stroll in a black neighborhood in Washington, D.C., on June 6, 1868, wrote an entry in his diary:

In the course of two hundred years, the United States has civilized thirty-six states of America. The men and women who have been fully civilized are made slaves and servants. They dress like the others, but their accent is slightly different and belongs to a different kind of native tongue. . . . People from uncivilized states continue to dwell in caves in the wilderness and catch wild beasts for food. They paint their faces with five colors and wear bird feathers, and are known as the West Indians.[47]

---

45. For recent studies of Chinese racism, see Dikötter, *The Discourse of Race in Modern China*; and Johnson, *Race and Racism in the Chinas*.

46. Huang, *Renjinglu*, p. 130.

47. Zhang Deyi, *Ou Mei huanyou ji*, p. 659.

蓋合衆國二百年來，已化阿美里加三十六邦，已化男女令爲奴僕，服與衆同，惟語音稍异，爲另種土語……其未化諸邦，仍穴居于野，攫獸爲食，面圖五色，身著翎毛，别之爲西印度。

Its many inaccuracies aside, this passage is noteworthy for its linguistic juxtaposition of a people, perceived as "uncivilized," with words such as "caves," "wilderness," "wild beasts," and "bird feathers."

The sanction of applying "civilizing influence" on a people who were considered less advanced in terms of technology, material wealth, and social organization brought the Chinese travelers unwittingly close to the discourse of colonialism. When Zhi Gang resisted the preaching of Christianity, he argued that Christianity was not necessary for an already morally superior people. "The practice of praying to God for blessings," he told an English missionary in Paris, "should only be applied to those stupid, ignorant, and uncivilized people living in the great wilderness or beyond the ocean's shores, such as the American Red Indians and the Australian or Malaccan aborigines, whose strong ones bully and devour the weak and who do not know remorse and fear." Belief in God, according to Zhi Gang, would help instill a sense of fear into those people; it was not, however, applicable to "people like you and me, who have long known rites and righteousness."[48] Zhi Gang's comment to the English missionary about the latter's having "long known rites and righteousness" just like the Chinese might have been a tongue-in-cheek one, but he obviously considered himself, as well as the English missionary, a cut above the "American Red Indians and the Austrialian or Malaccan aborigines."

What Zhi Gang could not possibly have known is that just fifteen years before his visit to Paris, a French diplomat and man of letters, Joseph Arthur de Gobineau (1816–82), published a work entitled *Essai sur l'Inégalité des Races Humaines*. In this work, de Gobineau, the man who predicted that the Chinese would eventually drive out their Manchu conquerors just as they did the Mongols, developed his theory for a racial demography. De Gobineau divided the human races into the white, the yellow, and the black. He allowed the yellow race to be superior to the

48. Zhi Gang, *Chu shi Taixi ji*, pp. 317–18. This appears in the entry for the second month of the eighth year of the Tongzhi era (March 13–April 11, 1869).

black race, but placed the white race at the top of the hierarchy.[49] A Chinese diplomat like Zhi Gang may decry de Gobineau's classification as absurd and insist on placing the yellow race on top, but as long as he espouses a classification and gradation of human societies, he always runs the risk of having such a system turned against himself.

I end this section with a final example. When traveling in neighboring Asian countries, the Chinese travelers found one more thing that troubled them: what they perceived as a lack of physical distinction between women and men. Bin Chun commented on the people of Saigon: "The men keep their hair and bind it in a chignon, and most of them do not have a beard. The women go about bare-footed and wear no hairpins and earrings. There is no telling male from female from what I see."[50] This so impressed Bin Chun that he wrote a poem about it:

青山短短髮垂絲	Their green hills are short, their hair is long;
跌足科頭一樣姿	walking bare-footed and hatless, they all look alike.
郎已及笄儂未冠	The boy has reached the age of donning a hairpin, the girl is not yet capped:
誰能辨我是雄雌	who can tell if I'm male or female?[51]

In the Chinese tradition, "donning a hairpin" marks a woman's reaching the age of maturity while wearing a cap marks that of a man's. Bin Chun reverses the order in the third line to make an ironic comment. Since the Confucian ideology places great emphasis on the separation of the sexes, perceived gender confusion among the Vietnamese constituted yet another trait of their foreignness and "barbarism" to the Qing Chinese.

The traveler in foreign lands feels a particularly urgent need for a symbolic order based on difference, exclusion, and segregation, so that a clear definition of the self can be maintained. For a Chinese traveler in a foreign country that was home to many Chinese settlers and traders, used Chinese as its written language, and had "the same kind of Chinese names for their commanderies and counties,"[52] there was perhaps an additional level of discomfort resulting from the Other's proximity to the Self. Bin Chun's observation of gender confusion in the former "vassal state" of the

49. de Gobineau, *The Inequality of Human Races*, p. 150.

50. Bin Chun, *Chengcha biji*, p. 214.

51. Bin Chun, *Haiguo shengyou cao*, p. 159.

52. Bin Chun, *Chengcha biji*, p. 214.

Qing evokes an age-old anxiety about gender transformation in the Chinese tradition. Dynastic histories from an early period on have recorded such "abnormal" occurrences as sex conversion or aberrance in clothing (*fu yao* 服妖), including, among other forms of what was considered deviant dressing styles, women wearing male-styled clothes or men wearing female-styled clothes.[53] Although a woman cross-dressed as male could be acting out of a noble and socially sanctioned motive (such as in the case of Mulan who joined the army to spare her aging father), a man cross-dressed as female was almost always regarded as morally suspicious except onstage—and even then, acting in premodern China was a profession scorned by society.[54] The Chinese author's disparagement of the people of Saigon for a lack of gender distinction bespeaks a sense of unease about the danger of emasculation.

Ironically, just as Bin Chun, Zhi Gang, and their entourages moved through distant lands and observed local customs, they were also being observed with great curiosity by the local people of those countries, and the onlookers were often confused about these foreign visitors' gender identity. Zhang Deyi recorded a number of such instances. In London, when Bin Chun, Zhang Deyi, and others toured the Crystal Palace, numerous sightseers were "overjoyed to see us, and said they had never seen any Chinese dressed like us. They followed us around; I wanted to speak with them but could not."[55] In Berlin, when they went out to purchase the Prussian King and Queen's portraits,

> Men and women who wanted to see the Chinese thronged in front of the store. There were about a thousand of them. After we went in, people who desired to see us also rushed in and filled up the room. The store owner had to stop them. After we finished, we almost could not make our way out. The store owner understood the situation and let us out from the back door. People found it out and all went through the store to go to the back door as well, so that the door-keeper could not even close the door. They followed us all the way to our hotel, and

---

53. See, for instance, Fang Xuanling, *Jin shu* 27.822–27. In one case it cites the Jin historian Gan Bao's comment: "The difference between men and women is the great principle of a country" 男女之別，國之大節. Disruption of the difference was believed to portend national disasters.

54. For an insightful discussion of gender transformation in Chinese tradition, see Zeitlin, *Historian of the Strange*, pp. 107–16.

55. Zhang Deyi, *Hanghai shuqi*, p. 503.

there was such a multitude that we could not enter the hotel. I had to wave my umbrella about to make some space and only then did the crowd begin to withdraw—I did that because I had asked them nicely in English but they would not leave. When I got back to my room, I looked out and saw that men and women, elderly and young, were still gathering like ants and had not yet left.[56]

店前之男女擁看華人者，老幼約以千計。及入畫鋪，眾皆先睹爲快，沖入屋内幾無隙地，主人強阻乃止。買畢，欲出不能移步。主人會意，引明向後門走。眾知之，皆從鋪内穿出，闍者欲閉門而不可得。眾人擁出，追隨瞻顧，及將入店之時，男女圍擁又不得入。明乃持傘柄揮之，眾始退，蓋因以英語浼之再三不去故也。 登樓俯視，男女老幼尚蟻聚樓下未去。

The most enthusiastic public welcome Zhang Deyi recorded took place in America, when the Chinese delegation was shown around Boston:

Men and women all opened their windows and looked out, took off their hats and waved their handkerchiefs, clapped their hands and threw flowers at us, and shouted "Hurrah!" Some were holding a Chinese umbrella, some were brandishing Chinese embroidered silk, some displayed opium tools and porcelain plates on a red blanket, and some wore Chinese autumn hats. In a word, anyone who possessed anything Chinese would show it off. Along the way there were so many onlookers that some sat over walls, some climbed on trees, and some stood on ladders.[57]

男女開窗眺望，免冠搖巾，擊掌飛花，口呼賀來。有舉中國傘者，有搖中土繡花綢緞者，有鋪紅被列煙具磁盤於窗下者，有戴中土秋帽者。總之，凡有些須華物，無不炫之。沿途人多，竟有騎牆跨脊、攀樹登梯者。

What turned out to be downright embarrassing for Zhang Deyi was, however, that he and the other young men in the delegation, being beardless, wearing a queue and dressed in long robes, were frequently mistaken for women. The first such instance occurred at Marseilles when they were leaving a tavern, accompanied by the Frenchman De Shan 德善 or De Yizhai 德一齋 (i.e., E. Deschamps), who was appointed the Right Secretary (*you xieli* 右協理) for this mission.[58] There are two versions of this

56. Ibid., p. 562.

57. Ibid., p. 687.

58. Similar incidents occurred once in Washington, D.C., and once in St. Petersburg. Zhang Deyi, *Ou Mei huanyou ji*, p. 659; Zhang Deyi, *Hanghai shuqi*, p. 553. Yuan Zuzhi 袁

incident. The following excerpt is taken from the edition included in the series of geographic works known as *Xiao Fanghu zhai yudi congchao* 小方壺齋輿地叢鈔:

When we were coming out from the door, there were seven or eight ignorant men and women. They asked De Yizhai, "Where do these people come from?" Shan said, "They are Chinese." They again asked, "The one with a beard is certainly a male; the beardless ones—are they women?" Shan said with a smile, "They are all men." Those who heard all laughed. On our way back, there were two or three children who, upon seeing us, shouted loudly: "Come quickly! Come and see Chinese women!" They shouted and ran away around the hedges on the road.[59]

出門有鄉愚男婦七八人，問德一齋曰："此何國人也？"善曰："中華人也。"又曰："彼長鬚者固是男子，其無鬚者是婦人乎？"善笑曰："皆男人也。"聞者咸笑。回時又有二三小兒，見彝等乃大聲呼曰："快來看中國婦人！"連聲跑過籬牆而去。

The compiler Wang Xiqi 王錫祺 (1855–1913) began to collect the editions included in the first series of *Xiao Fanghu zhai yudi congchao* in 1877. The version of Zhang Deyi's first diary represented in the *Xiao Fanghu* edition must have been published shortly after he came back from his trip, as its prefaces are dated 1867.[60] In the last years of his life, however, Zhang Deyi made a clean copy of his diary, and while doing so, he revised and edited just as a manuscript copyist was wont to do. Thus, the travel accounts from the nineteenth century not only bear the traces of their modern editor's expurgation, of which two examples are cited above, but were also censored by the author himself and, as we will see, by his nineteenth-century editor/publisher. In the cleaned-up copy of Zhang's diary, on which the modern *Zouxiang shijie congshu* edition is based, the passage quoted above appears as follows (the changes are marked in italics):

祖志 (1827–1900), who traveled overseas in the 1880s, observed in his *Xisu zazhi* 西俗雜誌, "Beardless men are often mistaken for women from China" 又每無鬚之男子，以爲中國之婦人. Cited in Lü Wen-tsuei, "Transcultural Travels in Late Qing Shanghai," p. 43.

59. Zhang Deyi, *Hanghai shuqi*, in Wang Xiqi, *Xiao Fanghu zhai yudi congchao*, 69a.

60. A manuscript copy made in 1870, now in the collection of Beijing University Library, is identical with the *Xiao Fanghu zhai* version in its content.

There were *several* ignorant men and women. They asked Deshan, "Where do these people come from?" Shan said, "They are Chinese." They again asked: "The one with *a fine beard and gray locks is certainly a man. The beardless youths with a charming demeanor—are they truly members of the fair sex*?" Shan said with a smile, "They are all *male*." Those who heard all *clapped their hands and* laughed. On our way back, *some people inquired about us, some pointed to us, some marveled, and some expressed envy, but all, from tender-aged lads and white-haired elders, vied to see us.*[61]

有鄉愚男婦數人，問德善曰："此何國人也？"善曰："中華人也。"又曰："彼修髯而髮蒼者，諒是男子。其無鬚而豐姿韶秀者，果巾幗耶？"善笑曰："皆男子也。"聞者咸鼓掌而笑。歸時一路黃童白叟，有咨詢者，有指畫者，有詫異者，有艷羨者，爭先睹之爲快。

Several things about the revisions stand out. First, the linguistic register of the original text is elevated. Thus, the more colloquial and plain *furen* 妇人 ("women") becomes *jin'guo* 巾幗, here translated as "members of the fair sex"; "the one with a beard" becomes "the one with a fine beard and gray locks"; even *nanren* 男人 (a man, a guy) is turned into *nanzi* 男子 (a male), a more elegant literary Chinese term. *Fengzi shaoxiu* 豐姿韶秀 ("with a charming demeanor"), a conventional phrase describing a good-looking young man, is inserted as an attribute for the "beardless youths." "Clapping hands" is added to the description of the men and women's reaction to Deschamps' reply, as this is a positive phrase that expresses cheer, wonder, or admiration, and serves to bring more clarity to the ambiguous act of "laughing," which could otherwise indicate pure ridicule. The other noticeable change is the deletion of the children's remarks. In its stead, we have a much more flattering portrait of onlookers "marveling" at the Chinese travelers and even "expressing envy."

While the senior Manchu official Bin Chun observes with a sense of superiority and unease the lack of gender distinction in Saigon, especially in beardless men with long hair (which the Han Chinese men used to have before the Manchu conquest), Zhang Deyi, the young Chinese bannerman, was mistaken for a woman as he traveled around the world.[62]

---

61. Zhang Deyi, *Hanghai shuqi*, p. 481. It is in the entry for the nineteenth day of the third month in the fifth year of the Tongzhi era (May 3, 1866).

62. In one such instance, recorded in the entry for the third day of the twelfth month of the seventh year of the Tongzhi era (January 15, 1869), Zhang explained that "only the two senior officials [Zhi Gang and Sun Jiagu] have beards, and the rest are all [beardless]

In his original diary entry, Zhang Deyi recorded the incident in a matter-of-fact tone; but when he was copying out his diary later on, he tried to make the incident sound more becoming and dignified. His revisions show that being the object of foreign gaze was not a concern for the Chinese traveler, as long as the gaze was that of amazement, wonder, and envy; what unsettled him was having gender confusion directed at him personally.

In 1867, about a year after Zhang Deyi's first visit, Wang Tao arrived in England. While traveling in Scotland, he was also mistaken for a woman.

Children in the north who had never seen a Chinese person pointed to me and said: "This is a *Zaini lidi*." Some said, "No, she is Zhan Wu's *weifu*." The English dialect refers to China as "Zaini" [i.e., Chinese]; *lidi* means "woman" [i.e., lady] and *weifu* means "wife." At the time, Zhan Wu was still with us, which was why they said that.[63]

北境童稚未睹華人者，輒指目之曰："此載尼禮地也。" 或曰："否，詹五威孚耳。" 英方言呼中國曰載尼，其曰禮地者，華言婦人也。其曰威孚者，華言妻也。時詹五未去，故有是説。

Wang Tao responded with a rather long-winded philosophizing:

Alas, I am a virile and extraordinary man, but when I encounter those who do not recognize me, they take me for a woman. I have the honor of being a male, but am now suffering the fate of being confused with a female—who can see me for what I truly am? It is bewildering indeed. I have thrown my body onto the ocean's gray waves, and lodged my feet in a foreign country; instead of flying like a cock, I am crouching like a hen. When I heard what the children said about me, I could not help feeling that it might in fact be a prophecy for the rest of my life!

噫嘻！余本一雄奇男子，今遇不識者，竟欲雌之矣。忝此鬚眉，蒙以巾幗，誰實辨之？迷離撲朔，擲身滄波，托足异國，不爲雄飛，甘爲雌伏，聽此童言，詎非終身之讖語哉！

Like Zhang Deyi, Wang Tao recorded the incident because it was psychologically disturbing, and he tried to make it sound more dignified by using a level of rhetoric that far surpassed the triviality of the situation. More specifically, Wang Tao combined two traditional rhetorical moves:

---

youths, so the locals mistook us for women" 當時惟兩欽憲有鬚，餘皆少年，故土人妄以爲女也. Zhang Deyi, *Ou Mei huanyou ji*, p. 731.

63. Wang Tao, *Manyou suilu*, p. 144.

one was to complain that nobody recognized his true self and his true talent; the other was to attach much importance to children's songs or children's words as a portent. Because of his associations with the Taiping rebels, Wang Tao was wanted by the Qing government; he first sought refuge in Hong Kong, and then went abroad. Here Wang Tao used gender confusion as a symbol of his exile status, comparing himself to a "hen" lying low. The phrase *mili pushuo* 迷離撲朔, here translated simply as "bewildering," evokes the famous "Ballad of Mulan" ("Mulan ci" 木蘭辭) from early medieval times. The last four lines of the ballad read,

雄兔腳撲朔	The male hare's legs have a nervous spring,
雌兔眼迷離	the eyes of the girl hare wander;
雙兔傍地走	but when two hares run side by side,
安能辨我是雄雌	who can tell if I'm boy or girl?[64]

In the "Ballad of Mulan," Mulan served in the army for ten years, traveling to the far northern frontiers, crossing the Yellow River and Black Mountain; only after she came home did she finally begin wearing women's clothes again. For the nineteenth-century Chinese travelers, that horrible anomaly of gender confusion, whether in their own case or in the case of the Other, could only take place far away from home in a foreign land.

The Problem of Gender and Sexuality

> The other is my (own and proper) unconscious.
>
> Julia Kristeva, *Strangers to Ourselves*

In Confucian ideology, gender segregation was considered one of the basic elements in the maintenance of the moral caliber of individuals and of the society as a whole. In late imperial China, when a male member of the literati elite socialized with women, it was either with kinswomen or with prostitutes. Outside of a family or brothel context, a male elite member had relatively few opportunities to mingle with women of equal

64. Owen's translation. *An Anthology of Chinese Literature*, p. 243.

social status who were not objects of sexual interest. This created intriguing consequences for gender relationships in Chinese society, as well as caused much astonishment among the nineteenth-century Chinese visitors to Europe and America.[65] Zhang Zuyi's remarks betray his surprise upon seeing mixed gender company on social occasions:

When they invite a guest, if the guest has a wife and daughter, the wife and daughter are invited as well. According to their custom, women are present at all court assemblies and state banquets, for they claim that *yin* is of the same entity as *yang* and must not be neglected.[66]

凡延客，有妻女者必並延之。其俗朝會筵宴大典皆有婦人，謂陰陽一體，不容偏廢也。

Since one of the primary purposes of gender segregation is to prevent sexual promiscuity (under the assumption that mixed gender company leads to moral decrepitude), the Qing Chinese travelers were amazed by the fact that the upper-class Western women could freely mix with men and yet observe sexual propriety. Wang Tao's remarks are representative of the general impressions of his compatriots:

Daughters of renowned families and young married women do not avoid male company even upon first meeting. They share the same table with men at meals and ride in the same carriage when going out. They exchange toasts with men and sit with them in close proximity, without feeling the least bit of discomfort. And yet, just as their appearances are beautiful like flowers, their hearts are pure like white jade; they abide by morality and adhere to the principle of chastity; they can read and write, and they observe propriety. Exercising caution in their behavior and cherishing their virtue, they truly cannot be compromised or violated.[67]

名媛幼婦，即于初見之頃，亦不相避。食則幷席，出則同車，觥籌相酬，履舄交錯，不以爲嫌也。然則花姸其貌而玉潔其心，秉德懷貞，知書守禮，其謹嚴自好，固又毫不可以犯干也。

Zhang Deyi expressed similar sentiments:

---

65. For a discussion of this issue, see Teng, "The West as a 'Kingdom of Women,'" pp. 110–11.

66. Zhang Zuyi, "Lundun zhuzhici," 4a, in Xu Shikai, *Guanzide zhai* 24; Wang Shenzhi and Wang Zijin, *Qingdai haiwai*, p. 210.

67. Wang Tao, *Manyou suilu*, p. 135.

I hear that in the English capital women walk on the street every night, and that men caress and kiss them playfully but do not engage in improper behavior. This is truly quite amazing.[68]

聞英都每夕女子街行，有男子狎抱，接唇爲戲，而不爲無禮者，殊堪詫異。

By "improper behavior" (*wu li* 無禮), Zhang means sexual intercourse, but it is difficult to tell whether he was more amazed by the degree of sexual freedom allowed or by the degree of self-restraint practiced.

It may be tempting to conclude that these Chinese men were simply more "conservative" in their view of gender relations than their Western counterparts, but this is not what I am trying to suggest. The structure of male power and desire remains fundamentally the same in all patriarchal societies, but is played out in different ways in different cultures. The nineteenth-century Chinese travelers' puzzlement about gender and sexuality in the West was no more than a projection of their own desires and fears. The mixed gender company witnessed in some foreign countries brought to the surface the Chinese men's anxieties about gender confusion and emasculation discussed in the preceding section.

The Chinese travelers, with their limited experience of Western social life, tended to read deep meanings into light-hearted banter, and sometimes the Western social etiquette led them to believe that women enjoyed a fundamentally superior status in the Western society. In a diary entry Zhi Gang recounts a visit from the wife of a British governor:

She was accompanied by her husband's younger brother. During our conversation, he pointed to his sister-in-law and said, "This is the great ruler of our family." The Westerners esteem women, but this incident seems to show that they are not necessarily happy with the situation.[69]

其夫弟隨之。談次，指其嫂曰："此我家之大君主也。"西人貴女，以此觀之，未見其甘心也。

Bin Chun observed with some contempt that European husbands on the ocean liner would "wait upon their wives every day," and that the wives

68. Zhang Deyi, *Ou Mei huanyou ji*, p. 719. This is in the entry for the twenty-second day of the tenth month of the seventh year of the Tongzhi era (December 5, 1868).

69. Zhi Gang, *Chu shi Taixi ji*, p. 297. This is in the entry for the fourth day of the ninth month of the seventh year of the Tongzhi era (October 19, 1868).

would "arrogantly order them about like maids or concubines" (*ruo bi ying ran* 若婢媵然).[70] In regards to the last four characters, "like maids or concubines," a late Qing printed edition of Bin Chun's diary reads "obeyed their commands respectfully" (*feng ling wei jin* 奉令惟謹). This variant mitigates the harshness of the observation by removing the unmanning simile, but in doing so also calls attention to it.[71]

During his first overseas trip, Zhang Deyi remarked in his diary: "The Western custom is such that both men and women are able to travel in foreign countries."[72] Another diary entry from his second overseas trip makes a disapproving comment on American women:

> The women of the United States do not have much feminine manners. No matter whether they are married or not, they intervene in everything outside of their household. I am afraid that it is unavoidable that they breach moral codes and violate moral principles. Even a young woman is allowed to live alone in the outside world and follow a male acquaintance to travel for ten thousand miles, and her parents do not utter a word of disapproval. Instead of crouching like a hen, they fly like a cock; though women, they act like men.[73]

> 合眾女子少閨閣之氣，不論已嫁未嫁，事事干預閫外，蕩檢逾閑，恐不免焉。甚至少年婦女聽其孤身寄外，並可隨相識男子遠游萬里，爲之父母者亦不少責，不爲雌伏而效雄飛，是雌而雄者也。

If we recall how many times Zhang Deyi was mistaken for a woman during his overseas travels, this passage seems particularly fraught with a deep-seated anxiety about gender reversal.

The nineteenth-century Chinese travelers found Western women's freedom of movement threatening, as it violated their sense of the proper order of things. Since they were separated from their family for months and even years during their travels, they also felt envious of couples travel-

---

70. Bin Chun, *Chengcha biji*, p. 101.

71. This edition, most likely from the late nineteenth century, is in the collection of the Harvard-Yenching Library. Unfortunately, it is impossible to establish the precise date or place of the publication of this edition, which is block printed on double leaves and contained in a case. It is also unclear whether it was Bin Chun himself or the editor/publisher who had effected the change.

72. Zhang Deyi, *Hanghai shuqi*, p. 550. This is in the entry for the third day of the sixth month of the fifth year of the Tongzhi era (July 14, 1866).

73. Zhang Deyi, *Ou Mei huanyou ji*, p. 670. It is in the entry for the eighteenth day of the fifth month of the seventh year of the Tongzhi era (July 7, 1868).

ing together. No. 8 of Huang Zunxian's poetic series, entitled "Various Responses on an Ocean Voyage" ("Haixing zagan" 海行雜感) and written during his trip to San Francisco from Japan in early 1882, conveys the poet's ambivalent attitude:

每每鴛鴦逐隊行	Every now and then a pair of mandarin ducks join the ranks,
春風相對坐調箏	sitting face to face in spring breeze, they tune the harp.
才聞兒女呢呢語	Just as we hear boy and girl sharing lovers' words in a whisper,
又作胡雛戀母聲	they again make the sound of Tartar whelps whining for their mother.[74]

A note appended to this poem explains: "Many Western passengers take their wives along on their journey. The Russian ambassador and his wife sit face to face every night, playing piano and singing together. Their songs are quite touching."[75] The last line of the poem is taken almost verbatim from the Tang poet Li Qi's 李頎 (ca. 690–751) poem on listening to a "Tartar whistle" performance, except that the phrase *hu'er* 胡兒, "Tartar children," is changed to *hu chu* 胡雛, "Tartar whelps."[76] The word *chu* means "chick" and, unlike *er* (human child), is often used to refer to young birds or animals. The poem betrays a sense of envy for the foreign couple, and yet, the terms in which the poet describes them are tainted with a slight tone of condescension.[77]

To downplay the threat posed by Western women's freedom of movement, Bin Chun also chose to portray them in terms of "birds"—harmless, innocent creatures of nature:

---

74. This line evokes the story of Cai Yan 蔡琰 (fl. ca. 170–215). During the chaos of the late Eastern Han, Cai Yan was abducted and married to a Xiongnu chieftain; she lived with him for twelve years and bore two children. When she was ransomed to return to the Han, she had to leave her two children behind. A "Song of the Tartar Whistle in Eighteen Stanzas" (*Hu jia shiba pai* 胡笳十八拍) is spuriously attributed to Cai Yan, in which the speaker laments her separation from her "Tartar children" (*hu'er* 胡兒).

75. Huang Zunxian, *Renjinglu*, p. 125.

76. Li Qi, "Ting Dong da tan Hujianong jianji Fang jishi," in *Li Qi shi pingzhu*, p. 215.

77. This poem may be contrasted with No. 11, in which Huang Zunxian playfully refers to himself as "Old Man Huang" (Huang gong 黃公) who takes along "Old Woman Huang" (Huang nai 黃嬭)—a sixth-century term for "books."

After two meals, they sometimes walk about a hundred paces on the arms of their husbands; when they are tired, they lie down on a chair side by side with their husbands. They whisper into their husbands' ears like chirping swallows on a beam, or mandarin ducks folding their wings. They are completely innocent and show no uneasiness about other people.[78]

兩餐後，或掖以行百餘武，倦則橫兩椅并臥，耳語如梁燕之呢喃，如鴛鴦之戢翼，天眞爛漫，了不忌人。

As early as the second century, "bird talk" was a term used to refer to the language or languages spoken by the non-Han people in south and southwestern China. Bin Chun used "bird talk" to describe the Western women's speech because to his ears their speech was both incomprehensible as a foreign language and senseless as female chatter. Bin Chun wrote a poem about a young woman he met in London:

彌思小字是安拿	Miss's pet name is Anna,
明慧堪稱解語花	sparkly and bright, a talking flower.
嚦嚦鶯聲夸百囀	A twittering oriole makes a hundred tunes:
方言最愛學中華	of all dialects, she loves the most to imitate Chinese.[79]

In this poem "Miss Anna" is compared to a flower and then a bird that loves to imitate Chinese talk, here implicitly represented as human speech as opposed to the language of flowers and birds. Bin Chun was not a colonial officer, and yet, when it came to the depiction of foreign women, he superimposed the natural onto the human, a rhetorical move often found in colonial romances.

As condescending as Bin Chun's poem is, it is one of the more benign versions of the Qing Chinese travelers' representations of gender and sexuality in foreign countries. Some nineteenth-century travel writings about foreign women are much more sarcastic, even venomous. To those writers, nothing seemed to better demonstrate the moral decrepitude of a

---

78. Bin Chun, *Chengcha biji*, p. 101.

79. Bin Chun, *Haiguo shengyou cao*, p. 168. "Anna" was likely the elder sister of Edward Charles MacIntosh Bowra (1841–74), who was the British interpreter appointed in the Chinese Maritime Customs at Canton. He helped arrange Bin Chun's tour. Zhang Deyi transliterated Anna's name as Bao E'nuo 包婀娜. *Hanghai shuqi*, p. 534. "A talking flower" is said to have been used by the Tang Emperor Xuanzong 玄宗 (r. 712–56) to refer to his favorite consort, Lady Yang Yuhuan 楊玉環 (719–56). See Wang Renyu 王仁裕 (880–956), *Kaiyuan Tianbao yishi*, in *Tang wudai biji xiaoshuo daguan*, p. 1737.

foreign culture than despicable sexual mores. In their observation of these sexual mores, their gaze was almost invariably focused on the female body that represented to them the source of decadence. Their writings generally branch off into two extremes: at one end of the spectrum, Wang Tao extravagantly praised the absolute chastity and virtue perceived in Western women; at the other end, Zhang Zuyi saw licentiousness and lust in any male-female relationship.

When he was in Paris, Bin Chun made the following observation after attending a dinner party:

> The wives of various officials arrived gracefully, all wearing sumptuous long dresses and glittering jewelry, with their arms and breasts exposed. Gauze and silk filled the hall, with candles casting light and shadow—it made me wonder if I was in the sea-god's palace decorated with shells and pearls.[80]
>
> 各官夫人姍姍其來，無不長裾華服，珠寶耀目，皆袒臂及胸，羅綺盈庭，燭光掩映，疑在貝闕珠宮也。

If Bin Chun's travel diary is full of language that evokes an earthly paradise, Zhang Zuyi's portrayal of Europe as a place of sexual degeneration and depravity in his "Bamboo Branch Songs on London" goes in the opposite direction, toward hell. The note appended to No. 12 of the "Bamboo Branch Songs" gives a lengthy description of the custom of holding parties, and the poem itself ends with a comment on the public appearance of female guests at such parties:

銀燭高燒萬盞明	Ten thousand silver candlesticks, all shining brightly;
重樓結彩百花新	fresh flowers in storied buildings decorated with colored ribbons.
怪他嬌小如花女	It is so strange that those slender flower-like women,
袒臂呈胸作上賓	with bare arms and exposed bosoms, are the honored guests.[81]

The presence of women and the female dress code at such parties take up only a few words in the lengthy prose note but become a major focus in the poem. It is the punch line designed to set a shocking contrast with the

80. Bin Chun, *Chengcha biji*, p. 110.

81. Zhang Zuyi, "Lundun zhuzhici," 3b, in Xu Shikai, *Guanzide zhai* 24; Wang Shenzhi and Wang Zijin, *Qingdai haiwai*, pp. 209–10.

first couplet, which depicts the magnitude of such lavish social occasions and thus better paves the way for the exposure of moral decrepitude.

No. 20 criticizes both the Western female body and women's clothes:

細腰突乳聳高臀	Slender waist, jutting breasts, a towering bottom,
黑漆皮鞋八寸新	brand new black leather shoes of eight inches long.
雙馬大車輕絹繖	In a carriage drawn by a pair of horses, with a light silk parasol,
招搖馳過軟紅塵	showing off ostentatiously, speeding through the soft red dust.[82]

The note appended to the poem explains to Chinese readers:

They [British women] bind their waists like bundled bamboo shoots, with two breasts sticking out from their bosom; behind their hip they fasten a soft bamboo frame, which holds up the skirt for about a foot high. This is considered beautiful. When a well-to-do family goes out, they ride in a coach drawn by two horses. Women carry a parasol while men do not.[83]

縛腰如束筍，兩乳突胸前，股後系軟竹架，將後幅襯起高尺許，以爲美觀。富家出遊必乘雙馬車，女子持日照繖，男則否。

There is not a word of explicit criticism, but the focus on waist, breasts, hips and feet, a particularly sexual object for the Qing men with their bound feet fetish, presents the image of an overly sexualized female body that is *zhaoyao* 招搖 (ostentatious, showy, and inappropriate). The statement "This is considered beautiful" conveys a strong sense of irony.

The Qing travelers were also struck by a number of professions held by women in the urban area. Zhang Zuyi's poem No. 40 is about female English teachers, who would "sit together with their [male] students, laughing and talking without the slightest of misgivings":

每日先零三兩枚	For three or two shillings a day,
朝朝暮暮按時來	every morning and every evening, she always comes on time.
豈徒教習英文語	Surely she is not just teaching English—

82. Zhang Zuyi, "Lundun zhuzhici," 5b–6a, in Xu Shikai, *Guanzide zhai* 24; Wang Shenzhi and Wang Zijin, *Qingdai haiwai*, p. 212.

83. Ibid.

别有師恩未易猜	a different sort of teacher's grace is not easy to guess.[84]

In the "*Fu* on Gaotang" ("Gaotang *fu*" 高唐賦) dated to the second century BCE, the King of Chu dreamed of the Goddess of the Wu Mountain making love to him and promising that she would be found under the Terrace of Light "every morning and every evening" as the "clouds of dawn" and the "passing rain."[85] In Zhang's poem, the phrase "every morning and every evening," taken verbatim from the poetic exposition, carries a sexual undertone.

No. 44 paints an equally derisive picture of nurses:

短榻縱橫臥病軀	Lying stretched on a short bed, a sick body
青衣小婢仗扶持	is taken care of by a little maid in dark clothes.
深情夜夜詢安否	Night after night, she inquires after his health with such affection,
浹骨淪肌報得無	her grace penetrates skin and bones—how could one ever repay?[86]

Indeed, Zhang's "Bamboo Branch Songs on London" describe cleaning women and waitresses as well as female shopkeepers and telegraph office workers in explicitly sexual terms without exception. Not only that, but hotels, buses, street corners, and public parks are all portrayed as places for trysts and love-making. He wrote with a particular relish about the London Aquarium, "a gathering-place for prostitutes":

銷魂最是亞魁林	The most soul-melting place is the Yakuilin:
粉黛如梭看不清	women with rouge and powder come and go in haste, hard to take a good look at.
一盞槐痕通款曲	With one glass of *huaihen*, she expresses loving affection,
低聲溫鎊索黃金	saying in a low voice, "*Wen bang*," she presses you for gold.[87]

84. Zhang Zuyi, "Lundun zhuzhici," 10a, in Xu Shikai, *Guanzide zhai* 24. Wang Shenzhi and Wang Zijin, *Qingdai haiwai*, p. 217.

85. Yan Kejun, *Quan shanggu sandai wen* 10.73.

86. Zhang Zuyi, "Lundun zhuzhici," 11a, in Xu Shikai, *Guanzide zhai* 24. Wang Shenzhi and Wang Zijin, *Qingdai haiwai*, p. 216.

87. Zhang Zuyi, "Lundun zhuzhici," 8b, in Xu Shikai, *Guanzide zhai* 24. Wang Shenzhi and Wang Zijin, *Qingdai haiwai*, p. 214.

The poem uses transliterations for English words: Yakuilin for Aquarium, *huaihen* for wine, and *wen bang* for one pound. It is certainly not because these words cannot be translated into Chinese, but because Zhang intends to add an exotic flavor to the poem. Without such foreign words, there would be nothing to distinguish such a scene from what one might encounter in Beijing, Tianjin, Chengdu, or any other Chinese city. Zhang himself must have been well acquainted with Chinese brothels, and he apparently paid visits to brothels in London and Paris as well, for this poem is followed by a lengthy note that recounts the various "phases" of being with a prostitute and their costs. The "heaven or hell" paradigm continues throughout, as Zhang wonders if one should consider a night spent with a London prostitute as "a land of sweet romance" (*wenrouxiang* 溫柔鄉) or "the kingdom of yakṣas" (*yecha guo* 夜叉國), and called a black prostitute in the French brothel "a true yakṣas" (*zhen yecha* 真夜叉), yakṣas being the term for a human-flesh-devouring demon in the Buddhist texts.

Zhang Zuyi's description calls to mind the "eroticization" of the non-Western world in Western colonial discourse. Although the backdrop is not exactly the same, the observations of the nineteenth-century Chinese travel accounts echo, in some ways, the observations of Westerners who traveled to colonized lands. One is tempted to cite David Spurr in his discussion of V.S. Naipaul's impressions of Africa: "My purpose is not to argue the correctness of Naipaul's impressions of African society—which in any case are of dubious values—but rather to consider the effect of these impressions on his audience and their place within a history of interpretation that defines the non-Western world *in visions of excess, as an uncharted, undivided territory of death and sensuality*" (italics mine).[88] If we substitute "Naipaul's impressions of African society" with "Zhang Zuyi's impressions of British society" and "the non-Western world" with "the Western world," we will get a more or less accurate description of this Qing Chinese traveler's impressions of London.

Prostitution in Victorian England was considered "the Great Social Evil" and was a topic of considerable contemporary interest.[89] My concern

88. Spurr, *The Rhetoric of Empire*, p. 182.

89. Interested readers should refer to Judith R. Walkowitz's study, *Prostitution and Victorian Society*.

here is not, however, about the actual number of "fallen women" walking the London streets in the Victorian era, but about the eroticized representation of women, "fallen" or otherwise, that is so prominent in Zhang Zuyi's bamboo branch songs. Of the ninety-nine quatrains, nearly half of them are about women, sexuality, and marriage customs. The series begins with several poems about none other than Queen Victoria herself, who is referred to as "kuiyin" 魁陰, an ingenious transliteration of "queen" that means the "leader of *yin*" in Chinese. In a poem composed upon Queen Victoria's Golden Jubilee celebration, Zhang derisively says of the Queen, "She was a beauty fifty years ago."[90] He also ridicules the Scottish courtiers for wearing kilts when being received by the Queen:

露膝更無臣子禮	Exposing their knees is no manners for a subject;
何妨裸體入王宮	why not simply enter the royal palace stark naked?[91]

Even funeral customs become an occasion for making pointed remarks about the immorality of English society, as Zhang Zuyi snickers at the custom of sending flower wreaths to the funeral as "'lusting after flowers' [i.e., pursuing women] even in death."[92]

In his diary entry for the fourteenth day of the ninth month of the seventh year of the Tongzhi era (October 29, 1868), Zhang Deyi recorded that he had heard many couples conducted their illicit love affairs in the public parks of London. He wonders:

> Although the gas lights are bright, it is always foggy at night. Is this caused by the rampant lascivious customs, so that heaven blocks its light as a warning? Or is this because the city is close to the ocean and the steam [from the ocean] causes the fog? I do not know the answer.[93]

氣燈雖亮，而入夜永系霧氣彌漫，不知淫風流行而天光蒙蔽，以示儆耶？抑或因地近海洋，而蒸汽使然耶？不可得而知也.

90. Zhang Zuyi, "Lundun zhuzhici," 1b, in Xu Shikai, *Guanzide zhai* 24. Wang Shenzhi and Wang Zijin, *Qingdai haiwai*, p. 207.

91. Zhang Zuyi, "Lundun zhuzhici," 2b, in Xu Shikai, *Guanzide zhai* 24. Wang Shenzhi and Wang Zijin, *Qingdai haiwai*, p. 208.

92. Zhang Zuyi, "Lundun zhuzhici," 11b, in Xu Shikai, *Guanzide zhai* 24. Wang Shenzhi and Wang Zijin, *Qingdai haiwai*, p. 217.

93. Zhang Deyi, *Ou Mei huanyou ji*, p. 708.

In Zhang Deyi's writings, London is configured as an eroticized space from the top down, where desire is rampant, uncontrolled, and overwhelming.

Such eroticization of foreign lands is not limited to writings about Western countries. A set of "Bamboo Branch Songs on the Local Customs of Japan" ("Dongyang fengtu zhuzhici" 東洋風土竹枝詞), written by a southern Chinese merchant under the name "Traveler on a Drifting Raft from Siming" (*Siming fuchake* 四明浮槎客) in the mid-1870s, contain many poems that disparage Japanese mores, particularly those regarding sex and gender.[94] Poems Nos. 23 and 82 denounce levirate marriage; the prose note appended to No. 23 exclaims contemptuously: "This is why the Japs are Japs" (*Ci Wonu zhisuoyi wei Wonu ye* 此倭奴之所以爲倭奴也). Nos. 72 and 73 express a sense of horror at the idea of a masseur performing massage on a woman, calling it a "lascivious custom." The author also maligns the Japanese dress code:

不穿褲子兩便當	They don't wear trousers—how convenient for both parties;
內系猩紅帕一方	underneath her skirt, the woman ties around a crimson kerchief.
好是衣裳風揭起	As a wind blows open her clothes,
愛他兩股白如霜	how one loves those thighs as white as frost.[95]

In his "Poems on Miscellaneous Subjects from Japan" ("Riben zashi shi" 日本雜事詩), written between 1877 and 1882 and subsequently revised and reprinted several times, Huang Zunxian wrote about the same topic, but he appended an erudite note tracing the history of trousers in China, arguing that the Chinese, too, wore no trousers in the antiquity and so there was nothing shocking about the Japanese sartorial custom. Huang's poem has a different focus from the poem cited above:

---

94. The author is otherwise unknown. A preface, dated the eleventh year of the Guangxu era (1885), was penned by an equally unknown figure under the pseudonym Loudong waishi 婁東外史. Siming is Ningbo 寧波; Loudong refers to Taicang 太倉 of Jiangsu 江蘇. The author had apparently received a low level of literary education and was a trader doing business in Japan. One of the poems mentions the death of the Tongzhi emperor (in early 1875), which indicates the author was in Japan in the mid-1870s. Wang Shenzhi and Wang Zijin, *Qingdai haiwai*, pp. 170–91.

95. Wang Shenzhi and Wang Zijin, *Qingdai haiwai*, p. 186.

六尺湘裙貼地拖	Six feet of *xiang* silk skirt trails on the ground;
折腰相對舞回波	she bends her waist toward the audience in a "whirling" dance.
偶然風漾中單露	Occasionally a wind blows, revealing her undergarment;
酒暈無端上頰渦	a tipsy blush, for no reason at all, appears on her cheeks.[96]

Huang Zunxian's poem appears to be more decorous, as it focuses on the Japanese female dancer's embarrassment rather than on the male onlooker's erotic gaze. And yet, in both cases the poet notices something "different" and "strange" in the foreign land, and tries to contain his sense of "shock and horror" (*jingguai* 驚怪), a phrase Huang uses in his note, by expressing it in verse—and in Huang's case also by rationalizing it in a scholarly note. The modern scholar and writer Zhou Zuoren comments that Siming fuchake "often set his eyes on such phenomenon as nakedness and bathing, for his mind was not clean, and as a result he saw unclean things."[97] It is remarkable how Zhou Zuoren's comment reiterates the early medieval belief that "what you are determines what you see."

In a way, Zhou Zuoren was quite right in calling attention to the psychological implications of the poems, which seem to be a projection of the poet's own fear about desire running amok. It is also noteworthy that the outcries about moral decrepitude in foreign countries are almost exclusively focused on the female body—from improper attire to its public presence—and on the danger of unchecked female sexuality. The eroticization of the Other is not restricted to the Western colonial discourse. The examples cited in this section demonstrate a negative eroticization by way of emphasizing, exaggerating, and dramatizing the sexual depravity perceived by the Chinese travelers in foreign countries. This is the darker side of late Qing Occidentalism that "typically represented the West by the image of a spirited, educated, and independent (if sometimes unruly, immodest, and overbearing) woman" as in Wang Tao's travel fiction, though it equally exemplifies what Emma Teng describes as the "fundamental adoption of 'woman'

96. Ibid., p. 144.
97. Ibid., p. 191.

as a flexible sign of difference, one that could index either the allure or the moral degradation of the other society."[98]

The threat posed by the Other is often mapped onto a sense of insecurity felt by the masculine sex in a power struggle with the feminine. This sense of insecurity drove Zhang Deyi to repeatedly record incidents of mistaken sexual identity, as if he felt an urgency to affirm his masculinity by the very act of writing. He also recorded several incidents in which he repudiated what he considered inappropriate remarks regarding women and sex. The first such incident occurred at Helsinki, also known as Helsingfors in Swedish (transliterated as Hanxingfo 漢興佛), then a part of the Russian Empire. Speaking to two elderly women in a public park, Zhang was approached by a man who teased him and called him "unlucky" for having to converse with elderly ladies instead of pretty young women. Zhang "smiled without saying a word." The man went on to ask him: "Don't you love girls?" To this Zhang gave a long-winded reply:

> Love is a human emotion. Love between man and woman is the uttermost emotion of human beings. But we prize the kind of love that does not deviate from the proper path. Within the four seas, all are brothers and sisters, and all the women in the world are no different from our sisters, so why indeed cannot I extend my love to them? But we are still young, our cultivation of character is not yet complete, and our willpower is not yet strong. How can we trust ourselves in such matters? It is far better not to have desire, so as not to give rise to love. Moreover, after parting we will each be in different places of the world, so what's the point of taking advantage of this momentary encounter and considering it fortunate? The reason why I speak to the elders is because I am a Chinese and we feel that to elderly and virtuous people we can speak of whatever is on our mind without inhibition. Do you understand this?

According to Zhang, the man was "embarrassed, apologized and left. Later I asked about him, and it turned out that he was an American traveling from Sweden whose name was Chalisi [Charles]."[99]

It is dubious whether Zhang Deyi could articulate his views so eloquently in English at that point of his life. More interesting are the con-

98. Teng, "The West as a 'Kingdom of Women,'" pp. 118, 120.

99. Zhang Deyi, *Hanghai shuqi*, pp. 549–50. This is in the entry for the third day of the sixth month of the fifth year of the Tongzhi era (July 14, 1866).

fused sentiments that come out in the lengthy speech carefully recorded in his diary, which is unusual because he had generally left out conversations. His didactic speech to the American tourist seemed to be directed more at himself and to his readers back home.

Another incident took place in a public park in Berlin. Zhang and the others went to a park "where there were many famous courtesans." He claimed that "several courtesans slowly approached us, striking all kinds of alluring poses, but we paid no heed to them." He did, however, notice their charms: "Their cherry lips were half open; their willow waists were slender. They were like flowers but could talk; they were like jade, but were more fragrant." After a British tourist teased him about his rigidity, Zhang launched into a discourse on how Europe had the greatest number of prostitutes in the world, and how he had heard that European men "reportedly must sleep with prostitutes when they reach the age of twenty." He congratulated himself on a narrow escape: "Fortunately I and the others were sitting upstairs with Messier Bin this evening, so not too many people saw us; otherwise we might have been trapped by them. So we hurried back to our hotel."[100]

Both incidents are recorded to have happened during Zhang's first overseas trip when he was only nineteen years old. Desire, self-denial, and self-glorification are all present in these comical everyday dramas in which Zhang Deyi stars as the chaste hero. Zhang plays his literary game particularly well in narrating the second incident, which structurally mimics early poetic expositions on seduction and the resistance of temptation.[101] In those poetic expositions, the description of female charm is an important element, because it serves as a foil for the male protagonist's extraordinary moral integrity. The two tourists who had supposedly tried to talk Zhang into enjoying himself and both conveniently spoke English also

100. Ibid., p. 564. This is in the entry for the fourteenth day of the sixth month (July 25, 1866).

101. See, for instance, "*Fu* on Remonstrance" ("Feng fu" 諷賦), attributed to Song Yu 宋玉 (fl. third century BCE), in Yan Kejun, *Quan shanggu sandai wen* 10.72–73; Sima Xiangru, "*Fu* on a Beauty" ("Meiren fu" 美人賦), in Yan Kejun, *Quan Han wen* 22.245.

fulfill a rhetorical function, since their questions and Zhang's answers evoke the literary form of "responses to questions" (*duiwen* 對問), an imaginary dialogue in which an interlocutor, usually a guest (*ke* 客), criticizes the author/host (*zhu* 主) and allows the author to defend his position. The difference is that Zhang Deyi himself was a guest (*ke*) in a foreign country, and he was trying to maintain the sense of a *zhu*—a subject and master—who was emphatically different from the foreigners who almost "trapped" him.

The apprehension about mixed gender company and loose morals in the West is sometimes intertwined with comical cultural misunderstandings, such as Zhang Deyi's mistaking the *droit de seigneur* (or the "right of the first night") for the local official's verification of a woman's virginity on her wedding day. Zhang believed that the abolishment of this law had led to the present state of affairs—that the bridegroom had no way of telling whether his bride was a virgin or not.[102] Back at home, however, boundaries were reestablished. The late Qing printed edition of Bin Chun's diary excised a large amount of material from the original text, most of which were records of Bin Chun's interactions with Western women. For instance, one diary entry notes that he paid a visit to a "Mr. Ye and his wife" (*Ye xing ji furen* 也姓及夫人); the later edition simply removed "and his wife."[103] Numerous remarks about female presence on social occasions were deleted this way, which seems to be an editorial decision made by the publisher rather than by Bin Chun himself. Gender segregation was thus performed on a textual level, and women were edited out of the social scene.

---

102. Zhang Deyi, *Ou Mei huanyou ji*, p. 739. This is in the entry for the twenty-fourth day of the twelfth month of the seventh year of the Tongzhi era (February 5, 1869).

103. Bin Chun, *Chengcha biji*, p. 118. This is in the entry for the twenty-seventh day of the fourth month of the fifth year of the Tongzhi era (June 9, 1866).

Mapping the Modern City

> Near to that part of the Thames on which the church at Rotherhithe abuts,[104] where the buildings on the banks are dirtiest and the vessels on the river blackest with the dust of colliers and the smoke of close-built low-roofed houses, there exists the filthiest, the strangest, the most extraordinary of the many localities that are hidden in London, wholly unknown, even by name, to the great mass of its inhabitants. To reach this place, the visitor has to penetrate through a maze of close, narrow, and muddy streets, thronged by the roughest and poorest of waterside people, and devoted to the traffic they may be supposed to occasion.
>
> —Charles Dickens, *Oliver Twist*

In contrast to the author of the "Bamboo Branch Songs on London" who was writing in the 1880s, earlier Chinese travelers were much more complementary in their accounts of the West. Wang Tao's verbal diagram ranks various regions and countries on a sliding scale: it begins with Hong Kong, which Wang found "unbearable" upon first arrival, and ends with the earthly paradise of Paris and London. Similarly, Bin Chun and Zhang Deyi's sense of wonder upon reaching Paris and London could only be paralleled by Marco Polo's amazement at the splendors of the paradisial East. Bin Chun used comparison as a rhetorical strategy and gave increasingly fantastic accounts of Marseille, Leon, and Paris. The steady geographical progress marks a process of gradually entering paradise:

[Marseilles] The streets and marketplaces are prosperous. All buildings are six or seven stories high. Carved railings and painted window screens reach to the clouds. At night gaslights are turned on and shine as bright as day, and there is no need for candles when one goes out. I hear that there are 500,000 residents in the city. Streets and alleys connect with one another, and the lights in the markets and shops are as dense as stars. Even the lights on the Lantern Festival at other places are not as numerous as these."

104. Rotherhithe is a port and a shipyard located on the south bank of the Thames in the southeast of London.

街市繁盛，樓宇皆六七層，雕欄畫檻，高列雲霄。至夜則煤氣燃燈，光明如晝，夜游無須秉燭。聞居民五十萬人，街巷相聯，市肆燈火密如繁星。他處元夕無此盛且多也。

[Leon] Lights fill up streets and shine as bright as day. The prosperity and splendor are twice as great as that of Marseilles.

燈火滿街，照耀如晝，繁盛倍于馬塞矣。

[Paris] The streets and marketplaces are prosperous and the city is grand, even more so than Leon. I hear that Leon has 600,000 people while the capital city has more than a million. . . . There is the sound of coaches rumbling, and the pedestrians are as numerous as ants, and yet they are all quiet and orderly and make no noise. At night the lights are as bright as day.[105]

街市繁華，氣局闊大，又勝于里昂。聞里昂人民六十萬，都城則百餘萬……車聲鄰鄰，行人如蟻，皆安靜無嘩。夜則燈火通明如晝。

Zhang Deyi expressed no less amazement about Paris: "Every morning is like a fiesta, and every night is like the Lantern Festival. It makes one marvel endlessly."[106] Zhang was a keen observer who was attentive to details, but when he tried to convey his general impression of a city, he frequently relied on established tropes. The saying that "Every morning is like a fiesta and every night is like the Lantern Festival" is, for instance, a stereotypical phrase. His description of Paris on his second visit two years later attests to the power of linguistic tropes even more clearly, as he repeats Bin Chun almost verbatim.

The streets and markets are prosperous, the buildings and terraces are tall and splendid, *and the city is grand. Day and night there is the sound of coaches rumbling, the pedestrians are as numerous as ants*, they are all tidy and neat in appearance, *quiet and orderly and make no noise*. Even drunks rarely burst into songs [italics mine].[107]

---

105. See the entries for the eighteenth, twentieth, and twenty-third days of the third month of the fifth year of the Tongzhi era (May 2, 4, and 7, 1866). Bin Chun, *Chengcha biji*, pp. 107–9.

106. Zhang Deyi, *Hanghai shuqi*, p. 490. This is in the entry for the twenty-third day of the third month of the fifth year of the Tongzhi era (May 7, 1866).

107. Zhang Deyi, *Ou Mei huanyou ji*, p. 727. This is in the entry for the twenty-first day of the eleventh month of the seventh year of the Tongzhi era (January 3, 1869).

街市繁華，樓臺峻麗，氣局闊大，晝夜車聲粼粼，行人如蟻，衣履修整，安靜無嘩，醉人亦鮮有歌唱者。

The last sentence offers an interesting detail that is meant to corroborate the foregoing statement rather than problematize it.

The introduction of "drunks" into paradise and the qualification of the statement ("rarely. . . .") cast a shadow on the Edenic discourse. As Zhang Deyi became a more frequent visitor to the European cities, he seemed to be better able to see them in shades of gray, although a lengthy stay was no guarantee for a true coming to terms with the human dimension of the Western world. After all, despite staying in England for two years, Wang Tao still sported an idealized view of the English society:

> The social customs of England are pure and good, and the material products rich and numerous. . . . Particularly enviable is the fact that people are modest and defer to one another, and that their hearts are honest and sincere. There is very little fighting and bullying in the mutual dealings of the gentry and commoners in the country. Foreign visitors are never harassed or cheated, but are treated with kindness and affection. There is very little suspicion and distrust. Be it in the Central Land or other foreign nations, I have rarely seen such customs and mores.[108]

英國風俗醇厚，物產蕃庶……尤可羡者，人知遜讓，心多慤誠。國中士庶往來，常少斗爭欺侮之事。異域客民族居其地者，從無受欺被詐，恆見親愛，絶少猜嫌。無論中土，外邦之風俗尚有如此者，吾見亦罕矣。

The contemporary British public, had they had chance to read this passage, would have found Wang's portrayal of their country quite unrecognizable. Befriended by James Legge and his family, Wang Tao was in a protected and privileged position from which he could afford to observe British society through a rosy looking glass. Just as "Marco's factual celebration of the East is the bright shadow of the West's own poverty and political factionalism, its famine and depopulation, its spiceless cookery and rigid sexual morality,"[109] Wang Tao's golden picture of a "pure and good" England was a projection of his own vision of a Utopia that had little to do with reality.

---

108. Wang Tao, *Manyou suilu*, pp. 111–12.
109. Campbell, *The Witness*, p. 111.

There was something else. The "heaven or hell" paradigm of seeing the foreign land was also a direct consequence of the segregation of social classes in the modern city. In 1844, Friedrich Engels wrote his well-known "The Condition of the Working Class in England" based on the sufferings of the underclass of Manchester, a great industrial city in the nineteenth century and a center for cotton processing. As this study points out,

> Owing to the curious lay-out of the town it is quite possible for someone to live for years in Manchester and to travel daily to and from his work without ever seeing a working-class quarter or coming into contact with an artisan. He who visits Manchester simply on business need never see the slums, mainly because the working-class districts and the middle-class districts are quite distinct. This division is due partly to deliberate policy and partly due to instinctive and tacit agreement of the two groups.[110]

Engels' remarks are uncannily borne out in a Qing mandarin's account of Manchester. Bin Chun arrived in Manchester by train on the evening of June 9, 1866; his diary entry reads: "In the distance, one could see the numerous lights of the city like the dense stars in the sky." The next day he stayed in his hotel room writing what he had learned of the place: "I hear that . . . this city has a population of 500,000 with prosperous streets and markets. It is the second largest harbor in England." The following day he visited a cotton mill, which had about three thousand workers, and expressed amazement at the speed with which cloth was woven from cotton and dyed. That evening, the younger members of his entourage, including Zhang Deyi, were invited to go to a park—it turned out to be the Belle Vue Gardens managed by John Jennison (1793–1869), transliterated rather ingeniously by Zhang as Bailiyou 百里游 (Roaming of a Hundred Miles)—and see its famous firework displays.[111] They came back around midnight, recounting to Bin Chun the "wondrous marvel of the fire-

110. Engels, "The Condition of the Working-Class in England in 1844," in *Engels: Selected Writings*, p. 27.

111. For the rise and fall of this famous garden/zoo/amusement park, see Nicholls, *The Belle Vue Story*.

works."[112] Zhang Deyi's diary entry gives a more detailed account of the firework show, calling it "something I truly have never seen before." He also recorded with admiration their visit to the local cotton mill, bank (housed in a "richly splendid" mansion), and court, and a shopping center in a five-storied building.[113] Bin Chun and his followers certainly never saw the poverty, the degradation, or the miserable, unsanitary working and living conditions of the Manchester working class. What they saw, as important overseas visitors, was the glossy side of things, the glittering surface.

We cannot ascertain the whereabouts of the Manchester hotel where the first Chinese delegation stayed or the cotton mill and bank they visited, but we know much more about their itinerary in London, thanks to the details provided by Zhang Deyi. Upon arriving in London on May 15, 1866, they stayed at the Dartmouth House, an impressive-looking town mansion located on Charles Street in the Haymarket area.[114] Charles Street is to the west of Regent Street and north of Piccadilly and St. James's Park, which is the oldest of the London royal parks and at the very heart of the nation's capital. It is close to all the fashionable haunts on Grosvenor Square, Bond Street, St. James Street, and Pall Mall. They were taken to see the Crystal Palace as soon as they arrived; on the following day, Edward Bowra invited Zhang to visit the Epsom Downs Racecourse and see the Epsom Derby. The identifiable places visited by the delegation include the British Library, the British Museum, the zoo in the Regent's Park, St. Paul's Cathedral, the Queen's Theatre, the London Tower, the

---

112. Bin Chun, *Chengcha biji*, p. 119. See the diary entries for the twenty-seventh, twenty-eighth, and twenty-ninth days of the fourth month of the fifth year of the Tongzhi era.

113. Zhang Deyi, *Hanghai shuqi*, pp. 529–30.

114. See the diary entry for the second day of the fourth month of the fifth year of the Tongzhi era. Zhang Deyi, *Hanghai shuqi*, p. 501. Zhang transliterated the name of Charles Street to Cha'er jie 茶餌街, and translated Haymarket as Caochang 草廠. Bin Chun also mentioned the name of the street as Cha'ersi si-te-li-te 叉耳思思忒力忒, though the modern edition mistakenly prints Cha'ersi as Yi'ersi 义耳思, *cha* 叉 and *yi* 义 looking very much alike. See Bin Chun, *Chengcha biji*, p. 120. The address of the Dartmouth House is 37 Charles Street. Remodeled and refurbished by Lord Revelstroke in the 1890s, it was bought by the English Speaking Union in the 1920s. Today it is considered a heritage building that is often rented for weddings, conferences, and other public occasions.

Westminster Abbey, the Parliament, Windsor Castle, and Buckingham Palace.

Zhang's second stay in London in the fall of 1868 was in a no less prestigious area. The Burlingame Mission was lodged in the Grosvenor Hotel adjacent to the Victoria Station, which had just been opened in 1862. The Grosvenor Hotel, described as the "No. 1 hotel in the English capital" and known as Thistle Victoria (still a four-star hotel) in modern days, is directly to the south of St. James's Park and within walking distance of Buckingham Palace and the House of Parliaments.[115] During this trip, it was decided that Zhang Deyi was to study English with a Mr. Ai-de-lin 艾德林 (which may have been transliterated from a name sounding like Eidlin), and Zhang thereupon moved in with his tutor, whose house he recorded as being on Bolingtan jie 柏靈坦街 (Burlington Street).[116] Old Burlington Street is not far from the hotel where Zhang stayed during his first visit to London; it is just to the west of Regent Street and located in the center of London's fashionable West End.

What does this all mean? In the words of Franco Moretti, who gives a brilliant analysis of the fictional geography of London in the nineteenth-century British novels, the London of the fashionable silver-fork novels flourishing between the 1820s and the 1840s was a "London as the West End": "This is not really a city: it's a class." The West End is the "first 'residential' area of the city, where inhabitants don't work (as they do in Gracechurch Street), but quite simply 'live.'"[117] Reading Bin Chun and Zhang Deyi's diaries, we are fascinated by the "level boulevards, flourishing parks and groves, neat alleys and lanes, and prosperous markets and shops" they saw in London.[118] We also realize that their sightseeing was largely limited to the west of Regent Street, which constituted the boundary to the shiny world of the silver-fork novels. We might very well ask, as

---

115. See the diary entry for the fourth day of the eighth month of the seventh year of the Tongzhi era (September 19, 1868). Zhang Deyi, *Ou Mei huanyou ji*, p. 697.

116. Zhang described "Bolingtan" as being "to the north of Hyde Park." In fact, Burlington Street is to the north of St. James's Park and to the east of Hyde Park. Zhang described the Regent's Park as being to the north of Bolingtan jie, which confirms that "Bolingtan" was indeed "Burlington Street." Zhang Deyi, *Ou Mei huanyou ji*, pp. 708–9.

117. Moretti, *Atlas of the European Novel*, p. 79.

118. Zhang Deyi, *Hanghai shuqi*, p. 501.

Moretti does, "But the rest of London? What is there, *what kind of stories* are there, east of Regent Street?"[119]

The answer can hardly be found in the Qing Chinese travelers' accounts. Their movement was confined within one particular social space, which belonged to the class of leisure and means. During his first visit to England, Zhang Deyi rarely went beyond the West End except for a trip to St. Paul's Cathedral near Cheapside, the neighborhood much scorned by the London elite in Jane Austen's *Pride and Prejudice*.[120] But when Zhang Deyi was in St. Paul's, he looked outward at London in the distance, and all he saw was the "towering height of the palaces, the majesty of the city, the prosperity of the markets, and the density of the population" 宮殿之巍峨，城池之雄壯，市廛之繁雜，人煙之稠密.[121] While staying with his tutor at Burlington Street, he thus described the West End and the city:

> This place is in the southwest of the newer part of the town (as there is an old part of London). There are few marketplaces but many residents. The houses are neat and sumptuous, neither narrow nor cramped; the buildings are like beehives, and there is no knowing how many hundreds of thousands apartments there are. The streets are wide and lined with shady trees. Even in wind and rain, there is never any worry about noises and dust such as in base and low dwellings.[122]
>
> 此地系倫敦新城（倫敦城有新舊之别）之西南，市廛少而人煙多，房宇整齊，華而不陋，樓似蜂窠，不知幾千萬落。街道寬闊，樹木連陰，雖經風雨，永無湫溢囂塵之患矣。

There is not a trace about the "old part of the town"—the poverty-stricken blind alleys of the East End, the scenery of urban misery and squalor. Zhang Deyi was not completely unaware of the poor and the unemployed in London, but he painted a rosy picture of a nearly perfect society, with a sense of wide-eyed marvel and amazement:

119. Moretti, *Atlas of the European Novel*, p. 83.

120. This is the famous, much quoted dialogue between Bingley and Darcy: "'If they had uncles enough to fill all Cheapside,' cried Bingley, 'it would not make them one jot less agreeable.' 'But it must very materially lessen their chance of marrying men of any consideration in the world,' replied Darcy." *Pride and Prejudice*, 8.

121. Zhang Deyi, *Hanghai shuqi*, p. 511.

122. Zhang Deyi, *Ou Mei huanyou ji*, p. 710.

The population of London is just under three million, and the needs of their livelihood are vast and numerous. Even the poor must have seven or eight ounces of silver to make a daily living. And yet, there are about thirty to forty thousand people who do nothing every day. I do not know how they support themselves. Even so, there are no beggars on the streets, and in the wilds there are no robbers. There is not even one person walking with bare feet or exposed head.[123]

倫敦居民不足三百萬，日用浩繁，貧者一人每日亦必需七八錢銀始可度活。而每日有三四萬人，游手無事，不知可以得食。雖然，街無乞丐，野無強盜，跣足科頭者更無一人。

Zhang Deyi's depiction of Paris similarly never strayed far from the glittering surface. Only during his second trip, as part of the Burlingame Mission, did he catch a glimpse of the less glamorous side of the "capital of the nineteenth century," as he moved his gaze from the northwestern part of the city, the wealthy area that had become the city center after Georges-Eugène Haussmann's (1809–91) massive city-renovation project, to the southeast:

To the southeast of the French capital, there is a Shumeng Park. In the area near the park, the alleys are narrow and the dwellings are base. When it is windy, the wind blows up dust that blocks the view; when it rains, the roads become muddy and difficult to walk on. The residents are largely poor and miserable, and most of them have uncombed hair like prisoners and unwashed faces as if in mourning. All day long men and women make much noises and children cry or laugh. Compared with Champs Elysées, the Boulevard de la Madeleine and so forth, this is completely different.

法京東南有述夢園。近園一帶，閭巷狹窄，房屋鄙陋，風則揚塵蔽目，雨則泥濘難行。居民率皆貧苦。大半囚首喪面，終日男女喧嘩，孩童泣笑，較之凱歌路、馬達蘭等處，迥不相同矣。

I have not been able to identify this park in the southeastern part of nineteenth-century Paris. I suspect, however, that Zhang Deyi was referring to Parc des Buttes Chaumont, as "Chaumont" sounds close enough to "Shumeng" 述夢 (literally, "relating a dream"). Parc des Buttes Chaumont was created by Haussmann in 1867 to the northeast, not southeast, of Paris. It was in a working-class neighborhood. Before being converted into a public park, it had been used as public waste ground.

123. Ibid., p. 721.

Dust and noise—these are the two elements missing from Bin Chun and Zhang Deyi's earlier accounts of Paris that sing the praises of its quietness and orderliness, and yet they are the very elements that mark the human condition. In his later diary entries, Zhang Deyi recorded a riot of the "poor people" of Paris, an event that foreshadowed the Paris Commune of 1871.[124] Then, during a still later visit to Paris, Zhang was caught in the middle of the Paris Commune, and witnessed much of the chaos brought about by this violent political episode. His early impressions of the European cities were, however, largely set out in paradisial terms. It was all heaven and no hell.

Bin Chun and Zhang Deyi's narration is a function of the received schemata of seeing the foreign land; it is also a function of the mapping of the modern city, where heaven and hell are sometimes separated by just one street. It is easy to adopt a binary scheme and see the foreign world as either a land of bliss or a land of evil or both; but it remained a challenge for the nineteenth-century Chinese travelers to go beyond the binary scheme and understand the West in human, fallible terms, not as a land peopled with either immortals or demons. "To reach this place," to quote the words of Charles Dickens, the visitor has to penetrate through more than just "a maze of close, narrow, and muddy streets."

124. Zhang Deyi, *Ou Mei huanyou ji*, pp. 786–87. This is in the entry for the second day of the fifth month of the eighth year of the Tongzhi era (June 11, 1869).

CHAPTER FIVE

Poetry and Experience in the Nineteenth Century

> But save for *ow*! or *ouch*!—for groans of pain, grunts or cries of orgasm, gasps of fear, bellows of rage, sobs of grief, laughter of being tickled—which might conveniently be called unmediated expression of something felt, I would maintain that most of what is called expression is in fact representation. . . . The work of poetry is not to try to say what *ouch*! or Horace's *eheu* or the Greeks' *pheu*!—or *aiai* or *oh*, or *ah*, or *oi*—"say" so purely and authentically. Poetry can be what emerges through a complex structure of channels and falls and pools carefully contrived and yet yielding always to discoveries occasioned by the act of construction. What leaks out of the helpless agent is not poetry.
>
> —John Hollander, *The Work of Poetry*

Between 1847 and 1849, Lin Qian, a native of Fujian, undertook a trip to America as an interpreter. Upon returning to Xiamen, Fujian, Lin Qian composed a long poem in the five-syllable line entitled "A Poem Record of My Travels in the Western Seas." A lengthy prose account written in the highly stylized "parallel prose" (*pianti wen* 駢體文) and interspersed with notes in plain prose introduces the poem. He published his writings under the collective title, *A Draft Record of My Travels on the Western*

Seas (*Xihai jiyou cao* 西海紀游草).[1] In the twentieth century, Lin Qian's travel account has been cited as evidence that traditional poetic form can no longer adequately articulate modern experience and must therefore be replaced by "new poetry" (*xinshi* 新詩) or vernacular poetry (*baihua shi* 白話詩). Critics have contended that Lin Qian's poem uses so much conventional terminology to refer to foreign novelties that the reader has to rely on the parallel prose introduction to fully understand the meaning of the poem; even then, parallel prose fails to effectively explain the novelties, and as a result, notes in plain prose become necessary for comprehension.[2]

Such a critique tells an all-too-familiar story about the origin of modern vernacular poetry and can even be regarded as a summary statement of a large amount of scholarly literature, especially in Chinese, that seeks to justify the "replacement" of classical poetry by modern vernacular poetry. The very act of justification, however, bespeaks an anxiety on the part of scholars of modern vernacular poetry. Inherited from the May Fourth generation that first began writing poetry in the modern vernacular as part of a crusade against poetry in the traditional form, this anxiety has by now long outlived its usefulness. In recent years, the work of modern Chinese literature scholars has largely succeeded in dismantling, in Ellen Widmer's words, the "sometimes oversimplified categories of May Fourth," and a new theoretical model must now be put in place to adequately deal with the history of modern Chinese poetry.[3] This is a particularly urgent task, since poetry in the traditional form, far from vanishing into thin air, continues to be written and read by a large number of people in Chinese communities

---

1. The printed version of *A Draft Record* includes two other items: an account of how, when in America, Lin Qian helped twenty-six Cantonese traders duped by a British human trafficker, and a biography of his grandmother. The printed edition also has a plethora of prefaces, colophons, and poems celebrating Lin Qian's travels; their dates range from 1849 to 1866, the year in which Bin Chun embarked on his voyage. *A Draft Record* is reprinted in Zhong Shuhe, *Zouxiang shijie congshu*, Vol. 1, pp. 25–59. For a translation and study of the account, see Eggert, "Discovered Other, Recovered Self."

2. See, for instance, Lin Gang, "Haiwai jingyan."

3. Widmer, "Foreign Travel through a Woman's Eyes," p. 787. See, for instance, David Wang's book, *Fin-de-siècle Splendor*, which effectively rebuts the May Fourth paradigm of modern Chinese literature. More recently, Theodore Huters' *Bringing the World Home* shows how the post-1919 radicalism obscured the contributions made during the unique period between 1895 and 1919.

across the world.[4] As both poetry in the traditional form and poetry in the modern vernacular are flourishing, it is imperative for scholars to consider the two in relation to each other rather than as two separate forms. For it is only when we view the two forms side by side that we can reflect on how such a coexistence affects both forms in modern and postmodern life.

In this chapter, my primary concern is with an implicit assumption about the nature of poetry and poetic language as demonstrated in the critique of traditional poetic form. This implicit assumption can be traced back to a canonical statement in traditional Chinese literary discourse: "Language is to be adequate to what is on the person's mind" (*yan yi zu zhi* 言以足志).[5] Sometimes, in the critique of traditional poetic form, a simple correspondence of language to objects and phenomena (for example, finding terms for modern inventions such as photography or the telegraph) is related to, and somewhat confused with, the question of the adequacy of classical poetic language to express one's emotional experience, a much more complex and much less black-and-white issue. We may ask, for instance, what is considered "adequate" and who is to be the judge? Furthermore, since we can only know of the poet's "experience" through his writings, who are we to say that the poet has failed to convey his "experience" through his poetry?

There are, of course, simpler ways of reconsidering the argument against traditional poetic form. Let me begin with the issue of genre. Lin Qian's account in parallel prose is similar to a poetic exposition or *fu*.[6] By the nineteenth century, providing a commentary on one's own poetic exposition had become a long-standing tradition in Chinese literary history, with the first writer to do so being none other than Xie Lingyun. It was also quite common for a poet to append short explanatory notes to his own poems, a practice that began as early as in the Tang. For a premodern Chinese reader, it was nothing unusual to read a poem with notes added by the poet between the lines. Classical poems can also have extensive narrative titles that sometimes run longer than the poems themselves, or lengthy prefaces that can stand alone as independent literary composi-

4. See Tian, "Muffled Dialect Spoken by Green Fruits."

5. This remark is attributed to Confucius. *Chunqiu Zuozhuan zhengyi*, the twenty-fifth year of Duke Xiang, 29.623.

6. See You Jingxian, "Yuejie yu youyi," p. 108.

tions; in fact, some prefaces are better known than the poems they precede. What critics construe as the failure of classical poetic language or of parallel prose is therefore no more than a continuation of generic conventions.

Something else is at stake here, and it is something much more important than proving the continuity of literary tradition. A poem and all its prosaic elements, from chatty title and lengthy preface to exuberant notes, were treated as a whole in traditional literary discourse, and the prosaic elements were never singled out as problematic. If it was accepted in the Chinese literary tradition that sometimes a poem must be accompanied by notes to make it more comprehensible to its contemporary and future readers, then the function of poetry could not possibly be limited to just the articulation of experience. One obvious question to ask about Lin Qian's *A Draft Record* would be: why did Lin Qian feel the need to relate his experience of America three times—once in parallel prose, once in poetry, and once in a plain prose record? If the articulation of experience had been his sole purpose, why could not a straightforward prose account suffice? What does poetry do in such a case? Was Lin Qian simply trying to reassure the reader of the "literary values" of his work and claim his place "at the core of his cultural tradition: *wen*," as Marion Eggert suggests?[7] If so, why is it that the highly stylized parallel prose alone could not satisfactorily perform the "function of literary embellishment"? And was not prose, especially plain classical prose (*guwen* 古文), at the core of "his cultural tradition" as much as poetry, and indeed considered by many late imperial literati members under the influence of neo-Confucianism to be better able to embody the Way than poetry? We must ask these questions because, as Cheng Yu-yu observes in her article on Huang Zunxian's poetry about Japan, "we cannot just discuss the modern things described by Huang Zunxian without examining the medium of his description or investigating his reason for choosing that medium."[8]

In this chapter, I argue that the genre of classical *shi* poetry shows an elasticity of functionality that can shed light on the nature of poetry in general. Nineteenth-century poems about overseas experience are particularly revealing in this aspect, because in visiting foreign lands far beyond their traditional sphere of movement, Chinese travelers came into a violent en-

7. Eggert, "Discovered Other, Recovered Self," p. 78.
8. Cheng Yu-yu, "Jiushiyu de dili chidu," p. 253.

counter with the world. The interplay of prosaic and poetic languages, genre, and experience becomes more complicated, more fraught with problems that would have otherwise been concealed from plain view, and more inventive.

Tension between Prose and Verse, or: Fear and Loathing in London

Explanatory notes appended to a poem are generally brief. They are subservient to the poem and assist the reader in grasping its meanings. Zhang Zuyi's "Bamboo Branch Songs on London" turn out to be quite different. In this series, the short poems and their lengthy notes form a sharp contrast in content and tone, creating an odd collocation that mirrors the author's ambivalent attitude toward the foreign land.[9]

Poem No. 57 is about tap water, a novel phenomenon for the nineteenth-century Chinese traveler.[10] The note reads:

> From large families to small households, people all use "water that comes of itself" for drinking and washing. The method is like this: a machine is placed by the river that draws the water up; then small iron pipes are buried underground or within the walls and take the river water to all households day and night. The river water is purified with some mechanical means, so it becomes unusually clean. A very low monthly fee is collected [from each household] for using the water.
>
> 大家小户飲濯皆用自來水，其法於江畔造一機器，吸而上之，復以小鐵管埋入地中或牆腹，達於各户，晝夜不竭。皆用機法瀝去渣滓，倍常清潔，每月收費也甚輕。

The note is descriptive in nature and neutral in tone. One even detects some admiration for the invention, which makes "unusually clean" water

9. A few years earlier, Huang Zunxian published his "Riben zashishi" 日本雜事詩, which included 154 quatrains with copious notes. Unlike Huang Zunxian, Zhang Zuyi rarely used complex learned allusions in his poems, but rather adhered to the conventions of "bamboo branch songs," which exhibit a more colloquial and "folksy" style. It is significant that Huang did not name his poem series "Bamboo Branch Songs on Japan." For an excellent study of Huang's "Riben zashi shi," see Cheng Yu-yu, "Jiushiyu de dili chidu."

10. Zhang Zuyi, "Lundun zhuzhici," 14b, in Xu Shikai, *Guanzide zhai* 24; Wang Shenzhi and Wang Zijin, *Qingdai haiwai*, p. 220.

for "very low" cost. The poem begins innocently enough, but ends with a surprisingly condemning judgment:

水管縱橫達滿城	Water pipes, horizontal and vertical, spread all over the city,
竟將甘露潤蒼生	drawing sweet dews to nourish the common people.
西江吸盡終何盤	Though the Western River is sucked dry, what good does it do?
穢俗由來洗不清	Their filthy customs can never be washed clean.[11]

The benefit of technology sketched out in the note is unexpectedly discredited by the moral decay of the society introduced in the poem.

The rhetorical strategy of contrast and shock is regularly deployed in Zhang's "Bamboo Branch Songs on London." In poem No. 60 describing the London zoo, the note appended to the poem is marked by a sense of wonder:[12]

There is a Garden of Ten Thousand Creatures that is several miles in circumferences and keeps all sorts of precious birds and strange animals. There are truly creatures that are not recorded in the *Classic of Mountains and Seas* or the *Erya*. One wonders where they were obtained.

有萬生園蓄各種珍禽異獸，周圍可數里，眞有山海經、爾雅所不載者，不知其何處得來也。

The poem again proceeds to turn that sense of wonder into an expression of disgust:

黃獅白象紫峰駝	Yellow lions, white elephants, camels with purple humps:
怪獸珍禽盡網羅	all strange animals and precious birds are captured here in the park.
都道倫敦風景好	Everyone says that London's fine;
原來人少畜生多	the truth is they have few human beings and many beasts.

11. The last couplet is based on a common saying, which appears in many variant forms but basically goes like this: "Even if using up the water of the entire Western River, / one can never wash away the shame one suffers." There are several major rivers named "Western River" in China; here the poet refers to the Thames, which of course is a "river in the West."

12. Zhang Zuyi, "Lundun zhuzhici," 15a, in Xu Shikai, *Guanzide zhai* 24. Wang Shenzhi and Wang Zijin, *Qingdai haiwai*, p. 220–21.

The rhetorical power of the last couplet comes from the evocation of the famous opening lines of Wei Zhuang's 韋莊 (ca. 836–910) *ci* lyric to the tune "Bodhisattva Barbarian" ("Pusa man" 菩薩蠻): "Everyone says that the Southland's fine, / in the South the traveler should stay till he's old and gray" 人人都道江南好，遊人只合江南老.[13] It leads the reader to expect a positive resolution and thereby intensifies the shocking effect of the last line.

The note to No. 58 describes a "machine factory":[14]

The machine factory is incomparably huge. All things, from big to small, can be produced by machines. The subtlety and profundity cannot be related in detail except by those who are deeply knowledgeable about its principles. Those Chinese who boast of understanding the machines are all lying. For when it comes to their learning, even as minor as one craft, one must study it continuously for a dozen years before one can grasp its essence and understand its advantages and disadvantages. If a Chinese calls himself an expert just because he has seen the machine wheels turn, picks up bits and pieces of their knowledge to make a book out of it, glides over the surface without sounding the depths and boasts of his extraordinary talent—and is actually considered an extraordinary talent by others—alas, that will make matters truly impossible.

機器廠其大無比，凡制造大小各物，無不有機器成之。精微奧妙，非深造者莫能細述。中國人自栩爲通曉機器者，皆欺人之語。彼其學雖一藝之微，亦非寢饋十數年不能得其要領，悉其利弊。若但見其機輪旋轉，便自命行家，竊取牙慧著爲論說，東塗西抹，奇才自負，人亦遂以奇才目之，嗚呼難矣。

In this note, the poet expresses open approval of the "subtlety and profundity" of the Western technology. The poem, however, metes out a judgment that undermines the approving tone:

爐錘水火奪天工	Furnace and hammer, water and fire, outdo Nature's art;
鐵屋迴環復道通	the house of iron winds along, connected by double passageways.

13. Wei Zhuang, *Wei Zhuang ji jianzhu*, p. 410.

14. Zhang Zuyi, "Lundun zhuzhici," 14b–15a, in Xu Shikai, *Guanzide zhai* 24; Wang Shenzhi and Wang Zijin, *Qingdai haiwai*, p. 220.

十丈輪回終日轉	The hundred-feet wheel of transmigration turns round and round all day long,
總難跳出鬼途中	but it is ever impossible to leap outside the path of ghosts and demons.

The poem presents a quintessentially Buddhist picture of hell: furnace and hammer, water and fire, and the house of iron that twists and turns like a labyrinth. The hellish nature of the scene is explicitly reinforced in the second couplet: the factory workers operating the machine wheels are compared to ghosts and demons that have no hope of ever escaping the wheel of transmigration and are doomed to suffer for all eternity. The image of the "foreign devils" is cleverly superimposed upon that of the miserable ghosts in hell.

The image of the "factory as hell" was not unfamiliar to nineteenth-century Europeans. Karl Marx used the term in his *Capital: A Critique of Political Economy*; his youngest daughter, Eleanor Marx, wrote a pamphlet entitled none other than *The Factory Hell*, decrying the miserable working conditions of factory workers.[15] The pamphlet was published in 1891. But Zhang Zuyi, the Qing mandarin, was no Marxist who harbored sympathy for the working class. For him, it was the factory workers' very foreignness that constituted their subhuman nature. The basic schemata of seeing heaven or hell in the foreign land is maintained but also complicated in his poetry: instead of either heaven or hell, we have both heaven *and* hell juxtaposed uncomfortably within one text, formally manifested as a tension between the appended prose note and the poem itself.

No. 67 of the "Bamboo Branch Songs," which describes the underwater tunnel of the Thames River, furnishes another example of the heaven/hell schema:[16]

A road was opened up underneath the Thames River so that people could go through. A bridge is above the river; in the middle there is water; underneath there is a tunnel. This is truly an amazing idea.

玳米司江底辟路一條，往來可通人行。上爲橋，中爲水，下又有隧道，眞奇想也。

15. *Capital*, p. 307. The "Factory Hell" image still appears often in media and popular culture in many nations.

16. Zhang Zuyi, "Lundun zhuzhici," 16b, in Xu Shikai *Guanzide zhai* 24; Wang Shenzhi and Wang Zijin, *Qingdai haiwai*, p. 222.

Qixiang 奇想, an unexpected but extraordinary idea, carries a tone of unmistakable admiration and wonder. As Mary Campbell says of the "quality of wonder" in Marco Polo's travel account, "A wonder partakes of another Nature. . . . And there is something essentially positive about it."[17] The poem, on the other hand, again expresses a completely different attitude:

水底通衢南北運	An open road under water connects north and south,
往來不喚渡頭船	people come and go, having no need for a ferryboat.
燈光慘淡陰風起	The lamplight is gloomy and dim, a cold wind arises:
未死先教赴九泉	though not yet dead, one is already transported to the Nine Springs.

The Nine Springs, also known as the Yellow Springs, refer to the netherworld. Once again the grim landscape of the second couplet undercuts the benefits brought by the technological wonder of the tunnel's architecture. Since in the original text the note comes after the poem, it may have been intended to mitigate the scathing effect of the poem, but in the final analysis the poem wins out because of the power of the image, and also because rhymed couplets, with their melodic rhythm, are much more memorable than prose. The tug of war between verse and prose in this case not only mirrors the poet's ambivalent attitude, but also realizes, in formal terms, the tension between heaven and hell in depicting foreign lands.

Despite his admiration of the foreigners' "cleverness" (*qiao* 巧), a word that itself implies an ambiguous value judgment in Chinese literary tradition, "loathing" is the basic mindset of Zhang Zuyi. Even cleverness can be perceived in a negative light. Upon visiting Madame Tussaud's wax museum, he marveled at the lifelike wax statues, but considered them an ill omen:

古來作俑猶無後	In the ancient days, even makers of terra-cotta figurines had no offspring;[18]

17. Campbell, *The Witness*, pp. 104–5.

18. Confucius was opposed to the burying of terra-cotta figurines with the dead. He said: "The first person who made terra-cotta figurines would probably have no offspring." *Mengzi zhushu*, p. 14.

此地將亡必有妖	as this country is going to fall, aberration is sure to appear.[19]

Poem No. 90 transforms an innocent experience into something sinister. The note tells us:

The English call the Chinese "Cai-ni-si" [Chinese]. If a Chinese walks on the street and encounters a group of children, they always clap their hands and sing loudly, "Qing-qing Cai-ni-si." I have no idea what it means.[20]

英人呼中國人曰菜尼斯。凡中國人上街遇群小兒，必皆拍手高唱請請菜尼斯，不知其何謂也。

The matter-of-fact narration in the note is turned into a militant threat in the poem:

一隊兒童拍手嬉	A group of children clap their hands and play;
高呼請請菜尼斯	they shout loudly, "Qing-qing Cai-ni-si."
童謠自古皆天意	From ancient times, children's songs have shown heaven's will;
要請天兵靖島夷	they are inviting our heavenly troops to conquer these island barbarians.

The poem appeals to the traditional Chinese belief that children's songs often portend important events such as the rise and fall of a dynasty. For the sound "qing-qing," Zhang chose to hear *qing* 請, which means "invite," rather than the more obvious "Qing" as in the Qing Dynasty. By doing so, he literally "made sense of" what to him was incomprehensible "barbarian" twittering, turning it into an "invitation" to the Qing troops to conquer England.

Once again, we see an interesting disconnection between the poem and its note. The note no longer merely supplies circumstantial information; it becomes a foil for the poem to work its magic. The poem impresses the reader with its imagery, rhyme, and rhythm, so that in the end the more somber and neutral prose note is entirely eclipsed by the fear and loathing of the "island barbarians."

---

19. Zhang Zuyi, "Lundun zhuzhici," 20b, in Xu Shikai *Guanzide zhai* 24; Wang Shenzhi and Wang Zijin, *Qingdai haiwai*, p. 225.

20. Zhang Zuyi, "Lundun zhuzhici," 22a, in Xu Shikai *Guanzide zhai*; Wang Shenzhi and Wang Zijin, *Qingdai haiwai*, p. 227.

Poetic Narration and Poetic Form

Writing is, as Derrida says, an act of violence. The canonical statement about poetry in Chinese literary tradition insists that "poetry articulates what is on the mind" (*shi yan zhi* 詩言志). The expressive function of poetry, in the simplicity and neatness of this formula, is certainly the theoretical principle that came to be taken for granted by generations of writers in later times. But the truth is that poetry is a way of ordering the world as the poet sees it, and a poet's vision can transform the world in strange ways.

Let us return for a moment to You Tong, the seventeenth-century historian and poet, and his textual travel and imaginary journeys. Chapter 4 mentions that You Tong composed two bamboo branch songs on Java.[21] The first one reads:

種傳罔象變獼猴	Descending from the elephant, transformed from monkeys,
生小啣刀不剌頭	since childhood they carry a dagger known as "bu-la-tou."
並駕塔車坐妻小	Driving a pagoda-carriage, with their womenfolk coming along,
竹槍會上鬥風流	they fight with such panache at the Bamboo Spear Assembly.

This poem alludes to four separate episodes in You Tong's sources, namely, the travel accounts by Gong Zhen, Fei Xin, and Ma Huan. One episode relates the putative origin of the native people of Java. Ma Huan's version of the story is as follows:

In the old days, there was a legend about a demon king with a blue face, a red body, and crimson hair, who stayed in this place and mated with an elephant spirit.[22] They begot over a hundred male offspring, who ate fish and meat. Many people were eaten by them. Then suddenly one day a thunderclap split a rock, in-

21. In Wang Shenzhi and Wang Zijin, *Qingdai haiwai*, p. 11.

22. *Wangxiang* 罔象 is a kind of water monster in early Chinese texts. Ma Huan used the term to refer to the elephant spirit in the local legend. Elephant, or *Gajah* in Indonesian, was considered a symbol of strength and has rich associations with the Majapahit Empire. The powerful minister of the Majapahit Empire from the fourteenth century was named Gajah Mada, meaning something like the "raging elephant."

side which sat a man. The people marveled at this and took the man to be their king, who commanded crack troops to drive away the monster elephant and its children. Later on, the people reproduced and flourished. Therefore even today the people here are tough and ferocious.[23]

舊傳鬼子魔王，青面紅身赤髮，止于此地與一罔象相合，而生子百餘，常啖血食，人多被食。忽一日，雷震石裂，中坐一人，眾稱異之，遂推爲王，即令精兵驅逐罔象等眾而不爲害，後復生齒而安焉。所以至今人好凶強。

Fei Xin's version is more or less the same but for one detail: the characterization of the demon king—blue face, red body, and crimson hair—is transferred to the elephant spirit.[24] Gong Zhen's version shows the greatest deviation: it is ambiguous in identifying the ancestry of the native people, and claims that the man in the rock, after being made king, surrendered to the elephant spirit.[25] This divergence is likely responsible for You Tong's statement that the natives descended from the elephant spirit.

The second half of You Tong's opening line, "transformed from monkeys," alludes to a story about the local monkey cult. Ma Huan and Gong Zhen's versions are identical in simply stating that local women prayed to a monkey god for fertility.[26] Fei Xin's account contains significantly different elements, and You Tong was certainly referencing Fei Xin's version when he wrote his poem:

There is an isle where several hundred monkeys gather. The local legend says that in the Tang there was a family of over five hundred members. Their men and women were all ferocious and fiendish. One day a Buddhist monk visited the family and spoke of good and bad omens. The monk then spewed water on the family, and all the family members except an old woman were turned into monkeys. The family's former residence still exists today. The local people as well as merchants from other places often brought food, drink, betel nuts, fruits, and meat to make offerings to the monkeys; otherwise bad things would happen to them.[27]

有洲聚猢猻數百。傳聞於唐時，其家五百餘口，男婦凶惡。忽一日有僧至其家，乃言吉凶之事。其僧取水噀之，俱化爲獼猴，止留其老嫗

23. Ma Huan, *Yingya*, p. 12.
24. Fei Xin, *Xingcha*, p. 13.
25. Gong Zhen, *Xiyang fanguo zhi*, p. 8.
26. Ma Huan, *Yingya*, pp. 9–10; Gong Zhen, *Xiyang fanguo zhi*, p. 7.
27. Fei Xin, *Xingcha*, pp. 14–15.

不化。今存舊宅。本處及商者常設飲食檳榔花果肉類而祭之，不然則禍福甚有驗也。

The second line of You Tong's poem, "since childhood they carry a dagger known as 'bu-la-tou,'" refers to the local custom of carrying a curved single-edged knife called kris, recorded in slightly different wordings in all three travel accounts. The third and fourth lines of the poem allude to an annual festival held at the beginning of spring. Both the king and queen appeared at the celebrations, each sitting in a horse-drawn "pagoda-carriage." Fights were staged in which contestants used sharpened bamboo poles to challenge each other. Their wives were present, and after the contestants battled each other three times, the wives separated the men with wooden sticks. If a man died, then the king gave a gold coin to the dead man's family, and his wife would leave with the winner. This custom is recorded in similar terms in Ma Huan and Gong Zhen's accounts, but not in Fei Xin's.

You Tong's poem pieces together four separate episodes scattered through the lengthy travel accounts to make a coherent linear narrative of the island men's lives: their origin, their childhood, and their adulthood, all marked with a wild strength and ferociousness. In order to present such a narrative, You Tong carefully selected from among his textual sources, adopting some elements from one version and some from another. The story of origin told in the opening line is designed to demonstrate the "beastliness" of the island people and "explain" their martial custom of encouraging boys to carry a dagger from childhood; the last couplet reinforces the impression of their warlike nature. While the prose travel accounts follow an entirely different narrative principle based on physical space traveled, a bamboo branch song with its highly compact quatrain form can easily make connections where there were none. In other words, a poetic line can create a relationship between two unrelated things simply by juxtaposing them; prose, especially that of a travel account, demands a more logical link.

The same rhetorical strategy is employed in You Tong's second poem about Java, which emphasizes the sensuality of island life:

新村市舶聖泉清	Traders' boats moor at the New Village, the Holy Spring is fresh;
喜聽番歌步月行	what a pleasure to listen to the native songs in the moonlight.

更喜彩禽能倒掛	Even more lovely is the colorful bird hanging upside down,
聞香時向夜深鳴	emitting a sweet aroma as it sings late at night.

The last couplet describes a local parakeet called the "hanging-upside-down bird" (*daogua niao* 倒掛鳥) in the travel accounts, while the second line of the poem refers to the custom that on the night of a full moon, local women would saunter in the moonlight and sing songs. This detail appears in Ma Huan and Gong Zhen's accounts, but not in Fei Xin's. The opening line of the poem turns out to be most interesting in its exclusion and juxtaposition of the sources. The New Village was about half a day's boat trip east from Tuban; its local name was transcribed as Ge-er-xi (Gresik). This was where a Chinese immigrant community lived, hence the name "New Village"; it was also where many foreign traders came to do business.[28]

The "Holy Spring" is, however, taken from an entirely different part of the travel accounts; it also refers to a different region of the island. According to all three travel accounts, the Holy Spring was located on the shore of Tuban. During the Yuan dynasty, in the year 1292, as two Chinese generals, Shi Bi 史弼 and Gao Xing 高興, were preparing to invade Java, their troops were dying of thirst on the ocean.[29] The two generals prayed on the beach and then struck their spears into the ground, where a spring of fresh water spouted. Fei Xin's account further states that the Yuan army then defeated the "barbarian troops," and "when they captured the barbarian soldiers alive, they stewed them and ate them, so that even today the local people claim that the Central Kingdom is cannibalistic."[30]

This gruesome detail about cannibalism is, however, completely absent from Ma Huan and Gong Zhen's accounts, and certainly from You Tong's poem. In You Tong's poem, the two names "New Village" and "Holy Spring," clearly located far apart according to the travel accounts, are brought into close proximity within one poetic line. Poetic language calls for no pragmatic road map or measure of physical distance; nor does

28. Ma Huan, *Yingya*, p. 9. Gong Zhen, *Xiyang fanguo zhi*, pp. 6–7.

29. For Shi Bi and Gao Xing's military campaign to Java, see Song Lian et al., *Yuan shi* 210.4665.

30. Fei Xin, *Xingcha*, p. 15.

it require any verb of action to produce a relationship among nominal elements as long as they are placed side by side.

A relationship is nevertheless produced. The hidden link between the two places is their association with the Han Chinese: the New Village was occupied primarily by Chinese immigrants, and the Holy Spring spouted for the Chinese troops (albeit sent by a Mongolian emperor). By linguistically juxtaposing the two places, far apart in geographical reality but connected by their common Han association, the second poem in the set subtly prepares the reader for a scene of sensuous sights, smells, and sounds—the "softer side" of Java. You Tong treated his prose sources like pieces of a puzzle: he picked and chose and moved them around to make the pastiche that was his poem. He did add one detail of his own invention, namely the singing of the parakeet late at night, a detail that is not found in any of the three travel accounts. This may have been a choice necessitated by the demands of the rhyme scheme, but by adding this detail, You Tong created a parallel between the native women singing in the moonlight and the native bird singing at night, evoking the familiar association between "barbarians" and their "bird talk."

Space is a key organizing principle in travel accounts. The author of a travel account often gives pragmatic instructions about how to get there from here. You Tong's poetic narration of Java substitutes the principle of space with that of time: an origin story, a fictionalized linear narrative of the Majapahit man's life, and an account of the local entertainment of one night *and* every night in the undifferentiated environs of a primitive island, with all the innocence, sensuality, and cruelty that characterizes its birds and animals. Poetry may not be concerned with the nitty-gritty details of road directions, but this is not to say that poetry does not play a role in the ordering of the world.

Familiarization: Wang Tao's Visit to Dollar, Scotland

The previous section discusses the way in which the poet orders the world by selecting and reorganizing material from textual sources. Textual sources are stable, and so are better able to demonstrate the artificial nature of the linguistic working of a poem that is based purely on the poet's textual experiences. For a poet who experiences a foreign land firsthand, especially a foreign land that has not yet accumulated a textual past in one's native literary tradition, writing poetry is likewise a way of ordering the world, albeit in a different manner. Simply put, it de-alienates that land in familiar tropes and images that provide the poet with the basic schemata of seeing the world; it is an attempt to not only make sense of an alien culture and people in familiar terms but also successfully transport it back to the home audience.

Insofar as seeing is inseparable from *seeing as articulated in language*, it is futile to contend that any poem is "inadequate" to articulating what the poet sees—or, for that matter, how the poet feels. If the "love of the strange" or exoticism, with its insistence on seeing only "strangeness" and "difference" in a foreign place, becomes the greatest impediment to a sympathetic understanding of the foreign, then conversely a positive aspect of the strategy of familiarization is that the poet humanizes the foreign land by presenting it in recognizable terms to people back home. The risk of doing so is to erase cultural difference, which only shows how difficult it is to achieve a balanced understanding of a foreign culture without assigning values, offering judgment, and, in the worst case scenario, demonizing it.

Several poems written by Wang Tao well illustrate the ambiguity of "familiarization" as a rhetorical strategy. Unlike Bin Chun, who was merely passing through, Wang Tao lived in England for well over two years. As Paul Cohen points out in his study of Wang Tao, "Wang T'ao was probably the first classically trained Chinese scholar in the modern era to spend a meaningful period of time in the West."[31] He formed a close friendship with the Scottish sinologist James Legge (Li Yage 理雅各) and his family, especially his third daughter, Mary, referred to as Miss Meili (Meili nüshi 媚梨女士) in Wang Tao's travel account. In early 1868, Wang Tao came to Scotland at Legge's invitation and stayed at the town of Dollar (Dula 杜拉). Near Dollar there is a small village called Rumbling Bridge (Xinglei qiao 行雷橋), so named because the River Devon falls over rocks and forms a series of cataracts that make a thunderous sound there, and also because of the unusual double bridge over the River Devon. About one mile downstream of the Rumbling Bridge is the famous Cauldron Linn Waterfall, or the "great wok" (*da huo* 大鑊) in Wang Tao's rendering. A popular guidebook, *Black's Picturesque Tourist*

31. Cohen, *Between Tradition and Modernity*, p.67.

of Scotland, reprinted not long before Wang Tao's visit, gives the following description:

> The river here suddenly enters a deep gulf, where, finding itself confined, it has, by continual efforts against its sides, worked out a cavity resembling a large cauldron. From this gulf the water works its way through an aperture beneath the surface into a lower cavity, where it is covered with a constant foam. The water then works its way into a third cauldron, out of which it is precipitated by a sheer fall of forty-four feet. The best view of this magnificent scene is from the bottom of the fall.[32]

In July of 1868, James Legge and his daughter Mary took Wang Tao on an outing to the Rumbling Bridge. Wang Tao wrote a long poem in the seven-syllable line to commemorate the trip.[33]

同治戊辰夏五月	The *wuchen* year of the Tongzhi era, summer, the fifth month:
我來英土已半年	it has been half a year since I came to the land of Britain.

The opening of the poem evokes the Tang poet Du Fu's 杜甫 (712–70) "Journey North" ("Bei zheng" 北征):

皇帝二載秋	Our Imperial Majesty's second year, autumn,
閏八月初吉	first day of the month, an adjusted eighth,
杜子將北征	I, Master Du, was to set on a journey north,
蒼茫問家室	over vast uncertain space to learn of my family.[34]

Du Fu, widely considered the greatest Chinese poet, wrote his poem after the An Lushan Rebellion that tore the Tang empire apart; he undertook a trip to reunite with the members of his family who had become separated from him during the war. Beginning an account with a date was a common narrative technique in dynastic histories. Du Fu's literary model might have been Ban Zhao's 班昭 (ca. 49–120) "*Fu* on My Journey East" ("Dongzheng fu" 東征賦), but he was the first to employ the technique

32. *Black's Picturesque Tourist of Scotland*, p. 194.

33. The Wang Tao citations in this chapter can be found in *Manyou suilu*, pp. 124–26.

34. Du Fu, *Du shi jing quan*, p. 159.

in poetry.[35] It lends a tone of solemnity to the narrative, as Du Fu painted an epic-scale portrait of the chaotic age in a poem of 200 lines.

In this context Wang Tao's opening for a poem on a summer outing might seem humorously grandiose—though not without precedent.[36] The most striking effect, however, is the poetic gesture that links him to Du Fu's loyalty to his emperor. Although staying in a more distant land than any Tang poet could possibly imagine, Wang Tao, by using the imperial reign of the Tongzhi emperor to mark time, affirmed his identity as a subject of the Qing Empire.

眼中突兀杜拉山	Abruptly towering in my sight, the mountain of Dollar;
三蠟游屐聽鳴泉	thrice I had waxed my clogs and listened to the music of its springs.
岩深澗仄勢幽阻	The crags were deep, the ravine narrow, and the hills secluded and steep,
飛泉一片從空懸	with a flying cascade hanging from heaven.
我臨此境輒叫絶	Whenever I went there, I marveled at its beauty:
頓洗塵俗開心顏	it washed away all the worldly dust from me and cheered me up.
居停主人雅好事	My gracious host loved to be helpful,
謂此不足稱奇焉	he told me that it was not worth being called remarkable;
去此十里有名勝	but about ten miles from here, there was a famous site:
風潭廣斥萬頃田	a wind-blown pool in a land of ten thousand acres;
上有飛瀑如匹練	above was a cascade like a bolt of silk,
下有雜樹相娟鮮	down below were all kinds of trees, fresh and fine.
爰命巾車急往訪	He had a coach ready for us to pay a visit,
全家俱賦登臨篇	so that the entire family could admire the wondrous view.
其日佳客踐約至	On that day this fine guest, true to his word, came along
遂與同載揚輕鞭	and rode with his host, who cracked his light whip.

35. Ban Zhao's *fu* begins with the lines: "In the seventh year of the Yongchu reign, / I followed my son on an eastward journey" 惟永初之有七兮，余隨子乎東征. Yan Kejun, *Quan hou Han wen* 96.987.

36. Another Tang poet Bai Juyi 白居易 (772–846) began his poem, "On Touring the Temple of Wuzhen" ("You Wuzhen si" 遊悟真寺), in a similar way.

The above stanza is reminiscent of priamel, a rhetorical device often found in ancient Greek poetry. It consists of a series of alternatives that lead to the true subject of the poem, revealed at last as better than all the previously listed alternatives. Here the poet expressed his admiration of the mountain of Dollar only to have it deflated by his "gracious host," who informed him of an even more breathtaking site.

初臨猶未獲奇境	When we first arrived, we did not yet see the marvelous realm,
漸入眼界始豁然	but the view gradually opened up, as we entered the hills.
意行不憚路高下	Following our whim, we did not mind the steepness of the path,
疏花密蔭如招延	as if sparse flowers and dense shade were beckoning us along.
澗窮路盡更奇辟	Where the ravine was exhausted, and the path ended, the landscape became even more extraordinary,
忽如別有一洞天	it was like having come into a grotto heaven.
水從石竅急噴出	Water spouted from the cavities of rocks,
勢若珠雪相跳濺	leaping and splashing like pearly snow;
至此積怒始奔注	here like a repressed wrath, it suddenly unleashed its power,
一落百丈從峰巔	falling a thousand feet from the mountain peak.
側耳但覺晴雷喧	Listening closely, I heard thunders rumbling in the blue sky,
聲喧心靜地自偏	the sound was noisy, my heart was calm, the locale naturally became remote.
徑穿犖確躡澗石	Following a trail through the ragged and broken, stepping on stones of streams,
獨從正面觀眞詮	I alone had a full frontal view of the true essence of this place.
四顧幾忘身世賤	Looking around, I almost forgot this humble life of mine
來往忽希逢飛仙	and began to cherish hopes of encountering divine beings.

In this stanza the echoes of Tao Yuanming are unmistakable. In Tao's Peach Blossom Spring account, the fisherman, after crawling through a dark hole in the hill, comes upon an open space, a quasi-immortal realm hidden from the world. After he returns home, he can never find his way back to the wondrous realm again. In Wang Tao's poem, there is the same process of accidental discovery, the "gradual entering of the realm of delight," as the Cauldron Linn Waterfall is being praised as an earthly paradise, a Daoist "grotto heaven" with "divine beings."

Another allusion is to the opening lines of Tao Yuanming's poem, No. 5 of "Drinking Wine," which is perhaps one of the best-known poems in the Chinese language:

結廬在人境	I built my cottage in the human realm,
而無車馬喧	yet there is no noise of horse and carriage.
問君何能爾	How then did you manage to achieve this?
心遠地自偏	When the heart is faraway, the locale naturally becomes remote.[37]

The implication is that Wang, too, was living in a self-imposed seclusion like Tao Yuanming, and that he had likewise achieved inner peace, which rendered all the sound and fury of the outside world trivial and meaningless. Though in a foreign country, the locale of the Rumbling Bridge was situated squarely in the "human realm," and was only "remote" because of the poet's mindset.

The poet also claimed to have grasped the "true essence" of the landscape: "Following a trail through the ragged and broken, stepping on stones of streams, / I alone had a full frontal view of the true essence of this place." The literary antecedent is the Tang poet Han Yu's 韓愈 (768–824) poem, "Mountain Stones" ("Shan shi" 山石), in which Han Yu described his visit to a Buddhist temple in the mountains. The poem begins with the line, "Mountain stones ragged and broken, tiny the trail I walked" 山石犖确行徑微.[38] After staying over at the temple for the night, the poet went off to see the mountain the next morning. Then he came upon a wondrous realm:

山紅澗碧紛爛漫	The hills were red, streams sapphire, Swarming with sparkling color,
時見松櫪皆十圍	at times I caught sight of oaks and pines, each one ten armspans around.

---

37. These lines are cited in Chapter 1.

38. Han Yu, *Han Yu quanji jiaozhu*, p. 107. Owen's translation. *An Anthology of Chinese Literature*, pp. 488–89.

當流赤足踏澗石	In the current I went barefoot stepping on stones of streams,
水聲激激風生衣	with sounds of the rushing waters, and the winds blowing my clothes.
人生如此自可樂	Moments like this in our lives being a joy in themselves—
豈必局束爲人羈	why must we stay fettered and tied, put in the harness by others?

Poems on visiting mountains or visiting Buddhist temples often end with the poet "acquiring" (*de* 得) the true spirit of the landscape and spiritual enlightenment. Han Yu followed the tradition; so did Wang Tao. Allusions to Tao Yuanming and Han Yu's poems that form the subtext of Wang Tao's poem reinforce a sense of spiritual freedom. As the poet claimed to obtain an insight (*guan* 觀) into the "true essence of the place," he was looking at the landscape with his mind's eye as well.

After the climax of enlightenment, the poem turns to the Legge family. The next stanza pays a compliment to the host's daughter, who had brought her painting tools that day and made a sketch of the landscape. The poet promised to do the same with his verbal art:

萬山擁翠忽環合	Myriad hills embraced us in azure, like a closed ring,
中有一朵芙蓉妍	in the midst of the hills bloomed a charming lotus flower.
惜非胸中具丘壑	I regretted that I did not have mountains and ravines in my breast
坐使腕底生雲煙	so as to make clouds and mist rise from my brush.
媚梨女士工六法	Miss Mary, skilled in the "six methods,"
定能寫此圖其全	could surely portray the scenery and reproduce its perfection.
勝情妙墨發奇想	With superior sentiments and wondrous ink, inspired by marvelous ideas,
盍將造化形神傳	why not transmit the shape and spirit of the natural transformation?
嗟予窮厄世所棄	Woe is me, down-and-out and abandoned by the world,
胸貯萬斛憂愁煎	tortured by ten thousand bushels of sorrow in my breast.

山靈出奇爲娛悅	The mountain god offered a miracle for my amusement,
令以文字相雕鐫	and commanded me to embellish it with words.

Earlier in the poem, Wang Tao introduced "this humble life of mine"; here again he lamented his "down-and-out" situation. Behind these lines is a long tradition of exiled Chinese literati going to lands far away from the center and finding comfort in the beauty of nature. Wang's situation was, however, somewhat different: rather than staying within the boundaries of the Qing Empire, he had voluntarily traveled to a foreign country, going farther than any earlier Chinese poet had ever gone.

我鄉豈無好山水	Is it that my homeland doesn't have beautiful landscapes?
乃來遠域窮搜研	That I should come to this distant region to search for marvels!
昨日家書至海舶	Yesterday a letter from home came by the sea,
滄波隔絕殊可憐	the gray waves—how piteous!—separate me from home.
因涉名區念故國	Upon seeing a famous site, I think of my native country;
何時歸隱江南邊	when can I go back and be a recluse in the Southland?

Throughout the poem, as well as in the lengthy prose account preceding the poem, the one word that keeps reappearing is *qi* 奇. The Rumbling Bridge is described as "secluded, *amazing*, and delightful" (*youqi kexi* 幽奇可喜); the host told the poet that the mountain at Dollar was not worth being called "*remarkable*" (*buzu chengqi* 不足稱奇); the hills of the Rumbling Bridge are referred to as a "*marvelous* realm" (*qijing* 奇境), "even more *extraordinary*" (*geng qipi* 更奇辟) as one moves on, a "*miracle*" offered by the mountain god (*chuqi* 出奇). Even Miss Mary's landscape sketch is "inspired by *marvelous* ideas" (*fa qixiang* 發奇想). All this is, however, a *qi* that belongs to nature, and as such it is no different from the "beautiful landscapes" of China that are so often depicted in the same terms of "wonder" and "marvel" in the literary tradition. The poem further displaces any alien element of the Scottish landscape by echoing earlier poetry. In this sense, *qi*, strangeness, has been completely domesticated. Indeed Wang Tao felt so much at home at Dollar that he ended his prose account with these words:

Ah, my situation was indeed difficult, and yet, the marvels of sightseeing, the extraordinary beauty of the landscape, the amusement brought forth by writings, and the predestined bond forged between me and my friends all afforded me sufficient reasons to feel proud, so much so that I almost forgot that I was living overseas.

噫，余處境雖厄，而遊覽之奇，山水之勝，詩文之娛，朋友之緣，亦足以豪，幾忘身之在海外也。

The key word is "almost" (*ji* 幾). In the "longing for home" narrative developed in early medieval times, there is always a moment that breaks the spell and causes discontent in paradise. For Wang Tao, that moment came when he received a letter from home. The timing of the letter remains ambiguous. At one point in the poem, we learn that the letter arrived "yesterday." But the prose account in which the poem is embedded states:

After the poem was completed, I suddenly received a letter from home, and I again composed two quatrains and attached them here.

詩成，忽得家書，復綴二絶句於後。

The first of the two quatrains is directly relevant to our discussion of the familiarization and domestication of the strange and the foreign:

一從客粵念江南	When I was visiting Canton, I always longed for the Southland,
六載思鄉淚未幹	for six years my tears of homesickness had never dried.
今日擲身滄海外	Today this body of mine is tossed beyond the dark green seas,
粵東轉作故鄉看	I now think of the Eastern Canton as my homeland instead.

This poem is based on a famous Tang poem entitled "Crossing the Sanggan River" ("Du Sanggan" 渡桑乾):

客舍並州已十霜	I was a visitor at Bingzhou for ten years,
歸心日夜憶咸陽	every day, every night, I longed to return to Xianyang.
無端更渡桑乾水	Then for no reason at all I crossed the Sanggan River,

卻望並州是故鄉 and I looked to Bingzhou
as my hometown instead.[39]

The poem has often been attributed to Jia Dao 賈島 (779–843), but many scholars believe that it was written by an obscure poet, Liu Zao 劉皂, under the title "Staying Temporarily at Shuofang" ("Lüci Shuofang" 旅次朔方). In the Tang poem, the poet travels farther and farther north: from Xianyang in Shaanxi, to Bingzhou (in modern Shanxi), and then across the Sanggan River (in modern Hebei). In Wang Tao's case, however, the poet was bound for the south, at least in the beginning, as he moved from the Southland to Canton. In both poems, the crossing of water turns out to be a crucial turning point: as soon as the poet crosses, his prior experience is romanticized, and the land on the other side, formerly strange and unbearable, now becomes the object of his nostalgia, while the place of origin recedes further into the distance.

Wang Tao did not cross a river, but crossed an ocean instead. The change from river to ocean marks the dramatic difference between the experience of the medieval poet and that of the modern poet. The medieval poet traveled from one region to another within one country, one empire; the nineteenth-century poet, on the other hand, traveled from one country to another, one empire to another. When seen from the vantage point of England, Canton, formerly a land for exiles, casts off its "barbarian" association and becomes part of "China." In some ways, we recognize a repetition of history, as the Southland had, as we have seen in the first part of this book, completed its own transformation from a land of "pestilential vapors" to a land of beauty in early medieval times. But here the difference is profound, as Wang Tao's poem is a quintessential expression of the newly formed notion of the nation-state. The poet loses the sense of the local but gains the sense of the national by traveling across the "dark green seas." By framing his quatrain within an earlier quatrain centered on the local, however, Wang Tao camouflages as well as familiarizes the fundamental strangeness of his experience.

---

39. Jia Dao, *Jia Dao ji jiaozhu*, pp. 336–37.

The Many Contending Voices of One Poet

Familiarization occurs in many forms and many genres. The Manchu diplomat Zhi Gang, for instance, kept a radically different sort of observation diary than that kept by Bin Chun or Zhang Deyi. Serious, troubled, cautiously curious, and ultimately conservative, Zhi Gang was constantly reflecting and rationalizing, trying to make sense of the Western world in both cultural and technical terms. Although familiarization is not the privilege of the poetic genre, poetry as a privileged genre in premodern China had a commanding presence in the cultural landscape. A premodern poet cherished some hope that one day, his or her poems might be on people's lips far and wide, as Zhang Deyi said of Bin Chun's poems: "Sire Bin's poems will be circulated on the five continents and certainly passed on to posterity for a thousand years."[40] He did not seem to anticipate as much for his own diary, even though it was his diary, rather than Bin Chun's poetry, that has been translated into English in the twentieth century as well as reprinted several times in China in the past decade.[41]

In this section, I turn to another aspect of the function of poetry. This is an aspect that defies the kind of prosaic rationalization seen in Zhi Gang's travel account. The poet reflects and his poem invites reflection, not because of what the poet speaks, but because of *how* he speaks. I focus on the case of Huang Zunxian, who, of the many members of the Chinese elite going abroad since the 1860s, makes the fullest use of the special nature and potential of the poetic genre. His poetry embodies and epitomizes a multitude of conflicting emotions and attitudes produced by the impact of fundamental changes that occurred in nineteenth-century China, when everything familiar was turned upside down and inside out.

Huang Zunxian is a versatile poet who, in his best work, subverts conventions and topoi even as he deploys them. His "Ballad of the Great London Fog" ("Lundun dawu xing" 倫敦大霧行) is a standard "hell" piece, filled with gloomy descriptions of the "black ashes left by the kalpa

40. Zhang Deyi, *Hanghai shuqi*, p. 539.

41. Frodsham, *The First Chinese Embassy to the West*; Johnstone, *Diary of a Chinese Diplomat: Zhang Deyi.*

fire of destruction" and "a stench wafting in the mirage city created by the gigantic clam."[42] Buddhist demonic terms are freely juxtaposed:

忽然黑暗無間墮落阿鼻獄 Suddenly darkness spreads without bounds as one falls into Avīci Hell;
又驚惡風吹船飄至羅刹國 then again one is taken by surprise when a gale rises, blowing one's boat to the kingdom of yakṣas.

At other times, Huang Zunxian adopts a paradisial scheme in his view of London, only to challenge and complicate that scheme. Poem No. 1 of "Moved by Events" ("Gan shi" 感事) gives an account of a grand party at Queen Victoria's court.[43] The poem begins with a scene of splendid luxury objects:

酌君以葡萄千斛之酒 I pour you, my lord, the grape wine in a thousand goblets;
贈君以玫瑰連理之花 I present you, my lord, with roses joined at roots.
飽君以波羅徑尺之果 I satisfy your appetite with the foot-long fruit of pineapple;
飲君以天竺小團之茶 I quench your thirst with small tea-cakes from India.
處君以琉璃層累之屋 I house you in a many-storied building with windows of glass;
乘君以通幰四望之車 I provide you with a carriage with curtains hanging on the four sides;
送君以金絲壓袖之服 I dress you in a robe with golden silk threads woven in its sleeves;
延君以錦幔圍墻之家 I invite you to a residence with brocade covering its four walls.

This stanza evokes the opening of the early medieval poet Bao Zhao's 鮑照 (414?–66) "Hard Travel" ("Xinglu nan" 行路難) No. 1:

奉君金巵之美酒 I present you, my lord, with ale in a golden goblet;
玳瑁玉匣之雕琴 a carved zither in a jade case decorated with tortoise-shell;

42. Huang Zunxian, *Renjinglu*, pp. 183–84.
43. Huang Zunxian, *Renjinglu*, pp. 188–89.

七彩芙蓉之羽帳	a feathered bed-curtain embroidered with lotus blossoms of seven colors;
九華葡萄之錦衾	a brocade coverlet with the pattern of lush grapes.[44]

Framing one's poetic lines in the verbal paradigm of early poetry is a rhetorical strategy of familiarization; it also calls attention to the elements that are new or different. In this case, we notice the exotic nature of the luxury objects—grape wine, roses, pineapple, Indian tea, glass windows, and wall hangings in Huang's poem. Huang's opening stanza is not only twice as long as Bao Zhao's enumeration but also more exotic and foreign.

The following lines plunge into a dramatic portrayal of the extravagant gathering of "devas, humans, and nāgas." Images of paradise and immortals abound:

紅氍貼地燈耀壁	Red carpet covers the floor, lamps shine on the wall;
今夕大會來無遮	tonight's grand assembly has no restriction.[45]
褰裳攜手雙雙至	Gathering up their dresses, holding hands, arriving in pairs,
仙之人兮紛如麻	a multitude of immortals descend, numerous as sands.[46]
繡衣曳地過七尺	Embroidered robes trail on the ground, with a train of over seven feet;
白羽覆髻騰三叉	white feathers decorating the chignon rise up like a trident.
襜褕乍解雙臂袒	Taking off their capes, the women expose their bare arms,
旁綴纓絡中寶珈	tassels hanging on the side, precious jewels in the midst.
細腰亭亭媚楊柳	Small waists, more charming than a willow branch,
窄靴簇簇團蓮華	a throng of slender boots like lotus blossoms.
膳夫中庭獻湩乳	Butlers serve sherbet in the courtyard,
樂人階下鳴鼓笳	musicians play drums and pipes below the stairs.

44. Bao Zhao, *Bao canjun shizhu* 鮑參軍詩注, p. 53.

45. "No-restriction assembly" (*wuzhe dahui*) is a large Buddhist gathering open to all people. It was first held in China in the Southern Dynasties.

46. This line is taken almost verbatim from Li Bai's 李白 (701–62) poem, "Mengyou Tianmu yin liubie" 夢遊天姥吟留別. *Li Bai ji jiaozhu*, p. 899.

諸天人龍盡來集 All devas, humans, and nāgas have gathered together;
來自天漢通銀槎 coming from the Heavenly River on a silver raft.[47]
衣裳闌斑語言雜 Wearing colorful clothes, speaking a motley of languages,
康樂和親懽不嘩 the crowd is joyful and agreeable; merry, yet not boisterous.

Making generous use of what J. D. Schmidt calls "paradisial allusions," the description seems an elaborate poetic rendering of Bin Chun's ecstatic diary entry about the court banquet.[48] But just as the lavish description culminates in the image of the "joyful and agreeable, merry, yet not boisterous" crowd, a climax point for the grand party itself, the poem abruptly ends on a note of melancholy:

問我何爲獨不樂 You ask why it is, then, that I alone am unhappy,
側身東望三咨嗟 turning to the side, gazing east, and heaving many sighs?

The ending couplet comes unexpectedly, and this intensifies its effect. The description of the splendid, joyful party becomes a foil to the poet's melancholy and sense of alienation. Paradise is spoiled.

The next two poems in the series reveal the poet's source of melancholy: the traditional world order as he knew it had been shaken up by the newly gained knowledge of "various great states," and the poet urges his fellow countrymen to forsake the "empty talk" (*xu lun* 虛論) of "Confucian scholars of Song and Ming" (*Song Ming zhu ru* 宋明諸儒) and strive to attain a true understanding of this brave new world:

古今事變奇到此 The changes from past to present are so very strange indeed!
彼己不知寧毋恥 If we remain ignorant about them and about ourselves, wouldn't it be a shame?[49]

Huang Zunxian was only too aware of the earth-shattering changes that had taken place "from past to present." Like Zhi Gang, he tried to make sense of the changes and figure out a way of dealing with the new reality.

---

47. This couplet refers to the foreign diplomats at the party.
48. Schmidt, *Within the Human Realm*, p. 120.
49. Huang Zunxian, *Renjinglu*, p. 191.

But Huang Zunxian himself changed in the process as well, as can be observed from his chronologically arranged poetic collection. It was not a quick and clear-cut transformation from A to B, but a gradual growth in intellectual and emotional complexity as the poet grew older, saw more and more of the world, and in the process understood more and more of it.

In 1874, the twenty-six-year-old Huang Zunxian decided to go to Beijing for the Court Examinations. He first took a steamer to the northern seaport of Tianjin 天津 (literally, "Heaven's Ford"), and then traveled to Beijing by land. This was the young poet's first venture into the world beyond his hometown; to his horror and discomfort, he discovered that he had to share the steamer with many foreigners, and that Tianjin, being open to foreign trade, was overshadowed by a large foreign presence. Huang wrote a poem entitled "Arriving at Tianjin on a Steamer" ("You lunzhou di Tianjin zuo" 由輪舟抵天津作):[50]

遙指天河問析津	Pointing to the Heavenly River in the distance, I inquire about the ford;
茫茫巨浸浩無垠	all I see is the great watery expanse— vast, open, limitless.
華夷萬國無分土	Chinese and barbarian, a myriad nations have no dividing boundaries;
人鬼浮生共轉輪	humans and demons in this floating life both ride the "turning wheel."
敵國同舟今日事	Sharing a boat with those from enemy states: that is what is happening today;
太倉稊米自家身	a tiny grain of rice in a great granary: this insignificant body of mine.[51]
大鵬擊水南風勁	The great *peng* bird roils the waters, the south gale is strong—
忽地吹人落軟塵	all of a sudden it blows this man down into the soft dust.

The third line evokes a couplet from Chen Gongyin's 陳恭尹 (1631–1700) poem, "Visiting the Temple for the Three Loyal Men at Yamen"

50. Ibid., pp. 44–45.

51. The general Wu Qi 吳起 advised the Marquis of Wei: "If you, my lord, do not cultivate your virtue, then even the people sharing the same boat with you would turn into your enemies" 若君不修德，舟中之人盡為敵國也. Sima Qian, *Shi ji* 65.2167.

("Yamen ye Sanzhong ci" 崖門謁三忠祠): "The waters of the sea still have a gate that distinguishes above and below; / yet rivers and mountains have no place for a boundary between Chinese and barbarians" 海水有門分上下，江山無地限華夷.[52] Chen Gongyin was the son of a Ming loyalist who died while resisting the Manchus. The "three loyal men" in the title are Wen Tianxiang 文天祥 (1236–83), Lu Xiufu 陸秀夫 (1236–79), and Zhang Shijie 張世杰 (d. 1279), three Southern Song loyalists who died resisting the Mongols; Yamen, a place in Guangdong, was where Lu Xiufu leapt into the sea with the baby Song emperor on his back. In writing this couplet, Chen Gongyin was lamenting the fact that the Manchus were overrunning China, but for Huang Zunxian, a subject of the Manchu Qing Empire, Manchus had long ceased being viewed as "barbarians"; his line is in fact a comment on the promiscuous mixture of Chinese and Westerners on the same ocean liner across a vast watery expanse that marks no boundary of any kind. The fourth line of Huang's poem makes use of a clever pun about the Chinese translation of a "paddle boat," *lunchuan* 輪船, which literally means a "wheel boat," and the Buddhist wheel of reincarnation and transmigration: the poet was riding on a wheel shared by humans/Chinese and demons/foreigners alike.

Sunzi, the master of war, once said: "The people of Wu and the people of Yue hate each other. But if they share the same boat crossing the river and encounter a storm, they work together like left hand and right hand."[53] And yet, to the young poet who had left home for the first time, the foreigners sharing his boat were nothing but "demons" and "enemies." Surrounded by strangers and the vast sea, he felt alienated and small: "a tiny grain of rice in a great granary: this insignificant body of mine." The subtext of this line is the "Autumn Floods" chapter of *Zhuangzi*, in which the god of the North Sea tells the god of the Yellow River: "When you come to think of the Middle Kingdom within the seas, isn't it like a tiny grain of rice in a great granary?" 計中國之在海內不似稊米之在太倉乎?[54] It seems that at the same time when the poet reflected on his own relative smallness, he was also contemplating the relative position of his country among "a myriad nations."

---

52. Liu Sifen et al., *Lingnan sanjia shixuan* 嶺南三家詩選, p. 181.
53. Sun Wu, *Sunzi jinzhu jinyi* 孫子今注今譯 11.197.
54. *Zhuangzi jishi*, 17.563–64.

The acute sense of smallness leads to the powerful and yet ambiguous image in the last couplet:

大鵬擊水南風勁	The great *peng* bird roils the waters, the south gale is strong—
忽地吹人落軟塵	all of a sudden it blows this man down into the soft dust.

The great *peng* bird, also an image from *Zhuangzi*, is a mythical bird of immense size that can "roil the waters for three thousand miles and soar into the skies on the whirlwind for ninety thousand miles."[55] At first it seems that the *peng* bird is a figure for the poet, but the last line complicates the picture. The poet is the man being blown into the "soft dust": a reference to the busy life of a metropolis, an indication of the beginning of his land journey, as well as a Buddhist term for the mortal world. The early medieval poet Lu Ji had famously lamented that the wind and dust of the capital Luoyang sullied one's clean clothes.[56] As the young Huang Zunxian was seeking his fortune in Beijing, he, too, must have felt the same anxiety about the temptations and uncertainties of life in the city and the complications of a public career. As the great *peng* bird has been transformed from a gigantic leviathan named *kun* in the *Zhuangzi* chapter, we have been led to expect a transformation. A transformation does occur, but only in the sense of defilement and degradation. In the end, the exaggerated sense of self as a *peng* bird is deflated: the bird may soar, but the man has fallen into a dangerously promiscuous world.

Sixteen years later, in early 1890, Huang Zunxian embarked on a journey to Europe as an attaché for the Chinese ambassador Xue Fucheng 薛福成 (1838–94). By this time, however, Huang Zunxian was already forty-two years old and had had years of experience working as an attaché in Japan and in San Francisco. Departing from Hong Kong, he followed the sea route that had been taken by all the others before him, including Bin Chun, Zhang Deyi, and Wang Tao. Upon preparing to leave Hong Kong, he wrote a poem, "Thoughts and Feelings upon Boarding the Boat from Hong Kong" ("Zi Xianggang dengzhou ganhuai" 自香港登舟感懷).[57]

55. Ibid., 1.1.
56. Lu Qinli, *Quan Jin shi* 5.682.
57. Huang Zunxian, *Renjinglu*, p. 161.

又指天河問析津	Once again pointing to the Heavenly River, I inquire about the ford:
東西南北轉蓬身	this windblown tumbleweed body of mine, from east to west, south to north.
行行遂越三萬里	Going on and on, I have already traveled thirty thousand miles in all;
碌碌仍隨十九人	hectically running around, this mediocre official still follows the trail of the "nineteen men."[58]
久客暫歸增別苦	After years of living abroad, a temporary home- coming only intensifies the sorrows of parting;
同舟雖敵亦情親	those sharing the same boat, though enemies, are endeared to my heart.
龍旗獵獵張旆去	As the dragon flag flutters in the wind, we embark on the journey;
徒倚闌幹獨愴神	leaning against the railing, I feel pained, alone.

The poem begins with "once again" (*you* 又), a reference to the past. In the Tianjin poem, "asking about the ford" has a pretentious connotation: every educated premodern reader would immediately recognize the allusion to the *Analects*, in which Confucius sends his disciple Zilu to ask a pair of farmer-recluses working the field for directions to the ford. The recluses answer that the entire world is overwhelmed by surging tides (therefore there is no point in asking about the ford), and that one had better retire from the world if one cannot change it.[59] Adding the adverb *you* ("once again"), however, tempers the somber tone of the allusion, and indeed even seems to bring a wry humor to it. In the Tianjin poem, the second line describing the vast waters continues the *Analects* association, but in the Hong Kong poem, the second line evokes another remark attributed to Confucius, who said, "Now I, Qiu, am a person of east, west, north, and south" 今丘也東西南北之人也.[60] The change of perspective

58. The Lord of Pingyuan of the State of Zhao was once preparing to go on a mission to the state of Chu in order to secure reinforcements for the besieged capital of his home state. He wanted to take twenty talented people with him, but found only nineteen. An obscure retainer of his, Mao Sui 毛遂, recommended himself to the Lord of Pingyuan, who agreed to take him. Sima Qian, *Shi ji* 76.2366.

59. *Lunyu zhushu* 18.165.

60. *Li ji zhushu* 6.112.

from the vast ocean in the earlier poem to one's own person in the figure of the much more limited and fragile image of tumbleweed in the present poem is only appropriate for the man who has fallen into the mortal world. This fallen man, who had endured his fair share of suffering through long separations from family and friends, began to regard his fellow passengers, "though enemies," with a more kindly eye. The world of "soft dust" had made the poet more human—in other words, more complicated and conflicted.

A long poem on arranging flowers exemplifies such complication and inner conflict. In 1891, Huang Zunxian was appointed general consul to Singapore, where he stayed until 1894. At one point, he suffered malaria and convalesced at the home of a local millionaire; during this time he picked several different kinds of flowers from the garden and put them in a vase. These flowers, each signifying a different season in China, bloomed all at once in the tropical climate of Singapore. Huang wrote a poem entitled "A Song on Arranging the Lotuses, Chrysanthemums, and Peach Blossoms in the Same Vase" ("Yi lian ju tao zagong yiping zuoge" 以蓮菊桃雜供一瓶作歌) about this experience.[61] The poem begins with an apparently impossible situation:

南斗在北海西流	The South Dipper appears in the north, the sea flows to the west;

The appearance of the South Dipper in the north indicates the "deep south" location of Singapore, but the sea flowing to the west recalls a line in a poem by Yuan Haowen 元好問 (1190–1257): "From past to present, who has ever seen the sea flow to the west?" 古今誰見海西流?[62] It is a rhetorical question meant to demonstrate absolute impossibility. In Huang Zunxian's poem, however, it is used to positively state a fact: the world order had been turned upside down; what had been thought impossible has already happened. The spatial disorder is paralleled by a blurred sense of time as the anomaly continues:

春非我春秋非秋	spring is not our spring here, autumn not our autumn.
人言今日是新歲	They tell me that today is New Year's Day;
百花爛熳堆案頭	a hundred flowers bloom in splendor on my desk.

61. Huang Zunxian, *Renjinglu*, pp. 214–16.
62. *Yuan Haowen quanji* 8.233.

Here the poet introduces a clear distinction between "me/us" (*wo* 我) and "them" or the "others" (*ren* 人). While "I" (*wo*) is confused about time and season, the "others" (*ren*), being the locals, are keeping clear track of time.

主人三載蠻夷長	For three years the master has served as chieftain of the barbarians;
足遍五洲多異想	his tracks have covered five continents, and he has many unusual ideas.
且將本領管群花	For the moment, he uses his power to take charge of the flowers,
一瓶海水同供養	nourishing them in one vase filled with seawater.

"Chieftain of the barbarians" is perhaps intended humorously, but the humor is undercut by the painfully real sinocentric sentiment and the irony of the contemporary political situation. The strange term here is *zhuren* 主人, meaning "master" or "host," for in no sense could Huang Zunxian be called a *zhuren*: he was not in China but in Singapore, which at the time was a British colony, and he was convalescing at Mr. She's house. In fact, in a note accompanying another poem about his recuperation experience, Huang properly referred to his stay as "taking lodgings as a guest" (*jieju* 借居) and to Mr. She as "the host" (*zhuren*).[63]

In the final analysis, the poet could be the "master" only of the flowers, which he placed in a vase filled with seawater. In his English translation of the poem, J. D. Schmidt emended "seawater" to "clear water," arguing that the word for "sea" (*hai* 海) must be a misprint for *qing* 清 ("pure"), because "the flowers would have wilted in seawater."[64] The point is well taken, though I suspect we are not dealing with realistic description in this case. The Tang poet Han Yu once said, "The sea is the biggest of all things between heaven and earth."[65] Since the sea is always considered the largest container for all the water in the world, a small vase filled with seawater seems to be an appropriate figure for the inclusion of different plant species as well as of human races.

---

63. Huang Zunxian, *Renjinglu*, p. 298.

64. Ibid., p. 278.

65. *Han Yu quanji jiaozhu*, p. 2407.

蓮花衣白菊花黄	The lotus wears white, and the chrysanthemum yellow;
夭桃側侍添紅妝	the peach blossoms attend to them on the side, dressed in red.
雙花並頭一在手	The paired flowers, head to head, are held together in my hand:
葉葉相對花相當	one leaf faces another leaf, one blossom matches another blossom.
濃如栴檀和眾香	Sweet-smelling like sandalwood mixed with various perfumes;
燦如雲錦粉五色	splendid like cloudy brocade decorated in five colors;
華如寶衣陳七市	sumptuous like jeweled robes on display in the Seven Markets;[66]
美如瓊漿合天食	delicate like jade ambrosia, a food fit for gods.
如競笳鼓調箏琶	They are like drums and pipes competing with one another, or harps and flutes played in harmony;
蕃漢龜茲樂一律	Tibetan, Chinese, and Kucha music, all performed in the same key;
如天雨花花滿身	they are like flower petals showering down from the skies and covering one's body;
合仙佛魔同一室	or immortals, Buddhas, and demons all gathering within one room;
如招海客通商船	or seafarers coming aboard the same merchant vessel;
黄白黑種同一國	or yellow, white, and black races sharing the same country.

A number of similes covering all senses—sound, sight, smell, touch, even taste—are used to describe the cohabitation of the different kinds of flowers in one vase. The similes are arranged in an orderly fashion just like the flowers themselves, and verbally imitate the flowers' diversity and abundance. "Tibetan, Chinese, and Kucha music," the seafarers from dif-

66. In Buddhist scriptures, the Seven Markets refer to the Grain Market, Clothes Market, Perfume Market, Food Market, Flowers Market, Crafts Market, and Prostitutes Market. They are used as a general reference to a large and prosperous marketplace.

ferent parts of the state or of the world, and "immortals, Buddhas, and demons" all prepare the way for the striking image at the end: "yellow, white, and black races sharing the same country." The bottle vase suddenly takes on a much larger dimension.

The poet is playing God in exercising freedom of creation. In the note accompanying another poem about the same experience, Huang lists the fourth kind of flower—the plum blossoms—but this poem omits it, since the three flowers with their colors of yellow, white, and red are perfect figures for the kind of racial classification based on skin color that was popular at the time and still quite novel to a nineteenth-century Chinese.

In the next stanza, the diversity of "species/races" (both *zhong* 種 in Chinese) is transposed onto the diversity of temperaments, attitudes, beliefs, and moods:

一花驚喜初相見	One flower feels happy surprise at this meeting with the others:
四千餘歲甫識面	for more than four thousand years, this is the first encounter;
一花自顧還自猜	one flower looks at itself and cannot help wondering:
萬里絶域我能來	how could I have traveled ten thousand miles to this distant place?
一花退立如局縮	One flower withdraws, as if coiling in fear:
人太孤高我慚俗	the others are too proud while I am ashamed of my commonness;
一花傲睨如居居	one flower smugly glances at the others and seems quite arrogant;
了更嫵媚非粗疏	yet it becomes more charming, neither casual nor coarse.
有時背面互猜忌	Sometimes, jealous and suspicious, they turn their backs on one another.
非我族類心必異	Those who are not of our own species must have a different mind.
有時並肩相愛憐	Sometimes they stand shoulder to shoulder and cherish one another:
得成眷屬都有緣	all those who are joined in wedlock are following their destiny and karma.
有時低眉若飲泣	Sometimes they hang their heads low as if weeping:

偏是同根煎太急	why are those sharing the same roots the worst bullies?[67]
有時仰首翻躊躇	Sometimes they turn their heads up as if in contemplation:
欲去非種誰能鋤	who could help us get rid of those who are of a different kind?
有時俯水瞋不語	Sometimes they bend over the water, sulking in silence:
誰滋他族來逼處	who has encouraged the other races to live so close to our territory?
有時微笑臨春風	Sometimes they smile in the spring breeze:
來者不拒何不容	we welcome whoever comes to us, accepting all of them.

That "those who are not of our own species must have a different mind from ours" is an ancient adage. In the context of its early appearance in the sixth century BCE, the phrase *zulei* 族類 indicated "clan" or "kinsfolk," but since then, its meaning has been broadened to imply a group of people sharing basic characteristics, a species or race.[68] The adage itself is one of those common sayings that have in the course of time achieved the status of a universal truth; and yet, it is offset by the Buddhist belief that any relationship is a result of karma and should therefore be cherished and cultivated. The loathing of "those who are of a different species" is tempered by the recognition that sometimes "those sharing the same roots" turn out to be the "worst bullies"; the fear and hatred of the "other races" living "so close to our territory" are countered by the call for tolerance and generosity. These attitudes and beliefs contradict and counterbalance one another, and yet they are inscribed within the same text, just as the flowers are put in the same vase.

In the next stanza, the poet emphasizes "flowerhood" as a general state of being shared by all flowers. He plays God to the flowers, arranging them "without discrimination or prejudice" and hoping the flowers agree with his arrangement.

---

67. This is a reference to the famous "Seven Pace Poem" attributed to Cao Zhi, in which he supposedly protests his older brother's persecution of him. Lu Qinli, *Quan Wei shi* 7.460.

68. *Chunqiu Zuozhuan zhengyi*, the fourth year of Duke Cheng, 25.439.

眾花照影影一樣	The flowers are reflected in water, their reflections look the same:
曾無人相無我相	there is neither perception of Other, nor perception of Self.
傳語天下萬萬花	I wish to pass a message to the myriad flowers in the world:
但是同種均一家	"You are all of one race, all of one family."
古言猗儺花無知	The ancients say nice things of them, the flowers do not understand,
聽人位置無差池	they let a human arrange them, with no discrimination or prejudice.
我今安排花願否	Are the flowers happy about my arrangement today?
拈花笑索花點首	Holding the flowers in my hand, with a smile I beg the flowers to nod yes.
花不能言我饒舌	The flowers cannot speak, but I am a chatterer,
花神汝莫生分別	so I ask the flower god not to create a hierarchy.

The poet then turns his thoughts to his homeland, and hopes that his fellow countrymen will also see such a marvelous phenomenon and will perhaps be enlightened, as he is, by the flowers' cohabitation. A pun is used in the first line of the following stanza: the Chinese are known as the "people of Tang" (*Tang ren* 唐人), and greenhouse flowers that blossom early are called "hall flowers" (*tang hua* 堂花):

唐人本自善唐花	The people of Tang are skillful gardeners of greenhouse flowers:
或者並使蘭花梅花一齊發	perhaps they can also make orchids and plums bloom together.
飆輪來往如電過	The steamer comes and goes, like whirlwind or lightning,
不日便可歸支那	in no time it can take this vase all the way back to China:
此瓶不乾花不萎	the water will not even dry, the flowers will not wither;
不必少見多怪如橐駝	there is no need to marvel at the sight like a country bumpkin and call the camel "a horse with a swollen back."

Since the modern world is full of such strange new things as the speedy steamer boat, the poet begins to contemplate other possibilities of change and transformation. Toward the end of the poem, the world turns into one gigantic "wheel of reincarnation" that spins around ever more quickly and exhilaratingly. The poet envisions the day when his body will turn into the flowers and the flowers into him, and he hopes this poem by "today's me" will be read to his future self.

地球南北倘倒轉	If one day the hemispheres of the earth are turned around,
赤道逼人寒暑變	the Equator will press on us, cold and hot seasons will switch.
爾時五羊仙城化作海上山	The Immortal City of the Five Rams will then become a mountain in the sea,
亦有四時之花開滿縣	and there will be flowers of four seasons blooming everywhere.[69]
即今種花術益工	Even today, the horticultural craft is increasingly refined,
移枝接葉爭天功	grafting branches and splicing leaves, we compete with heaven's achievements.
安知蓮不變桃桃不變爲菊	How then do you know that lotuses won't turn into peaches, and peaches won't turn into chrysanthemums?
迴黃轉綠誰能窮	Yellow changes into green— who could fathom the transformation?
化工造物先造質	When the maker creates things, he begins with atoms;
控摶衆質亦多術	to bring the atoms under control, he has many methods.
安知奪胎換骨無金丹	How then do you know there's no elixir to transmute the bones?
不使此蓮此菊此桃	No elixir to cause these lotuses, these chrysanthemums, and these peach flowers

69. Guangzhou is known as the City of the Five Rams, so named because of a local legend that tells of five celestial beings wearing robes of five colors who came to Guangzhou riding through the air on rams.

萬億化身合爲一	to metamorphose and join into a single body?
衆生後果本前因	For all sentient beings, effects are determined by causes,
汝花未必原花身	and you, flowers, do not necessarily have the bodies of the original flowers.
動物植物輪回作生死	Animals and plants live and die, they reincarnate many times;
安知人不變花花不變爲人	how do you know that humans won't become flowers, and flowers, humans?
六十四質亦么麽	The sixty-four atoms are tiny indeed,
我身離合無不可	my body will disintegrate and come together again—nothing is impossible.
質有時壞神永存	There is a time when even the atoms expire, but the spirit lives on,
安知我不變花花不變爲我	how do you know that I won't become the flowers one day, and the flowers won't become me?
千秋萬歲魂有知	If my soul retains awareness for thousands and thousands of years,
此花此我相追隨	then these flowers and this self shall follow each other for eternity.
待到汝花將我供瓶時	By the time when you, flowers, put me in a vase,
還願對花一讀今我詩	I only hope you will chant this poem written by today's me to those flowers.

At the beginning of the poem, the poet has expressed a sense of discontent and disorientation about the world order being turned upside down; toward the end, however, he celebrates change and the power of creation and transformation. Inspired by new scientific inventions and discoveries, the poet sets free his imagination and mixes the Buddhist idea of reincarnation, modern scientific concepts, and a traditional Chinese figure of drastic change—the mountains turning into the sea and the sea turning into land—all in one poem, which becomes a promiscuous textual "container" for contrasting and even conflicting elements, just like the bottle vase that holds different kinds of flowers.

Different voices, attitudes, and beliefs are not always easy to reconcile, but poetry affords the poet a form that is supple, resilient, and ideal for staging ambiguity. Huang's "A Ballad of Taiwan" ("Taiwan xing" 臺灣行),

written in 1895 after Taiwan was taken by Japan, is a wonderful example.[70] In this ballad, issues of dynasty and empire, race, kinship, and sovereignty are intertwined, and the poet's profound ambivalence about these issues is conveyed by the use of a voice of a persona in keeping with the ballad tradition. But there turns out to be more than one voice in the poem; the poet's own voice, superimposed at the end of the poem, becomes one of the many competing voices in the text, holding no final authority.

The poem opens with sound and fury: a thunderstorm of beating drums, cries to heaven, a passionate public speech and tears. The background is the Qing government's cession of Taiwan as a result of its defeat in the first Sino-Japanese War.

城頭逢逢雷大鼓	A booming sound of thundering drums came from the city wall;[71]
蒼天蒼天淚如雨	with cries of "Heavens!" tears fell like rain.
倭人竟割臺灣去	"The Japs have laid claim to the territory of Taiwan!
當初版圖入天府	When the map of Taiwan first entered the imperial storage,
天威遠及日出處	heaven's might spread as far as where the sun rose.
我高我曾我祖父	Our great-great-grandfathers, our great-grandfathers, and our grandfathers
芟刈蓬蒿來此土	had cut away bitter fleabanes and thistles to settle on this soil.
糖霜茗雪千億樹	With sugar like frost, tea leaves like snowflakes, myriads of trees,
歲課金錢無萬數	every year we paid taxes to the state in tens of thousands of gold.
天胡棄我天何怒	Why would heaven abandon us? Wherein lay heaven's wrath?
取我脂膏供仇虜	Wherefore would it take our blood and fat to give to our enemies?

70. Huang Zunxian, *Renjinglu*, pp. 245–47.

71. *Lei* (thunder) puns with *lei* 擂, to beat. The source of the line is a line from a Liang ballad, "Lyrics of Princess Julu" ("Julu gongzhu geci" 鉅鹿公主歌辭). Lu Qinli, *Quan Liang shi* 29.2153.

眈眈無厭彼碩鼠　Like huge rats, our enemies glare at us,
their greed knows no bounds,
民則何辜罹此苦　and yet what have we people of Taiwan done
to deserve such miseries?
亡秦者誰三户楚　Who destroyed the mighty Qin? It was Chu,
even with only three households left;
何況閩粤百萬户　not to mention that today we still have
a million households of Min and Yue.
成敗利鈍非所睹　Success or failure, victory or defeat,
these are not what we can know;
人人效死誓死拒　we only know we shall fight till death,
resist till our last breath.
萬衆一心誰敢侮　Ten thousand people with one heart:
who would dare to insult us?"
一聲拔劍起擊柱　With one shout of "Draw your sword!"
the sword strikes the pillar:
今日之事無他語　"There must be no disagreement
about what happens today!
有不從者手刃汝　Anyone dares to object—
I shall kill him myself."

This rousing speech in defense of their right to the land appeals to history and ancestry, as well as to the people's labor and time spent. The speaker is, ironically, a descendant of the Han Chinese colonialist settlers, one of the "million households of Min and Yue" (that is, Fujian and Guangdong) that regard the Qing court as "heaven." The aborigines of Taiwan could have easily said the same thing about these Chinese immigrants: "Like huge rats, our enemies glare at us, their greed knows no bounds."

The poem continues,

堂堂藍旗立黄虎　A majestic blue banner
embroidered with a yellow tiger:
傾城擁觀空巷舞　people all came out and danced for joy,
leaving lanes empty throughout the city.
黄金斗大印系組　A gigantic seal made of yellow gold
was tied with ribbons:
直將總統呼巡撫　the people were actually calling their governor
their President!

今日之政民爲主　“In today’s governance, the people are the master.
臺南臺北固吾圉　Tainan and Taibei have always been our territories,
不許雷池越一步　we shall not let the enemy go one step beyond.”

To resist Japan’s occupation, on May 25, 1895, a group of Taiwan officials proclaimed the Republic of Taiwan, and made the governor of Taiwan, Tang Jingsong 唐景崧 (1841–1903), president. The national flag of the Republic of Taiwan was a blue banner embroidered with a yellow tiger; the president’s seal was carved with the words: “The precious seal of the Republic” (*Minzhuguo zhi baoyin* 民主國之寶印). The use of *zhi* 直, meaning “actually,” in the fourth line deserves a pause: does it impart a tone of irony, or surprise?

In the end, an embroidered tiger was no match for the Japanese soldiers, and the short-lived Republic was crushed in the fall of 1895. Tang Jingsong and his poet-general Qiu Fengjia 丘逢甲 (1864–1912) were among the first to flee back to the Chinese mainland.

海城五月風怒號　In the fifth month at the seaport,
　　the wind was howling angrily;
飛來金翅三百艘　a fleet of three hundred vessels
　　flew here with golden wings,
追逐巨艦來如潮　tailing the grand battleship like a tidal bore.
前者上岸雄虎彪　The first who came ashore were more fierce
　　than tigers and tiger cubs;
後者奪關飛猿猱　those who followed forced open the pass,
　　speeding as nimbly as monkeys and gibbons.
村田之銃備前刀　The Murata guns served as the vanguard,
當輒披靡血杵漂　anyone who met with them fell back,
　　blood everywhere.
神焦鬼爛城門燒　Gods were charred, demons boiled,
　　the city gate set on fire.
誰與戰守誰能逃　Who could still fight or defend?
　　And who was capable of escape?

The ironic tone deepens in the next stanza, which describes Taiwan’s surrender:

一輪紅日當空高　A red orb of a sun rose high in the sky,
千家白旗隨風飄　white flags on a thousand houses fluttered
　　in the wind.
搢紳耆老相招邀　Officials and elders invited one another

夾跪道旁俯折腰	to kneel by the roadside and bend their backs.
紅纓竹冠盤錦條	Red tassels on bamboo hats, with brocade ribbons,
青絲辮髮垂雲髾	dark and silky braids of hair hanging behind.
跪捧銀盤茶與糕	Kneeling down, they held up silver platters filled with tea and cakes,
綠沈之瓜紫蒲桃	melons of green stripes and purple grapes.
將軍遠來無乃勞	"The general has come a long way and must be tired;
降民敬爲將軍犒	the surrendered people respectfully ask to feast the general."

While the red sun evokes the national flag of Japan, "white flags" of surrender now replace the blue and yellow colors of the flag of the Republic. In contrast with the earlier scene, in which people all came out to celebrate the founding of the Republic and "danced for joy," here "officials and elders" pour out from their houses and kneel by the roadside to welcome the Japanese army.

The following stanza conveys the general's speech, which in many ways forms a neat parallel to the rousing speech of the Taiwan official. It also appeals to "heaven" and cites history and ancestry to justify the Japanese rule in Taiwan. It makes a suggestive reference to Zheng Chenggong 鄭成功, the Prince of Yanping, also known as Koxinga (1624–1662), the heroic general who defeated the Dutch to claim Taiwan as well as fought against the Qing as a Ming loyalist. Koxinga's mother was a Japanese woman named Tagawa Matsu who died resisting the Manchu army. The speech resorts to the concept of the "yellow race," pointing out that the Japanese, unlike the Dutch colonialists, are an Asian people just like the Chinese. Thus, in a brilliant rhetorical move, the voice of the Japanese general reminds the Taiwan Chinese that they are bound together by race and kinship, and that the Japanese are in fact much closer to them than the Manchu. The Japanese monarch is compared to the Chinese sage emperor Yao, with a promise that he will treat the Chinese immigrants in Taiwan better than the aborigines.

將軍曰來呼汝曹	The general said: "You people, come hither.
汝我黃種原同胞	You and I are both of the yellow race, related by blood:
延平郡王人中豪	the Prince of Yanping was a hero among men;
實辟此土來分茅	he was the one who opened up this land, and he was enfeoffed here.
今日還我天所教	Today the land has been returned to us;

	this is heaven's will.
國家仁聖如唐堯	Our emperor is as benevolent and sagely as the sage emperor Yao,
撫汝育汝殊黎苗	He shall comfort you and nurture you, not like how He treats the Lis and the Hmongs.
安汝家室毋譊譊	Put your family at ease, and don't grumble anymore."
將軍徐行塵不囂	The general proceeded slowly, his horse stirred no dust;
萬馬入城風蕭蕭	ten thousand horses entered the city, yet only the sound of the wind could be heard.

The serenity of the Japanese army's procession and the order and discipline of the troops are contrasted with the earlier impassioned and boisterous scene. The most remarkable thing about this poem is that nearly every side is given an opportunity to present its perspective in the struggle over Taiwan. Neither the speech by the Taiwan official nor that by the Japanese general is caricatured. Both sound reasonable, persuasive. This is unusual in premodern Chinese poetry.

The people of Taiwan are readily persuaded:

嗚呼將軍非天驕	"Alas, the general is not one of those 'proud sons of heaven';
王師威德無不包	and the imperial army's might and virtue are able to contain us all.
我輩生死將軍操	Our lives are in the hands of the general,
敢不歸依明聖朝	how dare we not surrender to the wise and sagely dynasty?"

During the reign of Emperor Wu of the Han, the Xiongnu Khan sent a letter to the Han emperor in which it was written: "In the south there is the Great Han; in the north there is the powerful Hu. The Hu people are the proud sons of heaven."[72] The Taiwan people acknowledge that the Japanese are different from the "Hu" 胡—the traditional designation for "barbarians" and threatening foreigners, here referring to people of the white race, as opposed to the "yellow race."

72. Ban Gu, *Han shu* 64.3780.

It is noteworthy that in the last line, the word *chao* 朝, "dynasty," is used to refer to the Japanese. It is, of course, a rhyme word; and yet, it carries with it the implication that Taiwan is now ruled simply by another dynasty. In other words, against the backdrop of the "yellow race" versus the "white race," the changed rule over Taiwan is no longer a matter of Chinese versus "Wo ren" 倭人 (a conventional derogative term for the Japanese), but merely a matter of replacing one dynasty with another.

The poet's voice is finally heard at the end of the poem:

噫嚱吁，悲乎哉	Alas, how sad!
汝全臺	All of you people of Taiwan!
昨何忠勇今何怯	How loyal and brave you were yesterday, how cowardly today!
萬事反覆隨轉睫	As circumstances change and turn, you too change and turn in the blink of an eye.
平時戰守無豫備	In times of peace, there was no preparation for war and defense,
曰忠曰義何所恃	though loyal, though righteous, what can you depend on in a time of crisis?

In conclusion, the poet expresses sorrow and regret about the situation in Taiwan, and criticizes the Taiwan officials for their fickleness and unpreparedness. And yet, the ending seems curiously inadequate to the event and to the complicated representation of the multiple attitudes and perspectives throughout the poem. Significantly, the voice of the poet as narrator becomes one of the many voices in the poem, and so the narrator's voice becomes one of the many voices of the poet, conveyed through the passionate speech of the Qing official, the calmly reasoning address of the Japanese general, and the emotionally ambivalent narration of the founding of the Republic, the battles, and finally the Taiwan people's reception of the Japanese troops. Since poetic narration can skip over connections and leave gaps when representing an event, it is easier for poetry than for prosaic discourse to stage ambiguity and ambivalence. By entitling his poem as a ballad, Huang Zunxian also claims to be writing in the tradition of *yuefu* poetry, the one form of classical Chinese poetry that allows the voice of a persona—for instance, a soldier, a singing girl, or a grieving mother—other than the voice of the poet. Nevertheless, we rarely, if at all, see such a complicated mélange of voices represented within one poem, let alone in such an emotionally and morally ambivalent manner.

The only absent voice is that of the aborigines, referred to as "the Lis and the Hmongs," looming vaguely in the midst of the "bitter fleabanes and thistles" cleared away by the Chinese settlers. The fight for sovereignty over Taiwan happened among peoples of the "yellow race" as opposed to peoples of the "white race" such as the Dutch, the French, and the English, who had either occupied or coveted Taiwan; but it did not extend to the natives of the island, even though an incident between the aborigines and the Japanese had been a catalyst for these events.[73] Though a superior poet and a much more complex figure, Huang Zunxian followed Bin Chun and Zhang Deyi in adhering to the hierarchical ordering of the world in his geopolitical vision.

Sometimes, in Huang Zunxian's poetry, a multitude of voices completely drown out that of the poet-narrator. In another tour-de-force performance entitled "Inviting My Townspeople to Drinks on a Spring Night" ("Chunye zhao xiangren yin" 春夜招鄉人飲), the poet uses the length of the poem to mimic the overwhelming cacophony of voices in formal terms.[74] This is the poem he wrote in 1885 upon his return from an eight-year stay overseas, first in Japan and then in San Francisco. The opening stanza of the poem sets the stage:

春風漾微和	A spring breeze ripples in harmony,
吹斷簷前雪	blowing off the snow in front of the eaves.
寒犬吠始停	A cold dog barks, then stops,
衆客互排闥	as a group of guests push open the gate.
出甕酒子釃	I have jars of well-aged rice wine brought out;
欹壁燭奴熱	candlesticks radiate heat against the wall.
花豬間黃雞	A fatty piglet and a yellow chicken
亦足供餔餟	provide us with plenty of food.
團坐盡鄉鄰	Sitting around are all old neighbors;
無復苛禮設	there is no need for fastidious etiquette.
以我久客歸	Since I have just come back from a long trip,
群起爭辯詰	they vie with one another to ask questions.

73. *Qing shi gao* 清史稿 158.4623–624.

74. Huang Zunxian, *Renjinglu*, pp. 147–50.

Questions indeed follow; the first one is about Japan:

初言日本國	First someone mentions the country of Japan—
舊是神仙窟	"In the old days it was a grotto for immortals.
珊瑚交枝柯	The branches of coral crisscross,
金銀眩宮闕	gold and silver of the palaces dazzle the eye.
雲餘白傅龕	Clouds linger in Tutor Bai's shrine;
錦留太眞襪	Taizhen left her brocade stocking behind.[75]
今猶駿鸞來	Today their folks still come here, riding on simurghs;
眼見非恍惚	people have seen it, surely it's no mirage.
子乘仙槎去	You, my dear sir, went there on a celestial raft,
應識長生訣	surely you know all about their secret to long life?
靈芝不死藥	The elixir made of magic mushrooms—
多少秘筐篋	now how much is stored in your suitcase?"

This neighbor gives a fantastic account of Japan, which, in Chinese cultural lore, has often been identified with the legendary "immortal islands." He is, however, quick to point out that the fantastic element is "no mirage" because people have "seen" their folks come riding on simurghs.

Another neighbor asks about Columbus and his discovery of America:

或言可倫坡	Someone says, "That Columbus,
索地始未獲	he sought new land but could not find it at first.
匝月糧懼罄	They drifted for months, worried about running out of food;
磨刀咸欲殺	sailors all sharpened their knives and wanted to kill him.
天神忽下降	Suddenly a heavenly god descended,
指引示玉牒	pointing a way out, showing them a jade document;
巨鼇戴山來	A gigantic tortoise came with a mountain on its back,[76]

75. Tutor Bai was the Tang poet Bai Juyi, whose poetry has left a considerable influence on Japanese literature. Taizhen was Lady Yang Yuhuan 楊玉環 (719–56), the favorite consort of the Tang emperor Xuanzong 玄宗 (r. 712–56). Xuanzong ordered her execution during the An Lushan Rebellion, but it was rumored that she was in fact secretly transported to Japan and lived there for the rest of her life. An old woman supposedly found a stocking made of brocade that belonged to Lady Yang at the place where she died; later the old woman showed passers-by the stocking for a hundred cash each time and consequently became very wealthy. This story is recorded in Li Zhao 李肇 (fl. early ninth century), *Tang guoshi bu* 唐國史補, in *Tang wudai biji xiaoshuo daguan*, p. 165.

再拜請手接	the sailors all bowed to Columbus, asking to receive it.
狂呼登陸去	Shouting triumphantly, they landed on the shore;
炮鄉轟空發	cannons were shot toward the sky with a deafening sound.
人馬合一身	These men were one with their horses,
手秉黃金鉞	with golden axes in their hands.
野人走且僵	The people of the wilds ran or fell,
驚辟鬼羅殺	in shock and fear they fled from the yakṣas.
即今牛貨洲	That continent they found is today's Aparagoyāna;
利盡西人奪	all its benefits have been snatched away by Westerners.
金穴百丈深	A golden grotto of nine hundred feet deep
求取用不竭	surely cannot be used up!"

To an educated Chinese in 1885, Columbus was no longer an entirely strange figure. The description in this stanza echoes several books that were circulating in the late nineteenth century. Wei Yuan 魏源 (1794–1857) wrote, "The Continent of America should be the very Aparagoyāna recorded in Buddhist scriptures. This is not a mere speculation."[77] The statement that "These men were one with their horses" can be explained by referring to Xu Jiyu's *A Short Account of the Maritime Circuit*, first published in 1847 and reprinted many times since 1848: "This place [America] had had no ox, horse, sheep, pig, dog, and cat before. When the Spaniards first arrived, they went on the shore riding their horses. The people on the shore saw them and, thinking the men and their horses were of one body, fled in shock and terror."[78] In the section on "America," Xu Jiyu also records that the Andes range in South America is such a rich source of silver that it is called a "golden grotto."[79]

Another book that might have inspired Huang Zunxian's neighbor was a book on world history authored by a Japanese scholar, Okamoto Kansuke 崗本監輔 (1839–1904). Entitled *A History of the Myriad Nations* (*Wanguo shiji* 萬國史記), the book was written in *kanbun* and published in Japan in 1879. The Japanese edition was quickly transmitted to

---

76. That the fantastic isles peopled by immortals in the ocean were borne on the backs of gigantic tortoises is an old legend. See, for instance, *Liezi jishi* 5.153.

77. Wei Yuan, *Haiguo tuzhi* 海國圖志 74, in *Xuxiu siku quanshu*, Vol. 744, p. 343.

78. Xu Jiyu, *Yinghuan zhilüe*, p. 293.

79. Ibid., p. 292.

China, and the work was published in China within the same year and subsequently reprinted several times. Huang Zunxian himself had not only read the work but had also critiqued it.[80] Its narration about Columbus' discovery of the New World is more detailed than in the other two works. For instance, it relates how the sailors, first cursing Columbus for misleading them, bowed to him when they finally saw land; it also relates how Columbus, in order to intimidate the natives, made such thunderous sounds with gun and cannon that some of the natives collapsed in terror.[81] The descent of a heavenly god and the appearance of a gigantic turtle are the stuff of legend, but Columbus himself was the first to mythologize his adventure.[82] The stanza about the Americas in Huang's poem is a romantic portrayal of Columbus that comes from textual knowledge.

Another neighbor asks the poet about the extraordinary fish in the Pacific Ocean:

又言太平洋	Someone else talks about the Pacific Ocean,
地當西南缺	"It's located in the crack of the earth to the southwest.
下有海王宮	Down below is the palace of the ocean king,
蛟螭恣出沒	where dragons emerge and disappear at will.
漫空白雨跳	A white rain splashes all over the sky—
往往魚吐沫	a fish spewing foams from time to time.
曾有千斛舟	Once there was a colossal boat
隨波入長舌	driven into the fish mouth by the breakers.
天地黑如磐	Heaven and earth turned as dark as under a huge rock,
腥風吹雨血	a foul-smelling wind blew down the rain of blood.
轉腸入輪回	The sailors entered the reincarnation wheel of twisting intestines;
遺矢幸出穴	luckily they came out as fish excrement.
始知出魚腹	Only then did they know they were out of the fish belly;
人人慶復活	everyone congratulated themselves on their survival."

80. See the discussion of Huang Zunxian's view of this work in Liu Yajun, "Wan Qing xueren 'shijie lishi' guannian de bianqian," p. 98.

81. Okamoto, *Wanguo shiji* 19.2a–b.

82. See Mary B. Campbell's discussion of this point in Chapter 5 of *The Witness*.

This is material for an account of marvels, and yet it can be found in none other than Bin Chun's diary and poetry about his overseas experience. Printed after his return (with two of the three prefaces dated late 1869), his diary became so well known that it soon made its way to Japan and was reprinted there in 1872; it was also popular enough to be reprinted in China.[83] One of the diary entries records that he was shown the bones of a "gigantic fish measuring more than fifty feet in length" when he was in Sweden. Bin Chun recounts how he climbed a ladder and "entered the fish mouth and sat there for a little while."[84] He wrote a poem, "Viewing a Big Fish" ("Guan dayu" 觀大魚), to commemorate the marvel:

巨魚聞説可吞舟	I hear the big fish could swallow a boat;
皮化爲船六丈修	now its skin is made into one of fifty feet.
今日九人魚腹坐	Today nine people sit in the belly of the fish,
宛然游泳在中流	it is as if we were swimming in the midst of the waves.[85]

The neighbor in Huang Zunxian's poem who asks about the Pacific Ocean might very well have been inspired by this account.

Another neighbor's imagined version of the foreign experience can be entirely annotated by citations from earlier accounts of foreign travel, including Bin Chun and Zhang Deyi's diaries, both circulating in print by this time:

傳聞浮海舟	Someone says: "I've heard that those boats sailing the ocean
盡裹十重鐵	are all wrapped up with ten folds of iron.
疊床十八層	Eighteen layers of bunker beds
上下各區別	are divided into high and low.
牛羊豕雞狗	Oxen, sheep, pigs, chickens, and dogs,

83. The Japanese edition, *Jōsa hikki*, was published in the fifth year of the Meiji era (1872) by Fukuroya Kamejirō in Tokyo. This edition is currently in the Rare Book collection of Harvard Yenching Library. Lü Wen-tsuei ("Transcultural Travels," pp. 24–25) believes that the diaries kept by various Qing diplomats were rarely printed and not easily accessible to elite members or common readers, and that Zhang Deyi's diaries were the only ones among this group that circulated in the book market, but this was not necessarily the case.

84. Bin Chun, *Chengcha*, p. 127. This is the diary entry for the twenty-ninth day of the fifth month of the fifth year of the Tongzhi era (July 11, 1866).

85. Ibid., p. 174.

萬物萃一筏	ten thousand creatures all in one boat.
康莊九達間	On the boat there are nine wide avenues,
周廬千户辟	a thousand lodgings all have their doors open;
船頭逮船尾	from the head of the boat to the tail,
巡行認車轍	the guards make their rounds, following carriage tracks."

Zhang Deyi's diary contains detailed descriptions of ocean liners. One diary says: "The front half [of the boat] has 1,500 foldable iron beds for second-class passengers. On the left and right are sheep pen and chicken coop; the foul smell is unbearable."[86]

Another neighbor asks about architecture:

其人好樓居	"The foreign folks love to live in storied buildings
四窗而八達	with four or eight windows on all sides.
千光璧琉璃	A thousand strands of light radiate from glass,
五色紅靺鞨	red rubies shine in five colors.
傑閣高入雲	Towering mansions reach into the clouds,
明明月可掇	one could grab the bright moon with one's hands."

For these lines I must cite Zhang Deyi again: "The walls are all made of white stone, and the windows, of glass."[87] Another entry records, "There are millions of houses, big and small, in the French capital, and their windows are all made of glass without any paper. One can see through it from inside or from outside; it is all bright and transparent, and protects well against wind and rain."[88] The first Chinese visitors abroad were impressed by the glass windows, as Chinese windows were still constructed from paper pasted on wooden screens. They were also struck by the height of the buildings. Wang Tao commented in his *Jottings from Wanderings*: "The buildings in the capital city [London] were arranged in close formation like fish scales or the teeth of a comb. Those as high as several stories touch the sky and enter the clouds. When someone leans against the railing and gazes into distance, I almost suspect it is a divine being, who can be looked at from afar but cannot be approached."[89]

---

86. Zhang Deyi, *Ou Mei huanyou ji*, p. 629.
87. Zhang Deyi, *Hanghai shuqi*, p. 491.
88. Zhang Deyi, *Ou Mei huanyou ji*, p. 779.
89. Wang Tao, *Manyou suilu*, p. 103.

The topic then switches to another aspect of foreign life:

出入鬼仙間	"Coming and going amidst demons and immortals,
多具鎖子骨	many of them have 'chain-like bones.'[90]
曾見高絙伎	Someone once saw a performer on a rope high above ground,
行繩若飛越	who walked on that rope as if with wings.
犁靬善眩人	Those Lijian magicians are good at producing illusions;
變態尤詭譎	their transformations are particularly bizarre.
常聞海客談	We have often heard the seafarers' talk;
異説十七八	seven or eight out of ten are such strange stories.
太章實親見	You, a swift-footed Taizhang, have seen with your own eyes—[91]
然否待子決	whether the stories are true or not, we await your judgment."

The fascination with foreign acrobats and circus shows had had a long-standing tradition in China. "Lijian" is the Chinese name for the Roman Empire, which was famous for its performance of "many extraordinary illusions."[92] Chinese visitors to Europe and America recorded many viewings of theater and circus shows in extravagant language. In Huang's poem, the neighbor asks the poet to testify to the veracity of those fantastic stories with his own eyewitness account.

Another neighbor is interested in foreign food. It is noteworthy that every food term in the following stanza can be traced to some earlier literature, with "alfalfa" and "grapes" as the signature foreign foodstuff, even though they were imported from Central Asia into China nearly two millennia earlier.

90. "Chain-like bones" are believed to be a characteristic of those higher beings who had obtained the Way.

91. Taizhang 太章 was the swift-footed minister of the legendary sage emperor Yu 禹. He was ordered by Yu to measure the earth from east to west. Liu An, *Huainan honglie jijie* 4.132.

92. This was recorded in the account of the Roman Empire (Da Qin 大秦) in the third-century historian Yu Huan's 魚豢 *Wei lüe* 魏略, cited in the commentary to Chen Shou, *Sanguo zhi* 30.860. *Shi ji* records that the country of Tiaozhi 條枝 (Tajik) "was good at producing [magic] illusions" (*shan xuan* 善眩). Sima Qian, *Shi ji* 123.3163.

諸胡飽腥膻	"Those foreigners eat meat to their full,
四族出饕餮	the gluttonous Taotie is one of the four evil monsters.[93]
飣盤比塔高	Fruit platters pile taller than a tower,
硬餅藉刀截	hard cakes must be cut with a knife.
菜香苜蓿肥	They have lush alfalfa for their vegetable,
酒豔葡萄潑	and their wine is made from grapes.
冷淘粘山蠔	Cold noodle, 'hilly oysters' stuck together,
濃汁爬沙鱉	the sand-crawling turtle cooked in a heavy sauce.[94]
動指思異味	The index finger quivers, as one craves exotic flavors,[95]
諒子固不屑	but I suppose you did not care much for them?"

Yet another neighbor comments on the physical appearances of the foreigners and criticizes the poet for sporting a beard:

古稱美鬒眉	"The ancients praised 'a fine dark beard and eyebrows,'
今亦誇白皙	today we admire a fair complexion instead.
紫髯盤蟠虬	Those foreigners have purplish beards like a coiling dragon,
碧眼閃健鶻	green eyes flashing like a handsome hawk.
子年未四十	You are not yet forty years old,
鬑鬑須在頰	but you already grow some whiskers on your cheeks.
諸毛紛繞涿	'The many "hairy Maos" lived around Zhuo county'—[96]
東塗復西抹	putting some powder here, some rouge there.

93. This is a reference to the legend recorded in *Chunqiu Zuozhuan*. The sage emperor Yao sent the four monsters, including the gluttonous Taotie, into exile. *Chunqiu Zuozhuan zhengyi* 18.73 (the eighteenth year of Duke Wen).

94. Fruit platter, hard cake, alfalfa, grape, cold noodle, "hilly oyster" (so called because the oysters get stuck together and form a little "hill"), and sand-crawling turtle are all fancy delicacies.

95. That "the index finger quivers" was taken to mean one was going to enjoy delicious food. It comes from a story recorded in *Chunqiu Zuozhuan zhengyi* 21.368 (the fourth year of Duke Xuan); also see Sima Qian, *Shi ji* 42.1767.

96. "The many 'hairy Maos' lived around Zhuo county" is a reference to an anecdote in *Sanguo zhi* 42.1021. A heavily bearded minister was teased by the founder of the Shu Kingdom, who invented a story about many people with the surname "Mao" (which means "hair") living in Zhuo county.

得毋逐臭夫	Aren't you like those who loved stench and followed it around?[97]
習染求容悦	Are you, inured by habit, seeking to please them?
子如誇狄強	If you ever dare say the barbarians are any good,
應舉巨觥罰	you should be punished by drinking down a huge goblet."

Yet another neighbor expresses skepticism about the sizes of foreign countries:

謬稱夜郎大	"They brag about their countries like the small state of Yelang,[98]
能步禹跡闊	but could they truly follow the vast tracks of Yu?
試披地球圖	If we unroll the world map,
萬國僅蟣虱	myriad nations look like fleas.
豈非談天衍	Aren't they like Yan who discoursed on heaven,[99]
妄論工剽竊	talking nonsense and copying from others?"

Yu was the legendary sage emperor from high antiquity who traveled through the territories of China to implement waterworks during the Great Flood, and the phrase "Yu's tracks" is often used as a synonym for China in later times.[100] The neighbor's skepticism is reminiscent of a popular joke about some Manchu officials' refusal to believe the existence of so many foreign countries in the world. Wan Qingli 萬青藜 (1821–83), who served as the Minister of Defense in the early 1860s, had once burst out: "How could there possibly be so many countries in the world?!

---

97. This is a reference to a story about a man with a powerful unpleasant body odor. He lived alone by the seashore away from family and friends who could not bear the odor, but there were hoards of people who loved the smell and followed him around. Lü Buwei, *Lüshi chunqiu* 14.816.

98. *Shi ji* records that the Lord of Yelang (in modern Guizhou) asked the Han emissary: "Which state is larger, Han or Yelang?" Sima Qian, *Shi ji* 116.2996.

99. "Yan who discoursed on heaven" was Zou Yan 鄒衍, a man of Qi (modern Shandong) who lived in the third century BCE and reputedly loved discoursing on metaphysical topics. He believed that the Chinese land was only one of the nine great continents in the world. *Shi ji* 74.2348. In the nineteenth century, as the Chinese perception of the world broadened, Zou Yan was frequently evoked.

100. This is a reference to the *Zuozhuan* remark: "Vast are the tracks of Yu, who divided [China] into nine prefectures" 芒芒禹跡, 畫爲九州. *Chunqiu Zuozhuan zhengyi* 29.507 (the fourth year of Duke Xiang).

When you think about it, there are no more than two or three countries out there. One day they call themselves Yingjili [England], the next day they call themselves Yidali [Italy], and then the next day they call themselves Ruidian [Sweden]—all just to deceive China!"[101]

By this time the drinking party, just like the poem itself, has progressed to a climax. At the beginning of the poem, a spring breeze "ripples in harmony"; now the "harmony" has vanished into a din of voices that keep getting louder. The dog's barking is replaced by the "thunderous laughter" shaking the roof tiles loose. As the drunken neighbors "overturn cups and drop chopsticks," the absence of "fastidious etiquette" now lapses into complete chaos. In contrast, the poet himself becomes speechless.

一唱十隨和　One opens his mouth and ten chime in;
此默彼又聒　as soon as one falls silent, others begin.
醉喝杯箸翻　Drunkenly they overturn cups and drop chopsticks;
笑震屋瓦裂　thunderous laughter cracks open roof tiles.
平生意氣頗　All my life I have been quite the man,
滔滔論不歇　I can give as eloquent a discussion as anyone.
到此窮詰屈　At a time like this, I fumble for words,
口箝舌反結　my mouth is shut, my tongue is tied.
自作滄溟遊　Ever since I sailed on the gray waves,
積日多於髮　more numerous days had passed than one's hair.
所見了無奇　What I saw was not in the least strange,
無異在眉睫　indeed no different from what's before our eyes!
山經伯翳知　Boyi knew the *Classic of Mountains*;
坤圖懷仁説　Huairen explained "The Chart of the World."[102]
足跡未遍曆　My foot tracks have not yet covered the globe,
安敢遽排訐　how do I dare criticize and refute?

101. Wang Kangnian, *Zhuangxie xuanlu* 3.30a.

102. Boyi was the minister of the legendary sage emperor Shun. Boyi and Yu were in charge of "driving away birds and beasts, ordering mountains and rivers, categorizing plants and trees, and distinguishing waters and soils" 驅禽獸, 命山川, 類草木, 別水土. See the memorial to the throne accompanying the presentation of the *Classic of Mountains and Seas* by Liu Xin 劉歆 (53 BCE–23 CE), in Yan Kejun, *Quan Han wen* 40.346. Nan Huairen 南懷仁 was the famous Flemish Jesuit missionary Ferdinand Verbiest (1623–88), who came to China in 1659 and eventually died in Beijing. He was the author of *Illustrated Discussion of the Geography of the Earth (Kunyu tushuo* 坤輿圖説), published in 1674. See Smith, "Mapping China's World," p. 72.

大鵬恣扶搖	The great *peng* bird, with the whirlwind beneath its wings,
暫作六月息	is taking a rest after its six-month journey.
尚擬汗漫遊	I am planning another far roaming
一將耳目豁	to widen the scope of my ears and eyes.
再閱十年歸	After another ten years I will return,
一一詳論列	and then I will, one by one, give you answers.

This brilliant ending makes a brilliant poem, whose most important point lies in the deliberate contrast and subtle balance between the guests' and the host's perspectives. The guests, who have never been abroad, are apparently voracious and curious readers of contemporary overseas travel accounts. They seem to know so much about the "outside world" from reading and hearsay that their book knowledge reduces the only person with real experience of the foreign countries to silence. Upon close examination, however, much of their "knowledge" turns out to be either conventional fantasy about distant lands or excessively focused on the exotic aspects of life abroad, and in the end falls squarely within the heaven/hell paradigm of seeing the world, oscillating between "demons and immortals." Such knowledge is easy to articulate because it is already codified; in comparison, the poet is struck speechless by the complexities of *his* knowledge that has come from long years of experience. Because of his prolonged stay in the foreign countries, he has, on the one hand, become so used to "the strange" that he no longer considers it "strange"; on the other hand, a deeper understanding strips away the mirage effect from the foreign lands and peoples, enabling the poet to finally see their humanity that is "no different from what's before our eyes." This is a debunking of the "love of the strange" (*haoqi*), not by way of familiarization like in Wang Tao's case, but by way of deconstructing "the strange" itself.

The poet, of course, is not truly silent. He has his last word by representing his neighbors' views of the world in a poem. This poem is a self-conscious reflection on the possibility of writing about the foreign without being trapped by the topoi and tropes of encountering the foreign; it makes use of the rhetorical schemata of seeing to question and challenge such schemata. In this poem, what has seemed strange now becomes familiarly so and conventionally so, and hence ceases being strange; the "truly strange" is the human condition shared across cultures. This "truly strange" aspect is inexpressible exactly because it has gone beyond the traditional schemata of seeing the world.

The nineteenth century was a century of violent change worldwide. During this tumultuous century, China underwent, for the second time in its history, a profound cultural and intellectual transformation when it came into close contact with the foreign. In the early medieval period, the Buddhist cosmos seemed more an abstract principle than a tangible reality, and distant countries, unlike China's neighboring states, were still more a matter of hearsay, not something one could encounter face-to-face. Now things were different. Members of the Chinese elite, not just traders, sailors, interpreters, and clerks, embarked on voyages across oceans and saw with their own eyes the brave new world "out there." In the meantime, the Western powers made their way into China, bringing with them new technologies, knowledge, and concepts.

In *Bringing the World Home: Appropriating the West in Late Qing and Early Republican China*, Theodore Huters discusses "how China's crisis of accommodation worked itself out in the realm of literature—in particular, in narrative fiction and the critical work that accompanied the very self-conscious transformation of the genre of the novel after 1895."[103] As Huters demonstrates, during the late Qing and early Republican period, there was a self-conscious theorizing of "literature" (*wen*), especially fiction, as a central strategy, albeit deeply problematized, in the enterprise of national salvation. What I am more interested in is the role of poetry in China's negotiations with the new world order in the late nineteenth century. Although fiction came to occupy an increasingly prominent position in the literary realm as the "new novel" was regarded as "the key to national mobilization," poetry did not receive the same kind of wide critical attention in the late Qing, until it came under attack in the early twentieth century when the May Fourth intellectuals advocated for a new vernacular poetry. Huang Zunxian is frequently associated with the idea of a "poetic revolution" at the turn of the century, but, as it has been pointed out, Huang himself never used such a term in his extant writings.[104] In any case, in contrast with the weighty public role imposed on fiction, writing poetry turned out to be a largely private act, an attempt

103. Huters, *Bringing the World Home*, p. 15.
104. See Schmidt, *Within the Human Realm*, pp. 47.

made by an individual person to deal with an alien situation. Huang Zunxian's repeated emphasis on the expressive role of poetry highlights poetry as individual expression rather than in terms of its influence on public life.[105] This was certainly not characteristic of the conception of the role of poetry in China's long premodern tradition, but it has interesting consequences for our consideration of late nineteenth-century poetry.

In this chapter, my interest in the role of poetry focuses not so much on any critical writing about the genre as on the actual ways in which the genre works. In his classic study of literary form, Kenneth Burke proposes to think of poetry as "strategic answers" to "questions posed by the situation in which they arose." "These strategies size up the situations, name their structure and outstanding ingredients, and name them in a way that contains an attitude towards them."[106] Nineteenth-century poetry portraying overseas experience provides strategic answers to a situation both familiar and new: familiar, because this was certainly not the first time in Chinese history that people came into impactful contact with the foreign world; new, because the content of the situation had changed. The adoption of the poetic form, with its textual allusions and echoes of earlier literary works, is the very means by which the poet combats the sense of alienation thrust upon him. Just as Perseus had to fight Medusa, who turned anyone looking at her directly into stone, by observing her reflection, "the poet's style, his form (a social idiom), is this mirror, enabling him to confront the task, but by the protection of an indirect reflection."[107] To beleaguer poetry with the accusation of "formulaic" or "inaccurate" conveyance of information is to miss the point of literary studies, which is not just to ask *what* but also to ask *how*. In other words, form *is* content.

The paradigm of seeing the foreign world in either heavenly or hellish terms in earlier literature furnishes a basic framework for making sense of the strange and the unknown. And yet such a paradigm, while proffering a sense of comfort as well as a discursive means of articulating a difficult experience, proved inadequate for those elite travelers who, like Huang Zunxian, were sophisticated enough to discern the complexities of the

105. Ibid., pp. 53–55.
106. Burke, *The Philosophy of Literary Form*, p. 4.
107. Ibid., pp. 53–55.

foreign world they found themselves in. Poetry turned out to be an enabling genre because of its particular generic features. A successful poem incorporates complexities and contradictions that are not easy to reconcile and perhaps cannot ever be reconciled, because the condensation of the classical poetic form permits the juxtaposition of different, even contradictory, elements in a way that a discursive style of writing may not allow. A relation is constructed by this juxtaposition, but in a sophisticated work, the relation is supple, evocative, and full of interpretive potential. Interpretation is always the interplay of a text and its reader, but not all texts are created equal: in what they offer a reader, some texts are rich and some are impoverished.

The following poem by Huang Zunxian epitomizes many of the issues discussed here. This poem, simply entitled "My Little Daughter" ("Xiaonü" 小女), was written in 1885, at about the same time as "Inviting My Townspeople to Drinks on a Spring Night."[108] The poet was spending some quiet time with his long-separated family, after a sojourn spanning tens of thousands of miles and eight years.

一燈團坐話依依	My family sat around a single lamp, having an intimate chitchat;
簾幕深藏未掩扉	deeply hidden behind the drawn curtains, a door not yet closed.
小女挽鬚爭問事	My little daughter caressed my beard, asking me this and that;
阿娘不語又牽衣	then she tugged at her mother's clothes, who had fallen silent.
日光定是舉頭近	"The sun must be very close— one can see it just by raising one's head;
海大何如兩手圍	you say the ocean is big, but what if I cup it with both hands?"
欲展地球圖指看	I was about to unroll the world map and point at it for her to see,
夜燈風幔落伊威	when a breeze slipped into the curtains, flames flickered, and a moth fell.

Unlike in many of Huang Zunxian's poems, only the fifth line makes a textual reference that needs some explanation, taking us back to the early

108. Huang Zunxian, *Renjinglu*, p. 151.

medieval period again. In the early fourth century, Emperor Yuan of the Jin, who founded the new regime after the Jin royal house was forced to cross the Yangzi River by non-Han invasions, once held his young son, the future Emperor Ming, on his knees and asked him, "In your opinion, how far is Chang'an compared with the sun?" Emperor Ming answered, "Chang'an is closer, for I have heard people come from Chang'an, but I have never heard anyone come from the sun." Emperor Yuan marveled at the child's precocious intelligence. The next day he assembled his courtiers, and like any proud parent eager to show off a child's talent, he asked Emperor Ming the same question. This time Emperor Ming replied: "The sun is closer." Emperor Yuan's face fell. He said, "Why did you change your answer?" Emperor Ming said, "Well, I raise my head and see the sun, but I cannot see Chang'an."[109]

This is a story that would have been well known to any educated premodern Chinese reader. As such, it enables the reader to recognize a familiar framework for speaking of a child's precocity. It is, however, immediately followed by a line for which there is no literary precedence: "you say the ocean is big, but what if I cup it with both hands?" For all we know, the first line of the couplet, though apparently a textual reference, might have been a real utterance of the little girl, and the second line an imagined witticism. But it is impossible to recover the "real" world outside the poem to which this couplet refers. What we do know is that familiarity and novelty need each other: the first line, being a conventional literary trope of precocious intelligence, presents the reader with a well-established cultural-linguistic code; the second line, on the other hand, creates a "reality effect" by representing what is not standard, what is individual and personal. This couplet both comforts the reader with an existing discourse and jolts the reader out of it. In doing so, it calls our attention to its own constructed nature, and to the constructed nature of the imaginary space represented by the poem.

It is, we notice, an enclosed space: the family sits down in a circle around a single lamp—it is evening time, perhaps after dinner—and the curtains are drawn. It is a space that belongs to domestic life and to the womenfolk, marked by the wife's presence and the daughter's chatter. The poet establishes a boundary from the very beginning, a boundary

---

109. Fan Xuanling et al., *Jin shu* 6.15.

separating the inside from the outside, his family from the world, the women's domestic space from the man's public space. The former is intimate, warm, and peaceful: even the unrolling of the world map must be interrupted because it does not fit in such a feminine space—it is so small, so delicate, compared with the world outside.

And yet, the boundary is not rigid, and there are cracks everywhere. In the second line of the poem the poet tells us that a door is left open. Wind slips in, lamp flames flicker, and a moth is burned to death. The intimate, warm, and peaceful scene ends in a small act of violence and death. The outside world looms as a threatening force, a sudden gale blowing in from darkness.

But even before this climax, the outside world is already encroaching upon them, as the poet's little daughter is showing her intense curiosity about the world by asking him all sorts of questions: How far is the foreign land compared with the sun? Surely I can cup the ocean if I use both of my hands? What strikes us is the contrast between the smallness of the girl and the vastness of the ocean. The little girl's innocence seems touchingly fragile against the immensity and hardness of the world. The dynamics would presumably have been different if the poet were talking about his son: a boy would grow into a man, go out into the world, and soar like a *peng* bird, like his father; but a girl in nineteenth-century China had no such great expectations. Her mother's silence, in this context, is intriguing and yet revealing. It is an eloquent silence that coincides textually with the ultimate silence of the demise of the moth.

Suddenly, the poet seems awkwardly out of place in this domestic space. He himself represents the force of the outside world, even as he seeks refuge in his family home from the wind and waves of his ocean journeys and of national and international politics. He himself is an intruder into the space of the womenfolk, a stranger after an absence of eight long years. His masculinity is inscribed everywhere: in his beard, caressed by his little daughter; and in his world map, rolled up in the suitcase. He is no Odysseus—there are no suitors for him to slay—but he certainly has disturbed the domestic order and peace by bringing back with him new knowledge, charts, maps, and tall tales about the ocean and the brave new world. It is interesting that when he offers to show his little daughter the world map, the word he uses is *zhikan*: to point at it for her to "see." He seems to be implying that only by seeing it for herself can she comprehend the enormity of the world; but just then the wind blows in, the flames flicker, and a moth dies. The man is locked up in the loneliness of his newly acquired knowledge of the world that he finds impossible to communicate to the people back home—his neighbors, relatives, wife, and daughter—just as the woman is locked up in the loneliness of her domestic existence, and the girl in her innocence.

In the past, the phrase one commonly used to orient himself was *jia guo* 家國, "home and state"; but now it must become *jia shijie* 家世界, "home and the world." In many ways, the family home of the poet, and the enclosed domestic space described in the poem "My Little Daughter," is an allegory of China on the eve of an age of nationalism and internationalism. But the powerful, enigmatic image at the end of the poem, the burned moth falling from the lamp flames, interrupting the unrolling of the world map and distracting the little girl: *that* belongs to poetry, poetry of the best kind—and it intervenes between the poet and the foreign world he encounters.

Afterword

My main goals in writing this book are twofold. The first is to draw attention to the parallel between two important moments in Chinese history—namely, the early medieval period and the nineteenth century. In more ways than one, there exists a surprising similarity between the two, and the differences highlighted by such a similarity are equally illuminating.

A popular myth about imperial China is that it was isolated from the world, closed off until the Western powers forced open the gate in the nineteenth century. This belief presumes tradition to be a static site untouched by history, and it is, as this book demonstrates, far from the truth. Early medieval Chinese were frequently on the road; they had an insatiable desire to see the world and to see with new eyes. A paradigmatic structure of seeing and representing the world was established during this period and continued into the nineteenth century, all while sustaining a great deal of pressure and tension. While the two periods are generally similar, their differences lie in their respective peculiarities and their strategic responses to these peculiarities.

One of the key differences is the impact of technology, which was altering the world in the nineteenth century. In comparison with the technological equilibrium in early medieval times, scientific advances made by Western countries and the resulting advantages, both military and economic, to those countries were the main factors that changed the power equation between China and the West in the nineteenth century. While great transformations of the native cultural tradition took place voluntarily and gradually over the course of several centuries in early medieval

China, they occurred in the nineteenth century with speed and an unprecedented sense of urgency. Out of necessity, Chinese scholar elite traveled farther outside the empire than ever before, and even though they still fell back on the earlier heaven/hell framework, especially in their initial encounter with the Western world, what they saw increasingly could no longer be contained by it.

The cases of Xie Lingyun and Huang Zunxian form an instructive contrast. Xie Lingyun was an avid traveler, but he never stepped out of the bounds of the southern empire—in fact, his last stopping point, where he was executed, was Guangzhou. He belonged to the turn-of-the-fifth-century generation that not only was eager to see hitherto unexplored parts of the world, but, more importantly, prided themselves on seeing with new eyes. His was an epoch of deliberate expansion on geographical, cultural, and intellectual fronts, but this expansion happened in spatial terms with the temporal configuration of the cosmos largely remaining stable. In contrast, Huang Zunxian lived in an age when it was time, not space, that was undergoing the most dramatic transfiguration. The world space, uneven and diverse as it was, was subjugated to a universal narrative of linear progress and evolution, in the familiar story of modernity. As Xiaobing Tang put it, "Through temporalization, world geography is systematically narrativized and hierarchized, and world history can culminate only in Europe—'the center and end of the old world'—which is coterminous with the present."[1] Huang Zunxian traveled across time as much as across space, and the temporal disjunction was in many ways much more difficult to contend with than the spatial disjunction experienced by the earlier travelers.

Both Xie Lingyun and Huang Zunxian used poetry as a way of coping with change, and this brings us to the second goal of the book, which is an examination of the various responses to the great cultural transformations they lived through, with a particular emphasis on poetry. On the one hand, this book discusses different types of texts that cut across generic and disciplinary divisions in the hope of shedding light on common concerns with which the people of a given period were engaged; on the other hand, the book attempts to illuminate the ways of poetry by placing it alongside other types of texts that a literary scholar might normally over-

1. Tang, *Global Space and the Nationalist Discourse of Modernity*, p. 230.

look. While we should indeed investigate the situation out of which a poem is born and to which the poem constitutes a response, we must not forget that a poem is an intricate verbal art form with a nature of its own. The book asks how exactly poetry works as an act of self-protection, intervention, and thinking through the complexities of the poet's own, deeply personal situation, not just as an illustration of an issue of cultural history. Poetry *is* action, and it is the most elegant action in encountering the world.

In some ways, the study of late Qing poetry is itself a symbolic act. Compared with late Qing narrative forms, late Qing poetry is relatively understudied; one of the reasons for this is perhaps the belief, mentioned in the preceding chapter, in the impoverished and "exhausted" nature of classical-style poetry during this time, a belief that lends itself easily to the rationalization of the "rise of new poetry" in the early twentieth century. The underlying assumption is that literary forms also follow the model of evolution in European modernist discourse, which played a dominant role in the May Fourth mindset.

In early medieval China, the vast corpus of translated texts was primarily Buddhist scriptures. Although these texts served as a rich source of Chinese literature and produced a profound impact on it, they were never self-consciously acknowledged as such, nor were they considered part of the cultural sphere or the sphere of *wen*, which remained conceptually and bibliographically segregated from the realm of religious texts. Toward the end of the nineteenth century, foreign literatures for the first time emerged on the horizon as "literature" for the Chinese elite, even though the influence of Western poetry did not make itself fully felt until the early twentieth century. This was a significant new factor in China's encounter with the foreign in comparison with early medieval times, and it had interesting consequences. Literature became *Chinese* literature, situated side by side with other national literatures; it had to take on the task of reconciling the burden of its own past with its new role in the nation-building project that demanded severance from the past. When it came to poetry, the traditionally privileged genre with a much longer history and thus a heavier legacy than vernacular fiction, it seemed that nothing short of a complete break from tradition would be sufficient to construct the identity of a "modern" poetry.

In such a situation, old poetic forms tend to be either ignored or denigrated; indeed, the conception of "modern Chinese poetry" today still largely adheres to the outmoded May Fourth binary framework of "old versus new." The provocative question raised by David Wang in his ground-breaking study of late Qing fiction, "What modern genres, styles, themes, and figures have been repressed and suppressed by certifiably 'modern' Chinese literary discourse?" is uncannily pertinent to modern classical-style poetry.[2] The argument I offer for modern classical-style poetry is, however, *not* that the "old" genre is elastic and so could "contain new wine," because the very dichotomy of old/new remains trapped within the "framework of false essentialisms" invented at a specific moment of history for an ideological purpose.[3] Instead, I argue for a reconceptualization of modern Chinese poetry as a space marked by hybridity and diversity, a space where repressed modernities are being played out. In other words, what makes this poetry "modern" is not the supposed replacement of an old form with a new form defined negatively against the old form, but rather the coexistence and juxtaposition of different forms.[4] This juxtaposition itself characterizes the modern condition in the Chinese case.

Huang Zunxian's floral metaphor comes to mind. In his poem on flower arranging in Singapore, dislocation occurs on several levels. In local terms, the poet was a guest in another man's residence; in general terms, he was a visitor in the colony of another empire, far away from mainland China, on an island with a diversified population consisting of, among other Asians, Chinese, Malays, and Indians, as well as of Caucasians. A different spatial configuration leads to a different sense of time, as the tropical climate and the absence of seasonal distinction in Singapore, located barely one hundred miles north of the Equator, make possible the coexistence of flowers that are only considered markers of different sea-

---

2. David Wang, *Fin-de-siècle Splendor*, p. 15.

3. Chatterjee, *The Nation and Its Fragments*, p. 134.

4. By "defined negatively," I refer specifically to the fact that the verse form of modern vernacular poetry is free to be anything except classical. Therefore, a "new poem" can be rhymed or unrhymed, can have any number of characters/syllables in any given line, and can have any number of lines, but it cannot, for instance, appear in four lines with five or seven characters/syllable for each line. For a recent article on contemporary classical-style poetry, see Tian, "Muffled Dialect Spoken by Green Fruits."

sons at a different geographical location. While each flower retains its unique characteristics, their juxtaposition creates the effect of defamiliarization and enables the poet to see them with new eyes. In other words, each flower, each form, is changed by the presence of the others.

In Huang's poem, it is noticeably the poet who, playing host, functions as the agent in bringing the flowers together and then, in an act of imagination, sees into the future. The early medieval Chinese first stressed subjectivity and human agency—the power of the mind's eye—in discovering luminous patterns in mountains and waters. Now the late nineteenth-century poet, in a tour-de-force verbal performance, takes us on a visionary journey into the future that began with his present and our past.

Appendixes

APPENDIX I

*Xie Lingyun's "*Fu *on My Journey"* (*"Zhuanzheng fu"* 撰征賦)[1]

Xie Lingyun's "*Fu* on My Journey" begins with a preface in unrhymed prose. In the preface, Xie Lingyun relates the events that prompted him to compose the poetic exposition. In 416, the Jin general Liu Yu undertook a military campaign against the Later Qin (386–417) kingdom. According to Liu Yu's biography in *Song shu*, the army set out from the capital Jiankang on September 19, 416. Liu Yu camped at Pengcheng 彭城 (in modern Jiangsu). Prior to this, Liu Yu had sent his generals, Tan Daoji 檀道濟 (d. 436), Wang Zhen'e 王鎮惡 (373–418), and Wang Zhongde 王仲德 (d. 438), as vanguards. In October and November, the Jin troops recovered Huatai 滑臺 (in modern He'nan), a strategically important site, as well as the former Jin capital Luoyang, and repaired the tombs of the Western Jin emperors. In February 417, Emperor An of the Jin 安帝

1. The sources for this text are Shen Yue, *Song shu* 67.1743–53; Yan Kejun, *Quan Song wen* 30.2600–2603; Gu Shaobo, *Xie Lingyun ji jiaozhu*, pp. 250–62. There are three modern annotations of this poetic exposition: the earliest by Li Yunfu in *Xie Lingyun ji*, pp. 169–220; the second by Song Xulian 宋緒連 in *Li dai fu guangxuan*, pp. 76–128; and the third by Du Zhiqiang 杜志強 in *Li dai fu pingzhu*, pp. 23–75. Invaluable as these annotations are, they are incomplete and, in many places, inaccurate. In his "'Zhuanzheng fu bing xu' zhushi," Xiong Qingyuan has pointed out a number of errors in Li Yunfu's annotations. Du Zhiqiang is critical of the annotations in *Li dai fu guangxuan* (see his article "Xie Lingyun 'Zhuanzheng fu'"), although his own annotations in *Li dai fu pingzhu* contain many new errors and problems.

(r. 397–419) issued an edict promoting Liu Yu to prime minister and enfeoffing him as the Duke of Song.[2]

In December 416, Xie Lingyun was dispatched as the emperor's envoy to visit Liu Yu. He reported back to the court in March 417. He presumably began the writing of the poetic exposition during his return journey and completed it shortly afterward.[3]

蓋聞	I have heard that
昏明殊位	Darkness and light occupy different positions,
貞晦異道	Ill and good fortune go separate ways.
雖景度回革	Although luminosity and order return in the cycle of change,
亂多治寡	Chaos is predominant, and harmony rare.
是故	For this reason
升平難於恆運	It is difficult for peace to reign long,
剝喪易以橫流	But easy for destruction to spread wide.
皇晉鼎移河汾	The imperial house of Jin had moved its sacred tripod from the region of the Yellow and Fen Rivers
來遷吳楚	And relocated to the land of Wu and Chu.
數歷九世	Since then, it has been through nine rulers;
年踰十紀	It has lasted more than ten decades.[4]
西秦無一援之望	There was no hope for assistance from the western State of Qin;
東周有三辱之憤	The Eastern Zhou court had to suffer humiliations three times.[5]

---

2. Shen Yue, *Song shu* 2.36–41. Sima Guang, *Zizhi tongjian* 117.3695.

3. There are a few different theories about the dating of this piece: some scholars believe it was composed in 418 (see *Xie Lingyun shixuan*, p. 155; Su Ruilong, "Lun Xie Lingyun," pp. 48–49), while others argue it was composed as late as 419 (see Li Yan, *Xie Lingyun yanjiu*, pp. 139–40). I agree with Gu Shaobo (*Xie Lingyun ji jiaozhu*, pp. 372–73), who dates the piece to 417.

4. The Eastern Jin was established in 317 by Emperor Yuan 元帝 (r. 317–23). Emperor An was the tenth ruler after Emperor Yuan.

5. In 505 BCE, the King of Wu captured the capital of Chu; Shen Baoxu 申包胥 went to seek assistance from Qin. He cried for seven days and nights in the Qin court, and finally compelled Qin to agree. Sima Qian, *Shi ji* 5.197. The humiliations suffered by the Eastern Zhou refer to the exiles of three Zhou kings: King Hui, King Xiang, and King Jing. Each king relied on the assistance of the lord of Zheng or Jin to return to the Zhou capital. Sima Qian, *Shi ji* 4.151, 154, 157.

可謂積禍纏釁	One may verily say that our dynasty has been embroiled in disasters
固以久矣	For a very long time.
況迺	Not to mention
陵塋幽翳	The ancestral mausoleums were overgrown and concealed,
情敬莫遂	And it had been impossible to pay them heartfelt respect.
日月推薄	As days and months pressed on in turns,
帝心彌遠	The imperial pining was long-lasting.
慶靈將升	Then an auspicious aura was on the rise;
時來不爽	When the time was right, there was no deviation.
相國宋公	The prime minister, the Duke of Song,
得一居貞	In possession of the Way, followed the correct path.
回乾運軸	He turned back heaven by moving its axis.
内匡寰表	Within the empire, he lent aid to the land;
外清遐陬	Without, he cleared off far-flung areas.
每以區宇未統	Since the world was not yet unified,
側席盈慮	He was always filled with worries, unable to sit at ease.
值天祚攸興	Heaven bestowed upon us good luck,
昧弱授機	As the ignorant and weak received the state power.[6]
龜筮元謀	Divination by tortoise shell and *shi* plant yielded a good plan;
符瑞景徵	All signs pointed to a favorable outcome.
於是	At the time,
仰祇俯協	The Duke found peace above and accord below,
順天從兆	He respected heaven's will and heeded the propitious omen.
興止戈之師	Raising the army that would stop all wars,
躬暫勞之討	He personally embarked on the short-term campaign.
以義熙十有二年	On the *dingyou* day of the fifth month
五月丁酉	In the twelfth year of the Yixi era,[7]
敬戒九伐	The Duke declared the Nine Punishments for the wicked,
申命六軍	And delivered his command to the Six Regiments.
治兵于京畿	The troops set out from the suburbs of the capital,

6. Yao Xing 姚興 (366–416), the ruler of the Later Qin, died in 416, and his son, Yao Hong 姚泓 (388–417), succeeded him.

7. This was July 1, 416.

次師于汳上	And camped on the banks of the Bian River.[8]
雲檣千艘	There were a thousand ships with cloud-piercing sails,
雷輜萬乘	And ten thousand chariots with thundering wheels.
羽騎盈塗	Plumed riders filled the road;
飛旍蔽日	Flying banners concealed the sun.
别命羣帥	The Duke issued a separate order to the generals,
誨謨惠策	Giving them instructions in military maneuvers.
法奇於三略	His methods were more extraordinary than *The Three Tactics*;
義祕於六韜	His principles were more secret than *The Six Strategies*.[9]
所以	Thereupon,
鉤棘未曜	Even before the hooked halberds were applied,
殞前禽於金墉	The fast-fleeing fowls already met with their destruction at the Fort of Metal Walls;
威弧始彀	The bows had just been drawn
走鈒隼於滑臺	When the hawks were already retreating from the fort of Huatai.[10]
曾不踰月	Before a month was over,
二方獻捷	The news of victory came from these two places.
宏功懋德	The Duke's great achievements and virtue
獨絶古今	Were matchless from past to present.
天子感東山之劬勞	The Son of Heaven was moved by the toils of the Eastern Hills,[11]
慶格天之光大	And lauded the grand merit that touched gods.
明發興於鑒寐	At dawn, rising from a sleep with full clothes on,
使臣遵于原隰	An envoy began to traverse the plain.

---

8. Bian 汳 is also written as Bian 汴. The Bian River merges with the Si River 泗水 at Pengcheng.

9. *The Three Tactics* and *The Six Strategies* are both military works that were said to have been authored respectively by the Old Man of the Yellow Rock 黄石公 (see below) and Lü Wang 吕望, councilor to King Wen of the Zhou. Wei Zheng et al., *Sui shu* 34.1013.

10. Jinyong, the "Fort of Metal Walls," was a fortress in the northwestern corner of Luoyang. On November 27, 416, Tan Daoji captured Luoyang. Sima Guang, *Zizhi tongjian* 117.3696. Huatai at the time was in the territory of the Northern Wei; the governor of Huatai surrendered the city to Liu Yu's army without a fight. Sima Guang, *Zizhi tongjian* 117.3692.

11. The Son of Heaven refers to Emperor An. The poem "Eastern Hills" ("Dongshan" 東山) in the *Classic of Poetry* is supposed to be a depiction of the Duke of Zhou's military campaign against rebels in the east. *Mao shi zhengyi* 8.294–97.

余攝官承乏	I was temporarily employed to fill this office,
謬充殊役	Taking upon my unworthy self the extraordinary task.
皇華愧於先雅	The "Brilliant Splendor" of the emissaries was praised, though I could hardly presume to aspire to the former worthies of the Odes;[12]
靡盬頳於征人	Unceasingly laboring for the king's business, this traveler exerted himself no less than the foot soldiers.
以仲冬就行	Having set out in the second month of winter,
分春反命	I reported back in the midst of spring.[13]
塗經九守	My path took me through many commanderies;
路踰千里	My journey lasted more than a thousand miles.
沿江亂淮	Following the currents of the Yangzi, cutting across the Huai River,
遡薄泗汳	I went upstream on the waters of Si and Bian.
詳觀城邑	I observed cities and towns in detail,
周覽丘墳	And surveyed hills and mounds.
眷言古迹	As I looked back upon the sites of old,
其懷已多	Feelings swelled in my bosom.
昔皇祖作藩	In the old days, my august grandfather had served as the regional governor;
受命淮徐	He received the imperial command to take charge of Huai and Xu.[14]
道固苞桑	His way was as sound as the roots of a mulberry tree;
勳由仁積	His accomplishments came from the accretion of benevolence.
年月多歷	Many months and years have gone by,
市朝已改	The marketplace and court have changed;
永爲洪業	But the grand enterprise is everlasting,
纏懷清歷	And it is ever so clearly etched in my mind.
於是采訪故老	Therefore, during my travel I interviewed local elders,
尋履往迹	And traced the former tracks;
而遠感深慨	Stirred deeply by the past,

12. "Brilliant is the Splendor" ("Huanghuang zhe hua" 皇皇者華) is a poem from the "Lesser Odes" (*Xiao Ya* 小雅) of the *Classic of Poetry* that sings the praises of the imperial emissary. *Mao shi zhengyi* 9.318.

13. *Fenchun* 分春 refers to the second month of spring.

14. "My august grandfather" refers to Xie Xuan, who was made governor of Xuzhou 徐州 in 379.

痛心殞涕	I felt a pang in my heart, and tears fell.
遂寫集聞見	I then gathered what I had seen and heard, wrote it down,
作賦撰征	And composed the following poetic exposition to relate my journey.
俾事運遷謝	I hope when time passes and events recede into the past,
託此不朽	I will, by means of this work, obtain immortality.
其詞曰	The poetic exposition is as follows.
系列山之洪緒	My ancestors continued the great enterprise of Lieshan,
承火正之明光	And inherited the bright light of the Fiery Office;[15]
立熙載於唐后	The chief of the Four Mountains aggrandizes the accomplishments of the Tang emperor;[16]
申讚事於周王	And the Earl of Shen gave assistance to the kings of Zhou.[17]
疇庸命而順位	As repayment for carrying out the imperial commands and being obedient to the throne,[18]
錫寶珪以徹疆	Precious jade was granted to make the statutory division of land.
歷尚代而平顯	Throughout high antiquity, my clan was peaceful and prominent;
降中葉以繁昌	In the middle ages it flourished and prospered.

15. Lieshan refers to the legendary Emperor Shennong 神農 of early antiquity. See Zhang Shoujie's 張守節 (fl. seventh century) commentary in Sima Qian, *Shi ji* 1.3. The Fiery Office was held by Zhurong 祝融, the officer in charge of fire, during the time of another mythical emperor, Di Ku 帝嚳.

16. I have followed Sun Bin's 孫彪 (fl. 1890–1905) emendation in reading *li* 立 as *yue* 岳. See Shen Yue, *Song shu* 67.1744. "Yue" refers to the chief of the Four Mountains ("si yue" 四岳), the official in charge of the four mountains (Mt. Tai, Mt. Heng 衡, Mt. Hua, and Mt. Heng 恆) in the four directions under Emperor Yao (also known as Tang Yao 唐堯 because he had once been enfeoffed at Tang) in early antiquity. Sima Qian, *Shi ji* 1.20. The phrase "xi zai" 熙載 alludes to a remark made by Yao to the chief of the Four Mountains. *Shangshu zhengyi* 3.44.

17. The Earl of Shen was the descendant of the chief of the Four Mountains; he was enfeoffed at the Township of Xie 謝. See the poem "Grand and Lofty Mountain" ("Song gao" 崧高) in the *Classic of Poetry*. *Mao shi zhengyi* 18.669–71. Xie was believed to be the place of origin of the Xie clan.

18. The phrasing comes from Yao's remarks to the chief of the Four Mountains: "Oh, you chief of the Four Mountains, I have been on the throne for seventy years. You have been able to carry out my orders; I will yield to you my position" 咨, 四岳, 朕在位七十載, 汝能庸命, 巽朕位. *Shangshu zhengyi* 2.28. "Xun" 巽 is sometimes glossed as "shun" 順.

業服道而德徽	Its achievement lay in the cultivation of the Way and possession of fine virtues;
風行世而化揚	Its influence prevailed in the world, its moral impact was transmitted far and wide.
投前蹤以永冀	Following the tracks of my forefathers, I harbor eternal hope;
省輶質以遠傷	Reflecting on my own light substance, however, I feel a vast sorrow.
睽謀始于蓍蔡	Going against divination consultations, I did not carefully plan how things began;[19]
違用舍於行藏	And I deviated from the principle of "when employed, act; when neglected, go in hiding."[20]
庇常善之罔棄	Protected by the sage who excels in never abandoning people,[21]
憑曲成之不遺	I rely on him who follows every twist and turn of things without omission.[22]
昭在幽而偕煦	The sun illuminates those hidden, so they share in the warmth;
賞彌久而愈私	The longer the appreciation is, the more private it becomes.
顧晚草之薄弱	I gaze upon this fragile belated plant,
仰青春之葳蕤	And look up to the lush growth of the green spring.
引蔓穎於松上	Winding its extending tip around the pine,
擢纖枝於蘭逵	It sprouts slender tendrils over the orchid-covered path.
施隆貸而有渥	I have been showered with generous favor,
報涓塵而無期	I wish to repay such grace with a mere water drop and dust mote, but do not know when I will have the chance.

19. "Heaven and water operate in opposite ways: this constitutes the image of Contention. In doing things the noble man must carefully plan how they begin" 天與水違行, 訟, 君子以作事謀始. *Zhou yi zhengyi* 2.34.

20. Confucius told his disciple Yan Yuan 顏淵: "'When employed, act; when neglected, go in hiding.' Only you and I have achieved this" 用之則行，舍之則藏，唯我與爾有是夫. *Lunyu zhushu* 7.61.

21. This is a reference to *Laozi*: "The sage always excels in saving people, and does not abandon anyone" 聖人常善救人，而無棄人. *Laozi jiaoshi*, p. 109.

22. This is from the *Classic of Changes*: "[A sage] follows every twist and turn of things without omission" 曲成萬物而不遺. In other words, he deals with things as they come and adapts to change. *Zhou yi zhengyi* 7.147.

歡太階之休明	I rejoice in the magnificent clarity of the Grand Stairs Constellation;[23]
穆皇道之緝熙	With a sense of awe I revere the brightness of the Imperial Way.

At the opening of the poetic exposition, the poet traces his clan lineage and situates himself within a long and glorious family tradition. He also expresses regret about not having begun his official career well. Xie Lingyun had served under Liu Yi 劉毅 (d. 412), another powerful general who had vied with Liu Yu for power and was killed; afterwards, Xie Lingyun was briefly appointed as Liu Yu's aide before he entered the court as vice director of the Palace Library, but he was dismissed from office for some offense.[24]

In the following passage, the poet relates the reason for his mission, beginning with a reflection on the trouble that had been inflicted on the Jin royal house by the invasion of non-Han peoples.

惟王建國	When a king founds the state,
辨方定隅	He distinguishes the four directions and sets up the periphery.
内外既正	The inside and outside are established,
華夷有殊	The Han and non-Han are differentiated.
惟昔小雅	From the "Lesser Odes"
逮於班書	To Ban's work of history,
戎蠻孔熾	Records show that the *rong* and *man* peoples acted with impunity,
是殛是誅	They must be punished, they must be destroyed.[25]
是以	For this reason,
宣王用棘於獫狁	King Xuan of the Zhou applied halberds against the Xianyun;

---

23. The Grand Stairs is a six-star constellation. It was believed to consist of three levels, each level representing a particular social group or class. When the three levels worked well together, it signified order and peace in the world.

24. Shen Yue, *Song shu* 67.1743.

25. Many poems from the "Lesser Odes" of the *Classic of Poetry* describe military campaigns against non-Han tribes (referred to as "Xianyun" 玁狁) in the north, such as "Proceeding with the Chariots" ("Chu ju" 出車), "Gathering the Ferns" ("Cai wei" 採薇), and "The Sixth Month" ("Liu yue" 六月). "Ban's work" refers to Ban Gu's *Han shu*.

高帝方事於匈奴	The Exalted Emperor of the Han was engaged with Xiongnu.[26]
然侵鎬至涇	And yet, the Xianyun invaded Hao and advanced to Jing;
自塞及平	The Xiongnu made their way from the frontier to Pingcheng.
闚郊伺鄙	They cast greedy glances at the outer reaches of cities and peeped at border towns;
圍郭攻城	They surrounded boroughs and attacked metropolises.
慕攜王之矯虔	The enemy took advantage of King Xie's usurpation,[27]
階喪亂之未寍	And profited from the ensuing destruction and disorder.
竊彊秦之三輔	They snatched the three regions of the mighty Qin;
陷隆周之兩京	And captured the two capitals of the grand Zhou.[28]
雄崤澠以制險	They occupied Xiao and Mian and controlled an advantageous position;
據繞霤而作扃	Relying on Raoliu, they made it their gateway.[29]
家永懷於故壤	Families craved their former soil;
國願言於先塋	The state pined for the ancestral mausoleums.
俟太平之曠期	People waited for peace, which was slow in coming,
屬應運之聖明	And depended on the wise man who would respond to circumstances.
坤寄通於四瀆	The *kun* principle entrusts its unobstructed openness to the Four Watercourses;

---

[26] "King Xuan" refers to King Xuan of the Zhou, whose expedition against the Xianyun people is, according to traditional interpretation, the subject of the poem "The Sixth Month." The poem contains the lines: "[The Xianyun] invaded Hao and overrun Fang, / All the way to the north of Jing" 侵鎬及方，至于涇陽. *Mao shi zhengyi* 10.359. The Exalted Emperor refers to the founding emperor of the Han, who was besieged at Pingcheng 平城 (modern Datong of Shanxi) by Xiongnu for seven days. Sima Qian, *Shi ji* 384–85.

27. King Xie refers to Bofu 伯服, the son of King You of the Zhou and his favorite concubine. The king replaced the Crown Prince with Bofu; the Crown Prince's maternal grandfather, Marquis of Shen, attacked the Zhou capital and killed King You. Sima Qian, *Shi ji* 4.149. *Chunqiu Zuozhuan zhengyi*, the twenty-sixth year of Duke Zhao, 52.903.

28. "San fu" 三輔, literally "three assistants," originally indicates the three officials in charge of the capital regions in the Western Han; later it is used to refer to the capital region in general. The "two capitals of the grand Zhou" are Haojing (to the southwest of modern Xi'an) and Luoyang.

29. Xiao Mian refers to Mianchi 澠池 and Mt. Xiao 崤山 in modern He'nan. Raoliu is the name of a notoriously perilous winding road in Shaanxi.

乾假照於三辰	The *qian* principle lends its radiance to the Three Lights.[30]
水潤土以顯比	Water moistens the earth, demonstrating Closeness;
火炎天而同人	Fire blazes against heaven, exemplifying Fellowship.[31]
惟上相之叡哲	Our prime minister, wise and sagacious,
當草昧而經綸	Managed the state in a time of chaos.
總九流以貞觀	Governing the nine ranks of people according to the observation of what is true,
協五材而平分	He harmonized the Five Virtues, possessing them in equal portion.[32]
時來之機	Detecting the incipiency of an event when the time comes,
悟先於介石	He acted faster than those who are "harder than a rock";[33]
納隍之誡	Taking the warning of "pushing someone into the moat,"
一援於生民	He was eager to extend a helping hand to the common folk.[34]

---

30. The *kun* principle refers to the principle of earth; the *qian* principle, that of heaven. The Four Watercourses are the Yellow River, the Yangzi River, the Huai River, and the Ji River 濟水. *Erya zhushu* 7.120. The Three Lights are the sun, moon, and stars.

31. The Commentary on the image of the hexagram of Closeness ("Bi" 比) says: "Water on earth constitutes the image of Bi. In the same way, the former kings established the myriad domains and treated the feudal lords with geniality" 地上有水，比，先王以建萬國，親諸侯. *Zhou yi zhengyi* 2.37. The Commentary on the image of the hexagram of Fellowship ("Tongren" 同人) says: "Heaven and fire constitute the image of Tongren. In the same way, the noble man associates with his own kind and distinguishes among things" 天與火，同人，君子以類族辨物. *Zhou yi zhengyi* 2.44. These two lines stress the importance of making a distinction between "outside" and "inside" and of associating with one's own kind.

32. The five virtues are courage, wisdom, benevolence, trustworthiness, and loyalty. *Taigong liutao*, p. 108.

33. This is a reference to the hexagram of Contentment ("Yu" 豫), which states: "Harder than a rock, he does not let the day run its course. Constancy is auspicious" 介于石，不終日，貞吉. *Zhou yi zhengyi* 2.49. Confucius' commentary on the hexagram reads: "A gentleman acts as soon as he becomes cognizant of the incipience of something and does not wait for the day to run its course." 君子見幾而作，不俟終日. *Zhou yi zhengyi* 8.171. This line praises Liu Yu for his ability to seize an opportunity.

龜筮允臧	As divination turned up truly propitious results,
人鬼同情	Humans and spirits shared the same sentiments.
順天行誅	In obedience to the will of heaven, castigation was meted out;
司典詳刑	The officer in charge of statutes announced careful application of punishments.[35]
樹牙選徒	The commander's standard decorated with ivory was set up, the elite troops selected,
秉鉞抗旍	Axes were held in hand, banners raised high.
弧矢罄楚孝之心智	In matters of bow and arrow, the filial son of Chu exhausted his ingenuity;
戈棘單吳子之精靈	Master Wu depleted his mental energy regarding affairs of spear and halberd.[36]
迅三翼以魚麗	Warships of three different sizes sped up in fish-file formation;
襄兩服以雁逝	The chariot horses galloped like swift wild geese.
陣未列於都甸	Even before the army line was formed in the suburbs,
威已振於秦薊	The majesty of the troops already shook Qin and Ji.[37]
灑嚴霜於渭城	Savage frost descended upon the City of Wei,[38]
被和風於洛汭	A gentle breeze spread over the region of Luo.[39]
就終古以比猷	If we should seek a match for such accomplishments,

34. This is an allusion to Zhang Heng 張衡 (78–139), "A Poetic Exposition on the Eastern Capital" ("Dongjing fu" 東京賦): "If one person does not have a proper place, [the emperor] would feel as if he had personally pushed the person into the moat" 人或不得其所，若己納之於隍. Yan Kejun, *Quan Han wen* 53.766.

35. Poem No. 2 of Wang Can's 王粲 (177–217) "Joining the Army" ("Cong jun shi" 從軍詩) contains the line: "The officer of statutes declared the careful application of punishments" 司典告詳刑. Lu Qinli, *Quan Wei shi* 2.361.

36. "The filial son of Chu" might be a reference to Han Xin 韓信 (d. 196 BCE), the famous Western Han general who was enfeoffed as King of Chu. When he was still an impoverished commoner, he identified a burial site for his deceased mother that was spacious enough for ten thousand households guarding the tomb, a practice fit for a king. Sima Qian, *Shi ji* 92.2629–30. Master Wu was Wu Qi 吳起, a brilliant military strategist of the Warring States period. See his biography in *Shi ji* 65.

37. Ji is an old name for the region of modern Beijing.

38. The City of Wei was Xianyang 咸陽, the old Qin capital. Here it refers to the Later Qin capital Chang'an.

39. *Luo rui* 洛汭 refers to the point where the Luo River flows into the Yellow River; here it refers to the region of Luoyang.

考墳冊而莫契	Examining ancient and modern books we would find none.
昔西怨於東徂	In the past, those in the west lamented eastern journeys;[40]
今北伐而南悲	Now those in the south were saddened by northern campaigns.
豈朝野之恆情	How could this be the constant mood of the court and the people?
動萬乘之幽思	Yet it certainly aroused deep feelings in the Son of Heaven.
歌零雨於豳風	We sang of the "drizzling rain" of the "Airs of Bin,"
興采薇於周詩	And felt stirred by "gathering the ferns" in the Zhou poem.[41]
慶金墉之凱定	While we celebrated the victory at the Fort of Metal Walls,
眷戎車之遷時	We longed for the tarrying chariots that would not come home.
佇千里而感遠	We were moved when we looked across the vast distance of a thousand miles,
涉弦望而懷期	We craved a date for the troops' return, after the passage of days and months.
詔微臣以勞問	This humble subject was ordered by the imperial edict to convey His regards to the army,
奉王命於河湄	And I proceeded to carry out the king's command at the river shores.
夕飲餞以俶裝	After the evening's farewell banquet, I prepared my luggage;
旦出宿而言辭	In early morning I stayed outside home, having taken my leave.
歲既晏而繁慮	The year was getting late, concerns were many;
日將邁而戀乖	As the day was passing, I was affected by separation.
闕敬恭於桑梓	I would have been found lacking in serving my elders,
謝履長於庭階	And declined to spend the Winter Solstice Festival with my family.
冒沈雲之晻藹	Braving the darkness cast by heavy clouds,
迎素雪之紛霏	I greeted the flurries of white snow.

40. This refers to the poem "Eastern Hills" (see note 11 above).

41. These are two poems about military campaigns from the *Classic of Poetry* (see below).

凌結湍而凝清	Ice formed on fast-flowing water and congealed its purity;
風矜籟以揚哀	Wind raised its sound and spread sadness.
情在本而易阜	Feelings that touch the roots are easy to swell;
物雖末而難懷	Though external things may be insignificant, they are hard to bear.
眷余勤以就道	As I reflected upon the toils of traveling,
苦憂來其城頹	I felt a sorrow that could topple the city walls.

As the journey begins at Jiankang, the poet reflects on the dynastic history of the Eastern Jin. This section ends with another panegyric on Liu Yu.

爾乃	Thereupon
經雉門	I passed through the Pheasant Gate,
啓浮梁	And the Pontoon Bridge opened up for me;
眺鍾巖	I gazed far at Bell Mountain,
越查塘	As I sailed over Zha Pond.[42]
覽永嘉之紊維	I examined the law and order subverted in the Yongjia reign,
尋建武之緝綱	And traced the proper measure adopted during the Jianwu era.[43]
于時	At the time,
內慢神器	The divine vessels were scorned from within,
外侮戎狄	And the Rong and Di peoples were bullying us from without.
君子橫流	Noblemen were caught in the flood;
庶萌分析	Commoners were scattered and dispersed.
主晉有祀	But there was one in charge of the sacrifices to the Jin,
福祿來格	And blessings descended upon us.
明兩降覽	The Bright Sun sent down its illumination;
三七辭厄	The disaster of the "three sevens" was averted.[44]
元誕德以膺緯	Emperor Yuan, born virtuous, took up the imperial rule,

42. Zhatang refers to Zhapu 查浦 (to the south of the Stone Fortress), with "tang" (pond) being used for the purpose of rhyme.

43. Yongjia was the reign title of Emperor Huai 懷帝 of the Western Jin (r. 307–13); Jianwu (317–18) was the reign title of Emperor Yuan 元帝, the founder of the Eastern Jin.

44. Lu Wenshu 路溫舒, a Western Han official, foretold that the Han would suffer a calamity at the juncture of "three sevens." According to the *Han shu* commentary, the "three sevens" refers to 210 years, from the founding of the Western Han until the death of Emperor Ping of the Han 平帝. Ban Gu, *Han shu* 51.2372.

肇回光於陽宅	And began the return of sunlight in his residence.[45]
明思服於下武	Emperor Ming was bent on continuing the enterprise,[46]
興繼代以消逆	He rose as the successor and obliterated the rebels.
簡文因心以秉道	Emperor Jianwen with his intellectual mind adhered to the Way;
故沖用而刑廢	Thereupon harmony prevailed, and punishment was abolished.[47]
孝武捨己以杖賢	Emperor Xiaowu yielded himself to the worthies he relied upon;
亦寧外而治內	He, too, brought peace to outer regions, and ruled the realm well.[48]
覩日化而就損	As one observed the daily cultivation and daily reduction,[49]
庶雍熙之可對	Peace and harmony might still be encountered.
閔隆安之致寇	I was saddened by the rebellion in the Long'an era,
傷龜玉之毀碎	And lamented the destruction of the state's treasures.
漏妖凶於滄洲	The evil-doers escaped to the isles on the gray waters,
纏釁難而盈紀	The country was embroiled in chaos for a full decade.[50]

45. According to Emperor Yuan's biography, when he was born, there was "the extraordinary omen of a divine light, which illuminated the entire room" 有神光之異，一室盡明. Fang Xuanling et al., *Jin shu* 6.143.

46. Emperor Ming (r. 324–36) was the son of Emperor Yuan. He suppressed Huan Wen's revolt during his reign. The first line of the couplet refers to a *Shi jing* poem, "Xia wu" 下武 ("Succeeding the Forefathers"): "Succeeding their forefathers in the Zhou, / For generations there had been wise kings" 下武維周，世有哲王. *Mao shi zhengyi* 16.581.

47. Emperor Jianwen, the youngest son of Emperor Yuan, ruled from 371 to 372. His biography describes him as "tranquil and pure, with few desires, and particularly good at metaphysical discourse." Fang Xuanling et al., *Jin shu* 9.219.

48. Emperor Xiaowu (r. 373–97) was the third son of Emperor Jianwen. He appointed Xie An as his prime minister, who successfully fended off the Former Qin's attack.

49. "Daily reduction" is a phrase from *Laozi*: "In the pursuit of learning, one increases every day; in the pursuit of the Way, one reduces every day" 爲學日益，爲道日損. *Laozi jiaoshi*, p. 192.

50. Long'an was the reign title of Emperor An. The Long'an era lasted from 397 to 401. The Sun En Rebellion broke out in 399. Although Sun En died in 402, his brother-in-law Lu Xun 盧循 continued the revolt until his death in 411. Xie An's son, Xie Yan 謝琰 (d. 400), was among the many Eastern Jin officials killed in the civil war. Sun En often retreated to the sea when he encountered any setback in the revolt. See Fang Xuanling et al., *Jin shu* 100.2631–634.

時焉依於晉鄭	At the time, the court depended upon Jin and Zheng;[51]
國有蹙於百里	The state shrank more than a hundred miles a day.[52]
賴英謨之經營	We relied on the wise man to manage the state,
弘兼濟以忘己	Who extended beneficence to all people and forgot himself.
主寰内而緩虞	He took control in the capital region and relieved troubles;
澄海外以漬滓	He purged the outlying land of stains.
至如昏祲蔽景	At a time when a wicked aura blocked the sun,
鼎祚傾基	The foundation of the state was crumbling.
黍離有歎	There were sighs over the lush millet,
鴻雁無期	Yet the date for the wild geese was nowhere in sight.[53]
瞻天命之貞符	He observed the auspicious signs of the Mandate of Heaven;
秉順動而履機	Acting in accordance with the natural principle of things, he seized the moment.
率駿民之思效	All worthy people longed to devote themselves;
普邦國而同歸	The entire country stood unified as one.
盪積霾之穢氛	Clearing the filthy atmosphere of enduring sandstorms,
啓披陰之光暉	He opened the light to cleave the darkness.
反平陵之杳藹	He restored the lushness of the imperial mausoleums,
復七廟之依稀	And recovered the appearance of the ancestral temples.
務役簡而農勸	Bent on reducing labor and encouraging farming,
每勞賞而忠甄	He invariably rewarded the diligent and recognized the faithful.
變時雍於祖宗	He brought about the current peace of the ancestors;
布乂安於海甸	He spread order and concord to the farthest seashore.

51. When the Western Zhou collapsed, the royal house of the Zhou moved its capital east and relied greatly on the help of the feudal lords of Jin and Zheng. *Chunqiu Zuozhuan zhengyi*, the sixth year of Duke Yin, 4.71.

52. This line contains another allusion to a line from a *Shi jing* poem, "Shao min" 召旻, which laments the ruin of the state: "[In the past] The state expanded a hundred miles a day. / Now our state shrinks a hundred miles a day." 日辟國百里，今也日蹙國百里. *Mao shi zhengyi* 18.699.

53. These lines refer to two poems from the *Classic of Poetry*. The first is "Lush Millet" ("Shu li" 黍離), in which, according to the traditional interpretation, an official laments the ruined capital of the Zhou now overgrown with millet. The second is "Wild Geese" ("Hongyan" 鴻雁). According to the traditional interpretation, it praises King Xuan of the Zhou for bringing peace and rest to his people. *Mao shi zhengyi* 4.147–48, 11.373–74.

埽逋醜於漢渚	He wiped out fleeing bandits on the shores of the Han River;[54]
滌僭逆於岷山	He cleaned up the mutinous usurpers at Mt. Min.[55]
羈巢處於西木	He reined in those living in nests in the western grove;
引鼻飲於源淵	And drew near people drinking from ravines with their noses.[56]
惠要襋而思韙	He clothed people in fine attire, and they were grateful for his grace;
援冠弁而來虔	Holding ritual caps in hand, they submitted in sincerity.

As the poet passes through the Foundry City, he thinks of Wang Dao, the key figure in the founding of the Eastern Jin, who had set up his headquarters at the Foundry City when he was the magistrate of Danyang 丹陽.

視冶城而北屬	I gazed at the Foundry City, then I looked north,
懷文獻之收揚	I recalled the rise and withdrawal of Wenxian.[57]
匪元首之康哉	If not for the wisdom of the head of the state,
孰股肱之惟良	How could there be such a good minister?[58]
譬觀曲而識節	It was like observing the music and knowing the rhythm,
似綴組以成章	It was like weaving silk threads and creating a pattern.
業彌纏而彌微	His legacy has become increasingly entangled and increasingly diminished;
事愈有而莫傷	But his enterprise has become ever more distinct, and cannot be hurt.

Xie Lingyun's thoughts about Wang Dao might have been provoked by Liu Yu, who, just like Wang Dao, was the power behind the throne. But their differences were also unmistakable: Wang Dao had been good personal friends with Emperor Yuan before the latter took the throne,

54. This line refers to Liu Yu's defeat of Huan Xuan 桓玄 (369–404), the usurper of the Jin throne, in 404. Huan Xuan had fled from the capital to Jiangling, in the region of the Han River. Shen Yue, *Song shu* 1.10–11.

55. This refers to the conquest of Qiao Zong 譙縱, who had ruled Shu, in 413. Ibid., 2.31.

56. "Those living in nests" and "people drinking with their noses" refer to non-Han tribal people.

57. Wenxian was Wang Dao's posthumous title.

58. This is a textual allusion to a song recorded in *Shangshu*: "The head of the state is wise; the ministers, like the four limbs, are all good; various affairs are all in order" 元首明哉, 股肱良哉, 庶事康哉. *Shangshu zhengyi* 5.74.

and, despite his immense influence, had remained a loyal supporter of the Jin royal house till his death. In contrast, the current Jin emperor, Emperor An, was mentally retarded, and the Jin royal house was clearly in a precarious position at the moment when Xie Lingyun wrote the poetic exposition.

The poet next stops at the Stone Fortress, where he goes further back in time and recounts the Western Jin's conquest of the Kingdom of Wu.[59] Then he recalls Wang Dun, the son-in-law of Emperor Wu of the Jin (r. 265–90), who had had designs on the Jin throne in the early years of the Eastern Jin, and would have succeeded if he had not died from an illness. Wang Dun had camped at the Stone Fortress in his first military action against the Jin court in 322. The choice of these two incidents in association with the Stone Fortress, one positive and one negative in relation to the Jin, is worth noting. In the case of the conquest of Wu, Xie Lingyun especially sings the praises of Yang Hu, the visionary who supported the campaign against Wu and foresaw the unification of the empire; in the case of Wang Dun, the poet focuses his attention on Xie Kun 謝鯤 (281–323) and Zhou Yi 周顗 (269–322), the two ministers who disapproved of Wang Dun but met with different fates. Xie Kun was Xie An's uncle, one of the first members of the Xie clan who had enjoyed a high reputation. He managed to escape harm when serving under Wang Dun. These passages seem then to demonstrate Xie Lingyun's ideal: accomplish great deeds in the unification of the empire (Xie was a fervent supporter of undertaking northern campaigns),[60] but if the time is not right, then withdraw from public service and preserve one's life.

次石頭之雙岸	Mooring my boat at the banks of the Stone Fortress,
究孫氏之初基	I investigated the foundation of the house of Sun.
幸漢庶之漏網	Rejoicing in his survival as a commoner of the Han,
憑江介以抗維	Sun Jian took the south as his powerbase to uphold law and order.
初鵲起於富春	At first soaring like a magpie at Fuchun,
果鯨躍於川湄	In the end he leapt like a whale from the Yangzi River.

59. For an explication of the conquest of Wu related in the following passage, see Chapter 2, pp. 79–81.

60. Xie wrote a memorial to Emperor Wen of the Song (r. 424–53), urging him to undertake northern campaigns. Shen Yue, *Song shu* 67.1772–74.

匝三世而國盛	In three generations, the kingdom flourished,
歷五偽而宗夷	But the clan was finally destroyed after five pretenders to the throne.
察成敗之相仍	I examined the cycle of success and failure:
猶脣亡而齒寒	The teeth feel cold when the lips are gone—
載十二而謂紀	A period of twelve years is known as one full cycle;
豈蜀滅而吳安	How could Wu be safe when Shu had fallen?
眾咸昧於謀兆	Yet all remained oblivious to what was destined to be;
羊獨悟於理端	Yang alone recognized the sign from the beginning.
請廣武以誨情	With his sincerity, he convinced the Baron of Guangwu,
樹襄陽以作藩	And cultivated the city of Xiangyang as a fence.
拾建業其如遺	Taking Jianye was as easy as picking up something from the ground,
沿萬里而誰難	The army sailed ten thousand miles without encountering obstacles.
疾魯荒之詖辭	I loathed the lies of Duke Huang of Lu;
惡京陵之譖言	I detested the slandering of Jingling;
責當朝之憚貶	I disapproved of how those powerful men feared responsibility—
對曩籍而興歎	Facing the records of the past, I heaved a sigh.
敦怙寵而判違	Wang Dun, relying on imperial favor, betrayed the court,
敵既勍而國圮	As the enemy became powerful, the state fell into ruin.
彼問鼎而何階	By what means would he ask about the weight of the tripod?[61]
必先賊於君子	He must first destroy the upright gentlemen.[62]
原性分之異託	People's natures and temperaments are all dissimilar;
雖殊塗而歸美	Though they may follow different paths, they can be equally admirable.

---

61. The nine tripods of the Zhou represented the royal power, and asking about their weight implied that one harbored a design on the throne. See *Chunqiu Zuozhuan zhengyi*, the third year of Duke Xuan, 21.367. Wang Dun's *Jin shu* biography states: "[Wang Dun] had the intent to inquire after the weight of the tripod." Fang Xuanling et al., *Jin shu* 98.2557.

62. Du Zhiqiang believes this is a reference to the diviner Guo Pu 郭璞 (276–324), who was killed by Wang Dun because he refused to give Wang a satisfying answer about the outcome of his imperial ambition. See *Li dai fu pingzhu*, p. 43, n. 17. But in this context it could also be a general reference to Wang Dun's murder of those who did not support him, especially Dai Ruosi 戴若思 (see ibid., 69.1847–48) and Zhou Yi, whose deaths were particularly deplored by contemporaries because of their status and reputation.

或卷舒以愚智	Some may roll up and feign foolishness, or stretch out and apply one's intellect, with time;
或治亂其如矢	Some may be like straight arrows in rectifying disorder.
謝昧迹而託規	As Xie entrusted the model of conduct in concealing his tracks,
卒安身以全里	In the end he protected himself and preserved his principles;[63]
周顯節而犯逆	Zhou revealed his integrity and resisted the wicked,
抱正情而喪己	Cherishing righteous sentiments, he lost his life.[64]

The western side of Siwang Hill 四望山, to the northwest of Jiankang, looks toward the Yangzi River.[65] Xie Lingyun's river journey would have taken him right past the hill. Wen Qiao 溫嶠 (288–329) had built a fortress on Siwang Hill in 328, where he planned to set up an ambush for the rebel army of Su Jun 蘇峻 (d. 328) and Zu Yue 祖約 (d. 329).[66] But instead of tracing the early history of the dynasty, Xie Lingyun chooses to recall the more recent rebellion of Lu Xun 盧循 (d. 411) in 410, and gives another laudatory description of Liu Yu's accomplishments.

薄四望而尤眄	Approaching Siwang, I gazed into distance,
歎王路之中鯁	Lamenting the blockage of the royal progress midway.
蠢於越之妖燼	The remaining evil forces of Yuyue stirred like worms
敢淩蹈於五嶺	And dared to invade the Five Ranges.[67]
崩雙嶽於中流	As the twin peaks crumbled in mid-stream,

63. Xie Kun had served as a member of Wang Dun's staff. He did not approve of Wang Dun but knew he would not be able to change the state of affairs, so he abandoned himself to drinking bouts and tried his best not to get involved in Wang Dun's undertakings. Ibid., 49.1377–378. *Li* 里 shares the same pronunciation as *li* 理 in Middle Chinese. I agree with Xiong Qingyuan in reading it as *li* 理, meaning "principles." Xiong, "'Zhuanzheng fu bing xu' zhushi," p. 28.

64. Zhou Yi was a prominent minister at court, known for his outspokenness and executed by Wang Dun outside the south gate of the Stone Fortress. Ibid., 69.1852.

65. *Jingding Jiankang zhi* 景定建康志 17.1563.

66. Fang Xuanling et al., *Jin shu* 67.1793.

67. Yuyue is another name for Yue (modern Zhejiang). Sun En's rebel army had occupied Kuaiji (modern Shaoxing of Zhejiang) and caused much destruction in the Yue region. Ibid., 100.2632–33. The Five Ranges refer to the five mountains, Dayu 大庾, Yuecheng 越城, Qitian 騎田, Mengzhu 萌渚, and Dupang 都龐, at the boundaries between Guangdong, Guangxi, Hu'nan, and Jiangxi. After Sun En was killed, Lu Xun occupied Guangzhou and styled himself the governor in 404. Ibid., 100.2634.

擬凶威於荊郢　They pointed their heinous forces toward Jing and Ying.[68]
隱雷霆於帝坐　Lightning and thunder shook the throne;
飛芒鏃於宮省　Blades and arrows flew toward the royal palace.
於時朝有遷都之議　At the time, there was discussion about moving the capital
人無守死之志　And little intent to defend to the death.
師旅痛於久勤　The troops were wounded by their long toils;
城墉闕於素備　The city walls were lacking in preparations.[69]
安危勢在不侔　The odds were clearly in the enemy's favor,
眾寡形於見事　The inequality of power was manifested in the circumstances.
於赫淵謀　Ah, how profound and far-reaching was his foresight!
研其神策　He who had carefully investigated all the signs.
緩轡待機　He first relaxed his reins to wait for the opportunity,
追奔躡迹　Then he pursued the fleeing rebels, close on their heels.
遇雷池而振曜　At the encounter of Thunder Pond, he demonstrated brilliance;
次彭蠡而殲滌　Camping at Pengli, he brought total destruction upon the foe.[70]
穆京甸以清晏　He restored peace and leisure to the capital region,
撤多壘而寍役　By spreading numerous fortresses, he rested the soldiers.

Passing through the landmarks in the capital region, Xie Lingyun comes upon the White Stone Fortress. Once again, the poet aims for a

68. The "twin peaks" refer to He Wuji 何無忌 (d. 410), the governor of Jiangzhou 江州, and Liu Yi, both prominent Jin generals who were defeated by Lu Xun in 410. He Wuji died in battle. Lu Xun tried to take Jiangling 江陵, the provincial capital of Jingzhou 荊州 ("Jing and Ying"), but did not succeed. Shen Yue, *Song shu* 1.21.

69. Liu Yu's army had just returned from a northern military campaign and was worn out; there were only a few thousand soldiers in the capital region. In contrast, after defeating He Wuji and Liu Yi, Lu Xun had a hundred thousand men well equipped with warships and cavalry. Several ministers suggested leaving Jiankang and taking the emperor and the court north of the Yangzi River. Liu Yu would not listen. Shen Yue, *Song shu* 1.19.

70. Liu Yu defeated Lu Xun at Thunder Pond (Leichi 雷池, in modern Jiangxi); then, when Lu Xun was trying to find his way back to Yuzhang 豫章 (modern Nanchang 南昌 of Jiangxi), Liu Yu intercepted him at Zuoli (in modern Duchang 都昌 of Jiangxi) and vanquished his army completely. Lu Xun escaped with only a few thousand men. Pengli is the old name for Poyang Lake 鄱陽 in northern Jiangxi. Ibid., 1.22–23.

balance between the depiction of a recent event and the recounting of more remote history, as the following passage describes the revolt of Su Jun and Zu Yue in the early years of the Eastern Jin, and focuses on the key role played by Wen Qiao in its suppression. Wen Qiao, whose posthumous title was Zhongwu 忠武 ("Loyal and Martial"), had camped at the White Stone Fortress. He set up an altar there to make sacrifices to heaven and earth and the Jin ancestors, and gave an impassioned reading of the sacrificial address.[71] There also seems to have been a local shrine where the minister Yu Liang 庾亮 (289–340) had prayed during the battle with Su Jun.[72]

造白石之祠壇	I went to see the altar at the White Stone Fortress,
慭二豎之無君	And felt indignant at the audacity of the two wicked rebels.
踐掖庭以幽辱	They trampled and insulted the imperial harem,[73]
淩祧社而火焚	And set fire to the royal ancestral temples.[74]
愍文康之罪己	I sympathized with Wenkang, who blamed himself;[75]
嘉忠武之立勳	And appreciated the heroic undertakings of Zhongwu.
道有屈於災蝕	Although the Way was temporarily brought low by the eclipses,[76]
功無謝於如仁	The accomplishments were no less than Guan Zhong's endeavors.[77]

71. Fang Xuanling et al., *Jin shu* 67.1793–94.

72. Ibid., 95.2475.

73. Su Jun's soldiers entered the imperial palace and assaulted Empress Dowager Yu Wenjun 庾文君 (297–328) and other palace ladies. The empress dowager "died of sorrow." Ibid., 32.973, 100.2629.

74. Ibid., 65.1751: "After the rebellion was quelled, the ancestral temples and the palace compound were all burned down to the ground" 及賊平，宗廟宮室並爲灰燼.

75. Wenkang 文康 was the posthumous title of the minister Yu Liang, who blamed himself, rightly, for having mishandled Su Jun and provoked his rebellion. Ibid., 73.1919–920.

76. Eclipses of sun and moon were considered ill political omen.

77 .This is a reference to the *Analects*. Someone once wondered whether Guan Zhong 管仲 (ca. seventh century BCE), the minister of Qi, could be considered a benevolent man. "Confucius said, 'Duke Huan [of Qi] assembled the feudal lords nine times without using weapons and chariots. It was all thanks to Guan Zhong. Who could be like Guan Zhong in his benevolence! Who could be like Guanzhong in his benevolence!'" 如其仁，如其仁! *Lunyu zhushu* 14.126.

As Xie Lingyun continues east on the Yangzi River, he comes across the Falling Star Mountain to the northeast of Jiankang. On this mountain, Sun Quan had built a three-story structure, Falling Star Tower, in 232, the sight of which prompts the poet to lament the fate of the Kingdom of Wu.[78]

The last two lines of the following passage contain two allusions. The first is a reference to the ruler of Qi, who was having such a great time at a banquet that he wondered out loud what life would be like in the absence of death. His outspoken minister, Yanzi, replied, "If there were no death, then the ancients would be enjoying this feast now—how could you, my lord, take part in it? In the past, Shuangjiu had lived in this place; then Ji Ce succeeded him. . . . If there were no death, I am afraid the pleasure of Shuangjiu would not be something my lord would want."[79] The Wu poet Lu Ji's "Chant of Qi" ("Qi ou xing" 齊謳行) contains the couplet: "If Shuangjiu is already no more, / how could you, my dear sir, get to linger?" 爽鳩茍已徂，吾子安得停?[80]

The last line refers to a poem, "Hawthorn on the Mountain" ("Shan you shu" 山有樞) from "The Airs of Tang" ("Tang feng") in the *Classic of Poetry*.[81] The poem urges its listeners to enjoy themselves while they can, for once they die, their precious possessions will belong to others.

訊落星之饗旅	I inquired after the feasting of the troops at Falling Star Tower,[82]
索舊棲於吳餘	And looked for the Wu Leftover at the king's former residence.[83]
跡階戺而不見	I sought the stairs, but could not see any trace,
橫榛卉以荒除	As they were covered with weeds and bushes stretching across.
彼生成之樂辰	That happy hour, when the tower was first built,

78. Li Fang et al., *Taiping yulan* 176.989.

79. *Chunqiu Zuozhuan zhengyi*, the twentieth year of Duke Zhao, 49.861.

80. Lu Qinli, *Quan Jin shi* 5.663.

81. *Mao shi zhengyi* 6.217–18.

82. This is a reference to a line in Zuo Si's "Poetic Exposition on the Wu Capital" ("Wu du fu" 吳都賦): "They feast the troops at Falling Star Tower" 饗戎旅乎落星之樓." Yan Kejun, *Quan Jin wen* 74.1886.

83. The Wu Leftover (*Wu yu* 吳餘) is the name of a fish in the Yangzi River. According to a local legend, Sun Quan once dumped some leftover sashimi (sliced fresh raw fish known in Chinese as *kuai* 鱠) into the river, which turned into a fish called "Wuyukuai" 吳餘鱠. Li Fang et al., *Taiping guangji* 464.3821.

亦猶今之在余	Was surely just like these joyful times enjoyed today.
慨齊吟於爽鳩	I was moved by Shuangjiu of the chant of Qi;
悲唐歌於山樞	And felt pained by the mountain hawthorn of the ballad of Tang.

Xie Lingyun's journey takes him further down the Yangzi River. "Tu shou" 涂首 in the first line refers to the point where the Tu River 涂水 (now known as the Chu River 滁河) merges with the Yangzi.[84] In the following passage, Xie Lingyun ingeniously links the surrender of the Wu with the reestablishment of the Jin imperial house in the south.

弔僞孫於徐首	At the head of the Tu River I mourned the usurper Sun,
率君臣以奉疆	Who led his subjects in surrendering their territory.[85]
時運師以伐罪	At the time, the Jin sent armed troops to punish the immoral offender,
偏投書於武王	But he only sent his letter of submission to the Martial Prince.[86]
迄西北之落紐	At long last, a knot was tied around the northwest,
乏東南以振綱	But they still failed to catch the southeast in the net.[87]
誠鉅平之先覺	This was indeed due to the prescience of the Marquis of Juping;[88]
實中興之後祥	It also portended well for the future resurrection of the state.[89]

84. Tu 涂 is an emendation of Xu 徐. This follows Sun Bin, who emends *xu* 徐 to *tu* 涂 in his *Song shu kaolun* 宋書考論, cited in Shen Yue, *Song shu* 67.1748.

85. The usurper Sun refers to the last Wu ruler, Sun Hao (see Chapter 2). In 279, the Jin launched a massive attack on Wu, and Sima Zhou 司馬伷 (227–83) led an army from Tuzhong 涂中 (modern Chuzhou 滁州 of Anhui). In 280, Sun Hao sent a letter of submission and surrendered his seal to Sima Zhou. Fang Xuanling et al., *Jin shu* 38.1121.

86. Sima Zhou's posthumous title was "Wu" 武 ("martial"). Ibid., 38.1121.

87. "Net" is also a term for political control.

88. Juping refers to Yang Hu (see Chapter 2), the Marquis of Juping.

89. Sima Zhou was the grandfather of Emperor Yuan, so the fact that the last ruler of Wu offered his seal and letter of surrender to him instead of to other commanders of the Jin troops was considered an auspicious omen for the resurrection of the Jin.

據左史之攸徵	Evidenced by the omen recorded by the Left Historian,[90]
胡影蹟之可量	How could this be measured by mere shadowy traces?

Jiangsheng 江乘 was a county established during the Qin (to the north of modern Jurong 句容 of Jiangsu). His grand inspection tour undertaken in 210 BCE had taken the First Emperor of Qin through Jiangsheng.[91]

過江乘而責始	Passing through Jiangsheng, I was critical of the First Emperor,
知遇雄之無謀	Knowing how he had no good plans for encountering heroes.
厭紫微之宏凱	Weary of the grandeur and harmony of the imperial palace,
甘陵波而遠遊	He delighted in braving the beakers and roaming wide and far.
越雲夢而南泝	Crossing the Yunmeng Marsh, he sailed south;
臨淛河而東浮	Coming upon the Zhe River, he floated eastward.
彀連弩於川上	Pulling the cross-bow and shooting multiple arrows on the river,
候蛟龍於中流	waiting for dragons in mid-stream.

Sailing further east on the Yangzi River, the poet next reaches Guangling (modern Yangzhou of Jiangsu).

爰薄方輿	I approached the Square Hill,
迺屆歐陽	And reached Ouyang.[92]
入夫江都之域	I entered the territory of Jiangdu,[93]
次乎廣陵之鄉	And stopped at the city of Guangling.
易千里之曼曼	Scorning the distance of a thousand miles,
泝江流之湯湯	I went against the expansive flow of the Yangzi River.

90. The Left Historian recorded action while the Right Historian recorded speech. *Li ji zhushu* 29.545.

91. For the events narrated in the following passage, see Sima Qian, *Shi ji* 6.260–63.

92. Fangyu 方輿 is Fangyu 方嶼, the Square Hill. This Square Hill is different from the famous hill of the same name to the south of Jiankang. It is located on the north side of the Yangzi River, between Liuhe 六合 and Yizheng 儀征 (also known as Yizhen 儀眞). To the east of Yizheng is the Ouyang Fortress 歐陽戍. Li Daoyuan, *Shuijing zhushu* 30.2556.

93. The Guangling Commandery in the Jin was known as Jiangdu in the Han. During the Jin Jiangdu was a county in the Guangling Commandery. Fang Xuanling et al., *Jin shu* 15.451–52.

洊赤圻以經復	The tidal bore, billowing and flooding the Crimson Shore,[94]
越二門而起漲	Passed through the Twin Gates, swelling and surging.[95]

Guangling is the last metropolis in the poet's familiar territory. At this point, the poet pauses, looks to the road ahead, and, upon observing the freedom of the carefree creatures of nature, expresses a sense of wistfulness at his own toils.

眷北路以興思	I looked to the road north and thoughts stirred;
看東山而怡目	I gazed at the East Hill, which was pleasing to the eyes.
林叢薄，路逶迤	The grove was dense, the path winding;
石參差，山盤曲	the rocks jutted out, the hills twisted and turned.
水激瀨而駿奔	The water flew in swift currents and galloped on;
日映石而知旭	The sun shone on the rocks, and I knew it was dawn again;
審兼照之無偏	I observed how the universal enlightenment was impartial;
怨歸流之難濯	I resented how hard it was to sail on returning currents.
羨輕魵之涵泳	I envied the light-bodied striped fish that swam in the depths;
觀翔鷗之落啄	I watched the soaring gulls descending and scooping.
在飛沈其順從	The fowl and fish each followed its own nature;
顧微躬而緬邈	I looked at my humble self, so distant.
於是	Thereupon
抑懷蕩慮	I kept my homesickness in check, dismissed my concerns,
揚搉易難	And calculated the difficulties of the journey ahead.
利涉以吉	By heavenly auspices there would be a smooth crossing,
天險以艱	Though the natural barrier might prove challenging for travelers:
于敵伊阻	For the enemy such peril would certainly pose an obstacle;
在國斯便	But it proved advantageous to our state.

94. "Chi qi" 赤圻 refers to "Chi an" 赤岸, the "Crimson Shore," a place name that appears in the description of the famous "Guangling tidal bore" in Mei Sheng's 枚乘 (d. ca. 140 BCE) "Seven Stimuli ("Qi fa" 七發). The *Wen xuan* commentator Li Shan cites Shan Qianzhi's 山謙之 (d. ca. 454) *Account of South Xuzhou* (*Nan Xuzhou ji* 南徐州記), which locates the Crimson Shore in the section of the Yangzi River to the north of Jiangsheng. Xiao Tong, *Wen xuan* 34.1571.

95. The Twin Gates refer to the two hills in the Yangzi River, Songliao Hill 松寥山 and Yi Hill 夷山, known as "the two hills forming the Gateway to the Sea" (haimen ershan 海門二山).

勾踐行霸於琅邪	Goujian had achieved hegemony at Langye,[96]
夫差爭長於黄川	Fuchai vied for dominance at the meeting of Huangchuan;[97]
葛相發歎而思正	Minister Zhuge heaved sighs, longing for Fa Zheng,[98]
曹后愧心於千魂	And King Cao felt guilty at the thousands of perished souls.[99]

Before he resumes his journey in writing, Xie Lingyun's thoughts linger at Guangling awhile. Liu Pi 劉濞 (93–154 BCE) was the nephew of Liu Bang 劉邦 (d. 195 BCE), the founding emperor of the Western Han. He was enfeoffed as the king of Wu, with Guangling as his capital. According to Liu Pi's biography, Liu Bang was worried about the "quick and plucky" people of Wu and wanted to assign a mature family member to rule over them. He decided to send Liu Pi. Before Liu Pi left for Wu, Liu Bang had patted him on the back and told him: "There will be a revolt in the southeast fifty years after the founding of the Han. I wonder if it will be you. But people with the same surname are all from one family. I hope you will never rebel." Liu Pi kowtowed and said, "I shall not dare." But as the imperial court tried to reduce the territories of the various kingdoms and constrained their power, Liu Pi eventually did rebel in concert with six

96. Langye is in modern Shandong. Goujian, King of Yue (r. 496–65 BCE), had reportedly built a terrace at Langye in order to fulfill his ambition for hegemony in the north. *Wu Yue chunqiu* 6.176.

97. Huangchuan is Huangchi 黄池 (modern Fengqiu 封丘 of He'nan), here altered for the sake of rhyming. In 482 BCE, King Fuchai of Wu (r. 495–73 BCE) and the rulers of several states held a meeting there in which Fuchai sought to become the head of the confederation. Sima Qian, *Shi ji* 5.198.

98. After Liu Bei was defeated by Wu in 222 CE, Zhuge Liang 諸葛亮 (181–234), the renowned minister and military strategist of the Shu Han Kingdom, lamented that if Fa Zheng 法正 (176–220) had been alive, he would have been able to stop Liu Bei from undertaking the campaign. Chen Shou, *Sanguo zhi* 37.962.

99. The Cao King is Cao Cao 曹操 (155–220). His army was devastated by an epidemic at Baqiu 巴丘 (in modern Hubei) after his catastrophic campaign to Jingzhou in 208; many soldiers died. Cao Cao sighed and said that he would not have come to this if Guo Jia 郭嘉 (170–207), his councilor, had been alive. Chen Shou, *Sanguo zhi* 14.435. The "thousands of perished souls" in this line might also refer to Cao Pi's attempt on Wu in 225. When he came to Guangling and saw the Yangzi River, Cao Pi lamented, "Although Wei has thousands of cavalry, there is no way to deploy them." Chen Shou, *Sanguo zhi* 2.85, 55.1299. This reference and the ones above highlight the advantageous position of the south because of the Yangzi River.

other kings. The revolt was put down by the imperial army led by Zhou Yafu 周亞夫 (d. 143 BCE), Marquis of Tiao 條侯, and others.[100]

Although he criticizes the King of Wu for his mutiny, Xie Lingyun approves of the Han princes' eagerness to seek out men of moral principle and literary elegance. He especially sings the praises of Zou Yang 鄒陽 (ca. 206–129 BCE), Mei Sheng 枚乘 (d. ca. 140 BCE), and Dong Zhongshu 董仲舒 (ca. 179–104 BCE), who had all served at Guangling.

登高堞以詳覽	Ascending the towering parapets and scanning my surroundings in detail,
知吳濞之衰盛	I came to understand the rise and fall of Pi, King of Wu.
戒東南之逆氣	Warning him about the mutinous aura of the southeast,
成劉后之駭聖	The Liu emperor certainly awed the world with his foreknowledge.
藉鹽鐵之殷阜	The King relied on the richness and wealth of salt and iron;[101]
臨淮楚之剽輕	Furthermore, he ruled over a people who were plucky and tough.
盛几杖而弭心	The provision of an arm rest and walking cane appeased his heart;
怒抵局而遂爭	Angered by a game of chess, he was ultimately provoked into action.[102]
忿爰盎之扶禍	I was indignant at Yuan Ang for exacerbating the disaster,

100. Sima Qian, *Shi ji* 106.2821–34.

101. Liu Pi minted coins from a copper mine in his territory and produced salt from seawater; the kingdom profited from these things. Ibid., 106.2822.

102. During Emperor Wen's 文帝 (r. 179–57 BCE) reign, Liu Pi's son and designated heir had a dispute with the imperial Heir Apparent (later Emperor Jing 景帝, r. 156–41 BCE) over a game of chess, and was killed by the Heir Apparent. Since then, Liu Pi became resentful and refused to come to the imperial court under the pretext of illness. Instead of punishing him, Emperor Wen presented Liu Pi with an arm rest and walking cane (the traditional gift given to honor the elderly), and therewith appeased him temporarily. After Emperor Jing was enthroned, he took Chao Cuo's 晁錯 advice and reduced the territories of the various kings, which led to the revolt of the seven kingdoms. Ibid., 106.2823. Pan Yue's 潘岳 (247–300) poetic exposition "On a Western Journey" ("Xizheng fu" 西征賦) contains these lines: "He [Emperor Jing] destroyed the heir of Wu with a chessboard, / In a fit of anger roused by one game" 隕吳嗣於局下，蓋發怒於一博. Yan Kejun, *Quan Jin wen* 90.1983.

惜徒傷於家令	And regretted that the Household Provisioner was killed in vain.[103]
匪條侯之忠毅	If not because of Marquis of Tiao's faithfulness and stoicism,
將七國之陵正	The seven kingdoms would have overpowered the rightful rule.
褒漢藩之治民	I nevertheless appreciated the rule of the Han royal princes,
並訪賢以招明	Who sought out the worthy and beckoned the wise.
侯文辯其誰在	Wherein might eloquence and literary grace be found?
曰鄒陽與枚生	These were in Zou Yang, these were in Mei Sheng.[104]
據忠辭於吳朝	They offered loyal words to the prince of Wu,
執義說於梁庭	And gave righteous speeches at the court of Liang.
敷高才於兔園	They displayed their outstanding talent in the Rabbit Garden;
雖正言而免刑	Though they spoke their minds, they were spared from castigation.[105]
闕里既已千載	Queli's impact lasted for centuries,[106]
深儒流於末學	The Ru influence was profound even in the later generations.

---

103. Yuan Ang had served as King of Wu's prime minister. Chao Cuo had served as Household Provisioner to the Heir Apparent, later Emperor Jing, and persuaded Emperor Jing to reduce the territories of the various kingdoms. After the rebellion broke out, Yuan Ang advised Emperor Jing to kill Chao Cuo to appease the rebellious kings. Emperor Jing agreed, but that did not prove effective in stopping the revolt. Ibid., 101.2741–42, 106.2831.

104. Zou Yang and Mei Sheng were known for their literary and rhetorical talent. While serving in Liu Pi's court, they had tried to talk Liu Pi out of his mutiny plot, but their efforts were to no avail. They subsequently left Wu for the court of King Xiao of Liang 梁孝王 (r. 165–43 BCE), Emperor Jing's younger brother. The king aspired to succeed to the imperial throne, and Zou Yang kept advising him against it. At one point he was imprisoned for his directness but was ultimately released. See Ban Gu, *Han shu* 51.2338–65. The "Rabbit Garden" was reputedly the Liang king's pleasure park where he partied with his literary courtiers. Mei Sheng had supposedly written a "Poetic Exposition on the Rabbit Garden of the King of Liang" ("Liang wang Tu yuan fu" 梁王兔園賦). Ouyang Xun et al., *Yiwen leiju* 65.1162.

105. Ban Gu once commented on Zou Yang and Mei Sheng: "Zou Yang and Mei Sheng served turbulent kingdoms, but were eventually spared from punishment and execution, because they spoke righteously and plainly" 鄒陽枚乘游於危國，然卒免刑戮者，以其言正也. Ban Gu, *Han shu* 51.2372.

106. Queli (in modern Qufu 曲阜 of Shandong) was where Confucius grew up. See Sima Qian, *Shi ji* 47.1905.

欽仲舒之睟容	Admirable was the gentle bearing of Zhongshu,
遵縫掖於前躅	Who abided by the scholarly teachings of the ancients.
對園圃而不闚	Facing his family garden, he never even glanced at it;
下帷幙而論屬	Lowering the curtains, he devoted himself to teaching and writing.[107]
相端非之兩驕	He served as minister to two arrogant princes, Duan and Fei;
遭弘偃之雙慝	He came upon a pair of wicked men, Hong and Yan.[108]
恨有道之無時	How deplorable that he possessed the Way but did not encounter the right time;
步險塗以側足	Treading on a perilous path, he had to walk sideways.

As the poet lingers at Guangling, he focuses the following passage on Huan Wen and his heir, Huan Xuan. In 347, Huan Wen conquered the Cheng-Han kingdom in Shu; in 354, he undertook a campaign against the Former Qin and advanced as far as Bashang near Chang'an. In 369, upon returning from a failed northern campaign, Huan Wen moved his headquarters to Guangling.[109] Huan Xuan was Huan Wen's youngest son. He usurped the Jin throne in 403, and was defeated and killed by Liu Yu the next year.

聞宣武之大閱	I had heard of Lord Xuanwu's grand military parade,
反師旅於此塵	As the army under his command returned to this city.
自皇運之都東	Ever since the imperial fate settled on the capital in the east,

107. According to Dong Zhongshu's biography, he observed propriety in all his actions and manners; he taught *Chunqiu* to his disciples behind lowered curtains, and was so dedicated to scholarship that he did not set foot in his own garden for three years. Sima Qian, *Shi ji* 121.3127–128.

108. Dong Zhongshu was prime minister to Emperor Jing's sons, Liu Fei 劉非 (168–128 BCE), the King of Jiangdu 江都, and later to Liu Duan 劉端 (d. 108 BCE), the King of Jiaoxi 膠西. Liu Fei was described as "arrogant and extravagant," while Liu Duan was also self-indulgent and ruthless in executing many of his underlings. Hong and Yan refer to Gongsun Hong 公孫弘 (d. 121 BCE) and Zhufu Yan 主父偃 (d. 127 BCE), who were jealous of Dong Zhongshu and persecuted him. Sima Qian, *Shi ji* 121.3127–128; 59.2096; Ban Gu, *Han shu* 56.2525.

109. Fang Xuanling et al., *Jin shu* 98.2568–577.

始昌業以濟難	He was the first to glorify the royal enterprise, saving it from calamity.[110]
抗素旄於秦嶺	He held up white standards at the Qin Range;
揚朱旗於巴川	He raised the vermillion banners at the Ba River.[111]
懼帝系之墜緒	He feared the severance of the imperial lineage,
故黜昏而崇賢	Therefore he dismissed the dim-witted and honored the worthy.[112]
嘉收功以垂世	The lasting influence of his success was commendable,
嗟在嗣而覆旃	How regrettable that it was overturned by his own heir.
德非陟而繼宰	He occupied the position of ruler, undeserved by his virtues;
釁踰禹其必顛	When offerings made to him exceeded those to Yu, he would surely fall.[113]

The next stanza recalls Xie An, Xie Lingyun's great-grand-uncle, who built the New Fortress (Xincheng 新城) at Buqiu 步丘 to the north of Yangzhou. According to his biography, Xie An was a confirmed recluse who did not answer the summons to serve until his younger brother Xie Wan 謝萬 suffered a humiliating military defeat in 359 and consequently was demoted to a commoner. Xie An was already forty years old when he embarked on his official career. After the Jin army crushed the invading Former Qin army at the Battle of the Fei River in 383, Xie An planned to undertake further campaigns against the north; but Sima Daozi 司馬道子 (364–403), the emperor's younger brother, became increasingly powerful in court and clashed with him. To avoid him, Xie An left the capital

110. Huan Wen expanded the Eastern Jin territory by conquering Shu; he was also the first Eastern Jin general who recovered the former capital Luoyang, albeit temporarily, in 356.

111. The Qin Range is in north China; the Ba River is in Shu. This couplet refers to Huan Wen's campaigns against Shu and Qin respectively in 347 and 354.

112. In 371, Huan Wen dethroned the emperor ("Dismissed Emperor," Feidi 廢帝, r. 365–71) and established Emperor Jianwen.

113. This line might refer to the fact that when Huan Xuan was enthroned in 403, in his memorial to heaven he compared Huan Wen to the ancient sage emperor Yu 禹 (Fang Xuanling et al., *Jin shu* 99.2594). The comparison implied that Huan Xuan himself was like Yu's son, Qi 啓, who succeeded Yu to become emperor and thus began the tradition of hereditary monarchy (see Sima Qian, *Shi ji* 2.83). Xie Lingyun seems to be saying that Huan Xuan would surely encounter trouble if he put himself in Qi's position.

and camped at Buqiu in May 385. Intending to retire shortly afterward, he took his entire family with him, but he died in the same year.[114]

造步丘而長想	Upon reaching Buqiu, I was filled with nostalgic thoughts,
欽太傅之遺武	As I admired the remaining traces of the Grand Tutor.
思嘉遁之餘風	I reflected upon the lingering influence of his reclusion,
紹素履之落緒	Wishing to realize his aim of "treading with simplicity."[115]
民志應而願税	Responding to the common folk's desire, he wanted nothing but rest and peace;[116]
國屯難而思撫	But when the state experienced difficulty, he aspired to bring relief.
譬乘舟之待楫	It was like one who must use oars in rowing a boat,
象提鈞之假縷	And rely on a cord to reel in the fish.
總出入於和就	His service and withdrawal were guided by harmony and success,
兼仁用於默語	His benevolence was manifested in silence, his efficacy in speech.[117]
弘九流以揳四維	He expanded the nine schools of thought to govern the four principles of managing state affairs;
復先陵而清舊宇	He restored the ancestral mausoleums and cleared the former realm.
卻西州之成功	Dismissing his success achieved at the Xizhou Fortress,[118]
指東山之歸予	He anticipated his retirement to the Eastern Mountain.[119]

114. Fang Xuanling et al., *Jin shu* 79.2076.

115. "Treading with simplicity" is a citation from *Zhou yi zhengyi* 2.40: "Tread with simplicity, and there will be no calamity in setting forth" 素履往无咎.

116. The commentary on the image of the hexagram "Tread" reads: "Heaven above and lake below form the image of 'Tread.' In the same way, the noble man distinguishes between high and low and rectifies the common folk's desire" 上天下澤，履，君子以辨上下，定民志. Ibid., 2.40.

117. Ibid., 7.151: "The Master said, 'The way of the noble man is thus: he may go out or stay at home, he may remain silent or speak out'" 君子之道，或出或處，或默或語. This couplet states that Xie An did well both in his active participation in public service and in his withdrawal.

118. Xizhou (in modern Nanjing) was the headquarters of the Governor of Yangzhou 揚州, the capital region. Xie An was made Governor of Yangzhou in 375. Sima Guang, *Zizhi tongjian* 103.3269.

119. When Xie An was young, he lived in reclusion at the Eastern Mountain in Kuaiji. Fang Xuanling et al., *Jin shu* 79.2073.

惜圖南之啓運	What a pity that he was like the roc planning to fly south in having founded the basis of the great enterprise,
恨鵬翼之未舉	But did not have an opportunity to raise his pinions.[120]

After Guangling, the poet resumes his northbound journey.

發津潭而迴邁	I set out from Jin Lake on a long trip ahead;
逗白馬以憩舲	At the White Horse Lake, I rested my boat.[121]
貫射陽而望邗溝	Passing through Sheyang, I gazed at the Han Canal;[122]
濟通淮而薄角城	Crossing the waterway to Huai, I approached the Jiao Fortress.[123]
城坡阤兮淮驚波	The city wall went up and down, and the Huai had raging waves;
平原遠兮路交過	The plain stretched into distance, with crisscrossing roads.
面艽野兮悲橋梓	Facing the vast wilderness, I was grieved by tall and short trees;
溯急流兮苦磧沙	Going against the rapid currents, our boat suffered from sandy isles.
敻千里而無山	For a thousand miles there was not a hill in sight;
緬百谷而有居	Only where a hundred valleys came together were there some human dwellings.
被宿莽以迷徑	Paths were covered by evergreen plants, and the traveler got lost;
睹生煙而知墟	Only when I saw wisps of smoke did I realize a village was close by.
□□□□□□	[......]
謂信美其可娛	[This land] was truly lovely and could bring delight.[124]

120. This is a reference to the great mythical *peng* bird, depicted in the "Free Roaming" chapter of *Zhuangzi*. See *Zhuangzi jishi* 1.1.

121. Jin Lake (also known as Jing Lake 精湖; see Li Daoyuan, *Shuijing zhushu* 30.2557) and the White Horse Lake were at Baoying 寶應 (a county by the same name in modern-day Jiangsu), just north of Yangzhou. Jin Lake is nowadays part of Baoying Lake.

122. Opened by King Fuchai of Wu, the Han Canal connected the Yangzi River and the Huai River through the Sheyang Lake.

123. The Jiao Fortress (in modern-day Siyang 泗陽 of Jiangsu) was where the Huai and Si Rivers met. Li Daoyuan, *Shuijing zhushu* 30.2552.

124. This is a reference to Wang Can's famous "Poetic Exposition on Ascending the Tower" ("Denglou fu" 登樓賦), composed when he was away from his homeland: "Though truly lovely, this land is not my homeland; how could it be worth my while to

身少長於樂土	Having always lived in a happy world,
實長歎於荒餘	I lamented the territory ravished by disasters.
哀神形之具瘁	Sadly, both my body and my spirit were worn out
值歲寒之窮節	In this last month of the cold season.
視層雲之崔巍	I beheld the towering of layered clouds,
聆悲飆之掩屑	I listened to the howling of the sad wind.
彌晝夜以滞淫	It rained without ceasing, day and night,
怨凝陰之方結	I resented the continuous knotting of cloudy vapors.
望新晴於落日	I gazed at the setting sun finally breaking through,
起明光於躋月	And a bright light emitted from the ascending moon.
眷轉蓬之辭根	I felt sympathy for the tumbleweed parting from its roots,
悼朔雁之赴越	I pitied the northern wild geese flying to Yue.
披微物而疚情	Looking into these humble things of nature, I grew melancholy--
此思心而可歇	How could this heart of mine ever stop pining for home?[125]
問傜役其幾時	I asked how much longer this trip would last,
駭閱景於興沒	And was shocked by how often the sun had risen and set.
感曰歸於采薇	Moved by the anticipation to return in "Gathering the Ferns,"
予來思於雨雪	I had nevertheless embarked on my journey during snowfall.
豈初征之懼對	How could it be that I dreaded the hardship of travel?
冀鸛鳴之在垤	Yet I was hoping for the ibises' cries at the ant-hills.

The last four lines evoke two poems, "Gathering the Ferns" ("Cai wei" 采薇), and "Eastern Hills" ("Dongshan" 東山), from the *Classic of Poetry*. According to the traditional interpretation, "Gathering the Ferns" depicts a military campaign against the northern Xianyun people. Its opening lines read: "Gather the ferns, gather the ferns. / The ferns are just growing out. / When shall we return? When shall we return? / It will be late in the year" 采薇采薇, 薇亦作止, 曰歸曰歸, 歲亦莫止. Its last stanza contains these famous lines: "When we first set out, / the willows were hanging softly; / now when we are coming back, / the snow falls thickly" 昔我

tarry here?" 雖信美而非吾土兮，曾何足以少留. Yan Kejun, *Quan hou Han wen* 90.959.

125. Here I follow the variant in Ouyang Xun et al., *Yiwen leiju* 59.1072.

往矣，楊柳依依，今我來思，雨雪霏霏.[126] "Eastern Hills" speaks of the soldier's return: "Now we are coming back from the east, / A misty rain is drizzling. / The ibises are crying out on the ant-hills; / Our wives are sighing in their chambers" 我來自東，零雨其濛. 鸛鳴於垤，婦歎於室.[127] According to traditional interpretation, before it rains, ants emerge from their tunnels to avoid being flooded; ibises, however, are water birds and delight in the rain, so they cry out with pleasure. By saying "I was hoping for the ibises' cries at the ant-hills," Xie Lingyun is expressing his longing to go home.

Going further northwest, Xie Lingyun arrives at Xiapi 下邳 (in modern Suining 睢寧 of Jiangsu, to the southeast of Pengcheng). Xiapi was once the fief of Xizhong 奚仲, the Chief of Chariots in the Xia 夏 dynasty. The following passage recounts an incident recorded in *Zuozhuan*. According to *Zuozhuan*, in 509 BCE, several feudal domains participated in the construction of the city wall of the Eastern Zhou capital. The minister of Song, Zhongji 仲幾, tried to force several smaller domains, including Xue 薛, to work in Song's stead. The minister of Xue protested the slavish status imposed on Xue and argued with Zhongji. Citing the convention of Jiantu 踐土 organized by Duke Wen of Jin, he said that every domain participating in that convention was supposed to "return to its former post": "Xue's ancestor, Xizhong, lived in Xue, serving the Xia as the Chief of Chariots. Later, Xizhong moved to Pi, and Zhonghui 仲虺 lived in Xue and served Tang [the founding king of the Shang 商 dynasty] as Left Minister. If to return to one's former post is right, then we should be officers serving the king; why should we serve another feudal lord?"

At this point, Shimi Mou 士彌牟, the minister of Jin, intervened. He asked Song to do its share in the construction project, and promised to "check the old records" for precedent for Zhongji's request. Zhongji said, "Even if *you* cannot remember [any precedent], how could the ghosts and spirits of the mountains and rivers not remember?" Shimi Mou then delivered an angry speech: "Xue sought evidence from among the living, while Song sought it from among the dead. Song's crime is grave indeed. Besides, Zhongji had run out of arguments, and so he used gods and spirits to swindle me. The saying, 'One abuses favor and causes oneself hu-

---

126. *Mao shi zhengyi* 9.332, 334.
127. Ibid., 8.296.

miliation,' describes Zhongji perfectly. He has to be disgraced." He subsequently had Zhongji taken to Jin for punishment.[128]

停驂騑於踰宿	Pausing briefly at Suyu,[129]
騖吾楫於邳鄉	I then sped my oars toward Xiapi.
奚車正以事夏	Xizhong, the Chief of Chariots, served the Xia,
虺左相以輔湯	Hui acted as the Left Minister assisting Tang.
綿三代而享邑	The clan enjoyed the fief through three dynasties,
廁踐土之一匡	And took part in the confederacy of Jiantu.
嗟仲幾之寵侮	I disapproved of Zhongji, who abused favor and caused himself humiliation;
遂捨存以徵亡	He forsook the living, and sought proof among the dead.
喜薛宰之善對	I took delight in the eloquence of the minister of Xue,
美士彌之能綱	And appreciated Shimi's ability to impose discipline.

Xiapi was also where the general Han Xin set up his headquarters in 202 BCE after he was enfeoffed as King of Chu. A native of Huaiyin 淮陰 (in modern Jiangsu, about eighty miles to the southeast of Xiapi), Han Xin was impoverished when he was a young man. A local butcher boy bullied him in public, saying, "Either kill me, or crawl through my legs." Han Xin looked at him long and hard, then crouched on the ground and crawled through his legs. He was branded as a coward. Later, Han Xin served under Xiang Yu 項羽 (232–202 BCE), the Hegemon King of Western Chu. He tried several times to advise Xiang Yu, but Xiang Yu did not adopt his counsel, so Han Xin left Xiang Yu for Liu Bang. He was appointed commander-in-chief and played a crucial role in the founding of the Western Han. After he was enfeoffed as King of Chu, he summoned the butcher who had insulted him, saying: "When you insulted me, is it really true that I could not kill you then and there? But it would have been a pointless killing. I endured the shame so I could become what I am today." He subsequently made the butcher a lieutenant.

Quai Tong 蒯通, a man of Qi, had tried to persuade Han Xin to turn against Liu Bang; Han Xin refused. After the Han was founded, Liu Bang became distrustful of Han Xin, so he stripped him of military command

128. *Chunqiu Zuozhuan zhengyi*, the first year of Duke Ding, 54.941.

129. Yusu 踰宿 is probably Suyu 宿豫 (modern-day Suqian 宿遷 of Jiangsu), located halfway between the Jiao Fortress and Xiapei. The phrase *yusu* could also mean "staying overnight."

and demoted him to be Marquis of Huaiyin. Han Xin, feeling resentful, plotted with another general, Chen Xi 陳狶. Chen rebelled in 197 BCE and was defeated and killed; Han Xin was also executed.[130]

升曲垣之逶迤	Ascending the winding city wall,
訪淮陰之所都	I visited the former capital of the Marquis of Huaiyin.[131]
原入跨之達恥	I traced his endurance of the great insult of crawling through another's legs,
俟遭時以遠圖	And understood he was waiting for his time to come.
捨西楚以擇木	Abandoning the Western Chu in favor of a better lord,
造南漢以定謨	He served the Han instead, and found a place to apply his strategies.
亂孟津而魏滅	Once he crossed Mengjin, Wei was destroyed;
攀井陘而趙徂	As soon as he ascended Jingxing, Zhao was vanquished.
播靈威於齊橫	His magnificent power awed the King of Qi;
振餘猛於龍且	Even his remaining vigor was enough to daunt Longju.
覿讓通而告狶	And yet, seeing how he rebutted Kuai Tong first and then conversed with Chen Xi,
曷始智而終愚	I wondered why he was so wise in the beginning, yet so foolish at the end.

Xiapi evokes the memory of another Western Han figure, Zhang Liang 張良 (d. 187 BCE?). After a failed assassination attempt on the life of the First Emperor of Qin, a young Zhang Liang sought refuge at Xiapi.[132] On a bridge over the Yi River (which merges with the Si River at Xiapi), Zhang Liang had apparently met a poor old man. The old man deliberately dropped his shoes under the bridge and asked Zhang Liang to pick them up and put them back on his feet. Though surprised and angered by the old man's audacity, Zhang Liang felt compassion for him because of his age and complied with his request. The old man thereupon told Zhang Liang to come back to the bridge at dawn in five days. Zhang Liang went back at dawn five days later and found the old man was already there. He scolded Zhang Liang for being late, and told him to come back in another five days. In another five days Zhang Liang went again,

---

130. See Han Xin's biography in Sima Qian, *Shi ji* 92.2609–30.

131. There is a textual variant, *du* 睹 (to see), for *du* 都 (capital), so the line could read: "I visited what the Marquis of Huaiyin used to see."

132. See Zhang Liang's biography in Sima Qian, *Shi ji* 55.2034–48.

arriving before dawn. The old man was again already there, and he told Zhang Liang to come back in another five days. So in five days Zhang Liang went again, this time well before midnight. The old man appeared shortly afterward and was pleased to see Zhang Liang. He gave Zhang Liang a book of military strategy and told him that once he learned everything in the book, he would be fit as a teacher of kings. Before he departed, the old man revealed that he was the yellow rock at the foot of Mt. Gucheng. *The Three Tactics*, a military work attributed to "the Old Man of the Yellow Rock," is cited in the preface to Xie Lingyun's poetic exposition.

Zhang Liang went on to become one of Liu Bang's most trusted councilors. After the Han was founded, Liu Bang wanted to install his younger son, Ruyi 如意, in place of the Crown Prince, Liu Ying 劉盈 (210–188 BCE). The Crown Prince's mother, Empress Lü, asked Zhang Liang for advice. Zhang Liang recommended that the Crown Prince procure the help of the four old recluses who had refused Liu Bang's summons, so that when Liu Bang saw how popular the Crown Prince was, he would change his mind. The strategy worked, and the Crown prince succeeded Liu Bang as Emperor Hui 惠帝 (r. 195–188 BCE). In his old age, Zhang Liang cared little for honor and rank; instead, because of his frail health, he went on a no-grain diet and practiced breathing techniques in hopes of achieving longevity. Empress Lü, who was grateful to him, persuaded Zhang Liang to give up his diet, arguing that life was too short to live in such an abstemious manner.

The life story of Zhang Liang, narrated below, contrasts nicely with that of Han Xin.

迄沂上而停枻	Stopping my boat on the Yi River,
登高圯而不進	I ascended the high bridge and lingered there.
石幽期而知賢	The Old Man of the Yellow Rock recognized a worthy person and made a date with him;
張揣景而示信	Zhang Liang gave a good estimate of timing and demonstrated his sincerity.
本文成之素心	It had, however, been the constant wish of Marquis Wencheng

要王子於雲仞 To arrange a meeting with the Prince in the clouds.[133]
豈無累於清霄 It was not so much because he would be carefree in the clear sky;
直有概於貞吝 But rather because he was moved by the change of good and ill fortune.[134]
始熙績於武關 His first feat was accomplished at the Wu Pass,[135]
卒敷功於皇胤 And in the end he extended merit to the imperial heir.
處夷險以解挫 Whether in peace or war, he was able to solve problems;
弘憂虞以時順 He acted in accordance with the times to alleviate concerns.
矜若華之翳晷 He pitied the attempt to block the sun with the blossoms of the Ruo Tree,[136]
哀飛驂之落駿 He lamented the fall of the fleet steed.[137]
傷粒食而興念 Hindered by a diet of grain, he harbored brooding thoughts;
眷逸翮而思振 He looked fondly upon the aloof pinions and longed to beat his wings.

As if to continue the practice of balancing the events of the remote past with more recent history, in the following passage Xie Lingyun recalls Liu Yu's military campaign against the ruler of the Southern Yan 燕, Murong Chao 慕容超 (385–410), whose territory largely spanned modern-day Shandong. Murong Chao had attacked the Jin territory and captured over a thousand households from Suyu in 409. Setting out in the

133. Wencheng was Zhang Liang's posthumous title. The Prince refers to Prince Qiao 王子喬, an immortal.

134. That is, Zhang Liang, in Xie Lingyun's view, was not interested in immortality per se; he was trying to avoid the fate befalling many of Liu Bang's generals, such as Han Xin and Chen Xi, once they had served Liu Bang's purpose.

135. With Zhang Liang's help, Liu Bang entered the Qin capital through the Wu Pass (in modern Shaanxi) and captured the last Qin ruler.

136. In Chinese mythology, the Ruo Tree, also known as Fusang 扶桑, is a huge mulberry tree from which the sun arises. *Shanhai jing jiaozhu*, p. 260. The poem "Li Sao" contains the line: "I snapped a branch of the Ruo Tree to block the sun" 折若木以拂日兮. The traditional interpretation is that the poet tries to block the progress of the sun (symbolizing the passage of time). *Chuci buzhu* 1.28. Xie Lingyun's line is more closely modeled on Cao Zhi's couplet in his "*Fu* on Being Moved by Seasons" ("Ganjie fu" 感節賦): "I snapped the blossoms of the Ruo Tree to block the sun, and hope the vermillion light will always shine forth" 折若華之翳日，庶朱光之常照. Yan Kejun, *Quan sanguo wen* 13.1124.

137. This line refers to the chariot of the sun.

summer of 409, Liu Yu's army won a great victory at Linqu 臨朐 (in modern Shandong). They went on to besiege the Yan capital Guanggu 廣固 (in modern Shandong), conquering it in early 410.[138]

戾臣山而東顧	Ascending Mt. Ju and gazing eastward,[139]
美相公之前代	I admired His Highness's past accomplishments.
嗟殘虜之將糜	Alas, when the remaining barbarian forces were about to collapse,
熾餘焱於海濟	They fanned their last flames by the seashore.
驅鮐稚於淮曲	They drove the old and young from the bend of the Huai,
暴鰥孤於泗澨	And bullied widowers and orphans on the banks of the Si.
託末命於風雲	The people entrusted their imperiled lives to wind and clouds,
冀靈武之北閱	Hoping for the northern advance of the mighty imperial troops.
惟授首之在晨	Convinced that the enemy's surrender was destined,
當盛暑而選徒	At the height of the summer, the Duke selected his soldiers.
肅嚴威以振響	Rigorous and stern, he produced the sound of war,
漸溫澤而沾腴	But followed with gentleness and grace to the common folk.[140]
既雲撤於朐城	The enemy withdrew like scattered clouds at the city of Linqu;
遂席卷於齊都	The imperial forces occupied the Qi capital like a rolled-up mat.[141]
曩四關其奚阻	Though the four passes had been blocked in days of old,[142]

138. Shen Yue, *Song shu* 1.15–16; Sima Guang, *Zizhi tongjian* 115.3612–617.

[139] I have emended "Chen shan" 臣山 to "Ju shan" 距山 (alternatively written as 岠山 or 巨山 in modern day), a mountain at Xiapi also known as Mt. Geyi 葛嶧山. Li Daoyuan, *Shuijing zhushu* 25.2149–150.

140. At the battle of Linqu, Liu Yu beat the drum himself to encourage his troops. Shen Yue, *Song shu* 1.16. After he captured Linqu, he "comforted those who surrendered to him, and promoted the worthy and talented; both Chinese and non-Chinese were greatly pleased." Sima Guang, *Zizhi tongjian* 115.3617.

141. The Yan capital, Guanggu, was in the Qi region.

142. The "four passes" in the Luoyang area were the Chenggao Pass 成皋 to the east, Yique 伊闕 to the south, Mengjin 孟津 to the north, and Hangu 函谷 to the west. See

道一變而是孚 The Way prevailed with a total transformation,
and the entire world was converted.

Finally, Xiapi evokes the memory of Lü Bu 呂布 (d. 199), a ferocious but fickle general at the end of the Eastern Han. Originally serving Ding Yuan 丁原, the governor of Bingzhou, he soon betrayed Ding, killed him and pledged loyalty to Dong Zhuo 董卓 (d. 192), the powerful warlord who treated him generously and adopted him as his son.[143] But Lü Bu eventually betrayed and killed Dong Zhuo, too. For a short while Lü Bu gave allegiance to Liu Bei 劉備 (161–223), the governor of Xuzhou, and referred to Liu Bei as his "younger brother."[144] The alliance did not last long. In 196, Lü Bu assaulted Liu Bei and took Xiapi. When the warlord Yuan Shu 袁術 (d. 199) attacked Liu Bei, Lü Bu came to Liu Bei's rescue because he did not want Yuan Shu to become too powerful.[145] He continued to play the power game between Yuan Shu and Liu Bei until Cao Cao besieged him at Xiapi and had him executed at White Gate Tower (Beimenlou 白門樓).

傷炎季之崩弛 I felt pained by the dissolution of the Fiery Han:[146]
長逆布以滔天 It gave rise to the ever-expanding felony
of the mutinous Lü Bu.
假父子以詐愛 He faked filial love toward his adoptive father,
借兄弟以僞恩 And feigned fraternal benevolence
by claiming brotherhood.
相魏武以譎狂 Attempting to serve the Martial Emperor of the Wei
with wild lies,
宄謨奮於東藩 He devised his wicked plans at the eastern commandery.[147]

Lu Ji's *Account of Luoyang* (*Luoyang ji* 洛陽記), cited in Li Daoyuan, *Shuijing zhushu* 15.1350. There were four passes in the Chang'an area: Hangu to the east, the Wu Pass to the south, the San Pass 散關 to the west, and the Xiao Pass 蕭關 to the north. See Sima Zhen's 司馬貞 (fl. eighth century) commentary in Sima Qian, *Shi ji* 22.1120. Here the "four passes" are a general reference to the road blockage set up by the enemy state.

143. See Lü Bu's biography in Chen Shou, *Sanguo zhi* 7.219–27.

144. Sima Guang, *Zizhi tongjian* 61.1964.

145. Chen Shou, *Sanguo zhi* 7.222–223.

146. The element of fire was supposed to be the symbol of the Han dynasty.

147. Cao Cao held the last Han emperor under his power. For a while, Lü Bu turned against Yuan Shu and negotiated with Cao Cao in the hope of being officially made the governor of Xuzhou. But in 198, Lü Bu again forsook Cao Cao and formed an alliance

桴未譟於東郭	But before the war drum was beaten at the eastern city,
身已馘於樓門	He was already captured in front of the tower gate.

Soon after leaving Xiapi, Xie Lingyun reaches the destination of his journey, Pengcheng, the seat of Xuzhou. Always seeking to verify book knowledge against the landscape before his eyes, the poet traces the ancient history of Xuzhou in "The Tribute of Yu" ("Yu gong" 禹貢) from "The Book of Xia" ("Xia shu" 夏書) in the venerable *Classic of Documents* (*Shangshu* 尚書). He sees what he is prepared to see:

審貢牧於前説	I examined records of tributary gifts in former discourses,
證所作於舊徐	And found evidence for what was written in the old Xu territory.
聆泗川之浮磬	I listened to the floating chime stones in the waters of Si,
翫夷水之蠙珠	And played with the oyster-pearls on the shore of Yi.[148]
草漸苞於熾壤	Plants sprang up from the fiery soil, bushy and lush;[149]
桐孤榦於嶧隅	The *tong* tree grew its lone trunk on the slope of Mt. Yi.[150]
慨禹跡於尚世	I was moved by the ancient traces of Yu,
惠遺文於夏書	Who had bequeathed his writings to us in the *Book of Xia*.

The Si River coursed through Lü 呂 county, which was to the east of Pengcheng.[151] There was a stone bridge over the river in Lü, henceforth known as Lüliang 呂梁 (literally, "Lü Bridge"), which is famous for its association with a story recorded in *Zhuangzi*.[152] In the story, Confucius was sightseeing at Lüliang when he noticed a man dive into the raging water. He thought the man was going to drown and told his disciples to res-

---

with Yuan Shu. This led to Cao Cao's campaign against Lü Bu and Lü Bu's eventual demise. Chen Shou, *Sanguo zhi* 7.224.

148. "Near the banks of the Si River the chime stones [seem to] float in the water; the Huai and Yi Rivers produce oyster-pearls and fish" 泗濱浮磬, 淮夷蠙珠暨魚. *Shangshu zhengyi* 6.82. The stones that seem to be floating in the Si River are believed to make good chime stones.

149. "Its soil is red, clayey and rich; plants and trees spring up, bushy and lush" 厥土赤埴墳, 草木漸包. Ibid., 6.81.

150. Mt. Yi is Mt. Geyi 葛嶧 mentioned earlier in this poetic exposition. The *tong* tree growing solitarily on the southern slope of Mt. Geyi ("Yi yang gu tong" 嶧陽孤桐) is considered excellent material for making zithers and lutes. Ibid., 6.82.

151. Li Daoyuan, *Shuijing zhushu* 25.2148.

152. *Zhuangzi jishi* 7.656–58.

cue him, but the man subsequently emerged from the river, drying his hair and singing a song. Confucius asked the man if he had a way of treading water. The man answered, "I have no way. I began with what I was used to, grew up with my nature, and let things come to completion with fate. I go under with the swirls and come out with the eddies, following along the way the water goes and never thinking about myself. This is how I do it." Confucius asked him to further explain. The man said, "I was born on the dry land and felt safe on the dry land—that was what I was used to. I grew up with the water and felt safe in the water—that was my nature. I don't know how I do what I do—that's fate."[153]

紛征邁之淹留	With much lingering in the course of my journey,
彌懷古於舊章	Even more did I think on the past manifested in the writings of old.
商伯文於故服	Shang's lords cultivated the old territory beyond the capital,
咸徵名於彭殤	And both inherited their surname from the long-lived Peng.[154]
眺靈壁之曾峰	I gazed afar at the layered peaks of Lingbi;[155]
投呂縣之迅梁	I approached the bridge over the rapid waters at Lü county.
想蹈水之行歌	I envisioned the man who sang while treading water,
雖齊汩其何傷	How could the swirls and eddies cause him any harm?
啓仲尼之嘉問	He inspired the good inquiry of Confucius,
告性命以依方	To whom he told of adhering to nature and fate.
豈苟然於迂論	These surely were no casual and wild remarks,
聆寓言於達莊	And I heeded the parable of free-minded Master Zhuang.

Pengcheng was where Xie Lingyun's grandfather Xie Xuan served as governor. In the following passage, Xie Lingyun gives a detailed narration of Xie Xuan's accomplishments. In his youth, Xie Xuan had been fre-

153. I use Burton Watson's translation with slight modifications. Watson, *The Complete Works of Chuang Tzu*, p. 205.

154. Peng is Pengzu 彭祖, the mythical long-lived figure who was enfeoffed at Pengcheng. He and Shiwei 豕韋, also surnamed Peng, were both lords of Shang. See Wei Zhao's commentary, *Guo yu* 16.511–13. The phrase "Peng shang" 彭殤 in this line refers to "longevity and premature death," but here *shang* is clearly used for the sake of rhyme.

155. Lingbi was a county to the south of Pengcheng. Li Daoyuan, *Shuijing zhushu* 24.2023.

quently summoned to public service, but he steadfastly refused. He began his official career as a member of Huan Wen's staff. As Fu Jian 苻堅 (338–85), the ruler of the Former Qin, attacked the Jin frontier, Xie Xuan was highly recommended by Xie An, his uncle, to the court. In 383, Xie Xuan led the Jin army and fought the famous Battle of the Fei River (Fei shui 淝水) against Fu Jian's invasion. Taking advantage of Fu Jian's defeat, Xie Xuan advanced into the north and camped at Pengcheng, and captured a large part of the northern territory (mostly in Shandong and He'nan). He was subsequently appointed the governor of seven prefectures and enfeoffed as Duke of Kangle 康樂, a title inherited by Xie Lingyun. After Xie An's death in 385, Xie Xuan lost his support at court, and his request to continue to be stationed at Pengcheng in order to solidify the military victories in the north was rejected. Xie Xuan then fell ill, and repeatedly asked to be relieved from duty. He was made administrator of the Kuaiji Commandery, and so he returned to his home estate at Kuaiji. He died in 388.[156]

In two of his other works, Xie Lingyun expresses in much the same terms his admiration for his grandfather as well as his regret that Xie Xuan failed to conquer the north due to the power struggle at the Jin court. One of the works is his "Poetic Exposition on Dwelling in the Mountains" ("Shanju fu" 山居賦),[157] and the other is a poem entitled "Recounting the Virtues of My Grandfather" ("Shu zu de" 述祖德).[158]

於是濫石橋	Thereupon I looked at the reflection of the Stone Bridge,
登戲臺	And then climbed the Sporting Horse Terrace.[159]
策馬鈞渚	First speeding my steed at the fishing isle,
息轡城隅	I finally rested my reins at the corner of the city.
永感四山	Eternally touched by the four hills,[160]

156. Fang Xuanling et al., *Jin shu* 79.2080–85.

157. Shen Yue, *Song shu* 67.1754–72; Yan Kejun, *Quan Song wen* 31.2604–9. For a complete translation with annotations, see Westbrook, "Landscape Description in the Lyric Poetry," pp. 186–337.

158. Lu Qinli, *Quan Song shi* 2.1157.

159. This is the Xima tai 戲馬臺 constructed by Xiang Yu. See below.

160. "Yong gan" 永感 ("eternally touched") is a phrased often used when speaking of one's deceased parents. "The four hills" are not clear, but in the context of his subsequent reminiscence of his grandfather, Xie Xuan, I suspect Xie Lingyun is referring to the hills at his family estate at Shining, originally developed by Xie Xuan after he retired from public

零淚雙渠	I let my tears fall in two streams.
怨物華之推驛	How I resented the changes in things of nature,
慨舟壑之遞遷	And lamented the loss of the boat in the ravine.[161]
謂徂歲之悠闊	I recognized the infinite passage of time,
結幽思之方根	My pent-up feelings were knotted like vast roots.
感皇祖之徽德	I was moved by the fine qualities of my grandfather:
爰識沖而量淵	His insight was deep, his tolerance profound.
降俊明以鏡鑒	He pleased the outstanding talents with his keen perception,[162]
迴風猷以昭宣	He changed morals by propagating righteousness.
道既底於國難	He cultivated the Way during the crisis of the state;
惠有覃於黎元	He extended his grace to the common folk.
士頌歌於政教	Gentlemen sang the praises of his civilizing influence;
民謠詠於渥恩	Commoners composed ballads about his great generosity.
兼採芑之致美	He possessed the consummate grace depicted in "Gathering the White Millet,"[163]
協漢廣之發言	His conduct was fit for expression in "Han Is Wide."[164]
強虎氐之搏翼	He overpowered the tiger-like Di who spread their wings,
灟雲網於所禁	Tying a vast, cloud-like net to restrain them.
驅黔萌以蘊崇	The Di had driven people from their hometowns to fill their land;[165]

service. In his "Poetic Exposition on Dwelling in the Mountains," he mentions "the four hills" three times. Yan Kejun, *Quan Song wen* 31.2605, 2607. It may be roughly translated as "hills all around" or "hills on all sides."

161. "The loss of the boat in the ravine" refers to a famous passage from *Zhuangzi*: "You hide a boat in the ravine and a mountain in the swamp, and tell yourself that they will be safe. But in the middle of the night, a man of strength shoulders them and carries them off, and in your ignorance you have no idea what happened. It is proper to hide small things in big ones, and yet they get away from you." *Zhuangzi jishi* 3.243.

162. Chi Chao 郗超 (337–78) once said of Xie Xuan, "I had watched him appoint people: he always appointed the right men, even for minor tasks." Fang Xuanling et al., *Jin shu* 79.2081.

163. "Gathering the White Millet" ("Cai qi" 採芑) is a poem from the *Classic of Poetry* that celebrates the general Fangshu 方叔 and his military campaign against the Chu. *Mao shi zhengyi* 10.360–63.

164. "Han Is Wide" ("Han guang" 漢廣), another poem from the *Classic of Poetry*, is interpreted as a depiction of the spread of King Wen of the Zhou's moral influence to south China (the region of the Yangzi River and Han River). Ibid., 1.41–43.

165. *Yun chong* 蘊崇, a phrase from *Chunqiu Zuozhuan zhengyi* 4.71, the sixth year of Duke Yin, means "to accumulate." For moving households from territories, see Fang Xuanling et al., *Jin shu* 113.2889, 2893, 2898.

取園陵而湮沈	They had damaged the imperial mausoleums, which lay in ruins.[166]
錫殘落於河西	Xi was overwhelmed at Hexi,
序淪胥於漢陰	Xu was lost on the south shore of the Han.[167]
攻方城而折扃	They attacked the barrier wall to the north of Chu, and broke open the gate;
擾譙潁其誰任	They caused chaos in the region of Qiao and Ying, yet none could resist them.[168]
世闕才而貽亂	The world lacked talent, and this led to calamities;
時得賢而興治	When a worthy man was acquired, order was established.
救祖考之邦壤	To save the land of his forefathers,
在幽人而枉志	The recluse must yield his private aspiration.
體飛書之遠情	He understood the deep feelings of the man who had composed the letter conveyed by a shot arrow,[169]
悟犒師之通識	He grasped the comprehensive perception of the man who offered provisions to the army.[170]
迨明達之高覽	When it came to the penetrating insight of wise men,
契古今而同事	From past to present, they had much in common.
拔淵謨於潛機	He devised his far-reaching plan in incipiency,

166. The Former Qin capital was Chang'an, where the Han imperial mausoleums were located.

167. Xi refers to Zhang Tianxi 張天錫 (ca. 345–405), the Governor of Liangzhou 涼州 (in modern Gansu), who was captured by Fu Jian in 376. Xu is Zhu Xu 朱序 (d. 393), the Governor of Liangzhou 梁州, who was captured by Fu Jian at Xiangyang 襄陽 (in modern Hubei). Fang Xuanling et al., *Jin shu* 9.227, 229.

168. Qiao is modern Bozhou 亳州 of Anhui 安徽. Ying refers to the Ying River, which flows into the Huai River at Shouyang 壽陽 (modern Shou county 壽縣 of Anhui), where Fu Jian's army confronted the Jin army led by Xie Xuan.

169. This refers to Lu Zhonglian 魯仲連, a recluse living in the Warring States period who loved to help solve difficult political problems but refused to serve any public office. The Yan army took Liaocheng 聊城 (in modern Shandong) from Qi; a Qi general then besieged Liaocheng for over a year. Many soldiers died on both sides, with neither side being able to either capture the city or lift the siege. Lu Zhonglian wrote a letter to the Yan general, tied the letter to an arrow, and shot the arrow into the city. The Yan general committed suicide after he read the letter. Sima Qian, *Shi ji* 83.2465.

170. In 631 BCE, Qi invaded Lu. The Duke of Lu sent Zhan Xi 展喜 to offer provisions to the Qi army. Before he left, Zhan Xi received instructions on what to say from Zhan Qin 展禽, his father, a worthy man better known as Liuxia Hui 柳下惠. Zhan Xi's clever speech caused Qi to withdraw its army. *Chunqiu Zuozhuan zhengyi*, the twenty-sixth year of Duke Xi, 16.264. According to Mencius, Liuxia Hui conducted himself with propriety in every situation, whether as an official or as a recluse. *Mengzi zhushu* 3.67–68.

騁神鋒於雲旆	And drew out his divine blade under the cloud banners.
驅斥澤而風靡	The enemy was driven into salt marshes, falling with the wind;
蹙坑谷而鳥竄	Crowding ditches and valleys, they fled like birds.
中華免夫左衽	The Han populace was spared from buttoning their lappets on the left side;[171]
江表此焉緩帶	To the south of the Yangzi, people were able to loosen their sashes.[172]
既剋黜於肥六	Having crushed the enemy troops at Lu and Fei,[173]
又作鎮於彭沛	He proceeded to govern the region of Peng and Pei.
晏皇塗於國内	Bringing concord to the imperial way within the realm,
震天威於河外	He spread the might of heaven beyond the Yellow River.
掃東齊而已寧	Conquering the eastern Qi, he pacified the region;
指西崤而將泰	Pointing to Xiao in the west, he was about to effect peace therein.[174]
值秉均而代謝	But then the state power changed hands,
實大業之興廢	And the great enterprise began to decline.
心無忝於樂生	His mind might well be compared to that of Master Yue,
事有像於燕惠	But what was done to him resembled the act of King Hui of Yan.[175]
抱明哲之不伐	Cherishing the wise principle of not boasting of one's merit,
奉宏勳而是稅	He gave up the claim on his magnificent feat.
捐七州以爰來	Forsaking seven prefectures and coming home,
歸五湖以投袂	Resolutely he returned to the Five Lakes.[176]

---

171. Buttoning one's lappets on the left side was considered a non-Han Chinese dressing style.

172. That is, relax.

173. According to Li Yunfu, Lu refers to Lu'an 六安 (modern Lu'an of Anhui) in the Fei River region. *Xie Lingyun ji*, p. 212, n. 266. Modern Shou county is under the administrative district of Lu'an.

174. The eastern Qi refers to the region of Yanzhou 兗州 and Qingzhou 青州 (in modern Shandong). Xiao refers to Mt. Xiao 崤山 (in modern Luoning 洛寧 county of He'nan), to the west of Yanzhou and Qingzhou. Both were in the territory of the Former Qin.

175. Master Yue refers to the famous general Yue Yi 樂毅, who had won great victories for the State of Yan and was enfeoffed as Lord of Changguo by King Zhao. After King Zhao died, King Hui 惠王 distrusted Yue Yi, and Yue Yi fled to Zhao. Sima Qian, *Shi ji* 80.2429.

屈盛績於平生	All his life he had achieved numerous glorious deeds;
申遠期於暮歲	He finally realized his greatest aspiration in his old age.

The following passage goes back further in time to trace the early history of Pengcheng, which had been part of the state of Song during the Spring and Autumn period. In 573 BCE, the state of Zheng formed an alliance with Chu and invaded Song, advancing all the way to the Cao Gate (the northwestern gate of Song's capital). They took three Song cities—Zhaojia 朝郟, Chenggao 城郜, and Youqiu 幽丘—and went on to capture Pengcheng. They then installed five Song traitors, Yushi 魚石, Xiang Weiren 向爲人, Linzhu 鱗朱, Xiang Dai 向帶, and Yufu 魚府, in Pengcheng. The Song minister Xi Xuyu 西鉏吾 told people not to worry about the situation, pointing out that by stationing troops in Pengcheng, an important site on a major artery of traffic connecting the various feudal domains, especially Jin and Wu, Zheng and Chu would alienate the feudal lords and cause problems for themselves. Later that year, Song troops besieged Pengcheng but were defeated by Chu. Song asked for Jin's help, and a Jin army led by Han Jue subsequently forced Chu to retreat.[177]

訪曩載於宋鄙	I investigated the bygone years at the Song frontier city,
採陽秋於魯經	And gathered historical information in the classic of Lu.
晉申好於東吳	As Jin formed an alliance with the eastern Wu,
鄭憑威於南荆	Zheng relied on the military might of the southern Chu.
故反師於曹門	Therefore the Zheng army reached the Cao Gate,
將以塞於夷庚	Planning to block the level thoroughfare.
納五叛以長寇	They returned the five rebels to encourage the wicked;
伐三邑以侵彭	They captured three cities and invaded Pengcheng.
美西鉏之忠辭	I esteemed the loyal speech of Xi Xuyu,
快韓厥之奇兵	And took keen delight in Han Jue's speedy attack.

Liu Bang's archrival Xiang Yu, as king of Western Chu, had made Pengcheng his capital. He had ordered the construction of a terrace on a

176. This is a reference to Fan Li 范蠡 (fl. fifth century BCE), the minister of Yue who helped the Yue king conquer the state of Wu. Afterward, he withdrew from public service and spent the rest of his life leisurely roaming the Five Lakes (Lake Tai 太湖 and its adjacent four lakes). *Guo yu* 21.659. Xie Lingyun's second "Shu zu de" poem contains a couplet: "He bowed and declined the seven prefectures, / Dusting his clothes on the Five Lakes" 高揖七州外，拂衣五湖裏. Lu Qinli, *Quan Song shi* 2.1157.

177. *Chunqiu Zuozhuan zhengyi*, the eighteenth year of Duke Cheng, 28.485–89.

hill south of Pengcheng known as Sporting Horse Terrace (Xima tai 戲馬臺). Climbing the terrace, Xie Lingyun recalls the feats of Xiang Yu. While still an adolescent, Xiang Yu and his uncle were watching the First Emperor of Qin's procession when Xiang Yu reportedly said, "I could take that fellow's place." As an adult, he was said to have had an imposing physique and superhuman strength. He was twenty-three years old when he raised a rebel army against Qin.[178] In the end, Xiang Yu's personality flaws and misdeeds led to his tragic end. But Xiang Yu never seemed to acknowledge his personal failures. At the end of his life, he repeatedly claimed that "it is heaven that destroys me."[179]

追項王之故臺	Seeking out the former terrace of King Xiang,
跡霸楚之遺端	I traced the enduring accomplishments of the Hegemon of Chu.
挺宏志於總角	His great ambition stood out in his tender youth;
奮英勢於弱冠	He exerted his heroic force in early adulthood.
氣蓋天而倒日	His vigor overwhelmed heaven and turned back the sun;
力拔山而傾湍	His strength could uproot mountains and move rivers.
始飆起於勾越	At the beginning, he rose like a whirlwind at Gou Yue;[180]
中電激於衡關	Midway, he struck like lightning at the Heng Pass.[181]
興偏慮於攸吝	He gave way to thoughts of partiality and stinginess;

178. See Xiang Yu's biography in Sima Qian, *Shi ji* 7.295–339.

179. Ibid., 7.334.

180. Gou Yue refers to the old Kingdom of Yue. Xiang Yu and his uncle first raised the rebel troops in the Commandery of Kuaiji in the former Yue territory.

181. The Heng Pass (Heng guan 衡關) in the text should be emended either to the Han Pass 函關 (the Hangu Pass 函谷關) or the Tong Pass 潼關. The Han Pass, first established by Qin, was the key entry point to the Qin region and its capital Xianyang. In 206 BCE, Xiang Yu forced his way through the Han Pass. In 114 BCE, the Han Pass was moved to a different site. See Xu Guang's 徐廣 (352–425) commentary in Sima Qian, *Shi ji* 30.1435. The Tong Pass did not appear in historical records until the end of the Eastern Han (see Chen Shou, *Sanguo zhi* 1.34), but by Xie Lingyun's time, the Tong Pass had long eclipsed the (newer site of) Hangu Pass in terms of its strategic importance, and sometimes the Tong Pass and the (former site of) Hangu Pass became confused. See, for instance, Hu Sanxing's 胡三省 (1230–1302) commentary in Sima Guang, *Zizhi tongjian* 3.109, in which he claims that what Li Daoyuan, the compiler of *Shuijing zhushu*, means by "Hangu" is actually none other than the Tong Pass. The Tong Pass is also known as the Chong Pass 衝關. See Yang Shoujing's 楊守敬 commentary in Li Daoyuan, *Shuijing zhushu* 4.314. *Chong* 衝 and *heng* 衡 sometimes become mixed in textual transmission. See, for instance, Wei Shou, *Wei shu* 30.716.

忘即易於所難	He forgot to follow the easy course in things he found difficult.
忌陳錦而莫照	Worried about displaying brocade in the dark,
思反鄉而有歎	With many sighs he longed to return to his native soil.[182]
且夫殺義害嬰	Furthermore, he slew the Acting Emperor and took Ziying's life;[183]
而愎豐疑	[ ] harbored many doubts and was indecisive;[184]
紲賢不策	He held his worthy counselor in check without using his advice—
失位誰持	Who could then support him when he was deprived of power?[185]
迨理屈而愈閉	Losing moral ground, he became increasingly closed to reason;
方怨天而懷悲	Filled with anguish, he expressed resentment toward heaven.
對駿騅以發憤	Facing his handsome steed, he vented his bitterness,
傷虞姝於末詞	And lamented the beautiful Lady Yu in his last words.[186]

---

182. Instead of staying at Xianyang, Xiang Yu, a native of Xiaxiang 下相 (modern Suqian of Jiangsu), decided to make Pengcheng his capital, saying, "To be rich and noble without returning to one's homeland is like going out in embroidered clothes at night—who would have noticed?" Sima Qian, *Shi ji* 7.315.

183. After Xiang Yu entered the Qin capital Xianyang, he executed the last Qin king, Ziying 子嬰, even though Ziying had surrendered himself. He also killed the "Acting Emperor" (Yidi 義帝), a descendent of the former royal house of Chu, who had been established as the leader of the rebel army.

184. This line may have been corrupted.

185. Han Xin, who had first served under Xiang Yu and then defected to Liu Bang, summarized Xiang Yu's faults thus: "When King Xiang gives an angry burst, he can make a thousand men cower in fear, but he cannot appoint a worthy general. This is the bravery of a commoner. He is kind and respectful, and his words are gentle; if someone is sick, he weeps and gives him his own food and drink. But when someone has earned merit enough to be rewarded with an office, he begrudges the award and would rub the official seal in his hands until it is worn. This is the benevolence of a woman. Though he has become a hegemon and master to the various feudal lords, he did not stay within the Hangu pass, but chose Pengcheng as his capital instead. He betrayed his agreement with the Acting Emperor, and enthroned his favorites as kings. All the feudal lords are angry with him." Sima Qian, *Shi ji* 92.2612. The agreement with the Acting Emperor was that whoever entered the Hangu Pass first should be king. Liu Bang was the first to enter, but Xiang Yu failed to observe the agreement.

186. The last two lines of the passage refer to the song sung by Xiang Yu when he was besieged by Liu Bang's army. Xiang Yu had a favorite concubine, Lady Yu, who always fol-

In the above passage, the "worthy counselor" whose advice Xiang Yu did not heed is Fan Zeng 范增 (277–204 BCE), who had joined Xiang Yu's forces at the age of seventy. Xiang Yu respectfully called him "Father Fan" (Yafu 亞父) but rarely listened to his counsel. After Liu Bang tricked Xiang Yu into believing that Fan Zeng had had secret dealings with Liu Bang, Fan Zeng left Xiang Yu in anger. He died on his way home. His tomb is to the southwest of Xiang Yu's Sporting Horse Terrace in Pengcheng.[187] In the following passage, Xie Lingyun delivers a caustic judgment on Fan Zeng's failure to find a good lord from the start. Interestingly, the phrase used in this case is *moushi* 謀始 ("carefully plan the beginning"), the same phrase the poet uses to describe his own official career earlier in the poetic exposition.

陟亞父之故營	I climbed to see the former camp of Father Fan,[188]
諒謀始之非託	Truly he did not carefully plan his beginning, and entrusted himself to the wrong man.
遭衰嬴之崩綱	He happened upon the breakdown of the declining house of Ying,[189]
值威炎之結絡	But was in time for the Fiery Han's creation of order.
迄皓首於阜陵	Though his hair had already turned white in hills and mounds,
猶謬覺於然諾	He was still lacking in discernment in making commitments.
視一人於三傑	If we compare this one man with the Three Heroes,[190]
豈在己之庸弱	How could he be considered mediocre and weak?
置豐沛而不舉	But he failed to support the lord of Feng and Pei:[191]
故自同於俎鑊	It was like placing himself on a cutting board or in a cooking tripod.

lowed him in battle, and a fine piebald he always rode. His song goes: "My strength can uproot a mountain, my vigor tops the world; / The time is against me, and my piebald does not advance. / My piebald does not advance, and I let it be; / But Yu, alas Yu, what shall I do about you?" Sima Qian, *Shi ji* 7.339.

187. Li Daoyuan, *Shuijing zhushu* 25.2147.

188. "Ying" 營 (camp) might have been *ying* 塋 (tomb).

189. That is, the royal house of Qin.

190. The Three Heroes are Zhang Liang, Han Xin, and Xiao He 蕭何 (d. 193).

191. The "lord of Feng and Pei" refers to Liu Bang.

Significantly, the last historical figures evoked in the poetic exposition are not military or political personages, but Liu Jiao 劉交 (d. 178 BCE) and his scholarly descendants. Liu Jiao was Liu Bang's younger brother, who was enfeoffed as King of Chu after Han Xin was demoted. Liu Jiao was buried at the Tongxiao Hill 同孝山 to the west of Pengcheng. The hill is also known as King Chu's Hill 楚王山.[192] Considering himself the descendant of Liu Jiao, Liu Yu had had the tomb repaired.[193]

Liu Jiao had studied the *Classic of Poetry* in his youth and authored a commentary, no longer extant, known as *The Poems of King Yuan* (*Yuanwang shi* 元王詩). In the following passage, Xie Lingyun focuses on Liu Jiao's love of learning and singles out his cerebral descendants for praise.[194] There is no mention of Liu Wu 劉戊, Liu Jiao's grandson who had succeeded Liu Jiao as King of Chu but was killed in 154 BCE as a participant in the revolt of the seven kingdoms.

發下口而游歷	Embarking on an outing from the mouth of the Bian River,
迄西山而弭轡	I held in my reins at the western hill.
觀終古之幽憤	Observing the pent-up resentment and frustration over the centuries,
懷元王之沖粹	I could not help but pine for the gentility and purity of King Yuan.
丁戰國之權爭	Encountering the power struggle of the warring states,
方恬心於道肆	He calmly bent his mind on extending the Way.
學浮丘以就德	He studied with Fuqiu to perfect his virtue;
友三儒以成類	He befriended the three Ru scholars as his comrades.[195]
潔流始於初源	Clean currents can be traced to the source;
累仁基於前美	Accumulated benevolence is based on former integrity.
撥楚族之休烈	His descendants cultivated the fine enterprise of the clan of Chu,

192. Li Daoyuan, *Shuijing zhushu* 23.1986.

193. Fu Liang 傅亮 (374–426), his trusted secretary, had drafted on Liu Yu's behalf "Duke of Song's Command to Have King Yuan of Chu's Tomb Repaired" 爲宋公修楚元王墓教. Yan Kejun, *Quan Song wen* 26.2576.

194. For this passage, see Liu Jiao's biography in Ban Gu, *Han shu* 36.1921–972.

195. In his youth, Liu Jiao had studied the *Classic of Poetry* with Fuqiu Bo 浮丘伯; his fellow students were Shengong 申公, Baisheng 白生, and Musheng 穆生. After he was enfeoffed as king, he appointed Shengong, Baisheng, and Musheng to his court.

傳芳素於來祀	Whose fragrance and purity were transmitted to future generations.
彊見譽於清虛	Jiang was extolled for his high-minded quietude;
德致稱於千里	De received the acclaim of a "thousand-mile pony."
或避寵以辭姻	The latter avoided favoritism by declining a marriage proposal;
或遺榮而不仕	The former forsook worldly glory by refusing public service.[196]
政直言以安身	Zheng was direct in his speech and preserved himself;[197]
駿絕才以喪己	Jun possessed outstanding talent but lost his life.[198]
驅信道之成終	Driven by a desire to pursue the correct way at the end,
表昧世之虧始	He demonstrated how he, ignorant of the world, lacked a good beginning.
悟介焉之已差	Once understanding the infinitesimally small incipience of misfortune,
則不俟於終日	One must act immediately, without waiting till the day has run its course.[199]
既防萌於未著	Error should be forestalled before it sprouts;
雖念德其何益	Otherwise what advantage is there to merely long for virtue?

In the last six lines of the preceding passage, Xie Lingyun comments on the fate of Liu Xin, who had been a supporter of Wang Mang but turned

196. Jiang refers to Liu Bijiang 劉辟彊 (ca. 135–85 BCE), King Yuan's grandson. Like King Yuan, he was well versed in the *Classic of Poetry*. He devoted himself to learning and refused to serve public office for most of his life. His son, Liu De 劉德, was talented; Emperor Wu of the Han summoned him to an audience and praised him as a "thousand-mile pony" (*qianli ju* 千里駒) when he was still very young. The powerful minister Huo Guang 霍光 (d. 68 BCE) intended to marry his daughter to him, but Liu declined because he did not want to marry into such a prominent family. Ban Gu, *Han shu* 36.1927.

197. Zizheng 子政 was the courtesy name of Liu Xiang 劉向 (ca. 79–8 BCE), Liu De's son. He was an erudite scholar and writer. He frequently sent memorials to the throne offering candid advice which was never heeded, but his memorials were nevertheless tolerated.

198. Zijun 子駿 was the courtesy name of Liu Xin (d. 23), Liu Xiang's son, also a learned scholar. He was involved in a plot against Wang Mang, the usurper of the Han throne, and committed suicide when the plot was found out. Ban Gu, *Han shu* 99.4185.

199. Confucius thus comments on the hexagram "Contentment": "A gentleman acts as soon as he becomes cognizant of the incipience of something and does not wait for the day to run its course." *Zhou yi zhengyi* 8.171.

against him at the end. Citing the *Classic of Changes*, Xie Lingyun expresses regret that Liu Xin did not foster a good beginning and then only tried to correct his course when it was too late. Understanding the incipience of things and acting promptly according to it seems to be a recurring motif in the poetic exposition.

The awareness of the "sprouting" of error serves as a trigger for the subsequent description of the seasonal transition from winter to spring, a time of sprouting. The poetic exposition fittingly ends with the poet's return journey, and the poet concludes with the wish for a peaceful unified empire and, for himself, a life of reclusion and leisure.

爾乃孟陬發節	Then in the first month, the spring season has begun,
雷隱蟄驚	Thunderclaps shake the earth, hibernating creatures are startled.
散葉荑柯	Leaves are sprouting and budding on boughs,
芳藹飾萌	Sweet-smelling flowers decorate the newly-sprung plants.
麥萋萋於旄丘	Wheat grows lushly over the hills;
柳依依於高城	Willow branches softly dangle at the high city wall.
相睢鳩之集河	I observe the fish-hawks gathering by the river,
觀鳴鹿之食苹	I watch the crying deer nibble away at the wormwood.
沂泗遠兮清川急	Yi and Si flow into the distance, clear waters rushing forward;
秋冬近兮緒風襲	With autumn and winter not yet far gone, the remaining chilly air assails.
風流蕙兮水增瀾	An aroma nevertheless wafts on the breeze, and rivers are flooding;
訴愁衿兮鑑戚顏	I tell of my sorrow, and view my sad countenance in the mirror.
愁盈根而薀際	Sorrow swells like tree roots, accumulated underneath;
戚發條而成端	Sadness sprouts from branches, forming tips.
嗟我行之彌日	Alas, I have been traveling day in and day out;
待征邁而言旋	I look forward to completing my journey and coming home.
荷慶雲之優渥	I have received favor and grace from my superiors,
周雙七於此年	this year marking the fourteenth anniversary of my service.
陶逸豫於京甸	I will now enjoy a relaxed life in the capital,
違險難於行川	Saying farewell to the hardship of journeying on water.
轉歸舷而眷戀	And yet, as my boat turns back, I feel nostalgic,
望修檣而流漣	Gazing at the tall sail, I linger a while.

願關鄴之遄清	I wish that the northern land will soon be pacified,
遲華鑾之凱旋	As we await the triumphant return of the splendid princely chariot;
穆淳風於六合	That the customs will be harmonized throughout the realm,
溥洪澤於八埏	That grace shall be widely spread to the eight outlying regions;
頒賢愚於大小	That the wise and foolish will be ranked according to their natures,
順規矩於方圓	And proper measures be adopted to determine square and round;
固四民之獲所	That the four peoples will indeed find their rightful places,
宜税稷於萊田	And taxes be collected from the grain planted in uncultivated fields.
苦邯鄲之難步	As for me, I find the Handan manner of walking hard to imitate;[200]
庶行迷之易痊	Though I hope it will be easy to cure the one who has lost his way.
長守朴以終稔	Abiding by my unadorned nature and living out my natural lifespan:
亦拙者之政焉	This in truth is the task of an inept man.[201]

200. A young man from Shouling went to Handan and tried to imitate the Handan people's manner of walking; not only did he fail to master the skill, but he also forgot his own manner of walking and had to crawl back home. *Zhuangzi jishi* 6.601. The poet is saying that he finds it difficult to imitate someone who is skilled in being an official, and that his engagement in public service is like that of a man who has lost his way.

201. The last line is an allusion to Pan Yue's preface to his "Poetic Exposition on Living in Idleness" ("Xianju fu" 閑居賦). In the preface, Pan Yue keeps referring to himself as "an inept person" (*zhuozhe* 拙者) in terms of engaging in government as an official. At the end of the preface, Pan Yue writes: "Oh to be nothing but filial, and to be good to one's brothers: this is how an inept person exercises government" 孝乎惟孝，友于兄弟，此亦拙者之爲政也. Yan Kejun, *Quan Jin wen* 91.1987. Pan Yue is in turn alluding to the *Analects*: "Someone asked Confucius: 'Sir, why don't you engage in government?' Confucius said, 'The *[Classic of] Documents* says, "Oh to be nothing but filial, and to be good to one's brothers: this could be applied to the exercise of government." This too is a way of engaging in government. Why must one directly engage in government?'" *Lunyu zhushu* 2.19.

APPENDIX II

Shi Changhe[1]

Shi Changhe died and, after four days, came back to life.[2]

He said that after he died, he walked southeast and saw two men working on the road. They were always about fifty paces ahead of him; when he sped up, they, too, sped up. Both sides of the road were lined with brambles and thorns as sharp as eagle's claws. Shi saw throngs of people, old and young, running along among the brambles as if being driven. Their bodies were all wounded, and there was congealed blood on the ground. When they saw Shi walking alone on the flat road, they sighed, saying, "Happy is the Buddha's disciple—he alone walks on the thoroughfare."

Shi continued walking on the road and came to a mansion with tiled roof and seventy to eighty beams. There was a tower in the middle with windows and more than ten beams. In the tower sat a man with a three-foot-long square face, dressed in a black robe with four open slits. He sat under the north window; only his upper body was visible. Shi bowed to him. The man said, "Ah, the good Sir Shi is here. We have not seen each

1. There are two versions of the Shi Changhe story. This translation is based on the version in Liu Yiqing, *Youming lu*, in *Han Wei liuchao*, p. 746. The other version, slightly different, is from Wang Yan, *Mingxiang ji*, in Li Fang et al., *Taiping guangji* 383.3055–56.

2. The *Mingxiang ji* version gives a fuller account of Shi Changhe's background and the circumstances of his death and revival: "Shi Changhe, a man of the State of Zhao, was from Gaoyi [in modern Hebei province]. When he was eighteen years old, he was sick for over a month, and then he died. His family was poor and could not afford a coffin to bury him right away. After four days, he came back to life."

other for over twenty years."[3] Shi replied, "Yes, indeed." He immediately seemed to remember what it was like before.

The Magistrate of Pingyi, Meng Cheng, and his wife had died earlier. The man in the tower said, "Do you know Magistrate Meng?" Shi Changhe said, "Yes, I do." The man said, "When he was alive, Meng Cheng did not exert himself in following the Buddhist teachings.[4] So now he is sweeping the floor for me. His wife did the opposite, so now she is in peace and does not have to perform any official service." He pointed to a chamber to the southwest, saying, "Meng Cheng's wife is there now." Meng Cheng's wife then opened up a window and showed herself. She asked Shi Changhe, "When did you come here, good Sir Shi?" She also asked after her sons and daughters and every other member of her family, old and young: "Are they well? When you go back, please pay them a visit, and I will ask you to bear a letter for me." In a short while, Shi Changhe saw Meng Cheng come from the western side of the tower, with a broom and dust pan in one hand and a cane in another. He also asked after his family.

The man in the tower said, "I hear that Yu Long is diligent in following the Buddha's teachings. Is it true? What does he do?" Changhe said, "He does not eat fish or meat, and he does not drink a drop of wine. He always recites the venerable sutras and cures people of ills and pains." The man in the tower said, "I hope you are speaking the truth."

Then he asked the record keeper, "Has good Sir Shi lived out his lifespan? Or was he deprived of his life by mistake?" The recorder keeper replied, "According to the record, he has more than forty years left."[5] The man in the tower then ordered the record keeper to prepare an oxcart for Shi Changhe, with two officers on horseback to escort him. In a short while, the oxcart and the officers came from the east. Changhe bowed and took leave of the man in the tower, got into the cart, and returned home. On the road by which he had come, there were now way stations, officers and attendants, couches, food, and drink.

---

3. The *Mingxiang ji* version reads "two thousand years."

4. The term used in the Chinese text here is *jingjin* 精進(Skt. *vīrya*), which means continuous zealous self-cultivation.

5. The Mingxiang ji version reads "thirty years."

In an instant he was home. He saw his parents sitting by his corpse, which was swollen like an ox and emitted a foul smell. Unwilling to enter it, he walked around the corpse three times, sighing. Just as he was standing right in front of the head of the corpse, he saw his deceased elder sister, who gave him a push from behind. Shi Changhe stumbled and fell onto the face of his own dead body. Thereupon he was revived.[6]

6. The *Mingxiang ji* version has an additional passage at the end: "The Buddhist monk Zhi Fashan 支法山, who had not yet become a monk at the time, heard this account and was determined to join the Buddhist order. Fashan lived during the Xianhe 咸和 era [326–34]."

Reference Matter

Bibliography

Atwell, R. R. "From Augustine to Gregory the Great: An Evaluation of the Doctrine of Purgatory." *Journal of Ecclesiastical History* 38 (1987): 173–86.

Bakhtin, M. M. *The Dialogic Imagination: Four Essays*. Translated by Caryl Emerson and Michael Holquist. Austin: University of Texas Press, 1981.

Ban Gu 班固, comp. *Han shu* 漢書. Beijing: Zhonghua shuju, 1962.

Baochang 寶唱. *Biqiuni zhuan jiaozhu* 比丘尼傳校注. Collated by Wang Rutong 王孺童. Beijing: Zhonghua shuju, 2006.

———. *Lives of the Nuns: Biographies of Chinese Buddhist Nuns from the Fourth to Sixth Centuries*. Translated by Kathryn Ann Tsai. Honolulu: University of Hawaii Press, 1994.

———. *Biographies of Buddhist Nuns*. Translated by Li Rongxi. In *Lives of Great Monks and Nuns*. Berkeley, CA: Numata Center for Buddhist Translation and Research, 2002, pp. 69–154.

Baochang 寶唱, Senghao 僧豪, and Fasheng 法生, comps. *Jinglü yixiang* 經律異相. In *Taishō shinshū Daizōkyō* 大正新修大藏經 53.

Bao Zhao 鮑照. *Bao canjun shizhu* 鮑參軍詩注. Annotated by Huang Jie 黃節. Hong Kong: Zhonghua shuju, 1972.

Beal, Samuel, trans. *Si-yu Ki: Buddhist Records of the Western World*. London: Motilal Banarsidass, 1884.

Bin Chun 斌椿. *Chengcha biji* 乘槎筆記. In *Xiao Fanghu zhai yudi congchao* 小方壺齋輿地叢鈔 11, compiled by Wang Xiqi 王錫祺. Shanghai: Zhuyi tang, 1891.

———. *Chengcha biji* 乘槎筆記. In *Zouxiang shijie congshu* 走向世界叢書, edited by Zhong Shuhe 鍾叔河. Vol. 1. Hu'nan: Yuelu shushe, 1985.

———. *Chengcha biji (waiyizhong)* 乘槎筆記 (外一種). Edited by Zhong Shuhe 鍾叔河. Hu'nan: Hu'nan renmin chubanshe, 1981.

———. *Haiguo shengyou cao* 海國勝遊草 and *Tianwai guifan cao* 天外歸帆草. In *Zouxiang shijie congshu* 走向世界叢書, edited by Zhong Shuhe 鍾叔河. Vol. 1. Hu'nan: Yuelu shushe, 1985.

Black, Adam, and Charles Black. *Black's Picturesque Tourist of Scotland.* 15th edition. Edinburgh: Adam and Charles Black (Firm): 1861.

Boulton, Nancy Elizabeth. *Early Chinese Buddhist Travel Records as a Literary Genre.* Ph.D. dissertation, Georgetown University, 1982.

Burke, Kenneth. *The Philosophy of Literary Form: Studies in Symbolic Action.* New York: Random House, 1957.

Bush, Susan, and Hsio-yen Shih, eds. *Early Chinese Texts on Painting.* Cambridge, MA: Harvard University Press, 1985.

Bryson, Norman. *Looking at the Overlooked: Four Essays on Still Life Painting.* Cambridge, MA: Harvard University Press, 1990.

Cai Zhenfeng 蔡振豐. "Gu Kaizhi lun hua de meixue yiyi shitan" 顧愷之論畫的美學意義試探. *Zhongguo wenxue yanjiu* 中國文學研究 9 (June 1995): 137–50.

Cai Zongxian 蔡宗憲. *Zhonggu qianqi de jiaopin yu nanbei hudong* 中古前期的交聘與南北互動. Taibei: Daoxiang chubanshe, 2008.

Campany, Robert F. "Return-from-Death Narratives in Early Medieval China." *Journal of Chinese Religions* 18 (1990): 91–125.

———. "To Hell and Back: Death, Near-Death, and Other Worldly Journeys in Early Medieval China." In *Death, Ecstasy, and Other Worldly Journeys*, edited by John J. Collins and Michael Fishbane. Chicago: University of Chicago Press, 1995, pp. 343–60.

———. *To Live as Long as Heaven and Earth: A Translation and Study of Ge Hong's Traditions of Divine Transcendents.* Berkeley: University of California Press, 2002.

———. "Two Religious Thinkers of the Early Eastern Jin: Gan Bao and Ge Hong in Multiple Contexts." *Asia Major* 18.1 (2005): 175–224.

Campbell, Mary B. *The Witness and the Other World: Exotic European Travel Writing, 400–1600.* Ithaca: Cornell University Press, 1988.

Cao Wenzhu 曹文柱. *Zhongguo liumin shi* 中國流民史. Guangzhou: Guangdong renmin chubanshe, 1996.

Cao Xueqin 曹雪芹. *Chongjiao bajia pingpi* Honglou meng 重校八家評批紅樓夢. Edited by Feng Qiyong 馮其庸. Nanchang: Jiangxi jiaoyu chubanshe, 2000.

Cen Zhongmian 岑仲勉. *Zhongwai shidi kaozheng* 中外史地考證. Beijing: Zhonghua shuju, 2004.

Chatterjee, Partha. *The Nation and Its Fragments: Colonial and Postcolonial Histories.* Princeton, NJ: Princeton University Press, 1993.

Chen Chuanxi 陳傳席. *Liuchao hualun yanjiu* 六朝畫論研究. Taibei: Xuesheng shuju, 1991.

Chen, Jack W. "On the Act and Representation of Reading in Medieval China." *Journal of American Oriental Society* 129.1 (January–March 2009): 57–71.

Chen Jiarong 陳佳榮, Qian Jiang 錢江, and Zhang Guangda 張廣達, ed. *Lidai zhongwai xingji* 歷代中外行記. Shanghai: Shanghai cishu chubanshe, 2008.

Chen Jinfeng 陳金鳳. *Wei Jin nanbeichao zhongjian didai yanjiu* 魏晉南北朝中間地帶研究. Tianjin: Tianjin guji chubanshe, 2005.

Chen Sen 陳森. *Pinhua baojian* 品花寶鑒. Ji'nan: Qi Lu shushe, 1993.

Chen Shangjun 陳尚君, ed. *Quan Tang shi bubian* 全唐詩補編. Beijing: Zhonghua shuju, 1992.

Chen Shou 陳壽, comp. *Sanguo zhi* 三國志. Beijing: Zhonghua shuju, 1959.

Cheng Yu-Yu 鄭毓瑜. "Jiushiyu de dili chidu: Yi Huang Zunxian 'Riben zashishi' zhong de diangu yunyong weili" 舊詩語的地理尺度: 以黃遵憲日本雜事詩中的典故運用爲例. In *Kongjian yu wenhua changyu: Kongjian yidong zhi wenhua quanshi* 空間與文化場域：空間移動之文化詮釋,

edited by Wang Ailing 王瓊玲. Taibei: Hanxue yanjiu zhongxin, 2009, pp. 251–92.

Chuci buzhu 楚辭補注. Annotated by Hong Xingzu 洪興祖. Beijing: Zhonghua shuju, 1983.

Chunqiu Zuozhuan zhengyi 春秋左傳正義. In *Shisanjing zhushu* 十三經注疏.

Cohen, Paul A. *Between Tradition and Modernity: Wang T'ao and Reform in Late Ch'ing China.* Cambridge, MA: Harvard University Press, 1974.

Collins, John J., and Michael Fishbane, eds. *Death, Ecstasy, and Other Worldly Journeys*. Chicago: University of Chicago Press, 1995.

Cosmas Indicopleustes. *The Christian Topography of Cosmas, An Egyptian Monk.* Translated by J. W. McCrindle. London: The Hakluyt Society, 1897.

Daoshi 道世, comp. *Fayuan zhulin* 法苑珠林. Collated by Zhou Shujia 周叔伽 and Su Jinren 蘇晉仁. Beijing: Zhonghua shuju, 2003.

Daoxuan 道宣, comp. *Guang hongming ji* 廣弘明集. In *Taishō shinshū Daizōkyō* 大正新修大藏經 52.

de Gobineau, Joseph Arthur. *The Inequality of Human Races*. Translated by Adrian Collins. New York: G. P. Putnam's Sons, 1915.

Derrida, Jacques. *Of Grammatology*. Translated by Gayatri Chakravorty Spivak. Baltimore: John Hopkins University Press, 1998.

Dikötter, Frank. *The Discourse of Race in Modern China*. Stanford: Stanford University Press, 1992.

Dīrghāgama Sūtra 長阿含經. In *Taishō shinshū Daizōkyō* 大正新修大藏經 1.

Douglas, David C., ed. *English Historical Documents*. New York: Routledge, 1979.

Drake, Fred W. *China Charts the World: Hsu Chi-yu and His Geography of 1848.* Cambridge, MA: Harvard East Asian Research Center, 1975.

Du Fu 杜甫. *Du shi jing quan* 杜詩鏡詮. Annotated by Yang Lun 楊倫. Shanghai: Shanghai guji chubanshe, 1962.

Du Zhiqiang 杜志強. "Xie Lingyun 'Zhuanzheng fu' 'Shanju fu' de zhushi wenti" 謝靈運撰征賦山居賦的注釋問題. *Liaodong xueyuan xuebao* 遼東學院學報. 10.5 (2008): 62–67.

Egeria. *Egeria's Travels to the Holy Land.* Translated by John Wilkinson. Revised edition. London: Ariel Publishing House, 1981.

Eggert, Marion. "Discovered Other, Recovered Self: Layers of Representation in an Early Travelogue on the West (*Xihai jiyou cao*, 1849)". In *Traditions of East Asian Travel*, edited by Joshua A. Fogel. New York: Berghahn Books, 2006, pp. 70–96.

Elsner, Jaś, and Joan-Paul Ribiés, eds. *Voyages and Visions: Towards a Cultural History of Travel.* London: Reaktion Books, 1999.

Engels, Frederick. *Engels: Selected Writings.* Edited by W. Henderson. Harmondsworth, England: Penguin 1967.

Erya zhushu 爾雅注疏. In *Shisanjing zhushu* 十三經注疏.

Fang Xuanling 房玄齡 et al., comps. *Jin shu* 晉書. Beijing: Zhonghua shuju, 1974.

Farmer, Michael J. *The Talent of Shu: Qiao Zhou and the Intellectual World in Early Medieval Sichuan.* Albany: State University of New York Press, 2007.

Faxian 法顯. *Faxian zhuan jiaozhu* 法顯傳校注. Annotated by Zhang Xun 章巽. Shanghai: Shanghai guji chubanshe, 1985.

———. *Faxian zhuan kaozheng* 法顯傳考證. Annotated by Adachi Kiroku 足立喜六. Translated from the Japanese by He Jianmin 何健民 and Zhang Xiaoliu 張小柳. Shanghai: Shangwu yinshuguan, 1937.

———. *Das Gaoseng-Faxian-Zhuan als religionsgeschichtliche Quelle: der älteste Bericht eines chinesischen buddhistischen Pilgermönchs über seine Reise nach Indien mit Übersetzung des Textes.* Translated by Max Deeg. Wiesbaden: Harrassowitz, 2005.

———. "The Journey of the Eminent Monk Faxian." Translated by Li Rongxi. In *Lives of Great Monks and Nuns*, translated by Li Rongxi and Albert A. Dalia. Berkeley, CA: Numata Center for Buddhist Translation and Research, 2002.

———. *A Record of Buddhistic Kingdoms.* Translated by James Legge. New York: Paragon Book Reprint Corp., 1965.

———. *The Travels of Fa-hsien (399–414 A.D.), or, Record of the Buddhistic Kingdoms.* Translated by Herbert A. Giles. London: Routledge & Kegan Paul, 1959.

———. *Xinyi Foguo ji* 新譯佛國記. Annotated and translated by Yang Weizhong 楊維中. Taibei: Sanmin shuju, 2004.

Fei Xin 費信. *Xingcha shenglan jiaozhu* 星槎勝覽校注. Annotated by Feng Chengjun 馮承鈞 Shanghai: Shangwu yinshuguan, 1938.

———. *Hsing-ch'a-sheng-lan: The Overall Survey of the Star Raft.* Translated by J. V. G. Mills. Revised, annotated, and edited by Roderich Ptak. Wiesbaden: Harrassowitz, 1996.

Feng Weine 馮惟訥, comp. *Gushi ji* 古詩紀. *Yingyin Wenyuange siku quanshu* 景印文淵閣四庫全書, Vol. 1379. Taibei: Shangwu yinshuguan, 1983.

Fogel, Joshua A., ed. *Traditions of East Asian Travel.* New York: Berghahn Books, 2006.

Foshuo wuliang qingjing pingdeng jue jing 佛說無量清淨平等覺經. Translated by Zhi Loujiachen 支婁迦讖. In *Taishō shinshū Daizōkyō* 大正新修大藏經 12.

Frodsham, J. D., trans. *The First Chinese Embassy to the West: The Journals of Kuo Sung-t'ao, Liu Hsi-hung, and Chang Te-yi.* Oxford: Clarendon Press, 1974.

———. *The Murmuring Stream: The Life and Works of the Chinese Nature Poet Hsieh Ling-yün (385–433), Duke of K'ang-Lo.* 2 volumes. Kuala Lumpur: University of Malaya Press, 1967.

Fu Baoshi 傅抱石. "Jin Gu Kaizhi 'Hua Yuntai shan ji' zhi yanjiu" 晉顧愷之畫雲臺山記之研究. In *Fu Baoshi meishu wenji* 傅抱石美術文集, edited by Ye Zonggao 葉宗鎬. Nanjing: Jiangsu wenyi chubanshe, 1986.

Fu Liang 傅亮, Zhang Yan 張演 and Lu Gao 陸杲. *Guanshiyin yingyan ji sanzhong yizhu* 觀世音應驗記三種譯注. Annotated by Dong Zhiqiao 董志翹. Nanjing: Jiangsu guji chubanshe, 2002.

Gallagher, Catherine, and Stephen Greenblatt. *Practicing New Historicism.* Chicago: University of Chicago Press, 2000.

Ge Hong 葛洪. *Baopuzi neipian jiaoshi* 抱朴子内篇校釋. Annotated by Wang Ming 王明. Beijing: Zhonghua shuju, 1985.

———. *Baopuzi waipian jiaojian* 抱朴子外篇校箋. Annotated by Yang Mingzhao 楊明照. Beijing: Zhonghua shuju, 1991.

Ge Jianxiong 葛劍雄, Wu Songdi 吳松弟, and Cao Shuji 曹樹基, eds. *Zhongguo yimin shi* 中國移民史. Fuzhou: Fujian renmin chubanshe, 1997.

Gilles, Sealy. "Territorial Interpolations in the Old English Orosius." In *Text and Territory: Geographical Imagination in the European Middle Ages,* edited by Sylvia Tomasch and Sealy Gilles. Philadelphia: University of Pennsylvania Press, 1998, pp. 79–96.

Goethe, Johann Wolfgang von. *Italian Journey: 1786–1788.* Translated by W. H. Auden and Elizabeth Meyer. New York: Pantheon Books, 1962.

Gong Zhen 鞏珍. *Xiyang fanguo zhi* 西洋番國志. Edited by Xiang Da 向達. Beijing: Zhonghua shuju, 1961.

Gong Zizhen 龔自珍. *Gong Zizhen shixuan* 龔自珍詩選. Annotated by Liu Yisheng 劉逸生. Hangzhou: Zhejiang daxue chubanshe, 1982.

Guo Maoqian 郭茂倩, comp. *Yuefu shiji* 樂府詩集. Beijing: Zhonghua shuju, 1979.

Guo yu 國語. Shanghai: Shanghai guji chubanshe, 1978.

Han Yu 韓愈. *Han Yu quanji jiaozhu* 韓愈全集校注. Annotated by Qu Shouyuan 屈守元 and Chang Sichun 常思春. Chengdu: Sichuan daxue chubanshe, 1996.

Hawkes, David, trans. *The Songs of the South: An Ancient Chinese Anthology of Poems by Qu Yuan and Other Poets*. Harmondsworth & New York: Penguin Books, 1985.

Horiuchi Junichi 堀内淳一. "Nanbeichao jian de waijiao shijie he jingji jiaoliu: mapi yu ganju" 南北朝間的外交使節和經濟交流—馬匹與柑橘. In *Wei Jin nanbeichao shi yanjiu: Huigu yu tansuo* 魏晋南北朝史研究：回顧與探索. Wuhan: Hubei jiaoyu chubanshe, 2009, pp. 351–60.

Hostetler, Laura. *Qing Colonial Enterprises: Ethnography and Cartography in Early Modern China.* Chicago: University of Chicago Press, 2001.

Hou Xudong 侯旭東. "Dong Jin nanbeichao Fojiao tiantang diyu guannian de chuanbo yu yingxiang" 東晋南北朝佛教天堂地獄觀念的傳播與影響. *Fojiao yanjiu* 佛教研究 (1999): 247–55.

Hu Ying. "'Would That I Were Marco Polo': The Travel Writing of Shan Shili (1856–1943)." In *Traditions of East Asian Travel,* edited by Joshua A. Fogel. New York: Berghahn Books, 2006, pp. 144–66.

Huang Zunxian 黄遵憲. *Renjinglu shicao* 人境廬詩草. Annotated by Qian Zhonglian 錢仲聯. Hong Kong: Zhonghua shuju, 1963.

Huijiao 惠皎. *Gaoseng zhuan* 高僧傳. Annotated by Tang Yongtong 湯用彤. Beijing: Zhonghua shuju, 1992.

Huiyuan 慧遠 and Kumārajīva 鳩摩羅什. *Jiumoluoshi fashi dayi* 鳩摩羅什法師大義. In *Taishō shinshū Daizōkyō* 大正新修大藏經 45.

Huters, Theodore. *Bringing the World Home: Appropriating the West in Late Qing and Early Republican China.* Honolulu: University of Hawai'i Press, 2005.

Jia Dao 賈島. *Jia Dao shiji jianzhu* 賈島詩集箋注. Annotated by Huang Peng 黃鵬. Chengdu: Ba Shu shushe, 2002.

Jiang Yan 江淹. *Jiang Wentong ji huizhu* 江文通集彙注. Annotated by Hu Zhiji 胡之驥. Beijing: Zhonghua shuju, 1984.

Johnson, M. Dujon. *Race and Racism in the Chinas: Chinese Racial Attitudes toward Africans and African-Americans.* Bloomington, IN: Author House, 2007.

Kao, Karl S. Y., ed. *Classical Chinese Tales of the Supernatural and the Fantastic: Selections from the Third to the Tenth Century.* Bloomington, IN: Indiana University Press, 1985.

Knechtges, David R. "Poetic Travelogue in the Han *Fu.*" In *Proceedings of the Second International Conference on Sinology*. Taibei: Academia Sinica, 1989, pp. 127–52.

———. "Sweet-peel Orange or Southern Gold? Regional Identity in Western Jin Literature." In *Studies in Early Medieval Chinese Literature and Cultural History: In Honor of Richard B. Mather and Donald Holzman*, edited by Paul W. Kroll and David R. Knechtges. Provo, UT: T'ang Studies Society, 2003, pp. 27–79.

Knechtges, David R., trans. *Wen xuan or Selections of Refined Literature.* Vol. 1. Princeton, NJ: Princeton University Press, 1982.

———. *Wen xuan or Selections of Refined Literature.* Vol. 2. Princeton, NJ: Princeton University Press, 1987.

Kobayashi Taichirō 小林太一郎. *Chūgoku kaigashi ronkō* 中國繪畫史論考. Kyōto: Ōyashima, 1947.

Kristeva, Julia. *Strangers to Ourselves.* Translated by Leon S. Roudiez. New York: Columbia University Press, 1991.

Laozi jiaoshi 老子校釋. Annotated by Zhu Qianzhi 朱謙之. Beijing: Zhonghua shuju, 1984.

Le Goff, Jacques. *The Birth of Purgatory*. Translated by Arthur Goldhammer. Chicago: University of Chicago Press, 1984.

Lee, Sherman E. *Chinese Landscape Painting*. Ohio: The Cleveland Museum of Art, 1954.

Li Bai 李白. *Li Bai ji jiaozhu* 李白集校注. Annotated by Qu Tuiyuan 瞿蜕園 and Zhu Jincheng 朱金城. Shanghai: Shanghai guji chubanshe, 1980.

Li dai fu guangxuan xinzhu jiping 歷代賦廣選新注集評. Edited by Qu Delai 曲德來, Chi Wenjun 遲文浚, and Leng Weiguo 冷衛國. Vol. 4. Shenyang: Liaoning renmin chubanshe, 2001.

Li dai fu pingzhu: nanbeichao juan 歷代賦評注：南北朝卷. Edited by Zhao Kuifu 趙逵夫 and Tang Bin 湯斌. Chengdu: Ba Shu shushe, 2010.

Li Daoyuan 酈道元. *Shuijing zhu shu* 水經注疏. With commentary by Yang Shoujing 楊守敬 and Xiong Huizhen 熊會貞. Collated by Duan Xizhong 段熙仲 and Chen Qiaoyi 陳橋驛. Nanjing: Jiangsu guji chubanshe, 1989.

Li Fang 李昉 et al., comps. *Taiping guangji* 太平廣記. Beijing: Zhonghua shuju, 1981.

———. *Taiping yulan* 太平御覽. Taibei: Shangwu yinshuguan, 1975 reprint.

Li ji zhushu 禮記注疏. In *Shisanjing zhushu* 十三經注疏.

Li Jianguo 李劍國. *Tang qian zhiguai xiaoshuo shi* 唐前志怪小說史. Tianjin: Tianjin jiaoyu chubanshe, 2005.

Li Jiannong 李劍農. *Wei Jin nanbeichao minhu da liuxi* 魏晉南北朝民户大流徙. Wuhan: Wuhan bianyi weiyuanhui, 1951.

Li Qi 李頎. *Li Qi shi pingzhu* 李頎詩評注. Annotated by Liu Baohe 劉寶和. Shanxi: Shanxi jiaoyu chubanshe, 1990.

Li Yan 李雁. *Xie Lingyun yanjiu* 謝靈運研究. Beijing: Renmin wenxue chubanshe, 2005.

Li Yanshou 李延壽, comp. *Nan shi* 南史. Beijing: Zhonghua shuju, 1975.

Li Zhao 李肇. *Tang guoshi bu* 唐國史補. In *Tang wudai biji xiaoshuo daguan* 唐五代筆記小說大觀. Shanghai: Shanghai guji chubanshe, 2000.

Liezi jishi 列子集釋. Annotated by Yang Bojun 楊伯峻. Beijing: Zhonghua shuju, 1979.

Lin Gang 林崗. "Haiwai jingyan yu xinshi de xingqi" 海外經驗與新詩的興起. *Wenxue pinglun* 文學評論 4 (2004): 21–29.

Lin Wenyue 林文月. "Pan Yue Lu Ji shi zhong de nanfang yishi" 潘岳陸機詩中的南方意識. *Taida Zhongwen xuebao* 臺大中文學報 5 (1992): 19–36.

Liu An 劉安. *Huainan honglie jijie* 淮南鴻烈集解. Annotated by Liu Wendian 劉文典. Beijing: Zhonghua shuju, 1989.

Liu Sifen 劉斯奮 et al., eds. and annots. *Lingnan sanjia shixuan* 嶺南三家詩選. Guangzhou: Guangdong renmin chubanshe, 1980.

Liu Yajun 劉雅軍. "Wan Qing xueren 'shijie lishi' guannian de bianqian" 晚清學人世界歷史觀念的變遷. *Shixue yuekan* 史學月刊 10 (2005): 97–103.

Liu Yiqing 劉義慶. *Shih-shuo Hsin-yü: A New Account of Tales of the World*. With commentary by Liu Jun. Translated by Richard B. Mather. Minneapolis: University of Minnesota Press, 1976.

———. *Shishuo xinyu jianshu* 世說新語箋疏. Annotated by Yu Jiaxi 余嘉錫. Shanghai: Shanghai guji chubanshe, 1993.

———. *Youming lu* 幽明錄. In *Han Wei liuchao biji xiaoshuo daguan* 漢魏六朝筆記小說大觀. Shanghai: Shanghai guji chubanshe, 1999.

Liu Yuan-ju 劉苑如. "Sheyuan yu guifan: Faxian qiufa de xinglü xushu" 涉遠與歸返：法顯求法的行旅敘述. In *Kongjian yu wenhua changyu: Kongjian yidong zhi wenhua quanshi* 空間與文化場域：空間移動之文化詮釋, edited by Wang Ailing 王瓊玲. Taibei: Hanxue yanjiu zhongxin, 2009, pp. 319–54.

Liu Yuejin 劉躍進. "Liuchao senglü: Wenhua jiaoliu de teshu shizhe" 六朝僧侶：文化交流的特殊使者. In *Zhongguo wenxue yu diyu fengqing* 中國文學與地域風情, edited by Xue Tianwei 薛天緯 and Zhu Yuqi 朱玉麒. Beijing: Xueyuan chubanshe, 2005, pp. 33–57.

Liu Zhen 劉珍 et al., comps. *Dongguan Han ji jiaozhu* 東觀漢記校注. Annotated by Wu Shuping 吳樹平. He'nan: Zhongzhou guji chubanshe, 1987.

Liu Zongyuan 柳宗元. *Liu Zongyuan ji* 柳宗元集. Beijing: Zhonghua shuju, 1979.

Lu Ji 陸機. *Wen fu jishi* 文賦集釋. Annotated by Zhang Shaokang 張少康. Beijing: Renmin wenxue chubanshe, 2002.

Lu Qinli 逯欽立, ed. *Xian Qin Han Wei Jin nanbeichao shi* 先秦漢魏晉南北朝詩. Beijing: Zhonghua shuju, 1983.

Lü Buwei 呂不韋. *Lüshi chunqiu xin jiaoshi* 呂氏春秋新校釋. Annotated by Chen Qiyou 陳奇猷. Shanghai: Shanghai guji chubanshe, 2002.

Lü Wen-tsuei 呂文翠. "Transcultural Travels in Late Qing Shanghai: On Two Travelogues of Wang Tao and Yuan Zuzhi." *Chung Wai Literary Quarterly* 34.9 (2006.2): 7–47.

Lugard, Frederick. *The Dual Mandate in British Tropical Africa*. London: W. Blackwood and Sons, 1922.

Lunyu zhushu 論語注疏. In *Shisanjing zhushu* 十三經注疏.

Lynn, Richard John, trans. *The Classic of Changes: A New Translation of the I Ching as Interpreted by Wang Bi*. New York: Columbia University Press, 1994.

Ma Guangzu 馬光祖 and Zhou Yinghe 周應合, comps. *Jingding Jiankang zhi* 景定建康志. Beijing: Zhonghua shuju, 1990.

Ma Huan 馬歡. *Yingya shenglan jiaozhu* 瀛涯勝覽校注. Annotated by Feng Chengjun 馮承鈞. Shanghai: Shangwu yinshuguan, 1935.

———. *Ying-yai sheng-lan: The Overall Survey of the Ocean's Shores*. Translated by J. V. G. Mills. Cambridge, UK: Hakluyt Society, 1970. Reprint, Bangkok: White Lotus Press, 1997.

Mahāprajñāparamitā Sūtra 放光般若經. Translated by Zhu Shulan 竺法蘭 and Wuluocha 無羅叉. In *Taishō shinshū Daizōkyō* 大正新修大藏經 8.

Mao shi zhengyi 毛詩正義. In *Shisanjing zhushu* 十三經注疏.

Marx, Karl. *Capital: A Critique of Political Economy*. New York: Random House, 1901.

Mather, Richard B. "A Mystical Ascent of the T'ien-t'ai Mountains: Sun Ch'o's *Yu-T'ien-t'ai-shan Fu*." *Monumenta Serica* XX (1961): 226–45.

McClenon, James. "Near-Death Folklore in Medieval China and Japan: A Comparative Analysis." *Asian Folklore Studies* 50.2 (1991): 319–42.

Mei Xinlin 梅新林 and Yu Zhanghua 俞樟華, eds. *Zhongguo youji wenxueshi* 中國遊記文學史. Shanghai: Xuelin chubanshe, 2004.

Meng Jiao 孟郊. *Meng Jiao shiji jianzhu* 孟郊詩集箋注. Annotated by Hua Chenzhi 華忱之 and Yu Xuecai 喻學才. Beijing: Renmin wenxue chubanshe, 1995.

Mengzi zhushu 孟子注疏. In *Shisanjing zhushu* 十三經注疏.

Michihata Ryōshū 道端良秀. *Chūgoku Bukkyō shisōshi no kenkyū: Chūgoku minshū no Bukkyō juyō* 中國仏教思想史の研究: 中國民衆の仏教受容. Kyōto: Heirakuji Shoten, 1979.

Moretti, Franco. *Atlas of the European Novel, 1800–1900*. London: Verso, 1998.

Needham, Joseph. *Science and Civilization in China*. Vol. IV, Pt. 3: Civil engineering and nautics. With the collaboration of Wang Ling and Lu Gwei-Djen. Cambridge, UK: Cambridge University Press, 1971.

Nicholls, Robert. *The Belle Vue Story*. Manchester: Neil Richardson, 1992.

Okamura Shigeru 岡村繁. *Lidai minghua ji yizhu* 歷代名畫記譯注. Translated by Yu Weigang 俞慰剛. Shanghai: Shanghai guji chubanshe, 2002.

Okamoto Kansuke 崗本監輔. *Wanguo shiji* 萬國史記. Huaguo tang 華國堂, 1900.

Ouyang Xun 歐陽詢 et al., comps. *Yiwen leiju* 藝文類聚. Taibei: Wenguang chubanshe, 1974.

Owen, Stephen. *The End of the Chinese "Middle Ages": Essays in Mid-Tang Literary Culture*. Stanford: Stanford University Press, 1996.

———. "Gone South: Fantasies of the Eastern Jin Plebeian." Unpublished paper delivered at the Workshop on the Eastern Jin held at Harvard University on May 6, 2005. Chinese version: "Xia Jiangnan: Guanyu Dong Jin pingmin de huanxiang" 下江南：關於東晉平民的幻想. In *Xia Jiangnan: Suzhou daxue haiwai hanxue yanjiang lu* 下江南：蘇州大學海外漢學演講錄. Shanghai: Fudan daxue chubanshe, forthcoming.

———. "The Librarian in Exile: Xie Lingyun's Bookish Landscapes." *Early Medieval China* 10–11.1 (2004): 203–26.

———. *Readings in Chinese Literary Thought*. Cambridge, MA: Harvard University Asia Center, 1992.

Owen, Stephen, ed. and trans. *An Anthology of Chinese Literature: Beginnings through 1911*. New York: W. W. Norton, 1996.

———, ed. *The Cambridge History of Chinese Literature, Volume I: To 1375*. Cambridge, UK: Cambridge University Press, 2010.

Pei Qi 裴啓. *Yu lin* 語林. Annotated by Zhou Lengjia 周楞伽. Beijing: Wenhua yishu chubanshe, 1988.

Perdue, Peter. "Comparing Empires: Manchu Colonialism." *International History Review* 20.2 (June 1998): 255–62.

Pratyutpannasamādhi Sūtra 佛説般舟三昧經. In *Taishō shinshū Daizōkyō* 大正新修大藏經 13.

Qian Zhongshu 錢鍾書. *Qizhui ji* 七綴集. Shanghai: Shanghai guji chubanshe, 1985.

Qing shi gao 清史稿. Beijing: Zhonghua shuju, 1977.

Ren Jiyu 任繼愈, ed. *Zhongguo Fojiao shi* 中國佛教史. 3 volumes. Beijing: Zhongguo shehui kexue chubanshe, 1985.

Rockhill, W. W. "Notes on the Relations and Trade of China with the Eastern Archipeligo and the Coasts of the Indian Ocean during the Fourteenth Century, Part II." *T'oung Pao* 16.2 (1915): 236–71.

Sakanishi Shiho 坂西志保, trans. *The Spirit of the Brush*. London: Butler and Tanner Ltd., 1939.

Sarkar, Debarchana. *Geography of Ancient India in Buddhist Literature*. Calcutta: Sanskrit Pustak Bhandar, 2003.

Schafer, Edward. "Empyreal Powers and Chthonian Edens: Two Notes on T'ang Taoist Literature." *Journal of the American Oriental Society* 106.4 (October–December 1986): 667–677.

Schmidt, J. D. *Within the Human Realm: The Poetry of Huang Zunxian: 1848–1905*. Cambridge, UK: Cambridge University Press, 1994.

Shanhai jing jiaozhu 山海經校注. Annotated by Yuan Ke 袁珂. Shanghai: Shanghai guji chubanshe, 1980.

Shangshu zhengyi 尚書正義. In *Shisanjing zhushu* 十三經注疏.

Shang Yongqi 尚永琪. "3–6 shiji sengren de liudong yu dili shiyu de tuozhan" 3–6 世紀僧人的流動與地理視閾的拓展. In *Wei Jin nanbeichao shi yanjiu: Huigu yu tansuo* 魏晉南北朝史研究：回顧與探索. Wuhan: Hubei jiaoyu chubanshe, 2009, pp. 507–39.

Sengyou 僧佑. *Chu sanzang ji ji* 出三藏記集. Edited by Su Jinren 蘇晉仁 and Xiao Lianzi 蕭鍊子. Beijing: Zhonghua shuju, 1995.

Sengzhao 僧肇. *Zhu Weimojie jing* 注維摩詰經. In *Taishō shinshū Daizōkyō* 大正新修大藏經 38.

Shen Jie 沈杰. "*Sanyan* zhong daojiao shenxian gushi de xushi zhuti moshi" 三言中道教神仙故事的敘事主題模式. *Hebei daxue xuebao* 河北大學學報 29.2 (2004): 110–12.

Shen Yue 沈約, comp. *Song shu* 宋書. Beijing: Zhonghua shuju, 1974.

Shi Yuntao 石雲濤. *San zhi liu shiji sichou zhi lu de bianqian* 三至六世紀絲綢之路的變遷. Beijing: Wenhua yishu chubanshe, 2007.

Shisanjing zhushu 十三經注疏. Compiled by Ruan Yuan 阮元. Taibei: Yiwen yinshuguan, 1955.

Sima Guang 司馬光, comp. *Zizhi tongjian* 資治通鑑. Beijing: Guji chubanshe, 1956.

Sima Qian 司馬遷, comp. *Shi ji* 史記. Beijing: Zhonghua shuju, 1959.

Sishu zhangju jizhu 四書章句集注. Beijing: Zhonghua shuju, 1983.

Skandadhātvāyatana sūtra 陰持入經 (*Sūtra of [Five] Skandhas, [Eighteen] Realms, and [Twelve] Loci*). Translated by An Shigao 安世高, with a commentary by Chen Hui 陳慧. In *Taishō shinshū Daizōkyō* 大正新修大藏經 33.

Smith, Richard J. "Mapping China's World: Cultural Cartography in Late Imperial Times." In *Landscape, Culture and Power in Chinese Society*, edited by Wen-hsin Yeh. Berkeley: Institute of East Asian Studies, 1998, pp. 52–109.

Song Lian 宋濂 et al., comps. *Yuan shi* 元史. Beijing: Zhonghua shuju, 1976.

Spurr, David. *The Rhetoric of Empire: Colonial Discourse in Journalism, Travel Writing, and Imperial Administration.* Durham: Duke University Press, 1993.

States, Bert O. *Dreaming and Storytelling*. Ithaca: Cornell University Press, 1993.

Strassberg, Richard E., ed. and trans. *Inscribed Landscapes: Travel Writing from Imperial China*. Berkeley, CA: University of California Press, 1994.

Sullivan, Michael. *The Birth of Landscape Painting in China*. Berkeley: University of California Press, 1962.

Su Ruilong 蘇瑞隆. "Lun Xie Lingyun de 'Zhuanzheng fu' 論謝靈運的撰征賦." *Wen shi zhe* 文史哲 5 (1990): 48–52.

Su Shi 蘇軾. *Su Shi shiji* 蘇軾詩集. Beijing: Zhonghua shuju, 1982.

Sun Wu 孫武. *Sunzi jinzhu jinyi* 孫子今注今譯. Annotated and translated by Wei Rulin 魏汝霖. Taibei: Shangwu yinshuguan, 1972.

Sutra of Perfect Wisdom 道行般若經. Translated by Zhi Loujiachen 支婁迦讖. In *Taishō shinshū Daizōkyō* 大正新修大藏經 8.

Taigong liutao jinzhu jinyi 太公六韜今注今譯. Annotated by Xu Peigen 徐培根. Taibei: Shangwu yinshuguan, 1976.

Taishō shinshū Daizōkyō 大正新修大藏經. 101 volumes. Compiled by Takakusu Junjirō and Watanabe Kaigyoku. Taibei: Shihua yinshua qiye youxian gongsi, 1990.

Tang, Xiaobing. *Global Space and the Nationalist Discourse of Modernity: The Historical Thinking of Liang Qichao*. Stanford: Stanford University Press, 1996.

Tang Yongtong 湯用彤. *Han Wei liang Jin nanbeichao Fojiao shi* 漢魏兩晉南北朝佛教史. Beijing: Beijing daxue chubanshe, 1997.

Tang Zhangru 唐長孺. "Du *Baopuzi* tuilun nanbei xuefeng de yitong" 讀抱樸子推論南北學風的異同. In *Wei Jin nanbeichao shi luncong* 魏晉南北朝史論叢. Shijiazhuang: Hebei jiaoyu chubanshe, 2000, pp. 337–67.

Tao Yuanming 陶渊明. *The Poetry of T'ao Ch'ien*. Translated with commentary and annotation by James Robert Hightower. Oxford: Clarendon Press, 1970.

———. Soushen *hou ji* 搜神後记. Annotated by Wang Shaoying 汪紹楹. Beijing: Zhonghua shuju, 1981.

Teiser, Stephen F. *The Scripture on the Ten Kings and the Making of Purgatory in Medieval Chinese Buddhism.* Honolulu: University of Hawaii Press, 1994.

Teng, Emma Jinhua. *Taiwan's Imagined Geography: Chinese Colonialist Travel Writing and Pictures, 1683–1895.* Cambridge, MA: Harvard University Asia Center, 2004.

———. "The West as a 'Kingdom of Women': Woman and Occidentalism in Wang Tao's Tales of Travel." In *Traditions of East Asian Travel*, edited by Joshua A. Fogel. New York: Berghahn Books, 2006, pp. 97–124.

Tian, Xiaofei. *Beacon Fire and Shooting Star: The Literary Culture of the Liang (502–557).* Cambridge, MA: Harvard University Asia Center, 2007.

———. "Muffled Dialect Spoken by Green Fruits: An Alternative History of Modern Chinese Poetry." *Modern Chinese Literature and Culture* 21.1 (Spring 2009): 1–44.

———. *Qiushuitang lun* Jin ping mei 秋水堂論金瓶梅. Tianjin: Tianjin renmin chubanshe, 2005 (revised edition).

———. *Tao Yuanming and Manuscript Culture: The Record of a Dusty Table.* Seattle: University of Washington Press, 2005.

Tindall, Gillian. *Countries of the Mind: The Meaning of Place to Writers.* London: Hogarth Press, 1991.

Thompson, Laurence G. "On the Prehistory of Hell in China." *Journal of Chinese Religions* 17 (1989): 27–41.

Tomasch, Sylvia, and Sealy Gilles, eds. *Text and Territory: Geographical Imagination in the European Middle Ages.* Philadelphia: University of Pennsylvania Press, 1998.

Turner, Victor, and Edith Turner. *Image and Pilgrimage in Christian Culture.* New York: Columbia University Press, 1995.

Vimalakīrti-nirdeśa Sūtra 維摩詰所說經. Translated by Kumārajīva. In *Taishō shinshū Daizōkyō* 大正新修大藏經 14.

Walkowitz, Judith R. *Prostitution and Victorian Society: Women, Class, and the State.* Cambridge, UK: Cambridge University Press, 1982.

Wang Dayuan 汪大淵. *Daoyi zhilüe jiaoshi* 島夷志略校釋. Annotated by Su Jiqing 蘇繼廎. Beijing: Zhonghua shuju, 2000.

Wang, David Der-wei. *Fin-de-siècle Splendor: Repressed Modernities of Late Qing Fiction, 1849–1911.* Stanford: Stanford University Press, 1997.

Wang Jia 王嘉. *Shiyi ji* 拾遺記. Annotated by Qi Zhiping 齊治平. Beijing: Zhonghua shuju, 1981.

Wang Kangnian 王康年. *Zhuangxie xuanlu* 莊諧選錄. Shanghai: Zhongwai ribao guan, 1904.

Wang Qing 王青. *Wei Jin nanbeichao shiqi de Fojiao xinyang yu shenhua* 魏晉南北朝時期的佛教信仰與神話. Beijing: Zhongguo shehui kexue chubanshe, 2001.

———. *Xiyu wenhua yingxiang xia de zhonggu xiaoshuo* 西域文化影響下的中古小說. Beijing: Zhongguo shehui kexue chubanshe, 2006.

Wang Renyu 王仁裕. *Kaiyuan Tianbao yishi* 開元天寶遺事. In *Tang wudai biji xiaoshuo daguan* 唐五代筆記小說大觀. Shanghai: Shanghai guji chubanshe, 2000.

Wang Shenzhi 王慎之 and Wang Zijin 王子今, eds. *Qingdai haiwai zhuzhici* 清代海外竹枝詞. Beijing: Beijing daxue chubanshe, 1994.

Wang Tao 王韜. *Henghua guan shi lu* 蘅華館詩錄. In *Xuxiu siku quanshu* 續修四庫全書, Vol. 1558. Shanghai: Shanghai guji chubanshe, 1995–99.

———. *Manyou suilu* 漫遊隨錄. Changsha: Hu'nan renmin chubanshe, 1982.

Wang Yan 王琰. *Mingxiang ji* 冥祥記. In *Taiping guangji* 太平廣記, compiled by Li Fang 李昉 et al. Beijing: Zhonghua shuju, 1981.

Wang Zhongmin 王重民. *Lenglu wensou* 冷廬文藪. Shanghai: Shanghai guji chubanshe, 1992.

Watson, Burton, trans. *The Complete Works of Chuang Tzu*. New York: Columbia University Press, 1968.

Wei Jin nanbeichao shi yanjiu: huigu yu tansuo—Zhongguo Wei Jin nanbeichao shi xuehui dijiujie nianhui lunwenji 魏晉南北朝史研究：回顧與探索—中國魏晉南北朝史學會第九屆年會論文集. Wuhan: Hubei jiaoyu chubanshe, 2009.

Wei Shou 魏收, comp. *Wei shu* 魏書. Beijing: Zhonghua shuju, 1974.

Wei Yuan 魏源. *Haiguo tuzhi* 海國圖志. In *Xuxiu siku quanshu* 續修四庫全書, Vols. 743–44. Shanghai: Shanghai guji chubanshe, 1995–99.

Wei Zheng 魏徵 et al., comps. *Sui shu* 隋書. Beijing: Zhonghua shuju, 1973.

Wei Zhuang 韋莊. *Wei Zhuang ji jianzhu* 韋莊集箋注. Annotated by Nie Anfu 聶安福. Shanghai: Shanghai guji chubanshe, 2002.

Wen Qing 文慶, Jia Zhen 賈禎 and Bao Yun 寶鋆, eds. *Chouban yiwu shimo* 籌辦夷務始末. In *Xuxiu siku quanshu* 續修四庫全書, Vol. 419. Shanghai: Shanghai guji chubanshe, 1995–99.

Westbrook, Francis A. "Landscape Description in the Lyric Poetry and 'Fuh on Dwelling in the Mountains' of Shieh Ling-yunn," Ph.D. diss., Yale, 1972.

———. "Landscape Transformation in the Poetry of Hsieh Ling-Yün." In *Journal of the American Oriental Society* 100.3 (July–October 1980): 237–54.

Wheatley, Paul. *The Golden Khersonese: Studies in the Historical Geography of the Malay Peninsula before A.D. 1500.* Kuala Lumpur: University of Malaya Press, 1961.

Widmer, Ellen. "Foreign Travel through a Woman's Eyes: Shan Shili's *Guimao lüxing ji* in Local and Global Perspective." *The Journal of Asian Studies* 65.4 (2006): 763–91.

Wu Yue chunqiu jijiao huikao 吳越春秋輯校匯考. Collated by Zhou Shengchun 周生春. Shanghai: Shanghai guji chubanshe, 1997.

Xiao Tong 蕭統, ed. *Wen xuan* 文選. Shanghai: Shanghai guji chubanshe, 1994.

———. *Liuchen zhu* Wen xuan 六臣注文選. Beijing: Zhonghua shuju, 1987.

Xiao Zixian 蕭子顯, comp. *Nan Qi shu* 南齊書. Beijing: Zhonghua shuju, 1972.

Xie Boyang 謝伯陽, comp. *Quan Ming sanqu* 全明散曲. Ji'nan: Qi Lu shushe, 1994.

Xie Lingyun 謝靈運. *Xie Kangle shizhu* 謝康樂詩注. Annotated by Huang Jie 黃節. Taibei: Yiwen yinshuguan, 2005.

———. *Xie Lingyun ji jiaozhu* 謝靈運集校注. Annotated by Gu Shaobo 顧紹柏. He'nan: Zhongzhou guji chubanshe, 1987.

———. *Xie Lingyun ji* 謝靈運集. Annotated by Li Yunfu 李運富. Changsha: Yuelu shushe, 1999.

---. *Xie Lingyun shixuan* 謝靈運詩選. Annotated by Ye Xiaoxue 葉笑雪. Beijing: Gudian wenxue chubanshe, 1957.

Xiong Qingyuan 熊清元. "'Zhuanzheng fu bing xu' zhushi shiwu juli" 撰征賦並序注釋失誤舉例. *Huanggang shifan xueyuan xuebao* 黃岡師範學院學報 22.4 (2002): 27–31.

Xu Jiyu 徐繼畬. *Yinghuan zhilüe jiaozhu* 瀛寰志略校注. Annotated by Song Dachuan 宋大川. Beijing: Wenwu chubanshe, 2007.

Yan Zonglin 閻宗臨. *Zhongxi jiaotong shi* 中西交通史. Guilin: Guangxi shifan daxue chubanshe, 2007.

Yao Cha 姚察 and Yao Silian 姚思廉, comps. *Liang shu* 梁書. Beijing: Zhonghua shuju, 1973.

Yan Kejun 嚴可均, comp. *Quan shanggu sandai Qin Han san'guo liuchao wen* 全上古三代秦漢三國六朝文. Beijing: Zhonghua shuju, 1987.

You Jingxian 尤靜嫻, "Yuejie yu youyi: Wan Qing lü Mei youji de yuwai xiangxiang yu shuxie celue" 越界與遊移：晚清旅美遊記的域外想象與書寫策略, in *Wenxue xinglü yu shijie xiangxiang* 文學行旅與世界想象, edited by Ji Jin 季進 and Wang Dewei 王德威. Nanjing: Jiangsu jiaoyu chubanshe, 2007, pp. 92–119.

Yu Jianhua 俞劍華, ed. *Zhongguo hualun leibian* 中國畫論類編. Hong Kong: Zhonghua shuju, 1973.

Yu, Ying-Shih. "'O Soul, Come Back!' A Study in the Changing Conceptions of the Soul and Afterlife in Pre-Buddhist China." *HJAS* 47.2 (December 1987): 363–95.

Yuan Haowen 元好問. *Yuan Haowen quanji* 元好問全集. Edited by Yao Dianzhong 姚奠中 and Li Zhengmin 李正民. Taiyuan: Shangxi guji chubanshe, 2004.

Zeitlin, Judith T. *Historian of the Strange: Pu Songling and the Chinese Classical Tale.* Stanford: Stanford University Press, 1993.

Zha Zhilong 查志隆, comp. *Dai shi* 岱史. In *Daojiao yaoji xuankan* 道教要籍選刊, edited by Hu Daojing 胡道靜, Chen Liansheng 陳蓮笙, and Chen Yaoting 陳耀庭. Vol. 7. Shanghai: Shanghai guji chubanshe, 1989.

Zhang Deyi 張德彝. *Diary of a Chinese Diplomat: Zhang Deyi.* Translated by Simon Johnstone. Beijing: Beijing Literature Press, 1992.

———. *Gaoben Hanghai shuqi huibian* 稿本航海述奇匯編. 10 volumes. Beijing: Beijing Tushuguan chubanshe, 1997.

———. *Hanghai shuqi* 航海述奇 and *Oumei huanyou ji* 歐美環遊記 (*Zai shuqi* 再述奇). In *Zouxiang shijie congshu* 走向世界叢書, edited by Zhong Shuhe 鍾叔河. Vol. 1. Hu'nan: Yuelu shushe, 1985.

Zhang Keli 張可禮. *Dong Jin wenyi zonghe yanjiu* 東晋文藝綜合研究. Ji'nan: Shandong daxue chubanshe, 2001.

Zhang Tingyu 張廷玉 et al., comps. *Ming shi* 明史. Beijing: Zhonghua shuju, 1974.

Zhang Yanyuan 張彥遠. *Lidai minghua ji* 歷代名畫記. In *Jindai mishu* 津逮秘書. Vol. 7. Shanghai: Boguzhai, 1923.

Zhang Zuyi 張祖翼. "Lundun zhuzhici" 倫敦竹枝詞. In *Guanzide zhai congshu bieji* 觀自得齋叢書别集 24, compiled by Xu Shikai 徐士愷.

Zheng Cheng 鄭誠 and Jiang Xiaoyuan 江曉原. "He Chengtian wen foguo lishu gushi de yuanliu ji yingxiang" 何承天問佛國歷術故事的源流及影響. *Zhongguo wenhua* 中國文化 25–26 (2007.2): 61–71.

Zhi Gang 志剛. *Chu shi Taixi ji* 初使泰西記. In *Zouxiang shijie congshu* 走向世界叢書, edited by Zhong Shuhe 鍾叔河. Vol. 1. Hu'nan: Yuelu shushe, 1985.

Zhong Shuhe 鍾叔河. "Ji Qian Zhongshu zuoxu" 記錢鍾書作序. *Zhongguo bianji* 中國編輯 2004.5: 75–77.

———. *Zouxiang shijie: Jindai zhishifenzi kaocha xifang de lishi* 走向世界: 近代知識分子考察西方的歷史. Beijing: Zhongshu shuju, 1985.

Zhou Daguan 周達觀. *Zhenla fengtu ji jiaozhu* 真臘風土記校注. Annotated by Xie Nai 夏鼐. Beijing: Zhonghua shuju, 2000.

Zhou Hanguang 周瀚光 and Dai Hongcai 戴洪才, eds. *Liuchao keji* 六朝科技. Nanjing: Nanjing chubanshe, 2003.

Zhou yi zhengyi 周易正義. In *Shisanjing zhushu* 十三經注疏.

Zhuangzi jishi 莊子集釋. Compiled by Guo Qingfan 郭慶藩. Beijing: Zhonghua shuju, 1961.

Zürcher, Erik. *The Buddhist Conquest of China: The Spread and Adaptation of Buddhism in Early Medieval China.* Leiden: Brill, 1959.

Index

Harvard-Yenching Institute Monograph Series
(titles now in print)

11. *Han Shi Wai Chuan: Han Ying's Illustrations of the Didactic Application of the Classic of Songs*, translated and annotated by James Robert Hightower
21. *The Chinese Short Story: Studies in Dating, Authorship, and Composition*, by Patrick Hanan
22. *Songs of Flying Dragons: A Critical Reading*, by Peter H. Lee
24. *Population, Disease, and Land in Early Japan, 645–900*, by William Wayne Farris
25. *Shikitei Sanba and the Comic Tradition in Edo Fiction*, by Robert W. Leutner
26. *Washing Silk: The Life and Selected Poetry of Wei Chuang (834?–910)*, by Robin D. S. Yates
27. *National Polity and Local Power: The Transformation of Late Imperial China*, by Min Tu-ki
28. *Tang Transformation Texts: A Study of the Buddhist Contribution to the Rise of Vernacular Fiction and Drama in China*, by Victor H. Mair
29. *Mongolian Rule in China: Local Administration in the Yuan Dynasty*, by Elizabeth Endicott-West
30. *Readings in Chinese Literary Thought*, by Stephen Owen
31. *Remembering Paradise: Nativism and Nostalgia in Eighteenth-Century Japan*, by Peter Nosco
32. *Taxing Heaven's Storehouse: Horses, Bureaucrats, and the Destruction of the Sichuan Tea Industry, 1074–1224*, by Paul J. Smith
33. *Escape from the Wasteland: Romanticism and Realism in the Fiction of Mishima Yukio and Oe Kenzaburo*, by Susan Jolliffe Napier
34. *Inside a Service Trade: Studies in Contemporary Chinese Prose*, by Rudolf G. Wagner
35. *The Willow in Autumn: Ryutei Tanehiko, 1783–1842*, by Andrew Lawrence Markus
36. *The Confucian Transformation of Korea: A Study of Society and Ideology*, by Martina Deuchler
37. *The Korean Singer of Tales*, by Marshall R. Pihl

38. *Praying for Power: Buddhism and the Formation of Gentry Society in Late-Ming China*, by Timothy Brook
39. *Word, Image, and Deed in the Life of Su Shi*, by Ronald C. Egan
40. *The Chinese Virago: A Literary Theme*, by Yenna Wu
41. *Studies in the Comic Spirit in Modern Japanese Fiction*, by Joel R. Cohn
42. *Wind Against the Mountain: The Crisis of Politics and Culture in Thirteenth-Century China*, by Richard L. Davis
43. *Powerful Relations: Kinship, Status, and the State in Sung China (960–1279)*, by Beverly Bossler
44. *Limited Views: Essays on Ideas and Letters*, by Qian Zhongshu; selected and translated by Ronald Egan
45. *Sugar and Society in China: Peasants, Technology, and the World Market*, by Sucheta Mazumdar
46. *Chinese History: A Manual*, by Endymion Wilkinson
47. *Studies in Chinese Poetry*, by James R. Hightower and Florence Chia-Ying Yeh
48. *Crazy Ji: Chinese Rel igion and Popular Literature*, by Meir Shahar
49. *Precious Volumes: An Introduction to Chinese Sectarian Scriptures from the Sixteenth and Seventeenth Centuries*, by Daniel L. Overmyer
50. *Poetry and Painting in Song China: The Subtle Art of Dissent*, by Alfreda Murck
51. *Evil and/or/as the Good: Omnicentrism, Intersubjectivity, and Value Paradox in Tiantai Buddhist Thought*, by Brook Ziporyn
52. *Chinese History: A Manual, Revised and Enlarged Edition*, by Endymion Wilkinson
53. *Articulated Ladies: Gender and the Male Community in Early Chinese Texts*, by Paul Rouzer
54. *Politics and Prayer: Shrines to Local Former Worthies in Sung China*, by Ellen Neskar
55. *Allegories of Desire: Esoteric Literary Commentaries of Medieval Japan*, by Susan Blakeley Klein
56. *Printing for Profit: The Commercial Publishers of Jianyang, Fujian (11th-17th Centuries)*, by Lucille Chia
57. *To Become a God: Cosmology, Sacrifice, and Self-Divinization in Early China*, by Michael J. Puett
58. *Writing and Materiality in China: Essays in Honor of Patrick Hanan*, edited by Judith T. Zeitlin and Lydia H. Liu
59. *Rulin waishi and Cultural Transformation in Late Imperial China*, by Shang Wei
60. *Words Well Put: Visions of Poetic Competence in the Chinese Tradition*, by Graham Sanders
61. *Householders: The Reizei Family in Japanese History*, by Steven D. Carter
62. *The Divine Nature of Power: Chinese Ritual Architecture at the Sacred Site of Jinci*, by Tracy Miller
63. *Beacon Fire and Shooting Star: The Literary Culture of the Liang (502–557)*, by Xiaofei Tian
64. *Lost Soul: "Confucianism" in Contemporary Chinese Academic Discourse*, by John Makeham

65. *The Sage Learning of Liu Zhi: Islamic Thought in Confucian Terms*, by Sachiko Murata, William C. Chittick, and Tu Weiming
66. *Through a Forest of Chancellors: Fugitive Histories in Liu Yuan's* Lingyan ge*, an Illustrated Book from Seventeenth-Century Suzhou*, by Anne Burkus-Chasson
67. *Empire of Texts in Motion: Chinese, Korean, and Taiwanese Transculturations of Japanese Literature*, by Karen Laura Thornber
68. *Empire's Twilight: Northeast Asia Under the Mongols*, by David M. Robinson
69. *Ancestors, Virgins, and Friars: Christianity as a Local Religion in Late Imperial China*, by Eugenio Menegon
70. *Manifest in Words, Written on Paper: Producing and Circulating Poetry in Tang Dynasty China*, by Christopher M. B. Nugent
71. *The Poetics of Sovereignty: On Emperor Taizong of the Tang Dynasty*, by Jack W. Chen
72. *Ancestral Memory in Early China*, by K. E. Brashier
73. *'Dividing the Realm in Order to Govern': The Spatial Organization of the Song State*, by Ruth Mostern
74. *The Dynamics of Masters Literature: Early Chinese Thought from Confucius to Han Feizi*, by Wiebke Denecke
75. *Songs of Contentment and Transgression: Discharged Officials and Literati Communities in Sixteenth-Century North China*, by Tian Yuan Tan
76. *Ten Thousand Scrolls: Reading and Writing in the Poetics of Huang Tingjian and the Late Northern Song*, by Yugen Wang
77. *A Northern Alternative: Xue Xuan (1389–1464) and the Hedong School*, by Khee Heong Koh
78. *Visionary Journeys: Travel Writings from Early Medieval and Nineteenth-Century China*, by Xiaofei Tian